Praise for
Money for Nothing

"Do read this book. I would be surprised if you did not emerge from it with your understanding of the fundamental economic forces currently shaping our world, the opportunities and the threats, greatly enhanced."
Jill Leyland, The Business Economist

"Roger Bootle's analysis of the financial bubbles of the last few years and the hubris that they produced is penetrating and wise. Fortunately, he is optimistic about the potential for recovery for our newly globalised economy, but I hope that the policy makers will study his prescription as they try to steer us back to a more secure growth in wealth."
The Right Honourable Kenneth Clarke, QC, MP

"*Money for Nothing* is nothing short of a great economic vision and a magnificent blueprint for a global society."
Professor Dr. Norbert Walter, Chief Economist, Deutsche Bank Group

"Roger Bootle's latest book *Money for Nothing* is an extraordinary *tour de force* that starts with the shambles of the latest stock market bubble, warns us of the next clouds on the horizon—the property bubble, the coming pensions crisis and The Big One: global deflation compounded by international trade protectionism.
And Bootle sticks his neck out: no woolly-minded prevarication here. He makes his views clear and does not hedge his predictions and draws his lines firmly in the sand... If he is right—and he has been before, with his visionary book *The Death of Inflation* (1996)—the real good old days, the ones historians will look back on most fondly, are just around the corner. But we'll need leaders with vision and strong nerves. Let's hope that some of them take the time to read this troubling yet ultimately deeply reassuring book."
David Charters, Management Today

"There is much of value in this book. Anyone with an interest in economics will benefit from his clear description of the benefits of free trade and the dangers of deflation; private investors should read his chapter on the 'financial fantasies' evident in recent years. Few readers will finish without being stimulated and provoked."
Philip Coggan, Financial Times

"We saw it all. Now Roger Bootle tells us what it means and will mean for the future. This absorbing book tackles, head on, some of the greatest economic challenges of our time."
Sir Brian Pitman, Former Chairman, Lloyds TSB Group

Money for Nothing

Real Wealth, Financial Fantasies, and the Economy of the Future

Roger Bootle

NICHOLAS BREALEY
PUBLISHING

LONDON

This revised and updated paperback edition first published by
Nicholas Brealey Publishing in 2005

First published in hardback in 2003

3–5 Spafield Street
Clerkenwell, London
EC1R 4QB, UK
Tel: +44 (0)20 7239 0360
Fax: +44 (0)20 7239 0370

100 City Hall Plaza, Suite 501
Boston
MA 02108, USA
Tel: (888) BREALEY
Fax: (617) 523 3708

http://www.nbrealey-books.com
www.capitaleconomics.com

ISBN-13: 978-1-85788-283-0
ISBN-10: 1-85788-283-0

British Library Cataloguing in Publication Data
A catalogue record for this book is available from the British Library.

Printed in Finland by WS Bookwell.

Contents

Preface to the Paperback Edition

Money for Nothing is about the real sources of wealth—and the illusory ones. It is written not primarily for professional economists, but rather for general readers, millions of whom feel bamboozled, depressed, and downright confused after the events of the last few years. They were led up the garden path by the stock-market boom of the late 1990s and by the general sense of optimism about our economic future, and then let down by the stock-market collapse. Subsequently, as the market revived, the experts told them that it was safe to go back into the water. Now they don't know what to think.

This book is intended as a guide for all those disappointed millions: explaining how we have come to this pretty pass; what pitfalls and opportunities lie ahead; and what the economy of the future will be like.

It is divided into three parts. Readers who survive the dangers arising from the end of the wealth *illusion*, to which they are exposed in Part I, may be surprised at the contrasting message they encounter about the *real* sources of wealth, which forms the subject matter of Part II, and, I hope, intrigued and pleasantly surprised by the vision of the future that I depict in Part III.

The book has a wide scope, referring to both the structure and the behavior of the financial markets, the dangers of the present international conjuncture, the lessons of history about the sources of real growth, and the tantalizing economic prospects for the future. Some critics will doubtless say that this scope is too broad; but I feel that I must cover such a span, since these apparently disparate matters are closely interrelated.

Moreover, they all need to be addressed in order to meet the book's main objective. Over the last five turbulent years, umpteen people have, quite reasonably, asked me, as an economist known to have views about the future, "What is it going to be like?" or "Should we be worried about the economy?". I have wanted to give them an answer that does justice to the complexity of the future—and their stake in it. This book is my attempt to give that answer. Simply to cover the immediate dangers arising from financial bubbles and global imbalances without reference to the promise of the future, or to cover these without discussing the immediate dangers, would not only fail to reflect my own views sufficiently but, more importantly, would do the reader a gross disservice.

Relatedly, I am sure that I may be criticized for failing to give sufficient coverage to many important issues. I am profoundly conscious, for instance, that I have little to say about environmental matters. My defense is simply that this is a huge topic in its own right that could not possibly be dealt with adequately in this book, and that plenty of other books are dedicated to precisely this subject.

In keeping with the book's intention to serve the general reader, I have tried to avoid discussion of theoretical issues and relegated reference material to notes. But the notes are extensive. In order to keep this paperback edition within manageable proportions, and in keeping with much modern practice, the notes are not to be found at the end of the book but rather on my company's website, www.capitaleconomics.com.

Where I quote amounts of money I have rendered the sums in both dollars and pounds. This throws up the tricky question of the exchange rate. Between the first and second editions of this book the pound first rose sharply against the dollar and then fell steeply. At the time of writing it stands at about $1.75. For the sake of convenience, I have decided to stick with the original exchange rate of $1.50. If readers interpret this as an implicit estimate of the appropriate exchange rate, then so be it.

In some ways, preparing a new edition of a book two years after it first appeared is more difficult than preparing the original. This book is set in the here and now. Clearly, many things have happened since the first edition, some of which are in accordance with the analysis and predictions of the book, some of which are not.

What to do? Once you start to unpick a book, the whole structure may unravel and you are faced with the task of writing a new one. This I was loath to envisage—not just because I recoiled at the amount of work but also because the first edition of the book was such a success. I wanted a new edition of *this* book, not a new book. What I have therefore decided is, wherever necessary, to update examples, charts, and data throughout the book, and then to take a rounded view of the events of the last two years in the Finale.

In this paperback edition the Finale is mostly new. As well as reflecting on recent events, it addresses some key questions that the first edition threw up and that have come into closer focus since: why is a world blessed with so many economic opportunities rone to fall into recession and deflation; and why are interest rates so low across the world? I think that the answers I give relate Parts I and II more closely and explain the sequencing of troubles first, followed later by overwhelming opportunity, while also putting 2005's renewal of fears about an oil price-induced resurgence of inflation into perspective.

Bursting the bubble

The book grew out of my gathering anxiety in the late 1990s about the stock-market bubble and what I saw as the corruption of values and failure of public understanding about the sources of wealth that were associated with it. It seemed to me that there were close parallels with what happened in America in 1929. As I wrote in numerous newspaper articles, first for *The Times* and then for *The Sunday Telegraph*, I was full of foreboding about the stock market and what major weakness in it would do to the US economy and thence to the world.

Then the stock market plunged in the spring of 2000—and carried on downwards. In my view this was just the beginning. Admittedly, the stock market subsequently recovered, though to nowhere near its pre-crash levels. But, as I write this in mid-2005, there is a second bubble still inflating: in property, or what Americans call real estate. Like the earlier bubble in shares, the extent of overvaluation is different in different countries, but this is a global phenomenon. In the end, this bubble may be more serious than the primary bubble in shares. When it bursts, the world will tremble.

Today there are also threats of a very different sort to darken the sky. My view of the world is dominated by the prospective benefits of increased globalization and interdependence. Yet the threat of international terrorism could lead to consequences that would draw the world economy in a totally different direction from the one charted in this book.

There is little that I, like the rest of us, can do or say about such dangers, except face up to them and carry on. Whatever the threats, I believe that we will fulfill our destiny—and that involves both greater prosperity and greater interdependence. Perhaps these features of the economy of the future, which I analyze and discuss in this book, will even eventually help to deflect and then eradicate those dark forces that currently threaten not merely our economy but society itself.

Acknowledgments

Many people have helped me during the preparation of the book, both the original hardback and this paperback edition. Shaun Curtis was very helpful with some of the early research and Tim Condon supplied some useful comments. I am grateful to Brian Blackshaw, John Calverley, Mark Cliffe, Richard Holt, George de Nemeskeri Kiss, Chris Lewin, Ian Shepherdson, Don Smith, and Jack Wigglesworth, who read and commented on the typescript.

I would also like to thank my colleagues at Capital Economics for their help and hard work in relation to both researching and commenting on the book and maintaining the continued growth of our business. I should particularly mention Paul Dales and Adrian Thomas, who acted as my research assistants, and my senior colleagues, Martin Essex, Julian Jessop, and Jonathan Loynes, who provided many useful comments and ideas. I owe a particular debt of gratitude to my PA Joaly Smith who, as well as helping me enormously with the daunting task of managing the typescript, also steadfastly continued with running the office and administering Capital Economics, all with consummate aplomb.

Many of Capital Economics' clients unwittingly provided invaluable help in acting as a sounding board as I developed my ideas and being a source of ideas themselves. I am also grateful to Deloitte, to whom I act as economic adviser, for arranging a continuing stream of interesting conferences around the world at which I have spoken. From the comments and questions of Deloitte's clients and guests at these events, I have gained both insight and stimulation.

As with *The Death of Inflation*, I am extremely fortunate to have had Nicholas Brealey as my publisher. He has provided invaluable guidance and inspiration. Without him the book would never have been conceived, never mind published.

I cannot say that my children actually *helped* me in the preparation of the book, but I am conscious that they unwittingly bore some of its greatest burdens, in the form of my frequent absences as I tried to finish what I had begun. Now that they, and the book, are older and wiser, I hope they will forgive me.

Needless to say, none of the above-mentioned individuals or organizations is responsible for any of the book's errors or omissions. As always, these are the author's responsibility alone.

Roger Bootle
London
July 2005

PROLOGUE
The Crisis Point

The world is at a critical juncture, poised between a surge in wealth and descent into outright slump. It could go either way. Just as the fulfillment of our economic potential is enabling much higher living standards throughout the world, so dark forces are threatening a serious downturn.

How this tension is resolved will affect the very substance of our lives: our jobs and our leisure time, our savings and our pensions, our homes and our families. We are living at a moment when, like the characters in Tolstoy's *War and Peace*, we are acting out our everyday lives against the backdrop of a much bigger drama: the interplay of great historical forces, both political and economic, that dwarf us and threaten to overwhelm us. The *international* order that governed the world for half a century after the Second World War is collapsing in crisis. The new *global* order is yet to be born.

The Great Illusion

At the heart of the economic part of this crisis is the contrast between real and illusory wealth, a contrast that derives its resonance from something thoroughly human: the interaction between hope, greed, and delusion. During the 1990s, the western world was swept up in a great wave of enthusiasm for investing in shares as a source of enrichment. In the process, people lost sight of where real wealth comes from. Along with corporate managements and public officials, investors ceased even to ask the question. If the stock price was going up and up and up, who cared? *Real* wealth is for wimps. As the money cascaded into their laps without any strain or sacrifice, this was real enough for them. Indeed, it seemed all the more enjoyable for being so effortless.

A continually rising stock market is the greatest source of collective avarice known to man. Stock-market prices are driven by people seeking wealth in a hurry. Not for them the painful slog for paltry rewards that has been our lot since the beginning of time. What stock-market investors seek is to condense the productive potential of the infinite future into instant capital value. What they want for themselves is everyone's dream—money for nothing.

In the share-price surge of the late 1990s that is what they got. But it was all a gigantic illusion: the greatest bubble in previous financial history. A society cannot get richer through rising share prices. Societies can only get richer through becoming more productive. At best, rising share prices may *anticipate and reflect* future enrichment. Even then, it is the underlying real improvements, not the increases in share prices, that bring the wealth. All the stock market does is enable future benefits to be seen now—and allow some individuals to profit at the expense of others.

Given this, you might reasonably think that *falling* share prices should leave the economy unscathed, but it does not necessarily work that way. In the 1920s, the American stock market surged on a mood of boundless optimism about the technological advances of the time. However, it all went much too far and in 1929 came the Great Crash. Shortly afterwards, America was plunged into the Great Depression. Optimism about new technology gave way to the despair of the soup kitchen and the dole queue. In the 1980s, Japan was the miracle economy and its stock market soared— before collapsing into a decade-long slump, taking the economy with it. The stock market's importance at these critical times should not be surprising, for it is capitalism's hinge, linking present and future.

Now we all have to live with the consequences of recent stock-market excesses. The bursting of the bubble left wreckage strewn across the economic system. Over the period 2000–2002, the value of all the shares in the world fell by a total of $13 trillion—$13 million million, or $2,000 for every man, woman, and child on the planet.[1] In the UK, the value of the so-called with profits funds held by life assurance companies to cover long-term savings and personal pensions fell by about £50 billion in 2002 alone—equivalent to about £1,000 ($1,500) for everyone in the country.[2]

Yet the crash did not derail the economy. Why not? The short answer is that policies were deployed to stop it from doing so, especially the policy of 1 percent interest rates in the United States.

The long answer is that these polices transferred the bubble from equities to other assets—especially real estate. As investors lost their faith in equities, they found it redoubled in the asset that they had always trusted and that they thought couldn't let them down: property.

The bursting of the late 1990s bubble did not have more serious effects because it isn't all over yet. There is a second shoe to drop. What is happening in the real estate market is the second leg of the bubble. (If bubbles can have legs!)

And it is a global phenomenon. Since 1995, in real terms residential property prices have risen by more than 25 percent just about everywhere in the developed world except Canada, Italy, Germany, and Japan. In many countries they have increased by more than 100 percent. Just as in the share boom, hundreds of millions of people have thought that money would cascade to them from rising house prices, without effort or desert, merely by sitting there— money for nothing.[3] But a society can no more get rich through rising house prices than it can through everyone agreeing to take in each other's washing.

Even so, this illusion has enabled measured wealth levels to recover, and for all those people worried about their pensions it has provided a soothing balm. The bursting of the house price bubble will puncture this illusion and bring people face to face with the sober realities of their financial situation. The result can only be much weaker growth of consumer spending.

Deflation and Protection

The necessary adjustment following the collapse of the share and housing bubbles would be a heavy burden at the best of times, but we are not living at the best of times. In the middle of 2005, after sharp rises in oil prices, markets were again worrying about a resurgence of inflation but, not for the first time, they were looking in the wrong direction. In the 10 years since I wrote *The Death of Inflation*, there have been repeated scares about the re-emergence of inflation, but they have come to naught. This one is set to join the club. The reason is the strength of anti-inflationary forces that prevent a wage–price spiral from developing. Indeed, the end of the wealth illusion may readily bring about *deflation*. Japan, China, Hong Kong, and Singapore have already experienced it. In Europe and North America, there has not yet been generalized deflation but large sections of the economy are experiencing falling prices.

We are all familiar with the idea that the prices of high-tech goods such as computers and video recorders continue to fall, but deflationary trends have also affected long-established goods. In 1998, the average American car cost $25,500. Now it is $24,500. In 1983 that iconic symbol of America fast-food culture, the Burger King Whopper, cost $1.40. In 2003 it cost 99c.[4] In the UK between late 1997 and the summer of 2003, the average price of clothing and footwear fell by 18 percent, audiovisual equipment by 56 percent, and telephone calls by 13 percent. And deflationary trends have even infected the very medium through which you are reading these words: books. In May 2003 the average selling price of books in the UK was 5 percent lower than it had been two years previously.[5]

Moreover, in many western countries the overall rate of inflation is now perilously close to zero. In 2003, it fell as low as 0.6 percent in Germany and in the United States the core rate (that is, excluding erratic items) fell to 1.1 percent, a 37-year low. Even in the middle of 2005, after a huge increase in oil prices, inflation in these countries is only 1.9 percent and 3.2 percent. The writing is on the wall. Markets are currently more relaxed—again—about the risk of deflation. But such complacency is ill-judged.

So is the insouciance with regard to the dangers posed by falling prices that has been so common among commentators and investors. Deflation, they say, can be a good thing. Maybe, but not in today's economic circumstances. As I show in Chapter 3, in today's world the onset of a regime of falling prices would play havoc with the financial system, particularly pensions, which are looking extremely fragile and vulnerable after the stock-market collapse. In the US, employers' pension schemes are facing a short-fall of some $300 billion, while in the UK, pension schemes run by FTSE-100 companies are in deficit to the tune of £80–90 billion (about $130 billion),[6] or more than £20,000 ($30,000) for each of their UK employees.

The threat of deflation has appeared at a point when countries could readily resort to protecting their domestic economies through imposing trade restrictions; that is to say, shutting out foreign goods and services from their market in order to protect *home* suppliers. Indeed, despite decades of trade liberalization the world is still riven with trade barriers and new ones are regularly springing up in response to domestic pressure. America—which should know better—is one of the worst offenders. It is engaged in a long-running trade dispute with the EU but also, while paying lip service to the desirability of economic development around the world, by bowing to political pressure for the protection of some relatively unimportant sector of the American economy, it regularly promotes impoverishment in the developing countries. In January 2003, for instance, after heavy lobbying from American fish farmers, it imposed antidumping duties of 38–64 percent on imports of catfish from Vietnam. Vietnamese catfish exports to the US immediately fell by 30–40 percent and the Vietnamese catfish industry plunged into crisis.[7]

In the early months of 2003, the breakdown of friendly relations between America and Britain on the one hand, and France, Germany, and Russia on the other, made the protectionist danger all the more live and potent. Moreover, the weakness of the dollar against the euro threatened to intensify this danger. This exchange rate adjustment was welcomed in America as a way of reducing its huge current account deficit, but it did not cause much joy in Europe. It transferred demand for goods and services from the rest of the world, principally the eurozone, to the United States. Hardly surprisingly, other countries did not appreciate their loss. Despite a revival of the dollar in 2005, major dollar weakness remains a serious prospect in the years ahead. Other countries might readily seek to preserve their position, either by depreciating their currencies against the dollar or by imposing trade restrictions. Protection is the continuation of competitive depreciation by other means.

Nevertheless, one country's home market is another's export market. Protection by one country tends to lead to protection by others, with the result that trade is strangled in a tit-for-tat battle. All that a lurch into protection would achieve is a downward spiral of wealth and employment, just as it did in the 1930s. This is the way to impoverishment, not riches.

So how can we avoid the perils of a deflationary slump? If the origins of the crisis are thoroughly human, so is the solution. The key requirement is political leadership. Overcoming deflation is not technically difficult. The difficulties all lie in the human sphere of institutions, ideas, beliefs, and expectations. Similarly for successful resistance to protectionism. Protection is a pernicious influence in the world economy, but some may gain from it and countless millions may *think* they would. This is a political problem *par excellence* and, as I argue in the Finale, it has a political solution.

The great irony in this tale of woe and peril is that we face the threat of a deflationary slump at just the time that we stand on the brink of the greatest increase in prosperity in our history. This is not mere coincidence—the two are connected. The increase in productive potential and the relentless exposure to lower-cost competition, which are presenting the world with a continuing supply of deflationary shocks, are also part of the process that can bring boundless prosperity. Just as investors were getting caught up in the frenzy of the late 1990s stock-market bubble and thereby coming under the spell of an illusion of wealth, right under their noses the *real* sources of wealth were gathering their strength. *Then* markets got ahead of the economics. *Now* the economics are about to get ahead of the markets.

The Human Factor

From the beginning of time the physical has exerted an overwhelming pull over our economic life. Its substance has been the gathering, making, and amassing of *things*: things to eat, things to wear, things to live in, things to move us from here to there, things to play with, and now things to display with. The traditional language of economic thought is similarly "thingist." Output is supposedly determined by the three factors of production: land, labor, and capital.

Yet although thoughts and language are slow to change, the underlying economic reality is changing profoundly. As time has worn on it has become increasingly clear that there is something else besides those three thingist factors of production: the human factor. Economic history is the story of our painful escape from the barely physical to the mental—and now we are at the tipping point. The process of wealth creation is increasingly not about things, but rather about *nothings*, or intangibles—and it is the human factor that is at the root of this.

"Technological progress" may sound as though it is about the physical world of machines, but this is where it is applied, not where it comes from. Technological progress can best be thought of as improvements in the instructions for mixing together raw materials.[8] Those instructions, of course, come from the human mind.

And the conditions are now in place for the rate of accumulation of knowledge—and hence technological progress—to speed up. So far, the advent of computers, never mind their interconnection through the internet, has brought scant discernible benefit to productivity. This is about to change. Throughout history, the classic pattern is for innovations to take much longer than originally thought to have their full effect. This is what happened with railways, electricity, radio, and air travel. And it is about to happen with computers and the internet. Moreover, information and communications technology will greatly assist our ability to produce further advances in knowledge and to implement them more fully and more widely. What is more, the next great advance in knowledge is already with us and starting to bear fruit—biotechnology.

Biotech companies may not be as large or well known today as computer software companies, but then ten years ago computer software companies were not that large or well known either. But biotech companies are increasingly making their presence felt, especially in America. Amgen Inc. has revenues of some $5.5 billion and employs 7,700 people. Revenues for the stock-market-listed US biotech sector have risen by more than five times over the last decade to stand at over $25 billion per annum.[9]

These companies are fully part of the intangible economy. Their raw material is research and their output is knowledge: about how to improve production processes for food or how to improve our health. Already this output is starting to affect our everyday lives and our living standards. In years to come it may transform our health and greatly increase our longevity.

Biotechnology is a case of knowledge in and knowledge out. The preponderance of intangibles at both ends of the production process applies more and more widely across the economy. It is no longer simply a matter of the intangible sources of wealth helping to create things, for increasingly what we wish to spend our money on contains substantial amounts of intangibles too, whether it is the knowledge of how to put together a software program, how to entertain us, or how to make us better when we are ill.

The reason why intangibles are economically significant is that they have striking characteristics. They are like the biblical widow's cruse that never runs dry. Once we have the knowledge of how to make a plane or overcome a disease it can be used again and again to produce benefits at no further cost. Similarly, the intangibles we buy as part of our consumer goods, such as the design and styling of a car or the creative input into a Disney cartoon or a Harry Potter film, cost no more to produce for the millionth consumer than they did for the first. Intangibles give rise to what economists call increasing returns; that is to say when output expands, the total costs of production rise less than proportionately. Their increasing importance in the economy promises to bring enhanced prosperity—money for nothing. What this amounts to is a revolution: the Intangible Revolution.

The Wealth Spiral

If the potential of the knowledge economy is still not widely appreciated, at least the advantages of international trade are well established; and yet they have probably been widely underestimated too. Back in the eighteenth century the celebrated economist Adam Smith, the father of economics, had a theory of economic growth that is of major relevance to us today. The key to growth, he argued, was the size of the market; that is to say, the extent of the human sphere in which the deep-seated human desire to truck, barter, and exchange can be realized. For the bigger the market, the greater the degree of specialization, and hence, he argued, the lower the average cost of production. In other words, the economy was subject to increasing returns.

This, Smith thought, was the route to self-generating economic growth within a single country, but its relevance was multiplied by the interaction of countries through trade. Everyone's market could be expanded. And the gains are interactive: your enrichment expands my market, which enriches me; and my enrichment expands your market, which enriches you. This is the wealth spiral, which brings benefits to all, without effort and without sacrifice. While it may not be so quick or so spectacular as stock-market booms, it really is a source of money for nothing.

This is why the protectionist threat to which I referred above is so serious. Before this engine of prosperity has even got into first gear we could choose to shut it down. But if this threat is averted, as I show in Chapter 5, the wealth spiral now has massive scope to do its work as China, India, Russia, eastern Europe, and a host of other countries begin to play their full part in the world economy—indeed, to make it a truly *global* economy.

In other words, like it or loathe it, the great change from globalization is yet to happen. This should be a source not of anxiety, but of hope. Whether you live in a developed or developing country, globalization is good for you—and it is good for *them*. Or, at least, the right sort is. Globalization is simply the process by which producers and consumers come to treat the world as a single economic space. It merely continues the trend of widening horizons, increased specialization, and interdependence that has been taking place within countries for hundreds of years. Throughout our history this process has brought enhanced prosperity and it will continue to do so in the years ahead.

What the opponents of globalization fear, however, is the reduction of the rich diversity of independent nations into subjects of an ersatz American imperium. In view of America's domineering behavior at the beginning of the twenty-first century, their worries are understandable. Nevertheless, given American *leadership*, rather than domination, that is not what is in prospect. In fact, what lies before us is a shared prosperity that will release the poor countries of the world from both poverty and impotence—if the wealth spiral is given the chance to work its magic.

Good Governance

This makes it sound as though the process of enrichment is mechanistic. Just stir in the right ingredients and hey presto, up will pop growth and development. Yet as I show in Chapter 6, it is clear from economic history that there is nothing at all automatic about growth and development. On the contrary, they depend on a hidden third element: the human infrastructures of institutions, laws, values, and beliefs. These support two critical underpinnings of economic success: competitive markets and good government. The predominance of these two in the developed countries of the world largely explains their prosperity. The lack of them elsewhere in the world largely explains these countries' poverty.

There can be no better example than the contrast between North and South Korea—even though South Korea is no paragon of virtue. In North Korea, the percentage of GDP that is spent on the military is 25 percent, compared to 3 percent in the South. The share of international trade in GDP is 13 percent in the North and 62 percent in the South. These contrasts have their inevitable consequences for the relative size of the two countries' GDP. The South's GDP per capita is running at ten times the North's. Indeed, the North, a country that is able to produce long-range ballistic missiles capable of wreaking destruction on its neighbors, is incapable of feeding its own people. In the mass starvation of the mid-1990s, between 1 and 2 million people are thought to have died.

With regard to governance, too, the world is on the threshold of a great change. The greatest event of the late twentieth century was the collapse of communism, leading to the end of the Cold War. Although forms of communist government cling on in places, not least in North Korea, this spelt the end of an impoverishing ideology that held back economic growth and, in its extreme forms, trapped millions of people in needless poverty. The failure of communism was globalization's progenitor and its *sine qua non*.

Surprisingly, perhaps, the collapse of communism has also had profound effects within the capitalist countries: on the left of the political spectrum weakening the blind and rabid opposition to competitive markets as a means of organizing production; but also, on the right, making it possible for the supporters of competitive markets to criticize them and expose their limitations, thereby paving the way for an era of effective collaboration between markets and government.

The experience of the developed capitalist economies and the post-communist countries in Europe and Asia is going to have particular importance for the underdeveloped countries that have so far been largely excluded from the world's advancing prosperity. After decades of trying to boost economic development through foreign aid, the western countries have just about come to appreciate that pouring in money to boost investment is not enough to bring development. In short, what underdeveloped countries critically lack is the institutions that allow an economy to function effectively. But they will need help to build these. After years when the plight of Africa was quietly forgotten, in July 2005 it figured large on the agenda of the G8 summit at Gleneagles, Scotland—and debt relief plus an emphasis on governance were the results.

There is much to be done, but this was the crucial first step toward opening up the prospect of advance across swathes of the underdeveloped world, thereby giving the wealth spiral an even larger canvas over which to work its magic—and enabling the formerly excluded countries of the world, and their impoverished millions, to be brought within prosperity's embrace.

The Economy of the Future

The interaction between these forces opens up a new era. If the world manages to pull through the testing times that lie ahead, in the developed countries there is every prospect of a rise in the rate of economic growth to historically unprecedented levels. As a result of the intensity of competition and the empowerment of consumers, in complete contrast to the hopes and lusts of the bubble years, the gainers will largely be not companies or their shareholders, but hundreds of millions of ordinary people like you and me. Meanwhile, raising the poorer people of the world in Asia, Africa, the Middle East, and Latin America to take a full share in this wealth could be accomplished in a generation.

Nevertheless, as I show in Chapters 7–9, in the developed countries there will be profound changes in the way people earn their money. More and more of the traditional manufacturing activities will migrate to the developing countries, helping them to become more prosperous.* As the developing countries become increasingly sophisticated, more and more service-sector activities will migrate there as well. As a result, millions of people will be displaced from their existing jobs. Meanwhile, the intangibility of many aspects of the modern economy, and the associated scope for the rapid growth of e-commerce in areas such as agency and brokerage, finance, and information provision, will lead to millions more job losses in other industries—including among the various professions whose members helped to create the bubble.

Yet there will be no overall crisis of employment; quite the reverse. By 2025 China will probably have surpassed the United States as the largest economy in the world, and India will not be far behind. But this development, which so many people in the West fear, will be a source of great wealth. For the growing prosperity of these two waking giants, and other developing countries, will increase markets for the exports of the developed countries. Indeed, large numbers of western industries and their workers will come to depend on China and India for their markets.

And within the developed economies, as people get richer and richer, they will find new ways of spending their money, involving a shift of great significance in our economic history. The bulk of new jobs will appear predominantly outside the physical world and in the realm of the intangible—research and knowledge accumulation, caring, entertainment, pampering, and personal development.

Prosperity with a Human Face

But what will life be like in the economy of the future? The pessimists see an era of alienation and dehumanization as globalization homogenizes everything and destroys communities, while the progress of technology means that the real is supplanted not by the illusory but by the *virtual*. They imagine a world of virtual work, virtual leisure, and virtual relationships as technology takes over everything human and people shrink back into an isolated, impersonal world.

In Chapters 9 and 10 I reject this vision as yet another illusion. Although globalization will raise people to common levels of prosperity, it will support and encourage marked differences in how individuals and countries earn their living. The reason is simple: what drives it is specialization. Nor need globalization spell the end of communities. Rather, it will release the idea of community from the tyranny of the immediate locale. Even in the mundane worlds of work and leisure, never mind the realm of personal relationships, in the economy of the future the real and the human will remain supreme and the virtual will be recognized as second rate.

In economic history the human factor has become more and more important as a source of prosperity. Meanwhile, as regards the *ends* of economic activity, economic progress has widened the human sphere rather than diminished it. In the economy of the future, because the basic economic problem will have largely been conquered, the human sphere will be even wider. This will be an age of values and choices, offering us the opportunity for more leisure and allowing the pursuit of money to take a lower priority in our lives. Those values will include spiritual values and those choices will include moral choices.

This is no illusion. It is the destination of our journey in the next phase of economic history. Nevertheless, as I aim to show you in the succeeding pages, it is with an illusion that this journey begins.

---

* In what follows I frequently compare large groups of countries with regard to both past performance, current practice, and future prospects. It is clearly impossible to give lists of the countries each time. It is much more convenient to use group names as shorthand. Nevertheless, this is no easy matter. My criterion is essentially the level of current development. There is, however, a problem of terminology. Once the categorization has been drawn up, what should the groups be called? Sometimes it is tempting to refer to East and West, except that, geographically, Japan is in the East but economically it is in the West. And what about all those countries whose alignment is North–South? Furthermore, it seems to me that there should be *three* categories. In that case, is there to be an East, West, and North, with no South? Accordingly, I have decided to call my three categories of country developed, developing, and underdeveloped. I am sure that by so doing I am committing some political incorrectitude or other, but no offense is intended to anyone and it seems to me that this is the best solution for author and reader alike. The membership of my three categories is given in the Notes.[10]

Part I

Clear and Present Dangers

1

Financial Fantasies

At length corruption, like a general flood,
Did deluge all; and avarice creeping on,
Spread, like a low-born mist, and hid the sun.
Statesmen and patriots plied alike the stocks,
Peeress and butler shared alike the box;
And judges jobbed, and bishops bit the town,
And mighty dukes packed cards for half-a-crown;
Britain was sunk in lucre's sordid charms.

Alexander Pope on the South Sea Bubble of 1720[1]

The great stock market bull seeks to condense the future into a few days,
to discount the long march of history, and capture the present value of
all the future.

James Buchan[2]

In 1720, the physicist, astronomer, and mathematician Sir Isaac Newton, one of the greatest minds the world has ever been host to, was caught up in the speculative frenzy that we now call the South Sea Bubble. Seeing his South Sea holding rise appreciably in value and getting more nervous of a fall in the market, at one point Sir Isaac decided to sell. When asked by a friend when he thought the market would fall, he replied: "I can calculate the motions of the heavenly bodies but not the madness of the people."

How right he was. After Sir Isaac sold his stock, the market continued to rise and rise until eventually his nerve cracked again. He bought back in, this time with an increased stake. That was just before the market crashed. Sir Isaac Newton lost the then considerable sum of £20,000, which would be some £1.4 million or over $2 million in today's money. For the rest of his life, the discoverer of gravity, calculus, and much else besides could not bear to hear mention of the South Sea stock again.

By contrast, a bookseller whose claim to fame hitherto had been making a considerable amount of money by dealing in Bibles and Books of Common Prayer, one Thomas Guy, made a fortune out of South Sea stock. In April 1720 he held £54,000 of it, but over the following six weeks he sold his holding for £234,000, a sum that, in today's money, would be worth some £16 million or $25 million. Some good came out of all this. With his profits Thomas Guy founded Guy's Hospital, which is still treating patients in London today.

Sir Isaac Newton may not have been the first, or indeed the last, but he was surely the most intelligent victim of the lust after money for nothing. Since the beginning of time, while the daily reality has been relentless grind for paltry rewards, there have always been some who have dreamed of easy riches, wealth descending like manna from heaven. At various stages in our history the lust for easy riches has spread out from the afflicted few to consume whole classes of society. This happened in Holland in the seventeenth century when the road to riches was apparently strewn with tulips; in England in the eighteenth century when it wasn't so much a road as a seaway—to the South Seas; in England again in the nineteenth century when it was a railroad; in America in the early twentieth century when it was indeed a road, a railroad, and an airway combined; and in the late twentieth century when it was the information superhighway. All of these were "bubbles," a period of rapidly rising equity prices in a particular sector that are unfounded and are therefore liable to collapse equally rapidly.

In each case, for the individuals caught up in its vortex, the lust after money for nothing has typically led down the road to perdition. Sometimes a collapse of stock prices has occurred without apparently causing much harm to the economy at large. At other times, though, it has plunged the whole of society into crisis.

There is still a risk that in the aftermath of the bursting of the bubble of the late 1990s the world economy will fall into recession. In early 1994 the Dow Jones index stood at 3,600. At the start of 2000 it passed 11,700, a rise of 225 percent. Over this same period the key macroeconomic magnitudes—which you might think should be at least loosely related to the value of the stock market—rose by nothing like as much. US personal incomes and gross domestic product rose by about 40 percent and corporate profits rose by 60 percent. The widely watched measure of equity valuations, the price/earnings ratio on the S&P 500 Index, or P/E for short, hit 29 at the peak of the stock market in September 2000 (subsequently hitting 44 in May 2002), compared with a long-run postwar average of 16, easily outdoing the level it had reached on the eve of the Great Crash of 1929.

We should have learned the lessons of history and not been seduced by "lucre's sordid charms." How on earth did we come to this pretty pass? Can we at least learn from history how to stop the end of the dream becoming a nightmare?

The South Seas and Tulips

The South Sea Bubble of 1720 was largely a localized, purely English affair. It had some features in common with later bubbles, including the stock-market bubble of the late 1990s, but also some features that set it apart. It began as a scheme for privatizing England's national debt by offloading the government's liability to the South Sea Company. In return, the government made an interest payment on the debt and awarded certain monopolies in trading with the "South Seas," meaning in this case the Spanish colonies of South America. The South Sea Company then sought to persuade holders of the government debt to exchange these for its own stock. It was able to make a profit on the whole deal if it could succeed in driving the price of the stock above its face value.

The details of the scheme were complicated and need not detain us here, but the essential feature was that a higher price appeared to be in the interests of all concerned: the company, the holders of government stock, and the government. Initially the price of the stock rose mightily. However, the scheme had a fundamental weakness. It depended for its viability on the shares trading at a greater value than their intrinsic worth.

Carswell, a great authority on the Bubble, quotes one rational participant:

> *The additional rise above the true capital will only be imaginary; one added to one, by any stretch of vulgar arithmetic, will never make three and a half, consequently any fictitious value must be a loss to some person or other first or last. The only way to prevent it to oneself must be to sell out betimes, and so let the Devil take the hindmost.*[3]

As the South Sea stock soared and great enthusiasm was generated about its prospects, so a whole host of other companies were formed to take advantage of the public's lust for investing in new projects with the prospect of making a fortune. These eighteenth-century dotcoms subsequently became known as bubble companies. Many were outlawed by Act of Parliament— although not to protect the public but rather to maximize the appetite for South Sea stock.

The bubble companies invited subscribers to part with money on the basis of the most flimsy or ludicrous of prospectuses. My favorite is the one that said its purpose was: "For carrying on an undertaking of great advantage; but nobody to know what it is."[4]

When the crash came it was devastating for all involved. South Sea shares fell to 15 percent of what they had been worth at their peak, and even Bank of England and East India shares fell by almost two-thirds. Yet, despite the lamentations of many and the suicides of a few, the busting of the bubble did not appear to cause any great harm to the economy. The number of mercantile bankruptcies in 1721 was hardly higher than the previous year.

There were echoes here of an earlier localized bubble, the Dutch Tulipmania of the 1630s. What is so striking about the latter is that the extravagant prices paid for tulips had nothing to do with the idea that they could propagate themselves and thereby bring great wealth as a result of their productivity. As Chancellor puts it:

> The bulbous offshoots of a Semper Augustus would neither flower nor produce further offshoots for several years and there was no guarantee that they would exhibit the same special qualities of the mother bulb, since they were just as likely to revert to the plain breeder variety. Tulips did not even produce a cash yield (or 'dividend') since there was no trade in cut flowers at the time.[5]

Tulipmania was not excitement about the transforming power of technology, or contemplation of the output that would flow from a new piece of machinery, or even about the riches that would flow from international trade. It did not correspond to the alchemist's dream of turning base metal into gold. The value of the tulip bulbs derived from the beauty of the tulips they produced and the rarest of tulips acquired intense scarcity value. Essentially, tulips were being valued like Picassos. In 1624, a single Semper

Augustus fetched 1,200 florins; enough, at the time, to buy a small Amsterdam townhouse.[6]

However, once the price of the bulbs had started to rise sharply it seems clear that they then acquired speculative value. The higher the price rose, the more credible the price was. After all, it had a history. If someone paid $10,000 for an asset yesterday, you may well wonder whether you should pay $9,000 or $11,000 today. But the notion that the thing is actually only worth $100 is unthinkable. After all, it has a trading history somewhere near the asking price, so the price must be *roughly* right. This was as true for bulbs then as it was for internet stocks in 1999.

There is nothing peculiar about paying a fortune for something of beauty. Over the centuries people have done exactly that for paintings, furniture, and *objets d'art*. What marked out the tulip bubble was not the fact that people were prepared to pay these prices in order to acquire a thing of beauty, but rather that they were prepared to pay them in order to acquire something that they would then sell on to someone else for yet more money.[7]

Most importantly, perhaps, to us as early twenty-first-century survivors of the latest manifestation of such mass speculative psychology, again there is no evidence that the deflation of the tulip bubble caused any immediate distress to the Dutch economy, or any lasting damage to the fabric of the Dutch commercial system.

The Bubble as Mirage

The 1990s bull market in shares was not a localized affair at all. It was pretty much a worldwide phenomenon, but it had its origins in, and took its lead from, what happened in America. For the many millions who rode this bull market, this was a case not only of money for nothing but also of money *from* nothing. How did this collective madness take hold?

When the dust has settled there will doubtless be umpteen conflicting versions of how it happened, but if any one of them claims to have found *the* answer, in my view it will have failed. This was a historical event. As such, it was bound to have complex causes. Nevertheless, one factor stands out as fundamental, namely the fact that the bull market *began* as a reaction to improved economic circumstances. All the best myths have an element of truth and all the best bubbles start with something real.

Austrian economist Joseph Schumpeter believed that speculative manias often occur with the inception of a new industry or technology, when people overestimate the gains and underestimate the effects that the attraction of new capital will have in depressing returns. Charles Kindleberger, in his book *Manias, Panics and Crashes,* suggests something similar.[8] The first stage is a *displacement*, which excites speculative interest. This is followed by *positive feedback*, as rising stock prices attract new investors who then drive prices up further. The final stage is *euphoria*, when investors take leave of their senses.

The great 1990s bull market had its foundation in a combination of displacements, both economic and technological. The first of these, and arguably the most important, concerned inflation. The 1970s were a terrible time for the world economy. There were two huge increases in the price of oil that, in the context of labor militancy and accommodating monetary policy, sent the general price level rocketing and led to fears of hyperinflation, while output fell, unemployment soared, and the rate of productivity growth slumped. Governments seemed powerless to stop or reverse the deterioration in the economy. Economists for a long time seemed unable to explain it. Eventually, they did the next best thing. They invented a name for it: stagflation. People talked about "secular stagnation" or worse. The prosperity of the 1950s and 1960s had been an aberration, a one-off adjustment after years of world conflict. Now we were destined to lapse back into "normality;" that is to say, pedestrian rates of progress, or worse.

Even after the recovery from the recession of the early 1990s, in the US living standards appeared to be stagnating, or even declining, so that large numbers of people believed that their children would be less well off than they themselves had been. Ever-rising prosperity was believed to be part of the golden age that had passed. The title of a book by Wallace C. Peterson published in America in 1994 best sums it all up: *Silent Depression.*[9]

Within a few short years, though, all this was transformed. Not only were jobs plentiful, but inflation remained low. The beast of the 1970s was dead. Real living standards were rising—even for those at the bottom of the pack. The future was going to be better after all. Hey, even New York was getting better: cleaner, safer, and, well, *nicer.* Silent depression quickly gave way to "irrational exuberance."

Inflation illusion

When you think about it, both the conditions of the middle to late 1990s and the public perception of them made quite a contrast to the early 1990s, never mind the 1970s, and this contrast deserved a response. Some sort of celebration was in order. The stock market celebrated in style.

The trouble is that the high jinks went much too far. Despite the hype about the performance of the American economy, the performance of shares was out of all proportion. The stock market levitated above economic reality. Outside America the contrast was stronger because in the late 1990s economic performance in Europe was lackluster at best yet shares rose almost as much as they did in the US.

Somewhere along the line the market shifted from reacting rationally to the improved economic circumstances to building in wildly optimistic expectations for the future—what Kindleberger called "euphoria." Why did this happen?

It was partly because financial markets have an inherent tendency to extrapolate, as evidenced in that irritating expression "the trend is your friend." However, I think a good part of the reason is that investors did not appreciate the extent to which the substantial equity gains of the 1980s and early 1990s were the result of a one-off improvement, and they did not appreciate the inter-relationship with inflation. The death of inflation had allowed interest rates and bond yields to fall, thereby increasing the profits attributable to shareholders.[10] As the economy expanded without generating higher inflation, this gave a once-and-for-all boost to profits, just as it gave a once-and-for-all boost to employment levels. But although the unemployment rate could carry on falling for a while, it would eventually reach a limit—so would the accompanying rise in profits.

Who needs income anyway?

Moreover, the illusions created by inflation had a significant impact on the widespread popular view of equities. In short, the view took hold that since they had delivered fabulous returns over long periods, they were bound to do so in the future. After all, £100 invested in British equities in 1899, with the income reinvested year after year, would have grown by the end of 2000 to £1,209,836 (so $100 would have grown to $1,209,836).[11] The figures for American shares would be broadly similar.

These figures could launch a thousand savings schemes. Imagine the sales hype: "Save $100 with us and make your grandchild a millionaire. Save

$300 with us and make yourself a millionaire." Unfortunately, inflation has been up to its usual tricks. In 1899, $100 was just about equal to around half the average annual wage, so it was a little like putting aside $40,000 now for your grandchild—or $120,000 for yourself.

Admittedly, the performance of equities was pretty striking even after adjusting for inflation. That $100 would have turned into nearly $35,000 in real (i.e., inflation-adjusted) terms. By contrast, $100 invested in bonds would have grown to only $23,000, and only a little over $400 in real terms. However, this sparkling return in equities was due to some special circumstances and wasn't quite so sparkling when you made adjustments for bias in the data.[12]

Nevertheless, the result of apparently spectacular returns was to transform investment culture. Somewhere along the line the idea of investments as the source of a continuing flow of income got lost in the desire for capital gains, to the point where many investors really did not care about the income, and relatedly lost sight of the concept of risk. In short, they fell victim to the lust after money for nothing.

In the process, capital values lost their anchor. Once the importance of income has been eroded, what is there to limit, or even to set, stock-market values? We are then in the world of financial fantasies where asset prices depend wholly on views of the uncertain future, and stocks are seen as something akin to gambling chips.

This psychology went so far among investors that many lost all sight of the difference between investment and gambling. That difference can be summed up in a single word: fruitfulness. Assets can be compared to a tree that bears fruit each year. Investors who are only interested in capital gain are like farmers who ignore the harvest. The fruit need not necessarily be paid out as dividend but there should be fruit in some form; that is, there should be corporate earnings that *could* be paid in dividends.

By contrast, gambling is not a "fruitful" activity. It is a zero-sum game: for every winner there must be a loser. Individually, what drives it is the lure of money for nothing. Collectively, in a different sense, that is exactly the result—all that money and effort for no reward.

At the height of the dotcom mania, investing in stocks came very close to this as shares in businesses that had no profits, and in some cases no revenues, changed hands for huge sums. And some pretty strange businesses were set up. One company, AllAdvantage.com, paid customers to surf the web. That's right, it paid *them*. More precisely, it installed a program on their PC that pumped out a nonstop stream of banner advertisements. The idea was that AllAdvantage got paid by the advertisers so it could pay the surfer for putting up with having the adverts streaming across the screen. What I want to know is how it could be sure that subscribers were actually surfing the web rather than having some other program give the appearance of surfing, so that they were able to pick up the money while they went and did something useful like feeding the cat. (Have I stumbled on a new business idea, I ask myself?)

In any case, the troubles that hit this company proved rather more basic. The advertising revenues did not pour in quite as expected. The result is that it had to cut costs by reducing the fees paid to surfers. But to compensate, AllAdvantage introduced a *daily* $50,000 sweepstake, which was open only to qualifying surfers. Only in the topsy-turvy dotcom world could something like this be seen as a cost-cutting measure.[13]

In fact, the analogy with gambling was even closer. Although gambling is a zero-sum game to society as a whole, it is a *negative*-sum game to the gamblers, because they have to fund the house take, or bookies' margin. Similarly, with "investment" where the assets bear no fruit, the costs of transactions—the issuers' fees and the brokers' and market makers' take— ensure that it is a negative-sum game for the investors.

The way that many people "invested" clearly showed the links with gambling. During the dotcom mania the phenomenon of the "day trader" arose. These were people who traded stocks via the internet, typically aiming to buy and sell within the same day. As a result, the average holding period for Nasdaq stocks fell from 730 days in 1990 to 150 days ten years later. This connection between stock-market "investment" and gambling cannot be better highlighted than by the wording of a Connecticut billboard advertising offtrack betting, noticed by Robert Shiller. Its message was loud and clear: "Like the Stock Market, Only Faster."[14]

Mind you, the obsession with money for nothing and the blurring of the distinction between investment and gambling were not confined to the western side of the Atlantic. Another great popular scheme for making money recently emerged in the UK aimed specifically at women. It is believed to have begun in that well-known center of investment expertise the Isle of Wight, and from there it criss-crossed the country with lightning speed. Up to 15,000 investors were thought to have signed up for this scheme in pursuit of the promised eightfold return on an initial £3,000 (about $4,500) "investment," and officials believed that it could soon attract a million members.[15]

This is how it worked. New recruits were signed up to the scheme by a friend or family member and immediately handed over £3,000. You can guess the rest. Each new member was required to go out and sign up new members and when they did, the £3,000 was handed over to earlier joiners until they reached the magic £24,000 (about $36,000) payout, at which point they fell out and subsequent joiners rose in the pecking order to receive their money. It was money for nothing. Apparently the swarms of new members did not even see that on average the participants *could not possibly* make money, or if they did see this they simply believed, as all gamblers do, that they could beat the gun.

The old ones are the best! Sadly, you cannot overturn the laws of arithmetic, or escape the time-honored principles of real investment, merely by excluding men. Although they did not realize it at the time, by bidding up shares to ludicrous heights out of all proportion to underlying value, stock-market investors were engaging in essentially the same activity as the women on the Isle of Wight.

The Easy-Money Culture

There is no doubt that 1990s America was obsessed with money, and after the stock-price rises of the late 1990s being obsessed with money meant being obsessed with stocks. Between 1983 and 1999 the number of Americans with equity investments rose by 86 percent to nearly 80 million.

Their involvement went beyond the disembodied pursuit of profit. Advertisements proliferated and television and radio shows boomed, extolling the attractions, and the excitements, of investment. The stock market, which had previously been the home subject of only professionals or bores, became the stuff of every dinner-table conversation. Interestingly, John Kenneth Galbraith noted that something similar was true in 1929. He wrote: "By the summer of 1929 the market not only dominated the news. It also dominated the culture."[16]

In fact, in the late 1990s it went further than this. Americans, by and large, are a very religious people and they bring a religious fervor to the subject of making money. The lust after money for nothing went beyond the culture and entered the soul.

Moreover, mirroring what had happened in previous bubbles, the type of people drawn into stock-market investment also changed. Referring to the great British railway boom of the 1830s and 1840s, Kindleberger says that before 1835 railway shares were typically sold to local chambers of commerce, Quaker capitalists, and hard-headed Lancashire businessmen, both merchants and industrialists, who could meet not only the initial 5 to 10 percent payment but also any subsequent calls that might arise as the work of building the railway progressed. After 1835, though, professional company promoters, many of them rogues interested only in a quick profit, tempted a different class of investors, including "ladies and clergymen." Does this ring a bell?

The idea and the dream

Thus in the 1990s millions of investors deluded themselves. Still, there must have been something more than mere extrapolation and wealth illusion. There was. First of all, there was the money—lots of it. After a very difficult phase in the early 1990s when the US banking system was nearly brought down by a crisis over the insolvency of savings and loan institutions (roughly equivalent to British building societies), banks gradually recovered and soon found themselves benefiting hugely from the recovery in the economy. They were awash with capital. So they lent like the blazes and the supply of money and credit expanded rapidly.[17]

Nevertheless, investors needed the confidence in the future that leads to the desire to buy and the preparedness to borrow. In the late 1990s, this was supplied in the form of one of the most powerful drugs of all: an idea, or at least an expression masquerading as an idea. We do not know who first coined the expression "the new economy," but it will surely go down in the annals as embodying the spirit of the day. It was taken up by the armies of analysts on Wall Street whose job it is to drum up interest in stocks and quickly passed on to those who write news reports on the day's market movements. Soon stocks were openly classified as "old economy" or "new economy" and portfolios were constructed, prices evaluated, and stocks traded on the basis of this distinction.

The idea had a clear macroeconomic dimension, most notably the notion that the business cycle had been abolished, which I roundly dismiss.

But most investors would not be enthused by an essentially economic idea, even as the basis of an apparently economic concept like "the new economy." They would prefer something more solid and—particularly in America, which has an acute weakness for such things, akin to having a sweet tooth—they would prefer something more technological. They got it. The internet and all the technological gizmos associated with it supplied the missing ingredient: the dream.

The internet was the way by which the new-economy idea was made flesh. Costs would be cut, new industries founded, markets expanded, and hence profits driven up by the wonderful opportunities afforded by the new technology.

Fool's gold

What a letdown. Not long ago the world was supposedly on the brink of a technological revolution associated with the computer, the mobile phone, and the telecommunications links between them. We were about to undergo the e-revolution, which would sweep us all along to untold prosperity. New e-businesses were founded by the thousand. New fortunes were made, overnight, from nowhere and for nought. It was money for nothing.

Meanwhile, the owners and managers of older fortunes fell over themselves to transfer their cash to the new generation of e-ntrepreneurs. So great was the excitement about future wealth that professional firms such as solicitors and accountants were happy to accept equity in the new dotcoms in lieu of fees for their services. It was the economic equivalent of a magic carpet.

That was then. During the course of the year 2000 the magic carpet came down to earth—with a bump. Huge computer-related companies such as Intel saw sales plunge while mobile phone companies Nokia and Vodafone, which had been used to limitless growth, hit a brick wall. The British electronics company Marconi, formerly the staid GEC, almost collapsed, brought down by an ill-fated rush to snap up highly rated "new-economy" telecommunications companies that turned out to be little more than hollow shells. This really was a case of paying over money for nothing.

The really spectacular change came at the smaller end of the scale. Former highfliers in the dotcom world collapsed. So many dotcoms closed down that several internet sites were established to monitor them, and new companies, so-called vulture dotcoms, were set up to try to offload the assets of their ailing brethren. Not that there were normally many assets to be found. From the assets of liquidated Click Mango, an e-tailer for natural healthcare products, one juicy morsel stood out as a symbol of the whole sector: its inflatable boardroom, a sort of adult bouncy castle in clear plastic and opaque pink.[18] Any offers?

Fortunes so easily amassed quickly evaporated. Forget the magic carpet; it now looks more like an Indian rope trick. You would have thought that investors would have been aware of the risks of substantial misvaluation, and hence of big drops in stock prices, particularly after the sharp falls of 1998. But this is where the real magic ingredient comes in—the role of St. Alan.

The Saint

Excessive faith in central bankers is a special case of the wider species of exaggerated faith in individuals to control events. People are evidently uncomfortable with the idea that their lives are at the play of impersonal, dark forces, and happier with the notion that their fates are really in the hands of some super-talented, and preferably well-intentioned, human being. When Herbert Hoover became President of the United States in March 1929, there was a thriving personality cult around the 74-year-old Andrew Mellon who had been Treasury Secretary since 1921 and was thought able to walk on water. Hoover reappointed him, saying that he was "the greatest Secretary of the Treasury since Alexander Hamilton." Nevertheless, in February 1932 Mellon resigned in disgrace.

What the asset boom of the 1990s needed was someone to take on the role of saint/superhero/magician. Step forward the chairman of the Federal Reserve. Alan Greenspan took on mythical status. He was that most prized and dangerous of human types: the convert. He began as one of the doomsayers about the stock market, coining the phrase that surely captures the spirit of the age, "irrational exuberance," in a speech made on December 5, 1996, when the Dow was at 6,400. Subsequently, he became so convinced of the "new-economy" idea that his speeches were regularly peppered with references to the ability of the US economy to grow faster, and this was widely taken to be endorsement of the supposedly euphoric values on Wall Street.

He came to be regarded as a sort of a wizard-cum-saint, a man whose delphic utterances could decide the fate of billions—of dollars, if not people—

but whose noble aim was to steer the good ship *America*, followed by a flotilla of smaller vessels, many of them distinctly unseaworthy, across stormy seas to berth safely in the ports of foreign lands.

Belief in Merlin's abilities became so strong that he was widely credited with the ability to stop a major fall in the market from taking place. After all, it was he who had orchestrated the cuts in interest rates in 1987 that caused both the economy, and ultimately the markets, to rebound, he who had staved off disaster during the savings and loan debacle in the early 1990s, and again he who had organized the even more obviously successful turnaround after the global financial crisis of 1998.

The rude awakening

Was Greenspan's role even greater than I have suggested? From all past experience we can be sure that investors' reaction will be to seek out a scapegoat, someone to blame for the whole illusion. In advance you can never be sure who will ultimately be the focus of their ire, but from the history of speculative manias it is clear that it is often the selfsame individuals who were the heroes of the day just a few short illusions ago. As Galbraith relates, in the aftermath of the 1929 crash came "the eventual discovery of the severe mental and moral deficiencies of those once thought endowed with genius and their consignment, at best, to oblivion, but, more grimly, to public obloquy, jail or suicide."[19]

Even his fiercest critics could hardly claim that Alan Greenspan deserves that fate, and I reckon that in his time he has been an outstanding central banker, given the circumstances and pressures. Nevertheless, if it does all end in tears, on the basis of past experience, it would not be at all surprising if in due course the major villain of the piece was seen to be none other than the wizard himself. This would be particularly rich since most investors needed little encouragement from Greenspan to be taken in themselves.[20]

It is human nature to seek to shift the blame to someone else in order to hide the true extent of one's own folly—certainly from others, but most importantly from oneself. In his classic book, Charles Mackay provides a striking example of this phenomenon in 1720, when England was trying to come to terms with the excesses of the South Sea Bubble. He wrote:

> *...public meetings were held in every considerable town of the empire, at which petitions were adopted, praying the vengeance of the legislature*

upon the South Sea directors, who, by their fraudulent practices, had brought the nation to the brink of ruin. Nobody seemed to imagine that the nation itself was as culpable as the South Sea company. Nobody blamed the credulity and avarice of the people—the degrading lust of gain, which had swallowed up every nobler quality in the national character, or the infatuation which had made the multitude run their heads with such frantic eagerness into the net held out for them by scheming projectors. These things were never mentioned.[21]

Gearing and options

For all Merlin's powers, still you would have thought that investors, both professional and amateur, would have been worried about the *price* they were paying for their investments. But if they tried to come to terms with the question of what represented value in the stock market, they encountered a serious problem: the goalposts were being moved. To see exactly what was happening to corporate earnings you had to be something of a detective.

Share options were one of the main problems. Options were meant as a form of remuneration to senior employees, and in some of the new-economy enterprises to just about all employees. Options are a clear substitute for salary.[22] Yet during the great bull market options were not regarded as a cost when the accounts were constructed; that is to say, they were not charged to the profit and loss account. Only now are companies gradually coming to treat the value of options as an expense. Accordingly, the use of options artificially depressed recorded costs and boosted recorded profits. There were countless other sources of distortions, including variable treatment of pension funds and pension contributions (which I discuss in the next chapter) and the treatment of leasing operations, before we get on to the sort of skulduggery that occurred at Enron.

By the late stages of the stock-market mania, however, profits were not really what drove the market. Investors were sufficiently euphoric that they had scant regard for corporate earnings, let alone dividends, as a gauge of what a company was worth. This was most obviously true in the dotcom sector where companies rarely had any earnings, and in some cases did not even have any *revenues*. Investors who were keen to receive dividends from their investments were regarded as some sort of curiosum, a hangover from bygone days, to be indulged, perhaps, or merely pitied.

The comparative disregard for corporate earnings was also true, to some extent, of the whole market. You can see this most clearly in the behavior of the price/earnings (P/E) ratio, referred to earlier. At one point, companies the size of Cisco, Oracle, and America Online were selling for more than 100 times trailing earnings. In sharespeak, the market was now "more highly rated."

In the past, high P/E ratios had proved to be a good forecaster of imminent falls in the market; except when high ratings were applied to currently depressed earnings because of recession or a sudden and reversible rise in costs. But this was hardly the case in the late 1990s. The economy was booming and corporate earnings were surely near their cyclical peak— except, of course, that cycles had supposedly been abolished. So the P/E ratio was at an all-time high in relation to earnings figures, which were at an economic high, increased by the effects of gearing, overstated by favorable accounting treatment—and massaged by heaven knows what dubious accounting practices.

When the extent of those dubious accounting practices began to come to light in 2000–2003, the market was shocked and concern about the reliability of accounts became one of the most serious factors depressing share prices. This should not be surprising, because the reliability and probity of accounts are vital elements in the effective functioning of the capitalist system. It is through company accounts that we try to monitor the shifting, but all-important, continuous bargain that we strike between present and future.

Yet most market operators *were* surprised. This reveals an acute loss of collective memory. John Kenneth Galbraith had long before explained the way that financial standards lapsed in the boom years leading up to the 1929 crash. Things were accepted and even went unnoticed that, when they came to light after the crash, made hardened financiers wince.

How had these things been tolerated? Because financial euphoria is a sort of collective drug that causes people—even good, professionally competent people—to slip their moorings. Throughout the 1990s recovery, leading into the late 1990s boom, the leaders of corporate America, aided and abetted by the investment banks and nodded through by the accountants, had massive incentives to present the position of their companies in the most favorable light. Now the illusion is over we are seeing how their finances look in the cold light of dawn—and appreciating, once again, the wisdom of John Kenneth Galbraith.

Defending the indefensible

As the financial markets were structured, and in many ways still are, expecting professional market analysts to call time on the market was a bit like
expecting turkeys to vote for Christmas, except that when you consider
what these guys earned it is apparent that these were no turkeys—*we* were,
because we paid for them. Just about all of the analysts who gained notori-
ety in the bull market from regular appearances on TV and radio shows were
employed by major investment houses that had a strong interest in the continuation of the bull market; as did the individuals themselves. Lack of independence, major financial incentive, and a lack of accountability (except to
their corporate bosses, who were similarly compromised) inevitably produced a constant stream of bullish recommendations. They were definitely
on to money for nothing.

As you might expect, the armies of Wall Street analysts and commentators assembled a raft of arguments explaining why the high P/E ratios were
no barrier to ever-rising share prices. One of the most frequently advanced
was that low inflation improved the *quality* of earnings, and thereby justified a higher multiple. In some incarnations, this argument was little more
than a rehash of "the business cycle is dead" line.[23] The notion was that in
the past it was rising inflation that caused recessions, as it led the monetary
authorities to raise interest rates, which in turn hit real economic activity.
Yet just because inflation is quiescent at rates of capacity utilization and
rates of unemployment that would previously have led to surging inflation
does not mean that it will be quiescent at *any* rates of these variables. Even
in the brave new world it is possible to have a boom that goes too far and
leads to overheating. It is simply a matter of when.

Moreover, the notion that it has always been rising inflation, leading to
higher interest rates, that has killed the expansion represented a very narrow
reading of history—and only recent history at that. In the nineteenth century
it was overinvestment in capital equipment, and financial overstretch, that
subsequently caused the falls in real investment and financial retrenchment
that were at the heart of the cycle. This source of fluctuation is still with us in
the brave new world—and so are others. The sharp weakening of the US economy in early 2001 had little to do with rising inflation or rising interest rates.
As soon as Greenspan saw the signs he slashed interest rates, and continued
doing so, with some effect. Nevertheless, the signs of chronic weakness lingered
on. This had all the appearances of a classic nineteenth-century downturn.

But the apologists had another macro argument for higher P/Es: lower interest rates and bond yields. If you were accumulating capital in fixed-interest instruments, at each point in time your pile would be lower than it would have been under the earlier regime of higher interest rates. Accordingly, the same stream of prospective payments from an equity would overtake it all the sooner. So with the same risk factors and allowances for risk and risk preferences, equities should now be bid up in price until the prospective increase in accumulated capital was back on the same path relative to the accumulation of capital through holding fixed-interest assets.

The professionals have a convenient piece of jargon for this principle. It is called the "yield gap," referring to the gap between the yield on fixed-interest bonds and equities. As bond yields have fallen over recent years, they say, this tends to make the gap smaller and hence makes equities cheaper.

This relationship looks so simple that those who earn their megabucks from analyzing such things may feel somewhat embarrassed by it. Accordingly they have found ways to present it in more demanding form. It is common to refer not to the yield gap but to the yield *ratio*; that is, the ratio between the yield on bonds and the yield on equities. Immediately, all those investors who in their school days could master simple subtraction but were always uneasy with ratios fall back in wonder.

In fact it does not matter how you present this information. You can subtract one from the other, take the ratio, take the square root, or do a somersault with it if you like, but you cannot escape from its fundamental feature—and its fundamental, conceptual flaw. A given level of the gap between the two yields, or the ratio of the two yields, only makes sense given an assumption about the rate of inflation. If the inflation rate is changing, then the relationship between bond and equity yields should change also. The earnings on a bond are fixed in money terms, while the earnings on an equity can vary and should, in principle, change to reflect changes in the value of money. If bond yields have merely fallen in line with a fall in the prospective rate of inflation—that is to say, the real yield is unchanged—there is no reason why equities should be boosted.[24] At the peak of the equity market the real yield on US index-linked bonds was 4 percent, which would normally be regarded as a high rate, so there was scant support for fancy equity valuations from that quarter.

Suspend Your Disbelief

The most powerful argument assembled by the apologists for Wall Street's surge was essentially a plea for acceptance of a fervent agnosticism—the so-called efficient markets theory. This has been nothing less than the central orthodoxy in the field of finance for some 20 years or more. It holds that all the information available that could affect the market price is already embodied in the market price. So although the market may turn out to have been "wrong" in retrospect—in the sense that it priced a stock cheaply that subsequently soared, or priced expensively another one that subsequently plummeted—it is never wrong *prospectively*; that is to say, it never ignores or misuses information, leading to systematic mispricing.

Accordingly, if market prices diverged substantially from what traditional valuation models suggested *was* fair and reasonable, there must be something wrong with the traditional models. The search was on for new models suggesting that market values were fair and reasonable. Hence the idea of the "new economy" and the spate of new ways of valuing companies—especially those that did not make any profits and seemed unlikely to do so for the foreseeable future. Once companies were assessed on this new basis, it was evident that the emperor had some clothes on after all.

But what about the evidence of history, including the South Sea Bubble and Tulipmania? Some more enlightened souls accepted that gross mispricing may have happened *then* but merely argued that it could not happen *now*. Admittedly, that flew in the face of the evidence from what happened to Japan in the late 1980s, leading to the extended collapse of Japanese assets throughout the 1990s and the associated slump in the economy. Somehow, though, the investment professionals have always had a way of conveniently airbrushing Japan out of recent financial history.

The real zealots, though, went much further. *It could never have happened.* That's right, the supposed examples of financial bubbles in the past had been completely misinterpreted. They weren't bubbles at all. These rational market fundamentalists developed the concept of the "rational bubble." Even the apparently most obvious of speculative manias, such as Tulipmania, could be reinterpreted as the behavior of rational investors responding to the facts as they saw them.[25] And if manias and bubbles, as we had come to believe in them, had *never* existed, there was surely no reason to worry about being caught up in one now.

If this theoretical argument were not enough to dissuade you from trying to time your entry and exit from the market, there was the irrefutable evidence of investment history. Equities always did best in the end. It did not matter when you bought, the argument ran, if you waited long enough you always made money in stocks. Consequently, since you could not be sure when the market was overvalued or undervalued, the safest thing was always to be fully invested in the stock market. That way, you could never go wrong.

And if the market is always efficient, then why waste time thinking *which* stock to buy? That is best left to the market. The only scope for action left to investors is to decide on their taste for risk and then to assemble a portfolio that appropriately spreads risk to achieve the risk profile they desire. Then all they have to do is lie back and enjoy it—and let the market do the rest.

If you think about it, this efficient markets theory, for all its seductive allure, does have a few theoretical holes in it. Most notably, we are bound to ask who "the markets" are. They are supposedly the ever-watchful and all-seeing ones who set the right prices, given all available information. Yet everyone who might plausibly be thought to fulfill this role is induced by the theory into passivity through the injunction not to judge market prices and to leave that job to "the market." In short, for most of us to be able confidently to leave the job of setting the right price to someone else, there has to be someone who is *not* leaving it to someone else. Or to put it more provocatively, for the efficient markets theory to work there must be some people active in the market who do *not* believe it, and are able to disprove it by their actions.

In practice, in the boom of the late 1990s the markets were dominated by institutions who rarely thought about absolute value and instead, having their performance measured against benchmarks, thought about how they performed relative to their peers. The predominant fear was that they would not be fully invested in equities and would therefore underperform when the market rose.

Moreover, there is a little problem concerning that perennial bugbear of economic affairs—time horizons. The argument that stocks cannot be systematically mispriced because rational investors would be able to profit from the mispricing, and thereby correct it, fails to address the issue of how long the mispricing could exist. As Shiller puts it:

If indeed one knew today that the market would do poorly over the next ten or twenty years, but did not know exactly when it would begin to do poorly and could not prove one's knowledge to a broad audience, then there would be no way to profit significantly from this knowledge. There is thus no substantial reason to think that the smart money must necessarily eliminate such stock mispricing.[26]

These are the sort of criticisms one might level at the theory from an insider's perspective. At the wider human level, the criticism can be more trenchant. There is an enormous gulf between the academic discipline of finance and the way investors behave and think—or at least did, before they were brainwashed by the financial theorists. The divorce is so great that one is tempted to believe that it is intentional. Rationality is an a priori assumption rather than a description of the world.[27] Until recently, modern textbooks on finance typically did not even mention bubbles or the related phenomena, Ponzi or pyramid schemes, even though there are countless instances, including a recent scandalous example in Albania that caused great misery and outrage.[28]

Nor can we reasonably expect investment professionals, on whom poor old Joe Soap might rely for advice, to be immune to the gross mood swings of the market and always to adhere to the highest standards. Again, Galbraith is on the mark: "There is the possibility, even the likelihood, of self-approving and extravagantly error-prone behavior on the part of those closely associated with money."[29]

This judgment is certainly backed up by Bagehot's assessment of the events leading to the collapse of the firm of Overend, Gurney, which crashed on the day known as Black Friday, in May 1866: "These losses were made in a manner so reckless and so foolish that one would think a child who had lent money in the City of London would lend it better."[30] He should have lived to see the collapse of Barings Bank, brought on by the antics of the boy wonder from Watford, Nick Leeson.

Why *shouldn't* emotions like fear and greed, and the ebb and flow of fashion and ill-founded popular opinion, affect financial valuations? Just because human beings are rational does not mean that they are *only* rational. When the assembled throng at the Nuremberg rallies worked themselves into an ecstatic frenzy akin to a state of intense sexual excitement, does one suppose that this was the result of a discounted cost–benefit analysis of the results of the coming world conflict and its associated territorial acquisitions? Is it useful to consider how enthusiastic they were by assessing how their hopes for the future were grounded on a rational view of the prospects?

The whole of human history, on both an individual and a collective scale, is about the interplay between rational calculation and raw emotion. When you are dealing with high levels of uncertainty and long time horizons, it is often difficult to know where one ends and the other begins.

From Corporate Greed to Economic Peril

Given all the blandishments, arguments, and encouragements for Americans to hold stocks during the 1990s, you might be astonished to hear the identity of the major net buyers of stocks at the end of the decade. The answer speaks volumes about the US economy and the perils it may face in the years ahead. The buyers were US corporations themselves. This was doubly puzzling. It is not as though they were flush with cash. Quite the opposite, for although they were making good profits, as they should at this stage of the cycle (well, the accounts said that they were making good profits), they were investing boldly, thereby giving rise to the need to borrow. So by buying in their own stocks they had to raise still more borrowed money.

Moreover, it is not as though you could say that US stocks were cheap to buy in. This is, of course, the flip side of their not being cheap for investors to buy. On grounds of cost alone, corporations should surely have been issuing equity to fund their investments and retire debt.

The result was that the level of earnings per share was able to increase, but at the expense of traditional measures of balance sheet probity. In the jargon, companies were becoming more highly geared; that is to say, they had a higher ratio of debt to equity. This is generally regarded as more risky because if there were to be a downturn, companies would be obliged to carry on paying the interest on the debt, a burden that would now be borne by less equity. In really serious cases, the continued payment of interest could bust the company.

So why were they doing it? If corporate managements believed that the business cycle had been abolished, they could also believe that taking on more debt was justified because it was now less risky. Call me cynical, but somehow I doubt that this goes to the heart of the matter. There was at least one distinct advantage in companies pursuing this apparently risky strategy, namely that it had the apparent merit of boosting the share price. Could the increasing importance of executive share options have played a role in the choice of the apparently more risky strategy of issuing debt to buy in equity? Surely senior executives could not be putting their own narrow financial interest ahead of the company's, could they?

It remains to be seen how popular support for the American system of free enterprise holds up when the full results of this practice become known. For in doing this, and thereby sustaining the great bull market, the senior executives of American companies sought to pull themselves up by their own bootstraps. In the process, the wealth illusion was created for society as a whole, but the *reality* of untold riches was transferred from ordinary investors and prospective pensioners to those selfsame executives.

Money is blind

The illusion was so complete that the whole of society lost sight of the real sources of wealth. In the late 1990s it was common to hear people suggest that since equities returned, say, 20 percent per annum, we could *all* be better off if we piled into them. It was even suggested that, for this reason, the American Social Security Fund should be invested in equities.

Yet how could *everybody* gain from that? The return to equities derives from the profitability of companies and that in turn depends on the real performance of the economy. Unless that real performance were improved, or companies' share of it increased by greater participation in the equity market, collectively no real economic benefit whatever can come from increased purchases of shares. All that can happen is an increase in the price without real foundation, an increase that, as we have seen confirmed in recent years, would always be likely to collapse. In so far as equities have been able to deliver super returns in the past, it has been precisely because everybody was *not* holding them to start with. The holders of bank deposits, bonds, and other financial instruments could have their returns squeezed so that equity holders could have theirs boosted. If everyone held only equities this would no longer be possible.

If a pharmaceutical company successfully develops a new drug, it makes no difference to the real value of that development whether the company's shares rise as a result by $1, $10, or $100. All that this outcome affects is the degree of wealth illusion—and the distribution of wealth between investors and noninvestors. In the stock-market mania of the late 1990s, this simple thought hardly ever occurred to anyone caught up in the collective madness. If a firm's capitalization (i.e., its market value) soared by $1 billion, that was supposedly the same as $1 billion created any other way. The fact that this money had come from nowhere and corresponded to nothing in the economy was quite beside the point. Money was money. Investors then discovered the hard way that money conjured out of nothing by a collective bout of wishful thinking could just as easily shrink back to nothing.

Deflated hopes and inflated fears

Now it is clear that there was a whole rogue's gallery responsible for the investment disaster of 2000–2003. The share boom began as a reaction to some genuinely good economic performance and some interesting future prospects, not least concerning technology. But this grew into an absurd optimism in which the idea of technological transformation took flight.

Ordinary investors were certainly greedy and gullible, but they were egged on by an army of Wall Street professionals who had a strong self-interest in a rampant stock market. Meanwhile, umpteen professors of economics and finance were seriously culpable in developing and preaching the notion that bubbles could not happen; corporate executives were greedy for throwing everything, including some highly dubious accounting practices, in pursuit of short-term share performance and their own gain; and the accountancy profession was to blame for not sounding the alarm bells in the public interest. In some cases individual accountants apparently connived in cooking the very books they were supposed to be inspecting and approving.

Not for the first time, a whole society was consumed by the lust after money for nothing. The result was what all but the most purblind must now recognize as the greatest bubble in financial history—up to then.

But was it *all* an illusion, or was there something real at the bottom of the stock-market mania? Many of the participants thought there was. And the market visionaries *were* on to something. Admittedly, although the word globalization was all the rage, they hardly seemed to pay much attention to the transforming power of much increased international trade. They may have grossly overestimated the immediate potential of e-commerce, but they were alive to the eventual possibilities opened up by new technology. They may have been wrong about the death of the business cycle, but they were right to celebrate the death of inflation. They were naive about the new economy, but they correctly grasped the increasing importance of knowledge and the exciting ways in which it is different.

How could it simultaneously be true that the stock-market boom of the late 1990s was a gigantic illusion and yet the visionaries could eventually turn out to be right about the economy? There are three good reasons. First, the price. The stock market rose to such heights in the boom years that a wealth of future good economic news was discounted. It had to be fully as good as the ludicrous expectations implied by stock prices for the level of the market to remain unchanged. The market was discounting not so much the future as the hereafter.[31]

Second, the market seemed to assume that merely foreseeing future *economic* benefit was enough to justify higher share prices. But there is no reason why the bulk of the benefits of improved economic performance should fall to shareholders. Indeed, there are good grounds for believing that if the technological improvements about which the market was once so excited do bear fruit, the overwhelming bulk of benefits will fall to consumers: the increased competition and the increasing importance of human rather than physical capital as a source of economic growth. Whatever the employing company might think, its human capital walks out the door every night and this makes it extremely difficult for companies to get a return out of it, even if they have financed it. (Ironically, this is particularly true of investment bankers.) This increased tendency for employees or consumers to derive the benefits from economic progress may explain why so many businesses in 2002 seemed to be experiencing what can be described as a profitless recovery.

Third, the market was extremely naive about the life cycle of businesses and companies. Many of the companies that will eventually benefit from technological transformation and consequently high economic growth are not yet in existence and so their shares cannot be bought. Theirs is a wealth that cannot be transferred from the future to the present, but must remain forever over the horizon, beyond the grasp of those who would like to draw it down for themselves.

These three points have an important consequence. Just because stock markets made fools of themselves and their participants does not necessarily mean that the economic future is not going to be brighter. It is perfectly possible that as visionaries for the economy, the super-bulls will eventually turn out to be right, even though they were disastrously wrong about how to invest their, and your, money.

In short, this episode was not like Tulipmania or the South Sea Bubble. However, there is a good historical precedent for it: the mania for railway shares in Britain in the 1840s. The enthusiasts for these shares were convinced not merely that they were investing in assets that would bring them a profit, but that this profit arose from the transforming power of the new technology. Railways, it was thought, would transform not merely the economy but society itself. The irony is that the enthusiasts were right. Railways were the drivers of both economic growth and social change. They even transformed people's notions of time itself. Railway time became the arbiter of time for everybody. Nevertheless, people who bought railway *shares* still lost their shirts.

Consequences before Cures

Even if the visionaries of the 1990s were in essence right about the economy of the future, first we have to survive the bursting of the bubble. Many ordinary people hope, and some economists and financial professionals believe, that we will soon emerge unscathed and be able to waltz away from these recent troubled times. But we have just lived through a bubble greater than any other in previous history, a bubble whose values, both financial and moral, permeated every part of the financial system and even society itself. Somehow, I suspect that escape will not be so easy.

Much depends, of course, on what happens to the stock market from now on, and in that regard, as for Sir Isaac Newton in 1720, it is impossible for any of us to be sure of the future. Nevertheless, it is possible to say something. There may be a rally, a further crash, a continued slow slide, or merely a protracted period of share prices simply going nowhere. But I am pretty sure that there will not be a rapid return to the pre-crash levels of the market. And my suspicion is that the reality will be a good deal more testing than that. At the very least, the market will have to suffer a protracted hangover—a drawn-out period of investor disappointment and perhaps despair, accompanied by considerable risk of financial instability. As Warren Buffet has put it, the hangover may prove proportional to the binge that preceded it. And then there is the housing bubble, yet to burst.

The consequences that these bubbles are already bringing in their wake threaten to imperil not just the economy but society itself. Investors sowed the wind. We may all reap the whirlwind.

2
The Reckoning

History, which has a painful way of repeating itself, has taught mankind that
spectacular over-expansion invariably ends in over-contraction and distress.
Paul Warburg, investment banker, writing in March 1929[1]

Men, it has been well said, think in herds; it will be seen that they go
mad in herds, while they only recover their senses slowly, and one by one.
Charles Mackay, author of *Extraordinary Popular Delusions and the*
Madness of Crowds[2]

Some 200 years after the South Sea Bubble, Isaac Newton numbered among his many admirers and devotees the educator, philosopher, theologian, statistician, investment banker, forecaster, and economist Roger W. Babson, a worthy fellow, though *not* one of the greatest minds the world has ever been host to. Babson was mightily impressed by Newton's discoveries and especially his third law of motion: "For every action there is an equal and opposite reaction." He set about incorporating Newton's theory into many of his personal and business enterprises, going on to found the Gravity Research Foundation in 1948. In 1940 he even ran for President of the United States as the candidate of the National Prohibition Party, somehow managing to come third of eight candidates to Franklin Roosevelt and Wendell Wilkie.

All of this paled into insignificance beside his success as a forecaster. On September 5, 1929, speaking at a business conference, Babson observed: "Sooner or later a crash is coming, and it may be terrific." Warming to his theme he added: "…factories will be shut down… men will be thrown out of work… the vicious circle will get in full swing and the result will be a serious business depression."[3]

He was right, of course, but after a brief wobble Wall Street took no notice. His methods were thought questionable and investment weekly

Barron's denounced him, saying anyone acquainted with the "notorious inaccuracy" of his forecasts should not take him seriously. Anyway, there were other, higher authorities who had a much more soothing message.[4]

When the crash came it was devastating. In the first drop, to November 1929, prices fell by 34 percent, then recovered by 24 percent up to April 1930, then carried on falling until they hit bottom in June 1932, nearly three years after the crash began, with a cumulative fall of some 85 percent.

Most damagingly, there wasn't a rapid bounceback after the trough was reached. Someone who bought stocks on the eve of the Wall Street Crash would not have got their money back until 25 years later, in September 1954.

Yet the losses of stockholders in the early 1930s were nothing compared to the general losses to come. What came next was what we now know as the Great Depression. Although Babson may have been right about the nature of what would happen, he severely underestimated the extent. Even looking back, in most countries outside America people are still apt to underestimate it. For grim though things were more or less everywhere, except in Germany they didn't begin to approach the scale of what happened in America. There output fell by $9\frac{1}{2}$ percent in 1930, $8\frac{1}{2}$ percent in 1931, $13\frac{1}{2}$ percent in 1932, and by a further 2 percent in 1933. Unemployment reached 25 percent that year—one in four of the work force.[5]

Interestingly, two years after the Great Crash of 1929 the American economy appeared to be reviving, only to slip back again. In 1931 hardly anyone foresaw that America faced another *eight years* of depression and deflation. Could something similar happen now?

The Great Depression was not caused by the Wall Street Crash of 1929. Business was already vulnerable, indeed output in the US was already declining before the market broke. But the crash did undoubtedly play a significant part, eroding wealth, undermining balance sheets, ruining people and institutions, and, most important of all, shattering confidence.

The events that led up to the 1929 crash had a good deal in common with the great bull market of the 1990s. In much of Europe, the 1920s were a difficult period as countries sought to recover from the devastation of the war and grappled with unrest and political instability. In the United States, however, these were the "roaring twenties." The economy boomed and the promise of new technology burned bright. People talked of a new era. Asset prices soared—and then carried on going up.

Figure 2.1 The US stock market (S&P 500), 1922–1954 and 1993–2005
(Peak of market = 100)

Source: Based on data from R. Shiller, *Irrational Exuberance,* Princeton University Press, 2000; and Thomson Datastream

The shape of the bull market in the 1920s—and the subsequent collapse—was very similar to the shape of the market from 1993 to 2003, as Figure 2.1 shows. If you bought stocks at the 1929 peak, and held on, you had to wait until 1954 to get your money back—the equivalent this time of waiting until 2025. Of course, between 2003 and 2005 stocks rallied. Still, the game isn't over yet. After the market bottomed in 1932 there was a sharp rally. This time round the rally began from a much higher level. That may mean that the market has little scope to advance. It could easily take just as long to regan the previous peak.

What price must we pay for the irrational exuberance of the 1990s? If the South Sea Bubble of 1720 merely deflated egos and individual fortunes, the 1929 crash foreshadowed the appearance of the four horsemen of the economic apocalypse: slump, financial collapse, deflation, and protection. Will they ride again?

Collapse and Complacency

Many people evidently think that this question is hardly appropriate. Stock prices may have fallen, but so what? Life goes on. They are much too complacent about the dangers from a collapsed stock market. The conventional view is that stock-market values and the macro economy are separated, if not divorced. Even if there is some linkage from stock prices to the economy, it is likely to be weak. Accordingly even if stock prices continue to be weak or carry on falling, a short economic slowdown, never mind a recession, is all that should result. After that the world economy, suitably refreshed, should return to something like trend growth.

Admittedly, such complacency has some support from history. As I pointed out in Chapter 1, Dutch Tulipmania and the South Sea Bubble seem to have passed without causing a disaster to the economy of the time. But this was probably due to the restricted nature of the assets that had been speculated in and the relative lack of penetration, compared to today, of the financial world into the wider economy. By contrast, you could hardly argue that the US stock-market boom of the late 1920s or the Japanese asset boom of the 1980s left their economies unscathed. Quite the opposite: they contributed to a subsequent slump. It was similar for smaller phases of asset-price inflation such as late 1980s Britain and early 1990s Scandinavia. So why the complacency now?

The classic backing for a sanguine attitude comes from what happened in 1987. Most investors still believe that in October of that year the stock market crashed disastrously, wiping out fortunes. In fact, as any chart of stock prices readily shows, 1987 was a mere blip that now barely registers. If you had bought stocks on the first day of 1987 and held them through October's crash, you were still ahead of the game. More tellingly, even if you bought stocks the day *before* the crash and continued to hold them, before very long you were back in the money. In the US you only had to wait until January 1989 and in the UK until the following August—less than two years after the crash. And to have sold stocks and stayed out for the next decade would have been an appalling investment decision.

The events of 1997–98 provided another test. This was the time when several great stories were simultaneously playing themselves out on the world's investment stage. Russia defaulted on its debts and the rouble plunged. Meanwhile, several Asian countries, which had formerly been dubbed "Tigers" in recognition of their previous outstanding success, were caught up in a mammoth currency and financial crisis.

Most spectacularly, a hedge fund that hardly anyone had ever heard of before, called Long-Term Capital Management, almost went bust and thereby plunged the world into a financial crisis from which it was only just rescued by some panic reductions in interest rates by the Federal Reserve and other central banks. With two Nobel prize-winning professors of finance on its board, it made its business the identification of market anomalies. When it found one it bet the ranch on its ending. In 1998 it made a bet the size of a medium-sized country's GDP—and lost. After that lot you would have thought that the financial system would be seen to be vulnerable, but no. Because it turned out all right in the end, the aura of invincibility was *strengthened*.[6]

So the view that big falls in stock markets do not matter is now pretty well entrenched. It is also wrong. The sharp rally in share prices after the end of the conflict with Iraq was based on shaky foundations. It was accompanied by a major rally in bonds—continuing into mid-2005—that some observers likened to another bubble. If they are right, when it bursts there will be major capital losses and higher bond yields will undermine the equity market. Given the seriousness of the deflation risk that I detail in the next chapter, I do not think that this is a bond *bubble*. But the rally in equities is driven by the expectation of continued strong economic growth while the rally in bonds is driven by fears of recession and deflation. They cannot both be right. One way or another, markets are in for a very torrid time.

The Financial Time Bomb

For many professional observers and ordinary members of the public, the comparison of the current situation with the position after the Wall Street crash of 1929 is surreal, not least because one major element is apparently missing—a banking crisis. As I argue in the next chapter, however, the banking system may not be as robust as it looks. But history does not repeat itself exactly and this time the main financial threat comes from elsewhere: pensions and house prices.

Throughout the 1990s as the stock-market juggernaut rolled on, consumers were getting richer, without effort and without sacrifice. The investment professionals and corporate executives may have had their huge doses of money for nothing, but this provided the ordinary person's share—or at least the ordinary middle-class person's.

So why didn't the collapse of share prices in 2000–2003 have more serious adverse consequences immediately? Because the effects were heavily disguised within pension funds and offset by rising house prices. Even in a society like the US where direct share ownership is relatively high, but even more so in the UK, the effect of a drop in stock-market wealth falls largely on individuals' provision for the relatively distant and uncertain future in the form of pension funds and insurance policies. Although some people monitor the value of these policies reasonably closely, many do not, and indeed cannot, so great is the opacity of this form of saving.

Accordingly, the effect of a drop in such wealth is unlikely to come though quickly. Much of the effect of the stock-market's weakness in 2000–2003 is still to be felt. It will build up over time and the heavy burden of having to make extra provision for retirement will weigh like a millstone round people's necks. Pensions bring the ordinary man and woman face to face with the markets' attempts to put a value on the far future. If the countries of North America and Europe face a serious financial crisis, it will surely involve pensions and pension provision.

Because pension funds are so opaque, until recently they have seldom been subject to intense public scrutiny. They may be legally separate from their sponsoring companies (as in the UK), but the economic reality is that they are subsidiaries of their sponsoring companies and pension liabilities are like corporate debt. Meanwhile, pension fund assets are typically invested in the equity of other large companies, thereby effectively constituting a system of cross-holdings throughout the corporate sector.

Put that way, the comparison with Japan becomes clear. Moreover, the sheer size of corporate pension funds and their collective inter-relationship with the health of the stock market raises the specter of a pension doomsday machine. The vulnerability of pension funds to falling markets is Anglo-American capitalism's Achilles' heel. Weak investment performance worsens the pension funding position, and thereby weakens the profitability and ultimate viability of large numbers of companies. Accordingly their share prices fall, which sets the vicious circle turning again.

To most people working for large companies, this vulnerability must come as a huge shock. Until recently, pensions seemed pretty much cast iron. But this impression was built up in some very unusual circumstances. For nearly 20 years from the second oil shock in 1979–80 until the turn of the century, the economy operated in relatively favorable circumstances. The viability of pension funds was assisted by the full provision for the thousands of employees who, for one reason or another, departed early, thereby leaving the pension funds exceedingly well funded. More importantly, the investment performance was outstanding—to an extent that cannot possibly be repeated over the next 20 years.

Gradually, though, the generosity of pension schemes increased, as did their eventual costs. In the UK pensions in payment were uprated, frozen pensions were index linked, in many cases benefits were extended to widows, and pension funds bore the cost of waves of early retirements. "Never mind" was the attitude, since pension funds operated on a different sort of financial logic.

Pension provision was apparently cheap. You put in a little and the magic of the stock market transformed a little into a lot. It was money for nothing. In this way, until recently, the vulnerability of the whole system of pension provision, and thereby of the economy itself, was hidden not only from pensioners but also from the army of investment analysts who have been paid megabucks to analyze the financial health of companies. Meanwhile, even the actuarial profession, whose business this is, has been unable to come up with an agreed position on how pension funds should be valued.

Scarce wonder then that amid all the jargon and obfuscation, despite the huge sums involved and the enormous consequences for their companies, until recently most chief executives gave hardly a moment's thought to their companies' pension obligations. They simply buried their heads in the sand and hoped for the best. The pensions mess is not simply the outcome of the recent bear market. It has been an accident waiting to happen for years. And its root causes have been a deadly mixture of ignorance, incompetence, and optimism. Now comes the reckoning.

The end of the American dream
There are clear signs of the pensions crisis to come. In America millions of people are left wondering about their plans for retirement after they have seen the value of their "401k" (i.e., defined-contribution) retirement plans slashed. And these are the people who invested in relatively safe assets. Those who were taken in by the technology craze and the dotcom mania may have seen their savings decimated.

Admittedly, except for these unfortunate people most investors will have at least enjoyed gains in their investments in the late 1990s, so that by the end of 2002 they were simply back where they were in 1995 or 1996. But this is not as comfortable as it sounds. Throughout the western world the expected length of retirement is growing, yet people have not made increased provision for this. They certainly weren't doing it in 1995 or 1996. The stock-market boom provided a way to avoid facing this awful truth; you could let the stock market do your saving for you. Now, though, the chickens are coming home to roost.

The millions of people who are in final-salary pension schemes are apparently immune from stock-market weakness; it is their employers who must pick up the tab. They have had a cosy ride for many years as booming stock markets created a gap between the apparent benefit that employees would enjoy in the future and the apparent cost that companies had to shoulder now. Fear not, the stock market will provide!

The rules governing the accounting for pension liabilities in the US give companies enormous flexibility—which many have used to the hilt. They have allowed the gains on pension assets to feed into the bottom line. What is more, the system allows companies to amortize (i.e., spread out) any stock-market loss over several years, while still booking the expected gain on stocks to the current year's profits. So a company's pension assets might fall in value, but the company might still record this in the accounts as a gain. A Merrill Lynch study concluded that many companies' earnings would be reduced by more than 10 percent if pension income was not included. On the list were Bell South, Boeing, GE, IBM, Marsh & McLennan, SBC Communications, and Consolidated Edison.[7]

Standard & Poor's calculates that in the year to June 30, 2002, for the blue-chip components of the S&P 500 index, corporations' real adjusted net pension income was equivalent to a quarter of their reported earnings.[8]

Companies are still allowed to make some pretty optimistic assumptions about the returns on their pension assets, thereby flattering the profitability of the company in the short term. Many continue to assume 8 to 10 percent. In March 2003, BP announced that it had reduced the assumed rate of return on its American subsidiaries' pension funds from 11 to 8.5 percent, which remains on the optimistic side. In October 2002, General Motors warned of a deepening pensions shortfall, which UBS estimates put at over $22 billion. Mind you, at that point General Motors was sticking with its assumption of a 10 percent return on pension fund assets. It has sought to plug the gap in its pension fund by issuing $10 billion of bonds, although this is more like shifting money from one pocket to another. It has reduced liabilities labeled pensions by increasing the liabilities labeled bonds.[9]

According to Steven Kandarian, executive director of the Pension Benefit Guaranty Corporation (PBGC), US employers' pension funds are facing a shortfall of $300 billion. The PBGC provides a safety net for the under-funded defined-benefit schemes of bankrupt employers. This protection is far from complete, however. According to Mr. Kandarian, the liabilities of pension plans at risk had reached $35 billion, compared with the PBGC's assets of only $25 billion.[10]

The inappropriate accounting for pension liabilities, along with the non-expensing of employee share options, is a good reason still to be suspicious of the quality of US reported earnings, even after the post-Enron clean-up. Two Federal Reserve economists, Julia Lynn Coronado and Steven Sharpe, have concluded that in recent years US companies with large pension liabilities have been substantially overvalued by the stock market.[11] The growing realization of pension underprovision is going to be a powerful factor undermining confidence in the equity market, but it will also serve to undermine confidence in the pension system. Since pension assets are still heavily invested in equities, one tends to lead on to the other.

Occupational Hazards in the UK

Many of these points also apply to the UK, where the problems of pension provision are, if anything, less transparent but more acute. All those people who have been saving in so-called defined-contribution pension schemes are in a position analogous to those with 401k schemes in America. Most people in Britain, however, are not in this position. They are covered by occupational schemes that promise a certain proportion of final salary at retirement and, on the face of it, they are sitting pretty. But all is not quite as it seems. At the very least their employers are going to suffer a heavy blow, and in many cases they are going to transfer this blow to their employees.

The stock-market boom left many companies in the UK with a pension fund that was "overfunded" and this allowed them to take a pension contribution "holiday." According to the Inland Revenue, over three years between 1994 and 1997 employers took pension contribution holidays worth $4 billion.[12]

But the holidays are over. In the case of Unilever, both 15,000 UK employees and the company are experiencing end-of-holiday blues, after an extended vacation that, with the exception of a brief resumption of contributions in 1995–96, stretches back to 1991. Existing members of the fund had to make a contribution of 2 percent of salary from January 1, 2003, rising to 5 percent in 2004. Unilever started making contributions to the fund equal to about 7 percent of its UK payroll cost. This rose to 13 percent in 2004.[13]

Unilever is by no means the only company seriously affected. At the end of January 2003, according to Morgan Stanley, the member companies of the UK's FTSE 100 had a deficit on their pension funds of $130 billion, amounting to about 10 percent of their market capitalization. For some of these companies the shortfall is 90 percent of their capitalization. Many large schemes would be able to pay only a fraction of employees' pensions if they were wound up today.[14]

What is worse, some pension schemes are so big in relation to the companies that originally set them up that a substantial period of stock-market weakness could pose a serious threat to their continued existence. British Airways, for instance, has been described as a pension fund with a sideline in air travel. In late 2002, telecommunications company BT's pension fund was worth $40 billion compared to $24 billion for the parent company—and it had three times more members and pensioners than BT had staff.[15]

Nor have small companies escaped the problem. The average small company pension scheme is in deficit to the tune of £5.9 million (about $9 million). Since these firms typically employ fewer than 1,000 workers, this is an onerous burden.[16]

Now that companies are waking up to reality, they are recognizing how expensive and how dangerous pension provision is. The result is that in droves they are closing down final-salary pension schemes to new members, substituting money-purchase schemes that carry a lower contribution rate from them. They are thereby both reducing the costs to them and transferring investment risk to their employees. British companies that have done this include British Airways, ICI, and J. Sainsbury. In March 2003, according to the Association of Consulting Actuaries, nearly 75 percent of final-salary pension schemes were closed to new members.[17]

Corporate escape routes

Many companies are finding that simply closing their funds to new members is nowhere near enough to close the yawning gaps, and the size of the potential extra cash injections into them is horrifying. According to the *Financial Times,* in February 2003 BT Group was preparing to inject $2.3 billion into its pension fund, on top of its existing commitments. Some outside observers reckoned that the true size of the deficit could be as much as $9 billion.[18]

The next stage is for companies to reduce pension benefits, increase the retirement age, or ask for higher contributions. In February 2003, J. Sainsbury announced that to stay in the final-salary scheme, its employees had to increase their contributions from 4.25 percent of salary to 7 percent. Otherwise they would be moved to a career-average-salary scheme, whose benefits would, of course, be lower.[19] This switch is the equivalent of a permanent pay cut of 2.75 percent. Similarly, BAE Systems recently asked its 57,000 employees to pay £20 ($30) a week extra into its pension fund. In March 2003, Honda announced that it was raising the normal retirement age for 4,000 British employees at its Swindon plant from 60 to 62.[20] These are pretty concrete demonstrations of the losses caused by the collapse of the bubble hitting people where it hurts—in their bank balances.

The future for some members of final-salary schemes could have been even bleaker. In October 2002, it emerged that the pension fund of Sea-Land, a subsidiary of the international shipping group Maersk was being wound up. Maersk had decided that it was no longer prepared to fund the deficit in the Sea-Land pension fund even though Maersk was still very much in business. Despite the fact that the fund met the UK's statutory minimum funding requirement (MFR), some employees stood to lose up to 60 percent of their pension entitlement.

This is the ultimate way out for companies faced with severe financial pain, or even oblivion—effectively reneging on their promises to employees. In that case, of course, they have not eradicated the problem but merely transferred the burden to their employees. In fact, faced with enormous pressure, Maersk decided to meet Sea-Land's deficit in full. And the British government woke up to the iniquity of the situation and this particular escape route has now been closed. The government is now compelling companies to meet their pension obligations in full and has instituted an insurance scheme to provide most workers with 90 percent of their expected benefits if a company goes bankrupt.

This comes too late to ameliorate the plight of some very unfortunate individuals (see below). Although it may prevent the repetition of similar cases in the future, because it will raise costs to companies it will surely do even more to kill off final-salary pensions.

Meanwhile, some employees will bear the burden not only of increased contributions or diminished benefits, but also of higher taxes. It seems that in the UK taxpayers could be forced to pick up the bill for a $45 billion black hole in local authority pension schemes. The London borough of Wandsworth confirmed that the record increase in its council tax for 2003 was a direct result of a deficit in its pension fund.[21]

But there are other avenues for desperate companies. Some of them are planning to offload some of their pension liabilities to insurance companies and investment banks, which would then provide the pensioners with annuities. In most cases, however, the premiums that the companies would have to pay would be too high for across-the-board coverage. Instead, the idea is to restrict the plan to "affordable" groups, including elderly pensioners, workers from industries with poor health records, and people who live in districts with high mortality rates.

Many of the companies that have decided to close their final-salary schemes have blamed the accounting standard FRS17, which obliges them to show the state of any under- or overfunding of their pension fund on their balance sheet. But this is really a fig leaf. The underlying reason for closing final-salary schemes is now that the great equity illusion is over, companies are simply not prepared to bear the risk of final-salary pension provision that, stripped of all illusions, is clearly inordinately high.

Pensions penury

What happens when large numbers of companies go bust? No more top-ups and in some cases no more pensions. In the UK this danger is not acute for existing pensioners, who legally have first claim on a pension fund's resources,[22] but it *is* for all those yet to draw their pension. It is surely the prospect of substantial numbers of insolvencies that makes the underfunding of pensions potentially so dangerous. There has been a widespread attitude on company boards and among actuaries that pension underfunding was a much exaggerated problem because the ability to pay pensions depends on the income flow from the assets, rather than their current market value, and companies always had the option of making good any genuine shortfall in later years. But what if the company is no longer there?

Some individuals have already suffered greatly as a result of a pensions calamity.[23] One is Maurice Jones, the managing director of a Lancashire textiles company, who paid into an occupational scheme for 38 years. When his employer collapsed immediately before he was due to retire, he lost an expected income of £36,000 (about $54,000) a year. Others who had just retired were much luckier: they received almost their full entitlements.[24]

Mind you, not everyone is suffering. The senior managers of a typical large UK company retire on a final-salary scheme into which they have paid no contributions and whose benefits are index linked and extend to spouses. The pension of the former CEO of GlaxoSmithKline is very nearly £1 million (about $1.5 million) a year, the capital cost of which is almost £15 million (about $22 million).[25] Why haven't *these* schemes been closed down, I wonder?

For the 99.99 percent of the population who are not pampered in this way, the upshot is that the air of sanctity that formerly attached to pension funds is dissipating. The *fear* of pensions shortfall on a widespread scale is going to be a powerful factor deterring spending and boosting saving among the countless millions of pensioners-to-be—although probably not saving in pension schemes. Moreover, the inter-relationship of the key variables is deeply disturbing. A weak economy causes company insolvencies, which threaten the viability of large numbers of pensions, which causes consumer confidence and consumer spending to drop, which weakens the economy.

Long-term saving
Similar problems affect other forms of long-term saving. In the UK millions of people have saved in so-called with profits insurance policies, either to pay off a mortgage, provide life insurance, or build up a nest egg for retirement. Although they probably regarded these policies as giving a cast-iron guarantee of a good payout, in practice they were completely dependent on the performance of the stock market. Now many of these people are having to face the awful truth that their savings are not worth what they imagined they were. In some cases this means that they will be left having to pay off a large part of their mortgage when it matures, rather than relying on the proceeds of their policies.

There are also increasing worries about the solvency of some insurance companies. Weak equity markets are causing insurers' capital base to shrink, which forces them to sell equities and move into bonds—which worsens the downward pressure on equity prices, and thereby worsens insurers' capital base.

Interestingly, the realization that there are problems with many pension funds and insurance companies has led to widespread calls to make long-term savings instruments more transparent. In the long run, this must be the right thing to do. However, I am rather anxious about the timing. This is not the best time for people to be made aware of just how poor their long-term financial position is. While the long-term health of the economy and society may require people in North America and the UK (and parts of continental Europe) to save more, the immediate health of the world economy depends on them *not* doing this just yet. Indeed, from the standpoint of the macro economy a little less saving would not go amiss.

Continental Assurance?

There are some cases outside the Anglo-Saxon world of companies being able to do less saving because of the stock-market boom of the late 1990s—and now having to face the music. In the Netherlands companies are confronting a major pensions crisis. As a result of the fall in world stock markets and a tough regulatory regime covering pension funding, Dutch companies, including household names such as ABN Amro and Heineken, may be forced to add $15 billion annually to their pension funds over the next seven years.[26]

Nevertheless, the blow to pension funds, and thereby indirectly to their sponsoring companies, inflicted by stock-market collapse is largely an Anglo-Saxon phenomenon. In continental Europe, with the exception of the Netherlands, pension obligations are usually unfunded. In Germany for instance, although some companies such as Siemens have established an external fund and some such as RWE have a policy of holding significant financial assets to cover future pension liabilities, most companies do neither.[27] However, companies reflect their entire pension obligations on the balance sheet as provisions, and annual costs in relation to their pension plans are booked against profits.

This treatment means that there should be no pension surprises and the collapse of the equity market should have no direct consequences for German companies' pension obligations. In another sense, though, Germany is not so well placed. Those pension obligations are essentially like debt on the balance sheet, so German companies are more highly geared because of them. This means, of course, that they are more vulnerable to an economic downturn.

Theoretically, the position of the German employee is protected against the insolvency of his or her employer through an insolvency insurer (Pensions-Sicherungs-Verein, PSV) to which employers pay premiums. Quite how the institution would hold up in a severe economic downturn is another matter. The German economic system has grown up in a period of expansion and stability. The equity market may not be able to sink German companies through the pension system, but a general economic collapse would hit both German companies and German pensions.

In February 2003, credit rating agency Standard & Poor's issued a warning to a number of European companies that their credit ratings could be cut because of worries about their pension liabilities. The list included Deutsche Post, Linde, and ThyssenKrupp in Germany, as well as Arcelor, Michelin, and

Portugal Telecom elsewhere. Most worryingly, Standard & Poor's said that it had tried to assess the pension situation in 2002, but could not adequately do so because it could not obtain enough information from the 500 European companies interviewed.[28] In that case, what chance is there for the rest of us?

Europe's unfunded *state* pensions also present a significant financial challenge. According to the European Financial Services Round Table, Europeans need to save an extra $500 billion a year to preserve the level of retirement benefits while holding down the cost of public pensions. If policies remain unchanged, the cost of state pensions in the EU is expected to rise from 10.4 percent of GDP in 2000 to 13.6 percent by 2040.[29] In Germany, the VDR association of statutory pension funds has warned the government that contributions to the state pay-as-you-go pension system will have to rise to 19.9 percent of gross incomes.[30]

There have also been some severe problems with pensions in Japan. More and more Japanese companies are reducing the benefits from their employee pension funds because of declining investment returns. According to the Ministry of Health, Labor, and Welfare, by the end of the 2001 fiscal year benefits at 366 pension funds, or more than 20 percent of the total, were reduced. In some cases the cuts were more than 20 percent. Kubota slashed its standard pension benefit by about 25 percent. In most cases companies have only reduced the benefits that currently employed workers will receive in the future, but several companies, including Nisshin Steel, have reduced payments to existing pensioners.

The upshot is clear. With regard to pensions, the fallout from the stock-market crash will take many years to build up to strength. The full effect will come when umpteen millions of people realize that their pension is worse than it was, would have been, or should have been, leaving them anxious and wary about the future. These problems for pensions and long-term savings are bad enough now, in an era of next to no inflation, but they would be much more acute if the world enters a period of *deflation*, which I discuss in the next chapter.

Bricks and Mortar

I said that the hidden threat to pensions was the first reason for the comparatively modest response to the stock-market losses of 2000–2003. The second reason is closer to home, so to speak. Many people have been shielded from how awful their asset position could be in old age by the substantial gains they have been making on their houses and apartments. If pensions and insurance policies spread the gains from rampant asset prices deep into the middle class, strong property prices spread the gains even deeper into society. Every owner of a house or apartment, no matter how small, has had a share in the bonanza, their little bit of money for nothing.

In the US the acceleration in house-price inflation got going in 1997, with the rate peaking at 9 percent at the beginning of 2001—the fastest annual increase since the first quarter of 1980—before moderating slightly to 6 percent in 2002. But in the middle of 2005 the rate of increase was back up to 12.5 percent. These increases were more impressive in real terms. Previous big increases in house prices occurred during the inflationary era when the gains were in funny money. But this was the real stuff. In 2004 American house prices rose in real terms at the fastest rate since data began to be recorded in 1976. And the boom has continued. Over the 10 years 1995–2005, American house prices rose by 90 percent, or 50 percent in real terms.

On the face of it, in 2001–3 the gains in house prices were not enough to offset the losses on stocks. In the US, equities directly held by individuals are in aggregate worth about the same as the whole housing stock. Once you add in equities held in pension funds and insurance companies, total equity holdings easily exceed the whole of the housing stock. However, changes in household wealth deliver more bang per buck. The evidence is that whereas an increase in stock-market wealth of $1 raises spending by 3 to 5 cents, a comparable increase in housing wealth raises it by between 5 and 9 cents.[31]

Outside the US, increases in house prices have by and large been much bigger. In the UK they have recently been spectacular. Between 1995 and 2005 house prices increased by a total of 200 percent,[32] and in 2002 on one measure the annual rate of increase reached 30 percent. In Australia, in late 2002 prices were up by almost 20 percent over the year. There has correspondingly been a large increase in household debt. The debt to income ratio rose from 82 percent in 1996 to 122 percent in June 2002. According to a report by UBS Warburg, if prices were to return to their long-term average within three years they would have to fall by 22 percent countrywide, and by 36 percent in Melbourne.[33] But the boom continued. In mid-2005, Australian house prices were up over the previous 10 years by 123 percent, or 73 percent in real terms.

It is a popular misconception that home-ownership rates in continental Europe are very low, with the majority of people renting an apartment. This is an approximation of the truth in Germany, where the owner-occupation rate is only 40 percent, but elsewhere rates of home ownership rival or exceed the American or British levels (67 percent and 68 percent). They are particularly high in Ireland, Italy, Spain, and Greece (80, 77, 84, and 78 percent), but even in France and Belgium they are higher than you might imagine (54 and 65 percent).

And across much of continental Europe the recent rates of increase in property prices have been impressive. This is not the case in Germany, where even in the former West prices have only crept up, and in the former East Germany they have fallen sharply. However, between 1995 and 2005 property prices increased by 250 percent in Ireland, 120 percent in the Netherlands, 178 percent in Spain, 96 percent in France, 99 percent in Sweden, 104 percent in Denmark, 83 percent in Belgium, and 53 percent in Italy. In all of these countries except Italy, the increase in real terms was over 50 percent. Not bad—especially when you consider that the owners also enjoyed the benefits of living in their property.

The money maker
As property prices have gone up in leaps and bounds, it has been possible for many homeowners to say that they are making more money simply by living in their house than they are by going to work—money for nothing. This has undoubtedly boosted their spending. There are many ways in which the effect works. In America and Britain where the housing market is closely linked in with liquid financial markets in personal finance, the effect may be straightforward. Homeowners are not only wealthier, but they can readily realize that wealth by borrowing against it, either when they move home or simply by increasing the mortgage on their existing property.

This process of so-called equity withdrawal is nothing like so easy or attractive in most continental European countries. Nevertheless, even there people are surely affected by the same general factor that affects the Anglo-Saxon homeowner: the knowledge that their wealth has increased. This is bound to make them feel less inclined to save and more inclined to spend. After all, the increase in the value of their property will have a major effect on two of the more important reasons for saving: the provision for old age and the ability to pass on wealth to one's children.

So great has been the increase in housing values and so great the suspicion about pensions and pension funds in Britain that it is by no means uncommon to hear people refer to their property as their pension fund. In most cases, what they envisage is that when they retire they will move to a smaller property, or one in a less expensive area, and use the wealth thereby released to fund their retirement. In some cases they intend to stay put and merely avail themselves of an "equity-release" scheme, which gives the homeowner a guaranteed income for the remainder of their life in exchange for the institutional provider of this income (usually a bank or insurance company) taking some or all of the equity in the house when they die.

But to an increasing number of individuals in the UK (and also, interestingly, in Australia), an investment in housing is not merely a by-product of where they decide to live but part of a conscious decision about their portfolio. The "buy-to-let" market has taken off. Many a middle-class professional has taken out an extra mortgage—or two or three—to purchase investment property to be let out to tenants. So great have been the attractions of property and so inevitable the future rises in property prices that it has been a no-brainer—money for nothing. The result is that they have enjoyed strong gains during the bull market of the last few years—and are exposed to significant losses if the market should fall.

For some people investment in property has moved into the territory occupied a few years ago by the dotcom sector. I recently received a flier through my letterbox headlined "We'll prove you can make your fortune in Property." It began:

Dear Potential Millionaire: I'm (name withheld) and I've made millions of dollars in US real property. Now, after months of extensive research and careful planning I'm bringing my FREE property workshop to the UK. I want to invite you to a FREE TRAINING WORKSHOP in your locality where you can learn how to amass your own personal fortune. I'm not talking about a little nest-egg. I'm talking about wealth that assures lifetime financial security and comfort for you and your family! … We'll show you exactly how you can set a goal to quit your mundane 9–5 job and move on to a better way of life.

This was it: the epitome of the culture of money for nothing, and right there, sent through my letterbox.

Property illusions

For families owning properties that rise in value the increased wealth is real enough, but for society as a whole it is not. It is a pure wealth illusion— money for nothing. When property prices double no more real resources are being created and no extra services provided; not even any extra housing services. Indeed, for those people who do not currently own a property but would like to, or those who own a small one in relation to their lifetime needs, the rise in property prices actually makes them *worse* off.

In some ways increased wealth created by rising house prices is more clearly illusory than increases in stock-market wealth. Although the great stock-market boom of the 1990s was primarily about a higher valuation being placed on a given stream of future earnings, at least a rise in the stock market *may* correspond to genuine prospects for increased earnings in the future. And at least in part, the 1990s share boom *was* about the perception of increased earnings in the future.

In comparison, a property only produces a given flow of housing services and that is that. Valuing those services more highly is all very well, but it is essentially a reflection of relative scarcity and it effects a redistribution within society. For society as a whole the increase in wealth created by soaring house prices has been a financial fantasy; albeit one that has had major real consequences, not least the boost to consumer confidence and consumer spending.

The irony is that the immediate health of the economy in the US, UK, and several other countries depends on the illusion continuing for a while longer. In my view, it is now only the continuation of the housing illusion that stands between us and a world slump.

For it is only because consumers in America carried on spending freely in 2002–5 that the world avoided falling into recession. And they hold the key to staving off the recessionary danger in the years to come. That is why the threats to consumer finance from the pensions crisis and the coming weakness in house prices are so perilous. The American consumer is the world's spender of first resort.

Twin peaks

Why were property prices booming along with share prices? Some of the economic influences were the same. The genuine improvement in economic circumstances in the mid-1990s reduced unemployment and made us more prosperous. People were also affected by the same air of inveterate optimism about the future that drove the stock market. And the low level of interest rates had an even larger effect on housing than on shares.

Moreover, people probably suffered from an even greater wealth illusion over houses than they did over shares. Throughout the 1990s in money terms interest rates may have been very low by recent historical standards, but they were not *that* low in real terms. Yet while house prices continued to rise people did not think about *value*. Houses were highly "affordable," and since you could never go wrong buying property, who cared what the general rate of inflation was or what the so-called real interest rate was? From an investment point of view, when adjusting the nominal rate of interest to get a measure of the real rate, the appropriate deflator was not the rate of increase of retail prices but the rate of increase of house prices. That made the *"real"* rate of interest decidedly negative.

The result of the apparently irresistible case for property was that just like the stock market, the price of the asset looked extremely high in relation to the normal yardstick of value. In the case of houses, this was the ratio of house prices to the earnings of the people who were buying the houses and financing the mortgage payments.

Interestingly, the bears of the housing market in 2005 encounter a very similar refrain to the one met by bears of the stock market in early 2000: "You just don't get it. It's different this time." In relation to the housing market, what supposedly makes it *different this time* is the combination of relentless upward pressure on population (at least in North America and the UK) and low interest rates. However, to explain the short-term performance of the market the first part of this argument is bordering on the economically illiterate. Although the shortage of property in some countries, notably the UK, could reasonably argue for a rising real price of property over time, it could not account for rises of 30 percent per annum, any more than it could account for the 34 percent increase at the peak of the previous boom in 1988.

Will we never learn? Important structural factors, such as population growth and land shortage, affect the sustainable price in the medium term but change very little from one year to the next. In comparison, the state of the housing market can turn on a sixpence in six months. In 1988–89 in the UK it did precisely that. 1988 was a boom year when people would have paid the earth for the promise of a garage that could just about be converted into an apartment. In 1989 the same properties could not be offloaded for love nor money and the prices of even good properties plunged. Yet the

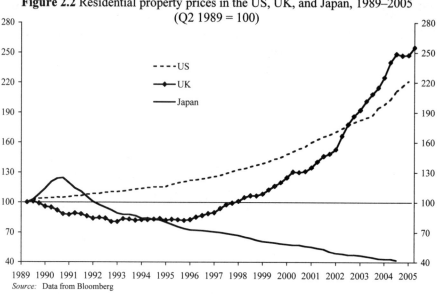

Figure 2.2 Residential property prices in the US, UK, and Japan, 1989–2005 (Q2 1989 = 100)

Source: Data from Bloomberg

population was the same, the prospects for population growth were the same, the shortage of land was the same, everything real was the same. All that had changed was the state of effective demand, driven by higher interest rates, a change in taxes, and a shift in price expectations.

By 2005, though, memories of this time had faded and the view was widely held among the UK's property-owning classes that property prices can never really fall—especially not in a small, overcrowded island like Britain. Nevertheless, the spectacular turn from boom to bust in Britain in 1988–89 was not a unique experience. Throughout the 1990s residential property prices fell in another overcrowded island, Japan (see Figure 2.2). From their peak in Q4 1990 to mid-2004, they fell by 66 percent. In a still more crowded island, Hong Kong, the falls are more recent but no less spectacular, as Figure 2.3 shows. Prices fell by more than 60 percent in five years, before recovering modestly in 2004 and 2005.

There have been periods of falling property prices elsewhere too. French property prices fell sharply in the early 1990s and at one point the annual rate of decline touched 13 percent. The cumulative drop in prices between the end of 1991 and the beginning of 1998 was 33 percent. In Sydney, Australia, house prices fell by 25 percent in the two years to the end of 1990. Swedish property prices were also chronically

Figure 2.3 The price of Hong Kong residential property, 1993–2005 (1993=100)

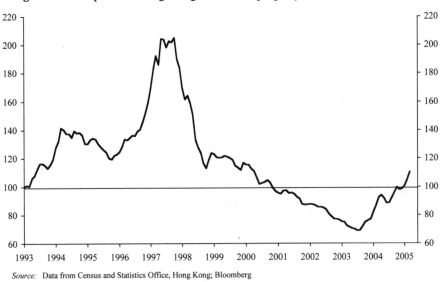

Source: Data from Census and Statistics Office, Hong Kong; Bloomberg

weak in the early 1990s. The annual rate of decline briefly exceeded 15 percent and the cumulative drop in prices from Q4 1991 to Q4 1993 was 18 percent.

In the US, the recent record does not show any year when house prices have fallen on average across the country. Nevertheless, there have been some huge swings and some pretty near misses. Whenever the rate of increase of house prices has got well out of line with the rate of increase of earnings, as it had by 2003, there has been a sharp fall-off in the rate of increase of house prices to well below earnings.

In the new world of low inflation, never mind in conditions of generalized deflation (which I discuss in the next chapter), occasional periods of falling house prices will be normal. The estate agents should be made to tell prospective purchasers: "Prices may go down as well as up and past performance may not be an accurate guide to the future."

Another bust?

To anyone burned by the stock-market crash this all sounds so distressingly familiar. The current housing-market boom *is* set to end in tears. You may wonder why the same fate should befall houses as shares, given that by the middle of 2003 share prices had been falling for more than three years while house prices continued to rise. Nevertheless, there are good reasons why house prices carried on going up and have continued rising since.

For a start, the housing-market boom got going later than the bubble in shares. It was also much more dependent on low unemployment and low interest rates. Indeed, the very weakness of share prices was a powerful factor behind the policy of continued low interest rates that helped to drive house prices upwards. Moreover, the experience of what had happened to shares helped to reinforce popular optimism about houses. After all, you couldn't go wrong with houses, could you? Why bother with all those pension plans, insurance policies, and so on? You were better off putting your money into bricks and mortar. They would never let you down. In this respect, the property boom is a bubble transferred.

A clear sign of this is the way that houses and apartments have replaced shares in the public consciousness. As Rosa Kim, a New York-based public relations consultant, puts it, "Amongst my friends, hearing people talk in the elevator in the office, you don't hear people talking about their stocks any more. If they're talking about finance, it's real estate, it's should I buy a place? Should I buy that summer home?"[34]

In fact it is quite common for booms in different assets to end at different times, as the end of the bubble in one market sends investors scurrying off to put their money into some other one, thereby creating yet another bubble. In the Japanese crash of the early 1990s, land and share prices fell at different points. Share prices peaked in January 1990 but land prices carried on rising for the next 18 months. In 1987 in the UK the stock market crashed in October, but throughout the following year residential house prices continued to rise sharply. It wasn't until the early months of 1989 that it became clear that the housing market was in deep trouble, and the worst year for price falls was 1990, by which time stock prices were recovering.

After the collapse of share prices in 2001–2003 the omens are not good for house prices. As with share prices, though, it is impossible to make confident short-term forecasts of house prices. Yet considerations of value do enable us to say something. One way or another, something like normal valuations in the housing market will have to be restored.

The comfortable scenario is one in which the rate of increase of prices drifts down gently toward zero and stays there for some time, thereby allowing earnings to continue to increase and something like the normal relationship between house prices and earnings to be restored gradually over an extended period. It is possible that this is how the market will behave in the years ahead, but if so adjustment will be a slow, drawn-out process. And this is not how it has behaved in the past. Rather, virulent booms have been followed by crashes. In the old days of high inflation, a crash in real house prices could occur without nominal prices falling. Continued high inflation would quickly erode the real value. But in today's world of low inflation, a comparable fall in real values would require a large drop in nominal house prices, thereby giving rise to the problems of "negative equity" that beset the British economy in the early 1990s. One way or another, the market has to make a major adjustment.

Once the property market has come down to earth people will have to face the awful truth—no more money for nothing.

The Savings Crisis

Coupled with low unemployment and apparently assured prosperity, these wealth gains in equities and property, conjured out of nothing, had a major result. In America and Britain, the proportion of incomes that people put aside as savings (the savings ratio) plunged. Why bother saving when the stock market and the housing market do it for you?

In the UK in 2000, the savings ratio fell below the ultra-low level reached at the peak of then Chancellor Nigel Lawson's boom in the late 1980s. In 2001 and 2002 it recovered somewhat, but remained pitifully low by normal standards. In America, at times the savings ratio appeared to be negative, although there was a minor cottage industry established among under-employed economists trying to recalculate it. Some even went so far as to include purchases of automobiles as saving, on the grounds that these were durable goods. Hey presto, if you are prepared to throw in the kitchen sink, there has not been a problem with low American savings. But the rest of us should be more circumspect.

The scale of the problem is staggering. In 2001 the US savings ratio was 2.3 percent compared to its long-run average of 8 percent. In May 2005 it stood at 0.6 percent. If the savings ratio were to return to the average this would reduce consumption by 7.5 percent, which would wipe 5.5 percent from American GDP. All that this requires is consumers to reduce their borrowing or increase their saving to levels that were the norm only a few years ago. And, of course, after the savings wipeouts of the last few years and in view of the uncertain future, they could readily decide to raise the savings ratio *above* the long-run average.

Corporate Caution

The boom years in America were not solely about consumer extravagance. Corporate investment was rampant. Between 1991 and 2000 the annual amount that corporations spent on real investment increased by 160 percent. It is easy to see why. The future was apparently full of opportunity, most particularly opportunity made possible by the new communications technology and the internet. The usual restraints apparently no longer applied. Meanwhile, final demand was extremely strong, driven by strong consumer spending. And finance was cheap and easily available. Low inflation and low short-term interest rates brought low bond yields. Moreover, the surging equity market made it possible to raise share capital on apparently cheap terms.

Then all of this went into reverse. In the first half of 2002 corporate investment in America and the UK collapsed. The main reasons were the overhang of excessive past investments (many of them poorly judged), weak balance sheets, and the sheer evaporation of confidence after the boom years. Suddenly the future no longer seemed a land of golden opportunity and corporate profitability plunged. Subsequently investment recovered, but whereas at the peak of the boom business investment in the US was running at 12.5 percent of GDP, it is now running at less than 10 percent—as it is in the UK.[35]

Now that the good times are over, company managers have to face up to a new, stark reality. One of the interesting characteristics of the combination of economic strength and the long bull market was the way that underperforming companies (and others) would be swept up by bigger corporate fish. The result was that often some of the best stocks to buy were ones whose long-term record was *not* good. Like old soldiers, bad companies never died—they just got taken over. All this could change, however. The combination of a weak economy and a pedestrian stock market would surely kill the mergers and acquisitions industry stone dead. This would leave both companies and their senior executives (as well as investors) facing the reality of the ultimate purgative of the capitalist system—bankruptcy.

The backlash

The pressures on the corporate sector are worse still. Just as there was in the 1930s, a revolt is under way against the worst excesses of the free enterprise system, after millions of people have lost so much money while the privileged few have pocketed fortunes. The backlash has begun. First in line are the financial companies, especially the investment banks, which are seen as having been complicit in the bubble that now seems so ruinous. But the anger has spread wider: against lax accounting standards, excessive executive pay, and poor vision and management.

What a difference a few years make. When the ramifications of the Asian/Russian crisis of 1997–98 threatened to bring down the international financial system, a spate of articles and papers appeared analyzing what had gone wrong. "Crony capitalism" was prime among the factors to blame. Why did Asian capitalism have to be shot through with dodgy practices? And why did it have to be so opaque? In short, why couldn't it simply be more like the crystal-clear, whiter-than-white American version? Now we know that the American version has all along had some huge stains on it. As the revelations of corporate wrongdoing continue to dribble out, so the public mood has changed.

The result is already legislation on executives' responsibility for the reliability of company accounts (the Sarbanes-Oxley Act), and there is mounting disquiet about the level of executive pay. Unsurprisingly, since in two decades the ratio of CEOs' to workers' pay has risen from 42:1 to 400:1 without any justification in US corporate performance.[36] Legislative intervention may well go further as public anger mounts and the intellectual climate continues to shift toward regulation.

On a different but related front, in late 2002 an American court awarded punitive damages of $28 billion against the tobacco company Philip Morris, more than the net worth of the company. Admittedly the damages were later reduced on appeal to $28 million, but in future businesses will not be able to rely on winning their appeals. And such damages may not be restricted to tobacco suits. They could extend to all sorts of corporate malfeasance, including accidental deaths or environmental damage.

The upshot of all this is that the social and legislative environment is shifting against business. This will be an added burden on shares and constitutes another reason why they will find it difficult to advance. It will also serve to intensify the corporate crisis and depress real investment. When executives face this sort of threat and deep uncertainty, the natural reaction is to batten down the hatches.

Deficits as Far as the Eye Can See

The combination of rampant consumer spending and high corporate borrowing led to the emergence of a huge financial deficit on the part of the US private sector (that is, companies and individuals combined). By early 2005, after a large improvement in companies' financial balances, the deficit of the private sector as a whole was 4 percent of GDP, and the public-sector deficit was a further 2.4 percent of GDP. The external counterpart of these domestic deficits is a deficit on the current account of the balance of payments of over 6 percent of GDP.

There are four recent examples of countries that have accumulated a private financial deficit on such a scale: Britain and Japan in the late 1980s, and Sweden and Finland in the early 1990s. In each case the subsequent retrenchment by companies and households plunged the economy into recession. In Japan's case it was a ten-year slump. Even if the private sector manages to reduce its deficit, if that is achieved by passing it to the public sector that hardly boosts confidence or sustainability.

These examples give the lie to an oft-heard defense of the American economy and advocacy of an optimistic short-term prospect, namely that a high level of investment has so contributed to the capital stock that the subsequent rate of productivity growth has been improved. Corporate investment was strong in these other examples too. More worryingly, precisely because of the distortions created by the boom, much of it was bad investment too—most obviously so in Japan. We should not be fooled by the description "investment." *Bad* investment is just like consumption—only without the enjoyment.

The dollar link

At some point the huge American current account deficit referred to above will have to be corrected, involving either a substantial drop in US aggregate demand, which would prompt a recession, or a massive fall in the dollar. The sharp fall of the dollar in 2003–4 raised hopes that adjustment will be confined to the latter. Although the dollar strengthened in 2005, this view could well be right, and it is possible that the US will even manage to grow well in the years ahead—despite the overhang from the bursting of the bubble. After all, the economy has had every form of stimulus thrown at it: huge tax cuts, interest rates reduced to 1 percent, and a weaker dollar.

But an even weaker dollar would transfer the burden to the rest of the world through lower US imports and more competitive US exports, or both. Whatever a weaker dollar may do to help the American recovery, it does next to nothing for the recovery of the world as a whole.

The strength of the dollar in the late 1990s was yet another American wealth illusion, and it helped to bolster the others by making investment in the US attractive to foreigners and keeping inflation low, thereby underpinning low interest rates and bond yields.[37] Given the history of massive dollar movements in the past,[38] you would have thought that late 1990s investors would recognize the dollar exchange rate as a roller coaster and not regard its current strength as at all secure. But no. Once again there were the excuses, the reasons why it was *different this time*. Mostly these were the same reasons adduced to justify the boom in American share prices: "the new economy" and rapid productivity growth. So the current account deficit could go hang.

But the lesson of late 1990s Britain and the Asian Tigers' experience of 1997–98 was that the current account matters because it needs to be financed. While America is running a deficit of 6 percent of its GDP it is requiring the rest of the world to supply savings to it of that amount, year after year after year. The world's investors are starting to say enough is enough. Yes, of course the deficit will be financed—but at a very different price. By the middle of 2005, even though this process has clearly begun, the dollar could still have a long way to fall.

The Sick Man of Europe

From boom to bust, bull to bear, euphoria to depression, it is easy to characterize the world's current economic and financial difficulties as essentially an American problem. But this is nowhere near a fair reflection of the truth. Although a major fall of the dollar would cause some difficulties for America, the end of the dollar illusion will on balance bring *benefits* to the US—but only by transferring the burden of adjustment to the rest of the world. Yet the rest of the world is in no position to take this up. Much of it is chronically weak. While the American asset-price boom of the 1990s and associated overspending by American consumers and corporations was a problem, without it the world would have faced a problem of a different sort. It would have suffered a deflationary slump then, as opposed to being *threatened* with one now.

The essential solution to both the world's problem and America's is the same—and it lies outside America. Some people characterize this as a problem of excess capacity. Supposedly, if we had less power to produce things we would be better off. Although it is true that there is excessive capacity in particular industries that it is difficult to imagine ever being matched by an increase in demand, generalized excess capacity is not the source of the economy's problems. The nub of the issue is that the world has suffered from a chronic shortage of aggregate *demand*. Its supply capacity has burgeoned but demand has not kept up.

Japan has been mired in a slump for the best part of a decade. The essence of its predicament is an excess of domestic savings over investment. With the population aging rapidly and people worried about the security offered by pensions and holdings of all financial assets, including even bank deposits, it is going to be difficult to get the personal savings ratio down.[39]

Stepping up corporate investment is hardly the solution. Japanese companies have been overinvesting for years, with the result that the capital stock is extremely high in relation to output and profitability is low. The process of reform necessary for Japan's long-term recovery is likely to involve *lower* levels of investment, not higher.

More government spending? In Japan this policy has been employed almost to excess and may now be close to the end of the line. The only factor left as a source of increased demand is net exports. This is exactly what would be encouraged by a lower yen exchange rate. However, in static markets an increase in Japanese exports implies lower sales and production for some other country. The upshot is that Japan is unlikely to be able to revive itself by an upsurge of domestic demand, never mind helping the world economy. Hopes for Japanese revival are likely to depend on the rest of the world.

The weakness of growth in the eurozone is emerging as another significant global problem. Unlike their Anglo-Saxon equivalents, people in continental Europe need no encouragement to save. On the contrary, they are doing plenty of it anyway. If economic conditions in the world deteriorate, the danger is that they might opt to do rather more of it. Part of the responsibility lies at the door of an institution: the European Central Bank (ECB).[40]

But Europe's problems are not restricted to monetary policy. There are also more deep-seated problems connected with over-regulation and inflexible labor markets. These have increased unemployment and deterred investment—except in labor-saving equipment. Meanwhile, consumer confidence has been held back across Europe by worries about the labor market and the future value and security of pensions.

Moreover, there is a severe structural problem in Europe's largest economy, Germany. This is probably the last country on earth where just about everybody still believes that the key to wealth lies in making *things*, and where the culture of money for nothing remains deeply alien. The share of manufacturing in GDP is still very high, but Germany cannot escape the logic of economic development. Manufacturing's importance has to fall there too, although the difference is that in Germany the service sector is still not developed enough to take up the slack.

The upshot is that as America flounders and Japan remains mired in recession, the world's second largest economic area, the eurozone, is in no position to take up the baton. Consequently, the world is threatened with a chronic shortfall of aggregate demand.

Save Us from Protection

The major loss of stock-market wealth, weak confidence, the fragility of international demand, the lack of leadership from key central banks—all that is strongly reminiscent of the 1930s. But there is something missing: another illusion. Wealth illusions are not confined only to the positive. An illusion that leads you to think that a threat to your prosperity may be fended off can be just as destructive of wealth and wellbeing. This is the threat the world now faces with regard to protection. And this threat emerges directly as a result of the weakness in the world's leading economies.

For all the talk about globalization, the world is probably no more globalized today than it was in the late nineteenth century and on some measures, such as labor mobility, it is less globalized. Between 1870 and 1914 international flows of goods, capital, and labor all increased dramatically. In the developing countries of Africa, Asia, and Latin America, the ratio of foreign capital to income more than tripled. Almost 60 million people emigrated from Europe, mainly to North America. In Asia a similar move took place as people left the densely populated parts of China and India and moved to Ceylon (Sri Lanka), Burma, Siam (Thailand), the Philippines, and Vietnam. It is estimated that during this period about 10 percent of the world's population left their homelands and settled in another country.[41] However, globalization went into retreat in the 1930s, turned back by a wave of protection.

In 1930 the US enacted the wide-ranging Smoot-Hawley tariff, which saw tariff rates on dutiable imports rise to their highest levels in over 100 years. Increases of 50 percent were common and some rates doubled. Other countries followed suit. The result was an enormous constriction of international trade. At the low point in 1942 imports into the US amounted to less than 2 percent of its GDP, compared with about 4 percent before Smoot-Hawley and about 14 percent now. As a share of GDP, Canadian imports almost halved, German imports fell from 15 percent to less than 5 percent, Italian imports from 12 percent to less than 5 percent, and British imports from just under 20 percent to less than 15 percent.

Globalization cannot be taken for granted even now. It could easily be put into reverse, just as it was in the interwar period. Protectionist sentiment is strong in many countries. As I argue in Chapter 5, the arguments for protection are fallacious, but that does not make them any the less pernicious.

There are ominous signs of what could happen. The US recently reaffirmed its tariff on steel imports to protect its ailing domestic steel industry; and it gives substantial subsidies to its agriculture. Moreover, America seems to be in a permanent running battle with the EU over just about everything from trade in bananas to the protection of intellectual capital.

Apocalypse now?

The threat of major trade wars is worse than it sounds. As I argue in Part II, international trade is one of the wellsprings of our prosperity. Restriction of trade would put the engines of prosperity into reverse. Coming on top of the financial collapse and the slump in aggregate demand, it was the third element that brought the international system to its knees in the 1930s.

What gave protection added appeal then was the fourth horseman: deflation. Fending off the protectionist danger now is going to depend greatly on how well the threat of deflation is resisted. Deflation and protectionism are close bedfellows—and, as all those forced to share such accommodation will attest, theirs is a bed of nails.

3
The Deflation Danger

We at the Federal Reserve recognize that deflation is a possibility.
Indeed, we now have been putting very significant resources in trying to
understand, without actually seeing it happen, what this phenomenon
is all about ... even though we perceive the risks as minor, the potential
consequences are very substantial and could be quite negative.

Alan Greenspan, 2003[1]

No one on the Committee has suggested that debt deflation is a prob-
lem either facing or likely to face the UK economy ... and part of our
task is to make sure it remains that way.

Mervyn King, Deputy Governor, Bank of England, August 2002[2]

On the eve of the Great Crash any investors who had been worried by the musings of Roger W. Babson had received considerable reassurance from an altogether more distinguished source, Irving Fisher: mathematician, inventor, eugenicist, health enthusiast, crusader, public figure extraordinaire, and professor of economics at Yale University; indeed, one of the greatest economists of the twentieth century. In 1929 he opined: "Stock prices have reached what looks like a permanently high plateau." Then the stock market plunged—taking a good part of Fisher's reputation with it. What made it worse was that Fisher stayed optimistic. In 1931 he praised President Herbert Hoover for his "calm reassurances to business."[3]

But when thinking about the economics of the Great Depression Fisher was on the ball. He even came up with a new theory: debt deflation. The key problem was excessive indebtedness and how this interacted with falling prices. In essence, by cutting back their spending to repay their debts people would cause prices to fall, thereby increasing the real value of what they owed. As Fisher put it:

The very effort of individuals to lessen their burden of debts increases it, because of the mass effect of the stampede to liquidate in swelling each dollar owed. Then we have the great paradox which, I submit, is the chief secret of most, if not all, great depressions: the more debtors pay, the more they owe.[4]

Mind you, this was a bit late for his own finances. Fisher had made a fortune out of inventing a card index system (now called a Rolodex™) and in 1925 his firm, which held the patent, merged with his main competitor to form Remington Rand and then Sperry Rand. His optimism on the eve of the crash cost him dear. He is estimated to have lost $10 million and thereafter he was never out of debt, much of it to his sister-in-law, who bailed him out. So great was his predicament that in order to save him from eviction, Yale University had to buy his house in New Haven and rent it back to him.

Perhaps this is one of the reasons why the theory of debt deflation, which Fisher did so much to pioneer, was pretty much neglected for so long—until the experience of the 1990s, notably in Japan, breathed new life into it and highlighted the hazards of falling prices.

Why Worry about the D-Word?

In order to be sure about the harm that deflation may do to incomes and living standards, we first need to be careful about what we mean by the term. Falling *output*, which is often referred to as deflation, obviously harms incomes and living standards, but that is not the same thing as falling prices, even though the two do sometimes go together. What I mean by deflation is falling *consumer prices*—and not just some prices. At low rates of inflation there are always some prices that fall. Over recent years we have become accustomed to the prices of electrical goods, telecommunications equipment, and even clothing and footwear falling year after year. However, because other prices have carried on rising, the overall level of prices has continued to increase. That is *not* deflation.

Deflation occurs when the general level of prices falls. In the extreme form prices of everything fall: goods and services, shares, houses, and labor. That is what happened in many countries in the 1930s. It is what happened in the 1990s in Japan. And it could happen in much of the world now.

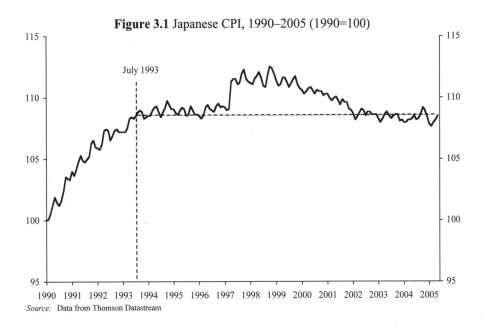

Figure 3.1 Japanese CPI, 1990–2005 (1990=100)

Source: Data from Thomson Datastream

As Figure 3.1 shows, in Japan the recent downward trend of consumer prices has meant that the consumer price level in 2005 is the same as it was 12 years earlier. And other prices that are traditionally more flexible and respond more quickly to shifts in demand—the prices paid to Japanese producers, as well as the prices of land, houses, and shares—have fallen much faster. This *is* deflation.

Should it be feared? In principle, deflation may be perfectly all right. In 1955, the US price index briefly dipped into negative territory, with the annual rate of deflation reaching 0.7 percent, without serious ill effects. And for much of the nineteenth century deflation was endemic but apparently benign. From 1812 to 1896, consumer prices in Britain fell by a half. In America they fell by more (see Figure 3.2). In the US from 1867 to 1896, producer prices fell on average by $2\frac{1}{2}$ percent per annum and consumer prices by 1.8 percent per annum. And there were some spectacular examples of falling prices. For instance, the introduction of new glass-making machines allowed the price of a dozen glass goblets to fall from $3.50 in 1864 to 40 cents in 1888. Yet real GDP increased at an average rate of $4\frac{1}{2}$ percent, 2 percent in per capita terms.[5]

Interestingly, this period of *prosperous deflation* saw the same combination of technological advances and increased globalization that is evident

Figure 3.2 UK and US price level, 1790–1939 (1800=100)

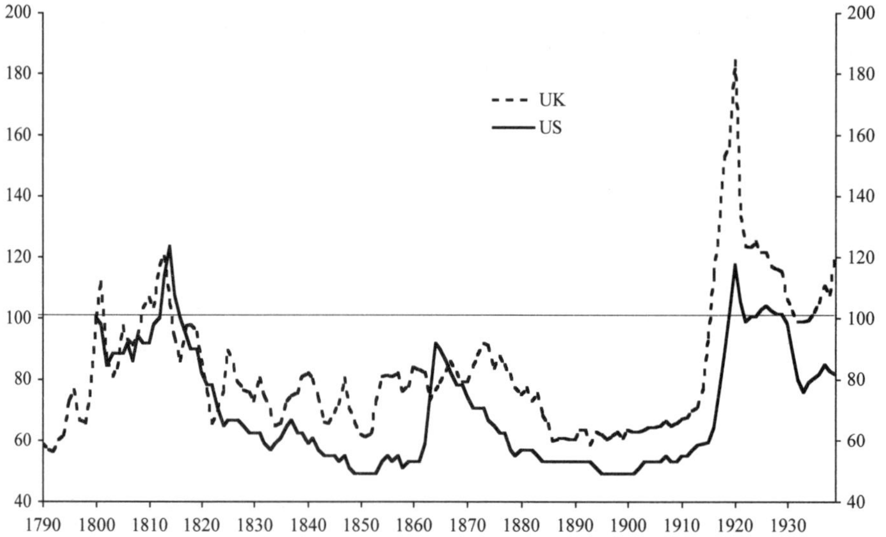

Source: Data from Global Financial Data and *Economist Book of Statistics*

today. This has led some commentators to draw a distinction between "bad deflation" and "good deflation." "Bad deflation" occurs as a result of asset-price collapses or bad monetary policy. "Good deflation" occurs as a result of increases in productivity growth or reduced costs stemming from an increase in international trade. Accordingly, recognizing these favorable factors at work now, these commentators are able to be optimistic about the future. If Europe and North America experience deflation, they say, it will be the "good" sort.

I find this analysis unconvincing and unhelpful. What happens if depressed asset prices, poor monetary policy, strong productivity growth, and cheaper imports occur simultaneously? What happens, indeed, if "good deflation" sets up forces that lead to "bad deflation"? This distinction will not do. To get the measure of deflation, we have to get to grips with those two human factors dominating economic life: what is in people's heads and what is in their institutions.

Expectations and practices
Rather like inflation, *if everything in the system is adjusted to it*, deflation need *not* be bad at all. In fact, according to some distinguished economists of yore, including the celebrated Milton Friedman,[6] a moderate rate of

deflation may be positively desirable. His idea was that if the price level was stable, and still more so if it was rising, people would hold too little of their assets in notes and coin, because they pay no interest. After all, they would be holding this money for nothing in return. This was "suboptimal" because money is costless to produce but helps to save resources by obviating the need for frequent trips to the bank. The solution was a regime where prices fell at the real rate of interest, say between 2 and 4 percent a year, thereby giving money holders due encouragement to optimize their money holdings.

OK, I admit it. In relation to the major issues at stake, this argument does rather seem like small change. It is the sort of debate that gives economists a bad name.

Older economists had seen different merits in a moderate rate of deflation. They argued that if prices fell at the rate of increase of productivity, this would impart stability to the wage structure. Rather than having to negotiate wages upwards all the time to benefit from productivity increases, all that workers had to do to benefit from the continual upward march of productivity was sit there and let falling prices do the job for them.[7] This regime was referred to as "the productivity norm." Advocates of the productivity norm had a point but, as I shall show in a moment, when thinking about deflation there are surely other, more important considerations.

Modern economists and central bankers have tended to argue that the ills of deflation are rather like the ills of inflation; that is to say, the uncertainty over money values that confuses consumers about relative prices and increases the perceived level of risk to do with all transactions that are spread over time, as well as so-called menu costs; that is, the costs incurred in altering slot machines and printing price lists.

While this is more like it, it is surely not quite right. It is still too comfortable a vision of the evil that deflation can bring. In short, it is a picture of the effects of deflation when all of the financial and economic system is adjusted to it. But typically the system won't be adjusted to deflation; and it certainly isn't now. On the contrary, companies and private individuals have scarcely considered it at all when framing their decisions. Until recently, many of them would hardly have encountered the word deflation, let alone known what it meant.

Moreover, in marked contrast to the second half of the nineteenth century, deflation now would come into a world riddled with debt, debt built up by households, companies, and governments with scarcely a moment's thought to the possibility that its real value could be driven up by a fall in the general level of prices.[8]

The result is that if, as I believe, some of the leading industrial countries do come to experience deflation, the effects will be profound. There will be a significant impact on corporate finances and levels of corporate failure, major effects on all asset classes, and it will cause disruption to the financial system, with serious implications for the solvency of financial institutions and the health of the real economy. In short, deflation poses a potent threat to the stability of the whole economic and financial system. Not good deflation, but deadly.

Deflation the destroyer

On the face of it, falling prices could leave companies pretty much unscathed—and many economic commentators, particularly those of the market fundamentalist bent, still thick on the ground in the US, take a relatively relaxed attitude to the prospect of deflation. They are wrong. In practice, deflation would be a machine for the destruction of much of corporate America, not to mention the corporate sector of just about every other developed country.

Although the downward flexibility of wage and salary costs has increased in recent years, it is still low in relation to selling prices, particularly as more products seem to have become commoditized. The result is that deflation will hit profits severely and unless it is extremely mild or short-lived, it is bound to bring on a wave of insolvencies. In this way the deflation of prices can easily lead to the depression of real output and employment.

In addition, the balance sheets of most companies are currently structured to lose out from deflation. All companies carry some real assets in the form of fixed capital, land, buildings, or inventory, and the market value of all of these can be expected to fall in nominal terms under deflation. Apart from shareholders' funds, however, almost all of the *liabilities* will be fixed in nominal terms, either short-term bank borrowings or debt of various kinds. So typically the corporate balance sheet is *un*balanced in relation to falling prices. The assets fall but the liabilities don't, with the result that the value of shareholders' equity falls.

Admittedly, if a company's debt finance is on variable interest rate terms there may be some relief. At least the interest rate on the debt can fall, reflecting the weaker trend of prices. Up to a point this means that a company holding real assets financed by fixed monetary liabilities with variable interest is hedged. After all, if the rate of change of the prices of the assets on the balance sheet moves from +2 to –2 percent but short-term interest rates fall by 4 percent, the company is no worse off.

However, there is a little problem about the number zero. Interest rates cannot fall below it, yet there is no such restraint on the rate at which prices can fall—including asset prices.[9] Thus real short rates are liable to *rise* in a period of deflation, thereby raising the cost of borrowing for individuals and the cost of finance for companies.[10] This means that even variable-rate funding offers no protection against anything other than the mildest deflation. After tax the increase will be even greater because nominal interest payments are allowable against profits when computing a company's tax bill, but no such allowance is made for the extra financial burden implied by falling prices under conditions of deflation.

Furthermore, as I pointed out in Chapter 1, the trend of recent years in America has been for companies to increase the gearing on their balance sheets by issuing more debt and even buying in equity. Accordingly, companies have restructured their balance sheets in a way that makes them more vulnerable to deflation.

Sharing in the corporate pain

Despite these acute dangers for the corporate sector, the historical evidence from the interwar period suggests that equities could hold up well in a period of deflation. This evidence is highly misleading, however, since in those days equities were lowly valued before the onset of deflation. And, of course, Japanese equities have done appallingly badly during the deflation that has lasted from the beginning of the 1990s to today. The Nikkei Index peaked at just under 39,000 at the end of December 1989. In mid-2005 it had not quite regained the 12,000 mark.

As they represent the ownership of streams of income that are variable with respect to changes in the general level of prices, you might easily think that equities *should* respond directly to the rate of inflation/deflation. On the usual simplifying assumption that everything adjusts to the change in the inflation environment, the result falls out that the price behavior of equities should directly mirror movements of the general price level, leaving real equity valuations unchanged. In that case, as long as you think in real terms, everything is tickety-boo.

In practice, though, matters are unlikely to be quite that simple. How equities react to deflation is clearly intimately bound up with how the corporate sector responds to it—and there, as I argued above, the answer is bound to be negative.

Moreover on past form, at first at least, bond yields are unlikely to fall sufficiently to reflect the full change in price prospects. Accordingly, with the onset of deflation real bond yields may rise. The markets use real bond yields to discount prospective future corporate earnings when setting the current value of equities. So higher real bond yields brought on by deflation would cause equity values to fall. (They would also temper what should otherwise be a favorable response of commercial property values to the onset of deflation.[11])

Swings and roundabouts

You might think that since the balance sheet problems of companies represent a redistribution of wealth through a mismatch of assets and liabilities, other parts of the system—notably the personal sector and the financial sector—must be gainers. In a narrow sense that is right. Personal and financial-sector holdings of company debt will rise in real value as deflation proceeds.

The constituency of the gainers will extend much more widely throughout society to the holders of all monetary instruments, including deposits in banks and savings institutions. Admittedly, in times of very low interest rates brought on by deflation their interest income would fall to virtually zero, as it has in Japan, but with prices falling year after year who needs interest? The real value of savings increases at the rate of deflation.

In principle, the gains would offset the losses. In some cases, indeed, the gainers would be the same individuals as the losers. So where is the problem? It is simple and stark. Who are companies except proxies for their ultimate owners, individual shareholders? It is impossible for society as a whole to gain by the corporate sector becoming worse off. But it can lose a very great deal if the extent of the corporate sector's problems is so acute that companies are forced to cut production, fail to service their debts, or go under.

Moreover, there is the little problem of the institutions that stand between the gainers and the losers, taking deposits from the one and making loans to the other. As borrowers fail to service their debts and cannot repay, while the assets against which the loans were secured fall in value, the solvency of these financial institutions is impaired. Eventually many would go bust.

The benefit of a high real rate of return on your savings is of no avail if the institution your savings are with goes bust. You will have saved all that money for nothing. In this way the pain of borrowers is transferred to savers, and the distress of both depresses consumer spending more, while the bankruptcy of some, and the feared bankruptcy of all, lending institutions causes the stock market to plunge still further, thereby destroying wealth and imperiling the solvency of other financial institutions, thus giving the deflationary spiral another twist.

Accordingly, the potential gain of the financial sector from deflation is a mirage. Worse than that, the financial sector ultimately becomes the repository of much of the pain caused by deflation, in the form of missed interest payments and bad debts. As the Japanese experience confirms, in deflationary conditions the financial sector is likely to perform particularly badly.

Furthermore, in anything other than a completely benign form of deflation where the rate was modest and it was fully anticipated, severe dislocation in the financial sector would be likely to restrict the supply of credit and contribute to a collapse of confidence and a deterioration of creditworthiness throughout the economy. Needless to say, all of this would be decidedly negative for equities.[12] Besides these calamitous consequences, the fact that Joe Soap's bank deposit would be worth more in real terms pales into insignificance.

A Cautionary Tale

This account of the ills that deflation can cause is not a fairy tale. Nor is it even a historical tale of the 1930s. On the contrary, it is a fair description of the deflationary process in modern-day Japan. After the collapse of the bubble economy, the 1990s saw a wave of financial bankruptcies caused by the interaction of collapsed stock markets and persistent deflation. 1997 saw the failure of Sanyo Securities, Japan's seventh-largest broker, Hokkaido Takushoku Bank, one of Japan's leading 20 banks, and, most spectacularly, Yamaichi Securities in the largest corporate collapse in history. In 2000 two large insurance companies, Kyoei Life and Chiyoda Mutual, went bust. And this has been during a relatively mild deflation and in an economy not noted for brutal financial adjustment.

Nor is such experience confined to the peculiar conditions of Japan. The perfect example of a disaster brought on purely by a change in the inflation regime is the venerable British financial institution Equitable Life, which for hundreds of years was used by the British professional middle classes for long-term saving. Now it is closed to new business and many of its policy holders are in a state of despair. Their plight has been brought about by the unforeseen transition to a regime of *low inflation* (well, unforeseen by most people).

Back in the inflationary era, the Equitable gave some of its policyholders the option of taking out a fixed-rate guarantee on its pensions, which effectively shielded the taker against the chance that long-term interest rates might fall dramatically and thereby cut back their pension entitlements.

At the time, the Equitable evidently took the view that a dramatic fall in long-term interest rates was unlikely given that inflation was ingrained in the system. Accordingly, it decided not to hedge its exposure. It continued with this stance even as inflation and long rates plunged, thereby raising enormously the value of the guarantees given to some policyholders. In the end, other policyholders in the so-called with profits fund, who were effectively taking an equity stake in the Equitable's investment strategy, footed the bill. Complex and extremely expensive legal action ensued, which bit into the value of policyholders' assets even more.

To cut a long story short, the Equitable is now a pale shadow of its once proud self and many a prospective pensioner is having to come to terms with much diminished prospects for their retirement. And this was simply from the transition to low inflation. The Equitable saga could prove to be a children's tea party compared to what might happen with the onset of deflation.

Not so Safe, after All

In the last chapter I emphasized the dangers posed to pensions by the bursting of the stock-market bubble. These problems would be far worse in deflationary conditions. Where pensions are set in relation to a salary, they are specified as either fixed payments or payments that can rise at a certain minimum rate per year. Under current arrangements in most countries they cannot be cut, regardless of what happens to consumer prices, wages, or the value of investments. This is a classic case of mismatch between assets and liabilities.

In order to provide for these pensions, funded schemes rely on their investments to rise. If the value of their investment falls, however, then once they have used up any cushion in the fund they are forced to find money from outside to be able to carry on paying the same pensions. This may mean increased contributions from existing members or a greater contribution from the sponsoring company.

Deflation also worsens the vicious interaction between pension under-provision, the stock market, and the economy, which I highlighted in the last chapter. It weakens investment performance but boosts the guaranteed real value of pensions, thereby transferring wealth to pensioners. As the size of this transfer mounts, it worsens the position of the corporate sector and thereby weakens share prices still more—and so on and so forth. Nor will there be an escape for the system as a whole if the threatened companies seek to get out of their predicament by slashing costs and employment levels, for that will simply intensify the deflationary pressure in the economy.

Pensions paid by so-called defined-contribution schemes do not experience quite the same problems, but they do experience problems. It is simply that the people who bear the impact of the losses are different. These schemes are a vehicle for stock-market investment where the prospective pensioner directly bears the investment risk. They will only get the pensions they thought they would if the stock market performs as expected. If deflation sets in, it will not. Admittedly, in this case there are no financial institutions in the middle whose existence may be imperiled. Nevertheless, the prospective pensioners will be decidedly worse off in money terms and, if they have considerable liabilities fixed in money terms, for instance through a mortgage (see below), *they* could be the ones whose solvency is in danger.

When occupational schemes are not funded, which is true in most of continental Europe, deflation is again deadly. Prospective pensioners will expect, and in many cases be entitled to, certain fixed sums, but as deflation proceeds, even if there is no real weakness in the economy, company revenues will be under downward pressure and company profits will probably fall, thereby making the burden of paying out the pensions all the greater. In this case the added burden is again felt directly by employers, who are liable to react by cutting costs, thereby intensifying the deflationary spiral.

State security?

Most people would naturally tend to assume that whatever problems deflation might cause for private-sector pensions, at least their *state* entitlements would be immune. I am not so sure. After all, under deflation tax revenues are likely to fall and so if the government cannot also cut its expenditure, its financial deficit must widen. In acute cases, the result will be a prospective level of debt that is unsustainable. Accordingly, prospective state pensioners would be right to be concerned about whether they will ultimately get what they think they have been promised. This is, after all, exactly what worries many people in Japan today.

There is a way out, but it hardly offers much succor to pensioners: namely reductions in pensions in line with falling prices. This has already happened in Japan, where in February 2003 the monthly pension was cut by 0.9 percent, in line with deflation in the shops. It would be open to other governments to adjust the nominal value of state pensions downwards or, if this were not deemed to be compliant with the existing "uprating" legislation, to pass new legislation allowing pensions to be tied to movements of the consumer price index, both up and down. There would, of course, be enormous resistance to this from pensioners, and perhaps even from the public at large. If this pressure succeeded in ensuring that state pension increases had a floor at zero while the state's tax take shrank in line with falling prices, deflation would cause the problem of burgeoning state pension liabilities to intensify.

You might think that a regime of *fluctuating* prices, where the average inflation rate was zero but years of inflation alternated with years of deflation, would escape this difficulty. However, if state pensions could not be cut, it would not. Pensions would remain constant in the years when the price level fell and rise in the years when it rose. In such a regime, the real level of the state pension (and its real cost to taxpayers) would ratchet up over time.

Redistribution between pensioners

Still, it's an ill wind and all that. The shift to deflation from a previous history of inflation would bring substantial gains for those who had retired on fixed pensions set earlier. In America and Britain, the outright winners would be members of defined-contribution pension schemes who retired when annuity rates were high, reflecting the markets' expectation of high inflation, only to find that deflation set in.

Equally, there is a category of outright loser. As I stressed above, if the countries of Europe and North America are set to experience deflation, this is probably not going to be a new regime of complete stability—a new steady state with a constant rate of deflation continuing year after year. After a period of deflation, these countries would probably undergo a bout of inflation. In fact, if the policy objective of the authorities were directed to maintaining a certain rate of inflation, or even to achieving and maintaining a certain price *level*, then after a period of deflation, policy would be set deliberately to deliver price increases. (After all, in inflation-targeting regimes it is explicitly recognised that inflation can be too low.)

The swing from deflation to inflation poses a really serious risk for pensioners. Suppose they retire at a time when the financial markets are worried about deflation, when annuity rates are set to reflect that, and when corporate and state uprating practices are also set to reflect it, but when, just around the corner, there lies a bout of *in*flation, perhaps stimulated by the authorities and perhaps virulent. Pensioners caught in this position would be in a similar situation to all those people who retired on fixed pensions in the postwar years only to find that those pensions' real value was substantially eroded by inflation. The problem is especially acute now that people typically face longer periods of living off a pension due to both earlier retirement and longer life.

Until recently this danger might have seemed pretty remote for most people working in large companies in the UK, because they would have been members of an occupational pension scheme whose retirement benefits would have been tied to final salary and subject to uprating with inflation, at least in accordance with statutory minimums and often uprated more generously. Now, as I emphasized in the last chapter, companies are rushing to close such schemes. Switching from final-salary to money-purchase arrangements may or may not be a good thing overall, but one aspect is clear. Compared to final-salary schemes, money-purchase schemes transfer risk from the employer to the employee—including inflation/deflation risk. In the UK, the way things are going, most people working in the private sector are going to be exposed to this risk—and it can be fatal.

Pensions and society
In the 1970s the plight of pensioners whose real incomes were ravaged by high inflation excited considerable public sympathy, but the onset of

deflation would bring the reverse. Imagine a situation where pay was static or falling for most of the population, while those living on pensions saw their incomes rising at 3 percent per annum. There would be considerable resentment. The high and rising real value of pensions currently being paid out to the retired would be paid at the expense of those still working. Some British companies are already expressing surprise and dismay that they are increasing the incomes of their pensioners faster than the incomes of their current employees, some of whom are on pay freezes or enjoying increases of only 1 or 2 percent.

These income-distribution and fairness effects would also be bound to cause considerable political difficulties. We are familiar with the idea of the population aging and gray power emerging as a political force. Yet we should not underestimate the continuing power of those in work, who will continue to be more numerous in the electorate even in the most graying of countries, and will continue to be capable of exerting a degree of economic power.

After the last bout of serious deflation in the interwar period there was a deliberate policy of reducing the real incomes of rentiers—those who live on the income from their investments—by cutting interest rates. In today's society, if we were to undergo a significant amount of deflation, pensioners would be the major beneficiaries and there might well be a comparable movement to reduce their entitlements. The scene would be set for a battle between the generations. How the problems of the pension system will pan out in the future is a subject I discuss in Chapter 7.

Mortgage Misery

Because of their long life, pensions are perhaps the most sensitive part of the economic system to a bout of deflation. However, mortgages must come a close second. Someone who takes out a mortgage is engaging in a trans-action whose value is determined by the interaction between one fixed money amount, namely the capital sum borrowed, and up to three variable amounts: the rate of interest (unless they take out a fully fixed mortgage), the rate of increase of their income, and the rate of increase in the value of the property.

The majority of people in the Anglo-Saxon countries have substantial mortgage debts. In the UK, the ratio of mortgage debt to GDP is 60 percent.

Admittedly in continental Europe such debts are typically lower, but they are still high. The average ratio of mortgage debt to GDP across the euro-zone is now 40 percent, and in Denmark and the Netherlands it is above 60 percent.

Deflation would raise the real value of these debts, making them more burdensome to repay. In the first instance mortgage holders might feel little affected, as nominal interest rates fell and their earnings still went up. But this is just the initial stage. In a full-blown deflation earnings would first stop rising and then would actually fall, as would the price of property. However, as I pointed out above, official interest rates cannot fall below zero and that means that mortgage rates could not plausibly be lower than, say, 1 percent and in all likelihood would be much higher than that. The problem is clear: a fixed burden of debt and debt interest payments while the ability to finance and repay debt is falling year after year.

This mismatch is the route to mortgage misery—and could lead to disaster for the economy as a whole. Millions of people in most of the world's leading countries would be facing financial ruin. Many would surely default, as they did in the 1930s. Even in the UK recession of the early 1990s, thousands of homeowners were unable to keep up their mortgage payments and lost their homes. As the value of the properties fell below the mortgage debts secured on them, there were many cases of people posting the keys of their property through the lenders' letterboxes and simply walking away. Why carry on forking out all that money for nothing?

Admittedly, then the pain was caused because interest rates had risen to insupportable levels. But pay was still rising. Under deflation, interest rates would fall to rock bottom and no more, while pay would continue to fall. This would bring exactly the same squeeze but from the opposite direction.

Deflation Experience

So in current circumstances deflation *is* to be feared—whatever the experience in Britain and America at the end of the nineteenth century, and whatever the textbooks say. But is it a realistic prospect outside Japan? Deflation is not a uniquely Japanese phenomenon. In 2002 China, Hong Kong, Singapore, and Taiwan also experienced it. In China this was the second bout of generalized deflation in five years and it came after only a short

Figure 3.3 Chinese inflation… and deflation, 1988–2005 (%y/y)

Source: Data from Thomson Datatstream

intervening period in which prices barely rose at all (see Figure 3.3). Together, these five countries account for about 20 percent of the global economy and an equivalent proportion of world trade. (Their share of world output is probably nearer 30 percent on a purchasing power parity (PPP) basis.)[13]

Moreover, the extent of the deflation in some of these countries is notable. In China, goods prices declined by 10 percent over five years. Hong Kong's measure of the overall price level (the GDP deflator) declined by 16 percent in five years.

Outside Asia, Switzerland, Sweden, Argentina, and Saudi Arabia have briefly experienced deflation in recent years. In the EU, the rate of price inflation has already touched very low levels in a number of countries, including Britain, France, and Germany. In the United States the rate has not yet fallen to very low levels, but until recently the country enjoyed strong economic expansion. Given the strength of the American boom in the late 1990s, inflation was remarkably low.

Moreover, the signs are that the American economy is now highly prone to deflation. In Q2 2002 the GDP deflator, just about the broadest measure of price pressures, was up only 1 percent over the previous year, representing a drop of 1.3 percent from the inflation rate prevailing at the cyclical peak, some six quarters earlier. That rate of inflation deceleration is about double

the norm in previous business cycles.[14] In early 2003 the rate of core inflation—that is, excluding the volatile elements of food and energy—fell to 1.5
percent, a 37-year low.

The prices of goods leaving British factories have been falling for years—
as have the prices of goods sold in British shops. It is only the continued
inflation of service prices that has kept deflation at bay in the UK.

Moreover, Asian deflation has a way of spreading into Europe and North
America, as prices are driven lower by the relocation of manufacturing, especially to China, where costs are a fraction of what they are in the developed
countries. For many products, once production is shifted to China the ultimate decline in prices might be 70–80 percent. So great is the overhang of
surplus labor in China that in the manufacturing sector China's prices are
going to become global prices. What is more, these effects are now starting
to spread into the service sector as European and North American businesses outsource to countries such as India such services as call centers,
email help desks, software design, accounting, network management,
billing, telemarketing, and transcription and translation services.

The zero margin

The weight of this evidence leads to a clear conclusion. For interest rates it may
be, but for inflation zero is most definitely *not* a magic number. Complete
price stability is an illusion. Policy makers have peddled a fantasy that we could
have gently rising prices for ever. But we have never had this, apart from the
extraordinary period of the first 25 years after the Second World War.

In Europe and North America this generation may be unused to deflation, but previous generations regarded it as part of normal experience. In
the UK deflation has alternated with inflation for centuries, leaving the
price level broadly stable over long periods. In 1932 the price level was marginally *lower* than it had been in 1795. Moreover, there were some periods of
very rapid price declines in the twentieth century. In 1921 prices fell by 21
percent in the UK and 10 percent in the US.

Until recently, this long historical experience with deflation was not only
unknown by most of the population but disregarded by economists and policy
makers. It occurred under a system that tied the value of money to gold (or some
other precious metal) and that therefore could not be managed. There were peri-
odic gluts and shortages of the precious metal that precipitated bursts of inflation and deflation, about which the monetary authorities could do nothing.

In the 1930s, however, countries abandoned the Gold Standard and afterwards national central banks managed their own monetary systems based on paper money and credit, the supplies of which were potentially unlimited. Central banks could readily create money for nothing. Accordingly in a modern monetary system, the experts thought, deflation was now impossible. The historical experience with deflation could be left to the history books. Then came the Japanese deflation of the 1990s (which I discuss briefly below). Now the historical experience of deflation no longer seems so irrelevant.

Even so, given that just about the whole world experienced prolonged low inflation in the 1950s and 1960s without any break into deflation, it is legitimate to ask what it is that makes deflation a serious possibility now. Why shouldn't the world simply carry on with a very low rate of inflation?

There are three factors that over the medium term are tending to cause countries to operate below full capacity, and these are closely associated with the main themes of Part II. First, as I argue in the Finale, large parts of the world are wedded to a policy of substantial current account surplus, thereby sucking demand away from the rest. Meanwhile, in the developed countries the intense competition unleashed by globalization is reducing the level of unemployment or unused capacity necessary to stop the economy from boiling over. Yet outside the US and the UK this change is barely acknowledged by the policy establishment.

Moreover, as I argue in Part II, the combination of globalization and a faster rate of knowledge discovery should unleash a higher rate of productivity growth. There are clear signs of this in the US, where productivity growth has remained very high even in the downturn, although outside the US this improvement in economic potential is hardly acknowledged. To be fair, outside the US there is not yet much sign of any improvement in the data. Nevertheless when the effect does appear, on all past form the central banks are likely to be slow to acknowledge it. The upshot may well be that policy will be run too tight, given the enhanced potential, with the result that the economy continually operates below capacity.

Greater flexibility

These factors give us the likelihood of unused resources, but why should this produce *deflation* as opposed to simply loss of output and increased unemployment? In *The Death of Inflation* I gave the answer. Prices are now more downwardly flexible than they used to be, so that weak aggregate demand will more readily result in falling prices. Globalization, a more competitive and more unstable business environment, and the growth of variable pricing practices have all contributed to a situation in which prices can more readily fall across wide sections of the economy.

With trade unions much weaker, it is more conceivable that even *wages* could fall. In the United States and Britain, but also increasingly elsewhere, a larger proportion of pay is now made up of variable components such as bonus and performance awards and profit-related elements. Even if "the rate for the job" is still sacrosanct, these variable elements mean that total earnings can fall—even in nominal terms, if there should be an adverse shock to aggregate demand. And there are an increasing number of wage cuts in particular sectors. In 2003, American Airlines agreed $1.8 million worth of wage cuts with its unions.[15] In the UK, Clifford Chance, the world's largest law firm, cut its pay rates for lawyers.

In Japan over recent years *average* earnings have been falling.[16] In 2002, average monthly pay fell by 2.2 percent. There are also many striking examples of wage cuts. Public-sector workers employed in Nagano recently accepted pay cuts of 12 percent over three years and Nissho Iwai and Nichimen, two trading groups that plan to merge, have asked their unions to accept pay cuts of 20 percent.

If my fears about the immediate outlook for the world economy prove justified and some industrial countries show next to no growth at best, one or more of them *will* experience deflation. In short, the countries of Europe and North America are one recession away from deflation. My only substantive doubt is whether that recession occurs sooner or later. But as I argued in the last chapter, there are powerful forces acting to bring it sooner.

Countries at Risk

Because of the extent of the loss of wealth in the stock market and the high level of flexibility for both pay and prices there, the United States is one of the most likely candidates for deflation. But until recently there has been a good deal of complacency about the prospect, even in high places. Glenn Hubbard, chairman of the US President's Council of Economic Advisers, dismissed the prospect on the basis of four spurious arguments.[17] The first is that US productivity growth has been strong, thereby underpinning strong growth in real incomes that in turn would sustain strong growth in consumption. Yet if consumption is strong because productivity growth is strong, this says *nothing* about the extent of inflationary or deflationary pressures. Indeed, the fact that productivity growth is strong is a priori an argument in favor of the prospect of deflation, because strong productivity growth *requires* that aggregate demand increase at a fast rate to prevent prices from falling.

The second argument is that the surge in US house prices is fully sustainable and underpins strong consumption growth. The reason for this is that high house-price growth stems from high levels of immigration and land shortage and high transaction costs deter speculative behavior in the housing market. Yet this completely ignores the points I made in the previous chapter about the vulnerability of the US housing market and the way the housing market works.

The third argument is that falling prices are not always bad. This is true, but so what? It is not an argument against the possibility of deflation occurring.

The fourth is that a sustained decline in prices that magnifies the real burden of debt is unlikely. But this assumes away the very thing whose likelihood is under debate.

One can only hope that the President receives better advice on other issues. At least the Fed is well up on the deflation risk and the markets are also keenly aware of it. Indeed, you could say that in 2003, at last deflation entered the mainstream of financial America and it has stayed there.

But unfortunately, awareness is not quite so acute elsewhere, even though it should be. Germany is in front of America in the deflation stakes because its starting point is so much lower, with core inflation below 1 percent in the first half of 2005 and dipping as low as 0.3 percent at one point. And the country looks uncompetitive. Moreover, since its partners in the eurozone are inflating only at very low rates, for Germany to regain competitiveness fairly quickly, prices there will have to fall. So far from being an accident, deflation in Germany could be said to be preordained. This situation is uncannily similar to what happened in the UK after it returned to the Gold Standard in 1925 at the old (now too high) parity.

Against this, German price and wage structures are more inflexible than in the US, so a downturn will probably have to be that much more severe to deliver falling prices. On the other hand, the German authorities are not able to set monetary policy to forestall the threat of deflation but have to rely on the ECB, acting in the interests of the eurozone as a whole.

This is a particularly alarming prospect that seems hardly to have been considered by all those advocates of the European single currency—or by many of those who worry about deflation. The main reason why conventional economists are so confident that deflation can be easily stopped is that the central bank can simply print money. But what happens if you haven't got a central bank with money-issuing powers? Germany still has the Bundesbank, but it can do virtually nothing. It is now no more than a branch of the ECB. Meanwhile, the ECB is not exactly the sort of central bank to undertake the radical steps that may be necessary to stop deflation. It seems to be frightened of its own shadow.

What is of special concern in the European case is that although monetary policy is conducted on a eurozone basis, monetary and financial institutions remain largely national. In Germany, for instance, the banking system has a preponderance of German debt on its balance sheets. The pensions and insurance systems are largely German: German providers and German takers. In other words, there is still a heavy concentration of nationally based credit and systemic risk in a monetary system that is being run on transnational lines.

Admittedly, deflation in Germany and France would not be able to go very far before the ECB was obliged by its remit to sit up and take notice, because these economies are so weighty in the eurozone economy and their inflation rates are an important component of the eurozone's inflation rate. But deflation could get going in these countries, and even more so in the smaller countries, while the ECB continued to be worried about *inflation* for the eurozone as a whole, not least because the fast-growing countries of the eurozone, especially Greece, Spain, Portugal, and Ireland, tend to have a much higher inflation rate for a systematic reason. Essentially, their price levels are catching up with those of central Europe. Arguably, their high inflation rates are therefore a different kettle of fish and should be excluded from the ECB's target, or the target should be raised to accommodate them.

Nevertheless, the point is that as things stand the ECB makes no allowance for this factor. The result is that if it succeeds in getting the eurozone's average inflation rate below the target of 2 percent, it will virtually guarantee that the German inflation rate will be just above zero. Pushing average eurozone inflation much lower, either by accident or design, would tip Germany into deflation. And this is not only a problem for Germany. Belgium, Austria, and Finland also have very low rates of inflation, and are closely tied into the Germany economy. They too are in acute danger of falling into deflation in the next couple of years. Even the Netherlands, which has tended to have a higher rate of inflation, would not be far behind.

The problem of divergent inflation performance has intensified after 10 further countries joined the EU in 2004, all of which tend to have high inflation rates for similar reasons. As and when some of these countries join the eurozone, the zone's inflation rate will rise, arguing for tighter monetary policy—which means even lower inflation in Germany and the rest of core Europe.

At first sight it is hard to see the UK being high on the list of possible deflators, but in fact there is a significant deflation risk there too. For a start, the UK's inflation rate has been extremely low—just about the lowest in the EU. On the common European harmonized measure, HICP, UK inflation has frequently been less than 1 percent. Furthermore, the UK is particularly exposed to a slump in residential property prices. As I stressed in the last chapter, UK house prices have risen a long way, look overvalued according to the usual yardsticks, and are particularly important as a determinant of consumer spending and therefore aggregate demand.

The UK's deflationary risk would be greatly increased if the country decided to join the euro at somewhere near the exchange rate ruling during the summer of 2005. The exchange rate of the pound against the euro was then much too high. If entry proceeded at that rate it could condemn British exporters to years of decline, and the overall economy to years of stagnation and falling prices. But as things stand, British entry looks a most unlikely prospect.

Foreseeing and Forestalling

So deflation is potentially deadly, it has occurred in Asia, and it could easily appear in the West. But could it easily be stopped by the policy makers? This is not the place to review the detailed policy options to defeat deflation, but some points of principle need to be established here.

The behavior of central banks is critical to the possibility of deflation in the modern world because, in contrast to the Gold Standard, monetary policy is now *managed*. Indeed, at least until recently it has been common to dismiss the possibility of deflation on the grounds that no government or central bank is aiming for it, nor is ever likely to—well, not yet anyway.

Although not many observers have particular faith in the ECB, there is still a good deal of faith in the powers of central banks in general—not least among central bankers.[18] This is why most people are inclined to be skeptical about the prospects for deflation in Europe and North America. The prevailing view among economists and market operators is that in the end we get the inflation rate not that we deserve, but that the central banks choose. In that case, what really matters is what the central banks (or, where appropriate, their political masters) want, how well they can anticipate the future, and how reliable their tools are for achieving their objectives. The prevailing view is that on all three counts there are grounds for reassurance. But I believe that on all three counts there are grounds for serious doubts.

The widespread market assumption has been that if the economy were ever in danger of sliding into a deflationary phase, which is itself the subject of some dispute, central banks would see the danger coming and take appropriate offsetting action. This is naive. After all, the world's central banks did not see the Great Depression coming, nor the Great Inflation of the 1970s. Nor has the Bank of Japan had a good record, either in foreseeing deflation ahead or taking appropriate action to forestall it. Nor, for that matter, did private-sector forecasters or financial markets see deflation coming in Japan. Japanese long-term bond rates remained as high as 5 percent right up to the beginning of 1995. Moreover, once the danger was upon them, the Japanese authorities still did not seem to appreciate how serious it was. Consequently, they did not act boldly enough and did not take out sufficient "insurance" against the special downside risks that deflation poses.[19]

But do the West's central banks now take the threat of deflation seriously? They certainly take it more seriously than they did when *The Death of Inflation* first appeared in early 1996. That book met with a barrage of criticism, especially from central bankers, particularly on the subject of deflation, which was widely felt to be beyond the realms of possibility in the West. Over the succeeding years, though, a number of central bankers have made statements suggesting that they now take the prospect seriously. In particular, the Bank for International Settlements (BIS), the central bankers' bank, said in June 1996: "The forces bearing on the price level are now more balanced than they have been for some decades."

Moreover, the speeches of Alan Greenspan at the Fed have been littered with references to the need to avoid deflation as well as inflation. But all is not sweetness and light. The ECB has also on occasion paid lip service to the deflationary threat, but it does not seem to give it due weight. In his comments at a press conference in June 2003, ECB president Wim Duisenberg said:

> *There are currently no forecasts indicating any deflationary risks. At a regional level a period of low price increases or indeed declines will improve that region's competitiveness in the monetary area.*
>
> *Within a monetary union deflation is not a meaningful concept when applied to individual regions, like New Hampshire or Germany.*
>
> *We are convinced that we don't have to prepare for deflation because we don't see deflation coming. Is the central bank prepared to deal with it if the situation were coming? The answer is yes.*[20]

At the Bank of England, even the arch-hawk, the then deputy governor Mervyn King, said in December 1998: "Central bankers should be as vigilant in counteracting deflation as in preventing inflation." Nevertheless, the doubts remain. After all, Sir Edward George, then governor of the Bank of England, said as late as August 2002: "I don't at this stage lose much sleep about deflation."[21] Let's hope his fellow central bankers don't need a wake-up call.

Weak tools

Not only do central bankers still tend to underrate the deflationary threat, but they are also overconfident of their ability to stop deflation if it appeared. Despite all the propaganda, their policy tools are not so finely honed and effective that central banks can be relied on to take exactly offsetting action when they do see a major shock coming.

In particular, central banks have fallen into the trap of overestimating the power of interest rates to adjust the economy, particularly when the recent history of financial fantasies has left companies with excess capital stock and consumers with weakened "balance sheets" so that they do not respond to reductions in interest rates in the normal way. For real efficacy, monetary policy has always relied on either very large movements in rates or the ability to deliver some sort of shock that affects expectations or the *supply* of credit. If confidence is lacking, reductions in interest rates of $\frac{1}{4}$ or $\frac{1}{2}$ percent, which have recently become the norm in the industrialized West, may have next to no effect.

Central bankers think and act as though the economy were some sort of finely tuned engine that only needs the sprockets adjusted and the right buttons pushed for it to leap into life, hover gently, or move up slowly to cruising speed—whatever the central bankers desire. In fact it is more like a wild animal: unpredictable, awkward, and sometimes downright dangerous.

Accordingly, as and when western central banks are confronted by emerging deflation, even though they might think that their responses are timely and forward looking judged by the potential speed of deterioration of sentiment, they are likely to be *slow* to reduce interest rates and the pace of reductions is likely to lag behind the pace of the deflationary process. This is usually characterized by falling confidence and a collapse of credit availability, against which minor reductions in interest rates may be next to useless. That, of course, means that interest rates will have to fall all the more and stay down that much longer—assuming, that is, that central banks do want to stop the deflation.

So what *do* central banks want?

It is not even clear that all central banks would want to stand resolutely against a small rate of deflation. The history of inflation fighting since the battle was first joined in earnest at the end of the 1970s is that the objectives have become more demanding as central banks have enjoyed more success. Far from relaxing as they succeeded in reaching their objectives, central banks have become more ambitious. At the moment across the world, something like an inflation rate of 1–3 percent is presented as the ultimate prize. But it is by no means clear that we have yet reached the final destination.[22]

Moreover, because of the history of high inflation over the last 30 years and more or less continuous inflation over the last 60, whatever they might think themselves central banks are still paranoid about their *reputation* as inflation fighters. The US Fed is an honorable exception, but in general, whereas central banks are inclined to see inflationary risks very clearly, they readily play down the chances of deflation. Accordingly, in the event of a major downward shock to demand, prompt offsetting action by central banks could not be taken for granted.

Meanwhile, the financial markets are also still supersensitive to the danger of inflation and accordingly tend to set long interest rates at a level that imposes high real interest rates on borrowers. Throughout the steep American economic slowdown in 2001, bond markets continued to fret, and sometimes to panic, about the threat of inflation.

How Could Deflation Happen?

The world is now stuck in a sort of low-inflation equilibrium in which continued downward pressure on a whole raft of prices is offset by continued upward pressure on others. A breakout will require some shock. Nevertheless, there is no mystery about what could cause a breakout downwards: adapting a phrase from President Clinton, it's the stock market, stupid; or perhaps more accurately, the stock market and the housing market.

Moreover, deflation in Japan could spread to North America and Europe. Most commentators and analysts in the West have become complacent about the Japanese slump. It may have lasted for a decade, and for the last several years this has been accompanied by deflation, but so what? Japan is not a substantial borrower from the rest of the world; it is a substantial net creditor. So who cares if the economy keeps contracting and prices keep falling? Anyway, Japanese deflation now seems to be ending.

This complacent view is wrong. The world will find it difficult to prosper when its second-largest economy is in the doldrums. We all need a strong Japan. And there are direct links from Japan's weakness to the rest of the world. In particular, a weak Japan threatens to destabilize the whole of East Asia, which is so critical for the West's prosperity. If Japan slipped back again, one way for it to overcome its deflation might be to export it to the rest of us via an ultra-weak yen.

If that ever happened, it would put pressure on the Chinese renminbi and other Asian currencies. (I briefly discuss Chinese exchange-rate policy in the Finale.) In short, there would be the danger of a mass depreciation of Asian currencies against the dollar and the euro—exactly the opposite of what is needed. Effectively Asia as a whole would be exporting deflation to the West. Meanwhile, the US would need the recent depreciation of the dollar to be accepted, and probably to go much further. The upshot would be substantial upward pressure on the euro—and downward pressure on prices in the eurozone.[23]

Could it be as bad as Japan?

Could countries in the West experience something as serious as the deflationary slump that has engulfed Japan? For most of the 1990s, as Japan floundered, it was common to believe that the answer was a categorical "no." Japan's problems were uniquely Japanese. Nothing like them could or would occur elsewhere.

To be fair, there have been some extraordinary features of the Japanese predicament that it is difficult to see readily repeated throughout the West, and there have been some glaring policy mistakes. Furthermore, the Japanese banking system has been a disaster beyond compare. The Japanese authorities first tried to deal with this problem by not admitting how serious it was, which in the end made matters worse. Only belatedly did they set about trying to clean up bank balance sheets sufficiently to facilitate flows of new credit. At the end of 2002, even official estimates put the ratio of bad debts to GDP at 8 percent, and the reality was surely worse.

By contrast, on the whole, banking systems in the West look relatively strong, even after the financial and economic crisis in America in 2001–2003. Still, complacency is to be avoided. It is in the nature of banking crises that they come and hit you when and where you are least expecting them. Banks have offloaded risks to other parts of the system through the use of derivatives, whose total face value, excluding contracts traded on exchanges such as the International Petroleum Exchange, comes close to $85 trillion.[24] It is always possible that major positions in derivatives, perhaps misunderstood or perhaps not even known about by bank managements, could cause some significant bank failures. The sage of Omaha, Warren Buffet, has said: "Derivatives are financial weapons of mass destruction. The dangers are now latent—but they could be lethal."[25] When Buffet is worried the rest of us should quake.

Moreover, not all of the western banking system even *looks* in tip-top condition. In late 2002 there were five continental European banks whose capital position appeared decidedly weak,[26] and at times there have been some strong market rumors that a major continental bank was on the brink of collapse. There are particular concerns about German banks that are suffering the deadly combination of a weak economy and incipient deflation on the one hand and a history of poor profitability on the other.[27]

Even in Britain, where the banks are highly profitable, generally well capitalized, and well managed, there are potentially serious problems. In December

2002 Standard & Poor's for the first time listed Britain as a country facing potential stress in its banking system if the housing bubble burst. It is right to have done so. *When* the housing bubble does burst banks will find themselves in much tougher conditions and this is bound to affect their lending policy.

In any case, as the source of all ills Japan's bad-debt crisis is not quite what it is cracked up to be. In the popular perception—sadly, perhaps also in the understanding of the Japanese authorities—there is a misguided tendency to give these bad debts an exaggerated causative role in the generation of Japan's deflation crisis. The prevailing idea is that they have eroded banks' capital and hobbled their willingness to lend. The implication is that alleviating the burden of bad debts is the solution to the problem. If only the Japanese authorities could muster the will and the funds to wipe the slate clean, all would be well.

Yet if the weakness of Japanese banks is the essential problem, why aren't foreign banks queuing up to make loans to the hoards of frustrated, creditworthy potential Japanese borrowers? The answer, of course, is that these hoards do not exist. *That* is the problem. The essential difficulty is the lack of creditworthy borrowers—and that is partly caused by deflation itself. What is the point of making loans if you know that you will not be repaid? You would be dishing out money for nothing.

In short, the majority of the banking system's travails are the *result* of weak aggregate demand and deflation rather than the independent source of those problems. Sorting out the banks' bad-debt problems is probably a necessary condition for full Japanese recovery, but it is certainly not sufficient. The same logic applies in Europe and North America. Relatively strong banks help to avoid deflation, but deflation has a way of rapidly turning strong banks into weak ones.

Japan the precursor?
Could we see deflation in Europe and North America emerging from similar causes as in Japan? Yes. Japan's deflation is a direct descendant of the bubble economy of the late 1980s. Stock and land prices then soared to extraordinary levels. When the crash came there was a devastating blow to wealth levels, to the balance sheet strength of both lenders and borrowers, and to confidence.

The land bubble has a clear parallel in the West in the spectacular housing bubbles in many countries. And the West's equity bubble in the late

1990s was directly comparable in type to the Japanese bubble a decade earlier. Moreover, there are strong similarities in the surge of investment in Japan in the late 1980s and the surge in the US in the late 1990s. In both cases this left companies with excessive levels of fixed capital, thereby sharply diminishing the subsequent incentive and desire to invest. Furthermore, there are some eerie similarities between Japan and Germany, including the rapid aging of, and then prospective fall in, the population.

Although policy in North America and Europe should be better conducted than it was in Japan, especially by the US Fed, my strong suspicion is that western central banks will easily fall prey to the problems that constrained the Bank of Japan. In particular, the ECB will be slow to see the deflation coming, slow to cut interest rates sufficiently, and very slow to embrace unorthodox monetary policies. Like the Bank of Japan it will be overly concerned with maintaining credibility and normality, inclined to minimize the dangers of deflation and maximize the dangers of the policies designed to overcome it. Again like the Bank of Japan, it will be inclined to see recovery, and an upturn in prices, just around the corner.

But not everything is the same. In some respects the Japanese predicament was much worse. In other respects, though, it was better. The Japanese authorities did not have to deal with the disastrous interaction between company pension provision and stock-market weakness that threatens to dominate economic prospects in several western countries.

In mid-2005 most financial market participants were fairly sure that deflation risks were minimal—as they were sure before the last deflation scare arose. The truth is that with aggregate demand so fragile, price-competitive pressures so intense, and the starting level of inflation so low, deflation is an ever-present danger. And if it materialises it could be deadly.

Central banks like to assure us that they and their policy tools are well up to the job—even if the job encompasses the overcoming of deflation. They had better be right, or the world economy will face catastrophe.

Part II

The Wellsprings of
Real Wealth

Introduction

While most of the developed world has been caught up in a great wealth illusion, the fundamental forces that throughout history have been the wellsprings of real wealth have been gathering and amassing their strength. To these past sources of real wealth we should pay close attention, since buried in our history lie the secrets of our future.

In Part II I examine the three principal sources of real growth, explaining how important they have been in the past and how they are coming together now to open up the opportunity for a period of boundless prosperity:

- The accumulation of knowledge about processes and materials, leading to increased productivity.
- The growth of international trade, leading to greater specialization and economies of scale.
- Good governance, reconciling private interests with the public good and enabling societies to gain maximum advantage from the economic opportunities open to them.

What the effects of the confluence of these great forces will be on finance, business, and our everyday lives is a subject that I take up in Part III, where I discuss the economy of the future. And quite how we manage to avoid the dangers and pitfalls that I identified in Part I and move into this period of great prosperity, I defer until the Finale.

Here in Part II I confine myself to the three great sources of wealth creation and the reasons that they provide for optimism about the world's economic future.

4
Mind over Matter

He who receives an idea from me, receives instruction himself without lessening mine; as he who lights his taper at mine, receives light without darkening me.

Thomas Jefferson, 1813[1]

We are slowly shedding the limitations of Matter to unleash the expansiveness of non-rivalrous Ideas.

Joseph Stiglitz, 1999[2]

In the closing years of the eighteenth century, booms and busts, bubbles and deflationary slumps were not the burning issues of the day in the sleepy little town of Albury, just south of London, England. There, Thomas Robert Malthus was pondering over what he thought was *the* burning issue, not merely then and there but for ever and everywhere: how the production of food could keep pace with expanding population.

Moralist, moral philosopher, disciple of Adam Smith, Cambridge Fellow, and the first man ever to be appointed as a professor of political economy, Malthus was no physicist and to the best of my knowledge he had no pretense to investment expertise. He was, though, an ordained minister of the Church of England and served as curate at Albury. Doubtless that gave him a unique perspective. Unusually for an economist, he took a keen interest in sex; or rather in its social consequences. He warned that the "passion between the sexes," if left unregulated, would result in misery and vice. He urged that the "consequences of our natural passions" be frequently brought to "the test of utility."

Malthus argued that population was closely circumscribed at a meager standard of living equal to mere subsistence. To put the matter in his own words:

The power of population is so superior to the power in the earth to pro-duce subsistence for man, that premature death must in some shape or other visit the human race. The vices of mankind are active and able ministers of depopulation. They are the precursors in the great army of destruction; and often finish the dreadful work themselves. But should they fail in this war of extermination, sickly seasons, epidemics, pesti-lence, and plague advance in terrific array, and sweep off their thou-sands and ten thousands. Should success be still incomplete, gigantic inevitable famine stalks in the rear, and with one mighty blow levels the population with the food of the world.[3]

It is this view, expressed in Malthus' *An Essay on the Principle of Population* published in 1798, which acquired for economics the description "the dis-mal science." But Malthus' contribution was greater than this implies. In October 1838 another Cambridge man, Charles Darwin, read Malthus' essay and, as he himself acknowledged, found the inspiration for the theory of natural selection. Given the struggle for existence everywhere, "favourable variations would tend to be preserved, and unfavourable ones to be destroyed. The results of this would be the formation of a new species. Here, then, I had at last got a theory by which to work."[4]

Ironically Malthus, the prophet of doom about the human condition on the grounds of its being constrained by earthy material circumstance, can thus be said to have spawned one of the greatest ever leaps forward in human *thought*. More modestly, he could also claim to be regarded as the father of economics, since his theory embodies what the layperson sees as the three essential elements of the modern subject:

- The conclusion is derived by relentless logic and elegant economy of reasoning.
- It induces a state of unrelieved gloom in all those who are exposed to it.
- It is outrageously wrong.

In a narrow sense, Malthus proved to be wrong because he underestimated the capacity of progress in food production to stay ahead of rising popula-tion. But his failure of vision went deeper. As agriculture gradually gave way to manufacturing in being the dominant employer and source of income, there were continued improvements in the standard of living over and above increases in the quantity and quality of food. Then, much later, came birth control. All of this was the product of the human mind.

In short, in concentrating on the limited supply of a key factor of production, namely land, and analyzing its interaction with the fecundity of men and women, Malthus had grossly underestimated the inventiveness of human beings; he had overlooked the human factor. In doing this he missed the essential spark in our history—and the key to our future. The evolution of economic man is a story of the increasing importance of the human factor and its triumph over the restrictions of material circumstance.

Lessons from the Past

When one contemplates the early economic history of humankind Malthus' obsession with the interaction between land and population is eminently reasonable. Population is where it all begins—in more senses than one. We may have been instructed by the Almighty to go forth and multiply, but to an early economist like Malthus the increase in the world's population was the cause of our impoverishment.

Back in one million years BC, when Raquel Welch roamed the earth, best estimates suggest that there were only some 125,000 souls to keep her company (and presumably about half of those were female). The population is estimated to have breached 1 million around 300,000 years BC and 100 million around 500 years BC. At the time of the birth of Christ it was about 170 million. Over the next 1,000 years it rose to 265 million. It then took some 600 years to double to about 550 million, then only 200 years to double again. The doublings then got faster: 120 years to reach 1,800 million in 1920, 50 years to reach 3.6 billion in 1970, with the next doubling to over 7 billion roughly 35 years later; that is, in 2005.[5]

Conventional charts of population growth fail to bring out the dramatic nature of this change. They simply show population shooting up in an explosive fashion.[6] Figure 4.1, though, gives a pretty clear picture. It shows the cumulative percentage increases in population over successive 100-year periods. The basic message is stark: world population took off only over the last two centuries; that is to say, *after* Malthus issued his dire warning.

More recently, although the world's population has continued to rise, the rate of increase has been falling. Nevertheless, this offers no support for the

Figure 4.1 World population growth from 2,000 BC to 2,000 AD
(% growth over successive 100-year periods)

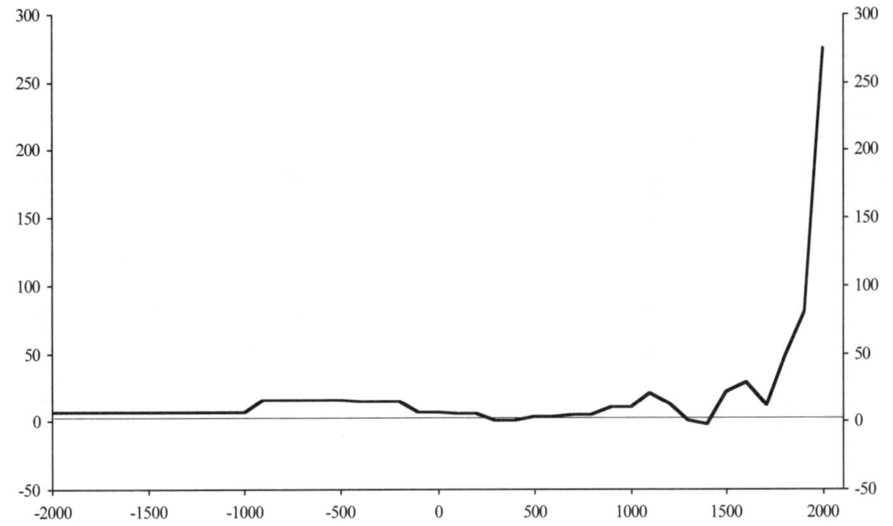

Source: Data from Michael Kremer, "Population growth and technological change: One million B.C. to 1990," *Quarterly Journal of Economics*, 2, 1993.

neo-Malthusians. It has been falling not predominantly because of increasing death rates (due to famine and malnutrition) but rather because of falling birth rates. These falls may themselves have been caused by higher levels of per capita GDP.

The changing importance of land
So how did this exploding population avoid collision with the limits imposed by the fixed amount of land? For a time it was possible to argue that it was the discovery, development, and cultivation of new land in America, Canada, and Australia that made all the difference. However, after the full development of these countries population kept on rising and still there was no Malthusian crisis.

It is striking that the amount of space per person has been declining sharply almost everywhere across the world with no deleterious influence on levels of per capita GDP, or their rate of growth. Moreover, as Figure 4.2 shows, across countries the amount of space per person has varied enormously without having any clear or decisive effect on GDP. After all, per capita GDP in Japan is higher than in Australia, even though Australia's

Figure 4.2 Total area per head of population, 1820 and 1987
(hectares per person; excludes Australia)

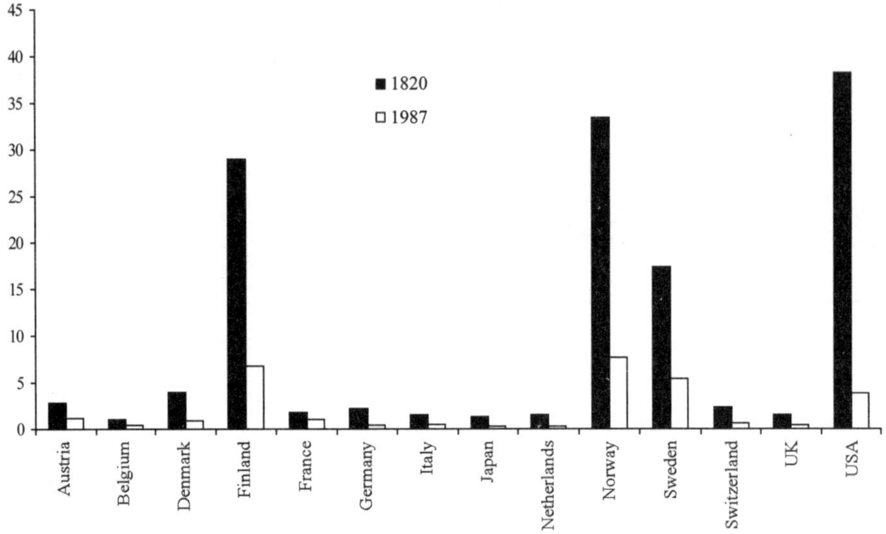

Source: Data from A. Maddison, *Dynamic Forces in Capitalist Development*, Oxford University Press, 1991

land resources are 150 times greater. (So much so that I cannot sensibly fit Australia on to the same chart![7])

The answer ought to be plain for all to see—Malthus was wrong. Not only was Malthus wrong about the constraints on the food supply, but also everyone before and since who has emphasized the fundamental importance of land and materials for wealth creation has also been wrong. This was slow to dawn on people in the nineteenth century and remarkably, even in the twentieth century, *land fetishism* had plenty of adherents, including Adolf Hitler. Hitler put control over land as the essential foundation of wealth and power. It was he, after all, who propounded the need for *Lebensraum* and saw Germany as hemmed in and restricted by its lack of territory. The British had their far-flung empire, the Americans had a huge continent, and Russia had both its own vast country and its empire in central Asia. Poor little Germany had nothing.

What Hitler did to acquire extra territory we all know. Most of us take for granted that his actions in pursuing his ambitions were evil. But it is not often considered that, from a modern economic point of view, they were also downright stupid. All the evidence is that the amount of space, with its access to food supply and raw materials, is not now a prime determinant of economic success—and has not been for some time. Trade, about which I have much to say in a moment, is what enables even the smallest, most barren territory to attain the highest standards of living.

Interestingly, it was the collapse of world trade and the growth of protectionism in the 1930s that gave Hitler the economic rationale for his conquests. In a world order where trade is suppressed and controlled, access to food and raw materials may be denied to particular countries. Germany, Hitler thought, had to secure its own large area that had ample supplies of food and raw materials. Japanese policy in the 1930s was infused with the same thinking, and related concerns about the supply of oil clearly influence American policy in the Middle East today.

One wonders what Hitler—or Malthus, for that matter—would have made of the fact that in 2000, at market exchange rates, the small, barren territory of Hong Kong had a GDP roughly two-thirds that of Russia, which has a land area roughly 16,000 times as large and a population roughly 20 times as large. Or what would they have made of the tiny island of Singapore, an area of only 647.5 square kilometers, yet a significant player in the world economy?

The climb out of poverty

You might think that guessing at population numbers as far back as one million years BC is pretty heroic (or foolhardy), but there have even been some superheroic attempts to estimate *per capita* GDP going back that far. To make any sense to us today, all these numbers need to be expressed in terms of a common money (dollars, of course) and, in order to abstract from the problems of changing money values caused through inflation, we need to express them in terms of the money prices of a given year. The figures quoted here use 1990 prices.

On this basis, in the year 2000 world GDP per capita was some $6,500 a year. With regard to its level in one million years BC, I hope the reader will be indulgent when I report that estimates differ. Indeed, they vary between $92 and $340.[8] (I must say, I do like the 2, don't you? It is important to value precision, even a million years ago.)

As to the rate of progress, there is a huge difference between the last five centuries and the rest of human history. From one million years BC to 1500 AD, per capita income probably rose by about 50 percent. This doesn't sound too bad at first blush, but it is not that good either, after more than a million years of struggle. Generations would come and go and things would remain the same, to the extent that someone who was reborn hundreds of years later would find both the way of life and the places in which they led it instantly recognizable. Mind you, over this period there was a considerable increase in the total level of output.[9] The trouble was that all "progress" was eaten up by the increases in population described earlier. In other words, up to that point Malthus was right.

After 1500 the tempo picked up. Between 1500 and 1820 there was probably no progress in Africa and Asia, but the growth rate of GDP per capita in western Europe may have been about 0.2 percent a year. At that rate, a doubling of living standards would take some 350 years. Then in the nineteenth century economic growth took off. GDP per capita more than tripled and in the twentieth century it rose some tenfold.

Figures for GDP per head can seem arid. It may be helpful to focus on a particular "good" that has been "produced" throughout history: lighting. We can measure productivity in the production of light precisely in terms of the output (lumen hours) per unit of input (Btu of energy). For a given unit of energy, today's lights are some 143,000 times brighter than the campfires used by the cavemen of prehistory. For the average person today, an hour's work purchases 45,000 times more lighting than it did 200 years ago.

Another way of conveying our economic progress is to look at life expectancy. In the year 1000, looking at the world as a whole, the average infant could expect to live for 24 years. A third of all children would die in their first year. In Europe, life expectancy in 1700 was not much greater than it had been at the time of the Roman Empire.[10] Up to 1820, the rise in average life expectancy across the world was almost imperceptible, and most of that was due to rises in western Europe. However, since the early nineteenth century life expectancy has shot up to the point where it has reached 66 years.[11]

When you put the increases in population together with the increases in per capita incomes, what happened over the last two centuries is even more impressive. Total world GDP one million years BC was some $10 million, believe it or not.[12] For the sake of facilitating a more interesting picture, Figure 4.3 begins only at 2000 BC. World GDP was some $19 *billion* at the birth of Christ and $30 billion a thousand years later. In 1800 the figure was still short of $200 billion, but over the nineteenth century total GDP rose more than fivefold. Over the twentieth century, though, GDP rose to 40 times its 1900 level.

Figure 4.3 World GDP growth from 2000 BC to 2000 AD
(% growth over successive 100-year periods)

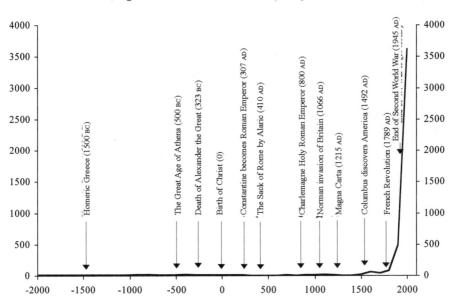

Source: Data from B. DeLong, "Estimating world GDP, one million B.C.–present," University of Berkeley, California; and Capital Economics

For the countries of what we might call the industrial world, from 1820 to 1989 the rate of growth of GDP was 2.7 percent and per capita growth 1.6 percent, about eight times as fast as in the proto-capitalist period.[13] The twentieth century was a period of economic advance the like of which the world has never seen—so far.

Figure 4.4 clearly shows the acceleration in the form of cumulative percentage growth rates in world per capita GDP over successive 50-year periods. The increase in world per capita GDP over the last 50 years has been a staggering 300 percent, easily outdoing the increase in the 50 years to 1950—and at the time that was the fastest ever.

Karl Marx certainly recognized the scale of the transformation. Writing in 1848, he said, "The bourgeoisie, during its rule of scarce one hundred years, has created more massive and more colossal productive forces than have all preceding generations together."[14]

Figure 4.4 Average world GDP per capita from 1500 to 2000
(% growth over successive 50-year periods)

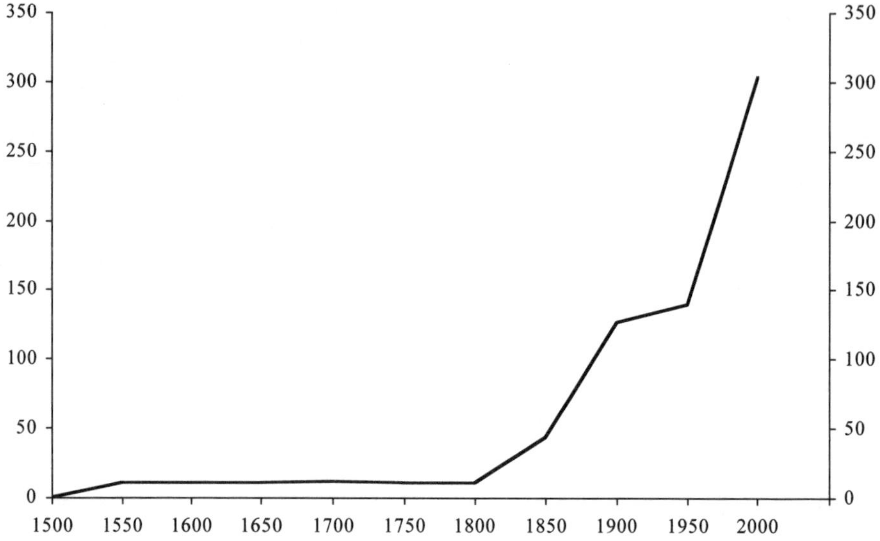

Source: Data from B. DeLong, "Estimating world GDP, one million B.C.–present," University of Berkeley, California

The Industrial Revolution: Miracle or Mirage?

The improvement in incomes and living standards has been a gradual process, but the historical breakpoint occurred in Britain with what we are accustomed to call the Industrial Revolution. Ironically this, and the improved crop yields and animal husbandry that appeared as a result of what we call the Agricultural Revolution, were already well under way when Malthus issued his dire warnings.

Mind you, the revisionists have been at it again. It is now fashionable to dismiss the notion of an Industrial Revolution. Jones[15] has argued that there was little economic growth in Britain in the second half of the eighteenth century, with growth identified with income per head.[16] This argument is not altogether convincing. This happens to have been a period when the population grew by a great deal as well. So a crisis of falling living standards and even starvation was averted "despite massive provocation from man's fecundity."[17] The "revolution" lay in the avoidance of a Malthusian calamity.

Moreover, we should not be misled by the apparently slow speed of change. Of course things did not change overnight. The use of the word "revolution" should connote depth, not speed.[18] Even some of the leading revisionists accept that the Industrial Revolution was a "historical discontinuity," and that over the period 1750–1850 the growth of the British economy was "historically unique and internationally remarkable."[19]

Another strand of modern thinking attacks the use of the word "industrial," and here the revisionists are on a sounder footing. There were a series of other "revolutions" in Britain that were arguably at least as important as the industrial one, and were perhaps pre requisites for the Industrial Revolution to happen at all: the agricultural, commercial, and political revolutions.[20] Nevertheless, this is in no way to diminish the importance of what we traditionally call the Industrial Revolution. As I shall show later in this chapter and the succeeding two, the changes of these critical years hold up a mirror to our own time. The economic advance of the Industrial Revolution was the result of the interaction of the three factors that throughout economic history have been the fount of economic progress and that hold forth the promise of great riches today: knowledge (leading to technological progress), international trade, and good governance.

The uniqueness of knowledge

As land and materials have been falling in relative importance as a source of wealth and prosperity, so *knowledge* has been increasing. The Malthusian nightmare was kept at bay primarily by our increasing knowledge, knowledge that enabled us to produce more output for the same quantity of inputs— money for nothing. And it is knowledge in all its forms—pure knowledge, skills embodied in human capital, and organizational capital—that explains why the economy of Hong Kong can be almost as large as that of Russia.

The increasing importance of knowledge as an input for companies can be seen in their rising ratio of sales to physical assets. Whereas for US Steel, which is still very much in the tangible economy, this ratio is just under 2, for Microsoft, a company quintessentially dealing in intangibles, the ratio is over 12.[21] More and more companies are moving to the Microsoft end of the spectrum.

Knowledge is different from land, materials, or physical goods—completely different in an economic sense. It is wholly outside the mean, desiccated, hobbled world of Malthusian economics. It possesses the magical quality of being able to produce money out of nothing. I do not mean this only in the sense that knowledge itself has no material form and hence any wealth that emerges from it has come, as it were, from nothing. This isn't quite fair, because the gaining of knowledge at least takes time and effort, if nothing else. (Because of this, economists would say that it has an *opportunity cost*.)

No, knowledge is special because it has the peculiar quality that if *you* possess it, this in no way reduces what *I* possess, and once possessed, it does not wear out, run down, or decay (although it may become obsolete). Once there, it continues to spew out benefits for the human race without further cost or effort. This is surely one of the main reasons why the accumulation of knowledge has been such an overwhelmingly important factor during our progress out of poverty.

What is more, the accumulation of knowledge operates on different principles to the accumulation of lumps of physical capital. Knowledge builds on itself. Advancing knowledge enables further advances to come. Isaac Newton himself acknowledged as much, saying: "If I have seen further it is by standing on the shoulders of giants."[22]

Productivity is the key to wealth and knowledge is the key to productivity. After all, what does it mean for productivity to increase? It means getting more output for the same quantity of inputs. Working harder won't give you this result, since that means increased inputs (of labor). Productivity growth is the result of working not harder but smarter. Future prosperity depends on working smarter still.

Knowledge Discovery

Why did the accumulation of knowledge over the centuries and the resulting improvement in productive capacity not happen faster? The answer reveals how different the present conjuncture is and why we can look forward to a faster rate of knowledge accumulation in the future.

Admittedly, part of the answer is that the rate of economic progress from the earliest times depended on other aspects besides the accumulation of knowledge. We surely had to go through a physical capital-accumulation phase that could not really have been shortened: houses, buildings, bridges, roads, boats, canals, machinery. Moreover, most production knowledge (technology) has to be embodied in capital goods. And accumulation of physical capital takes time, especially at low levels of income when the margin for saving is low. This is another example of the old adage that the richer you are the faster your riches can grow.

Mind you, you could say that throughout our history there has also been massive *destruction* of physical and human capital through wars. Moreover, earlier in our history a good deal of the investible surplus was wasted on public display rather than productive investment, for example the pyramids and the great cathedrals. (Arguably, though, these bore a return of a different sort.)

Yet on its own, this *thingist* explanation is not wholly convincing. After all, if technological progress had been faster then capital accumulation could have been accomplished more quickly. Higher income levels would have made accumulation easier and better techniques would have reduced the amount of capital needing to be accumulated to produce any given increase in output. So we are back with the question with which we began: Why wasn't the growth of knowledge faster?

The answer, to me, is that the "thinkers" of bygone ages labored under a welter of disadvantages. ("Thinkers" here should be understood to include pure thinkers, inventors, and the developers of new technology and processes.) Prime among them was that for much of human history the sort of thinking that leads to technological advance was either not esteemed or was severely constrained.

What did the Romans ever do for themselves?

Take the Roman Empire, for instance. It does not appear to have sustained a particularly high rate of economic progress, and perhaps no progress at all.[23] Yet the Romans still amaze us with the sophistication of their society and their civil and military architecture. In 100 AD Rome had better water supply, sewage disposal, paved streets, and fire protection than the capitals of Europe enjoyed in 1800.[24]

And in the classical period there were some extraordinary inventions. Among the devices credited to Hero of Alexandria (late first century AD) was the aeolipile, a working steam engine used to open temple doors.[25] The Antikythera mechanism, found on a sunken ship near Crete, is a geared astronomical computing machine built in the first century BC. Derek Price, who reconstructed the mechanism, said: "Men who could have built this could have built almost any mechanical device they wanted to."[26]

Perhaps most strikingly, it wasn't that classical civilization didn't discover any new techniques, but rather that when it did, it failed to extract anything approaching the maximum economic benefit from them. Inventions that could have led to significant economic changes were often left under-developed, forgotten, or lost. In some cases, innovations that failed to spread had to be reinvented independently.[27]

The reason for this apparent neglect of what we may call productive technology seems to be that the ancients placed very little value on engi-neering and other practical skills of economic worth. In other words, it was probably their value system or ideology that held them back.

The classical world did not esteem economic growth as such. Rather, it upheld other values: military, intellectual, administrative, artistic. "Production" was stigmatized as a lower-class activity, necessary but dirty, rather as refuse collection is regarded today.[28] Seneca pointed out that since only slaves were interested in such things it was natural that most inventions were the work of slaves.

Chinese decline
After the collapse of the Roman Empire in the West, the man from Mars would not have looked to any of the countries of western Europe as the probable economic leaders in the millennium ahead but rather to China.

The early superiority of Chinese technology over the West's is stagger-ing. The Chinese used paper before the birth of Christ, more than a mil-lennium before it reached the West. In the Middle Ages they used it for paper money and wallpaper, and according to one source as early as 590 AD they even used it in lavatories.[29] Printing probably began in China in the late seventh century. Wheelbarrows were used from 232 AD and quite possibly earlier, whereas it took until the twelfth century for Europeans to develop them. The examples go on and on.

Eventually, though, the Middle Kingdom slipped into backwardness and languished for centuries. In terms of per capita income, western Europe overtook China in the fourteenth century. Thereafter, China and most of Asia were stagnant until the second half of the twentieth century.[30] By con-trast western Europe, and later America, went on to initiate and then drive forward the Industrial Revolution and subsequently to enjoy remarkable increases in the standard of living.[31]

To most of the scholars who have studied the issue closely, at least a substantial part of the explanation for Chinese stagnation seems to lie firmly in the world of ideas, namely the prevailing set of values that stunted innovation and shut out foreign influences.[32] By about 1200, Europe had absorbed most of what China (and the Islamic world) had to offer. From then to 1500, Europe's technological creativity was increasingly original, whereas in China technology had become a "magnificent dead end."[33] This had an intellectual explanation: Chinese logic was based on historical analogy rather than on the "hypothetico-deductive" method of the West.[34]

Islamic stagnation

Similarly, the relative decline of Islamic civilization appears not to have a material explanation but an ideological one. It was the unquestioning acceptance of the status quo and the steadfast refusal to accept foreign innovations that stymied economic progress in the Muslim world. Admittedly, medieval Europe was just as hostile to Islam, but this did not stop it from adopting many inventions from Islamic civilization, including most notably Arabic numerals. The compliment was not readily returned.

In the seventeenth and eighteenth centuries, when the West had clearly pulled ahead of Islam technologically, Muslims allowed some European innovations to filter in, but only slowly and selectively. The first book printed in Arabic script appeared in Istanbul in 1729, almost three centuries after the invention of movable type. The Koran was not printed until the twentieth century, quite a contrast with the Gutenberg Bibles published in 1452–55. Perhaps most tellingly, although Muslim captains in the Arabian Sea operated *dhows* with sails that could be maneuvered against the wind, they nevertheless preferred to wait for the monsoons. According to an old Arab proverb, "No one but a madman or a Christian would sail to windward.[35]

Islamic tradition eventually came to believe that all useful knowledge had been acquired and all questions had been answered (in complete contrast to the early Muslim thirst for knowledge from all sources). From the later Middle Ages, in the Muslim world science consisted almost entirely of compilation and repetition.

Communication and numbers

In all the great civilizations of the past, technological advance was also held back by severe communications problems. Getting access to the thoughts of other thinkers was no easy matter before the advent of mass printing and even then there was the problem of transporting either the books to you or you to the books. The result was that a good deal of the thinking work would have to be done *ab initio*, constantly, as it were, having to reinvent the wheel.

What is more, knowledge could be lost. In the year 389, apparently spurred on by the Roman Emperor Theodosius, a mob attacked and very severely damaged the great library at Alexandria, in what is now Egypt. What survived this attack was lost when the library was destroyed by another mob in 642. This library housed the ancient Greeks' great works of philosophy, science, and literature. Of many of these great works there was just one copy in existence—in Alexandria. What has come down to us from the ancient Greek world is but a fragment of what the Greeks originally bequeathed to us.

Lack of communication with other contemporary thinkers would also have led to considerable duplication of effort, and equally, except in a few places where like-minded scholars got together, it would not be easy for thinkers to benefit from the tendency for interaction to produce results that any number of individuals kept separate could not achieve.

The advance of knowledge must also have been kept back by the relatively small number of people on the earth in bygone centuries—and by the small fraction of the population who could be freed from regular drudgery for "thinking." It is no surprise that societies living at the very edge of subsistence rarely produce technological advances or, indeed, advances of any kind. Every effort is expended on simply keeping alive.

Even 2,000 years ago, societies were nevertheless able to support some people who were free from material drudgery, but these were not necessarily the ones who were either gifted for, or inclined to, thinking. More often than not, these people would be supported to perform some religious or ceremonial duties rather than to advance the cause of knowledge.

In the past, moreover, knowledge discovery was largely unpredictable. "Discovery" is the appropriate word because the facts themselves, the raw material of knowledge, are always there, hanging in the air, rather like the notes of a Mozart symphony, waiting to be "uncovered" or revealed by someone who can "plug in" to the world of abstract truths. Economic history is littered with the names of technological Mozarts.

The importance of the contribution of key individuals has brought a certain unpredictability to the pace of technological and economic advance. To a degree, ideas have a life of their own and the extent of their flow, and of the knowledge they produce, cannot be predicted or prompted. In economic history there is often no good reason why an invention has been made at one particular time and not centuries earlier. (A good medieval example of this is the stirrup.[36]) One of the greatest technological advances, the printing press, was quickly disseminated largely as the result of an accident. In 1455 Johannes Gutenberg, its inventor, was in court for the nonpayment of debts. The asset his creditors seized was the world's first printing press.[37]

The speed-up of knowledge

So what will happen to the rate of knowledge "discovery" in the future? To some extent we are still bound simply to wait for new knowledge to appear. However, this is only part of the story, and a diminishing part at that. Now the advance of knowledge need not simply be a matter of serendipity. There are good reasons to believe that our society can produce, and exploit, knowledge at a faster rate than before.

For a start, western societies are now unencumbered by ideological or political restrictions in the pursuit of knowledge. Indeed, in many quarters the pursuit of knowledge for knowledge's sake is an over-riding objective. What is more, although there are some ideological challenges to free scientific thinking in Europe and North America, on a world scale the collapse of communism has resulted in a crumbling of restrictions on free thinking.

Secondly, one particular sort of knowledge has revolutionized our ability to access, possess, communicate, and accumulate all other sorts of knowledge. We have the ability through computers, and their extended use and connections through the internet, to research much more fully, quickly, and effectively.

Through computers, thinkers now have easy access to the *previous* thoughts of others. We are entering a world in which every sort of knowledge—whether it is an idea, a piece of music, a chemical compound, a design for a dress, the plans for a building, a photographic image, a great novel, or the assembled wisdom of the ages—not only cannot be lost but is instantaneously accessible by everyone in the world, whenever they want, always.

The world we are entering is the polar opposite of the situation that resulted in so much wisdom and learning perishing in Alexandria. Encyclopedias can now be stored on a $10 computer disk. If a bomb were to destroy all the physical capital and infrastructure in the world, those physical structures could be rebuilt in a generation, provided there were still people around to do the rebuilding.

Furthermore, information and communications technology enables researchers and thinkers readily to communicate with others working in the same field, thus greatly speeding up the interchange of ideas. It is easy to forget how utterly transformed the world is in this respect. As Joseph Stiglitz puts it: "In the days of the pony express, it took many horses, men and days to send a message from Kansas City to San Francisco whereas today it is done in the blink of an eye by a little quivering in an electromagnetic field."[38] This ability to communicate cheaply and quickly is particularly important given the large and developing *global* community of "thinkers," about which I shall say more in a moment. Without modern communications there would hardly be a global community of anything.

Even without communication with others, the modern thinker operating on his or her own enjoys huge advantages. Computers have the effect of leveraging up of the brainpower of all those working. The average modern computer has more computing power than was contained in all the computers in the entire world during the Second World War.

Scale effects

The third major advantage that the modern world possesses in the production of knowledge runs completely counter to the Malthusian emphasis on the link between population and limited food supply. The modern world's much larger population should produce a much larger number of "thinkers," and a much higher level of wealth and standard of living should enable us to support a higher number of people engaged in "thinking" (including research, invention, and technological application).

This apparent benefit may seem bizarre, not least because it runs counter to the current orthodoxy about the ills caused by high levels of population.[39] Yet the idea is surely more than plausible; it is almost self-evident. It is commonly found in the academic papers that developed modern growth theory[40] and one economist, Michael Kremer, has found considerable empirical support for the data in the historical record, at least up to the twentieth century. Notably, among societies with no opportunity for technological contact, those with higher initial population levels achieved higher levels of technological progress.[41]

Indeed, it is estimated that of all the scientists who ever lived, more than 90 percent are alive today.[42] Accordingly, the flow of ideas, and the knowledge that derives from them, should be faster. It is estimated that the stock of scientific knowledge is currently doubling every five or seven years.[43]

As with everything else in the human sphere, though, it is not simply a matter of sheer numbers. Millions of people living in complete isolation one from another will not be able to produce the same flow of ideas as the same number living together closely and working cooperatively. Here is the modern world's fourth distinct advantage, not only over previous centuries but even over the last few decades. I am not simply referring to the communications bonanza created by the internet, important though that is. My point here is that the end of the Cold War has opened up not only the trade in goods and services but also the trade in ideas. There has never before been a time when the bulk of humankind has lived in this degree of close communication, able and willing to contribute to the flow of new knowledge and to share its benefits.

For centuries after the Industrial Revolution, the combination of technological backwardness and cultural exclusion kept China separate from the West. This has continued right up to the present day. Yet China accounts for about a fifth of the world's population. And the Chinese were, after all, the source of so much early wisdom.

There has been no Chinese contribution to the stock of new knowledge in the West for centuries, except perhaps the transmission of some *old* Chinese knowledge such as acupuncture. A vibrant, fully developed China, integrated with the West in the pursuit of knowledge, could make an enormous contribution to the flow of new ideas.

Similar remarks apply to India, Russia, and the countries of eastern Europe. True, these countries have made a distinctive contribution to the stock of applied ideas available in the West through the export of large numbers of talented individuals, including mathematicians, scientists, engineers, computer scientists, and software engineers. Moreover, Russia managed to be a technological leader in some fields, even under the old Soviet system, although Cold War rivalry kept the two sets of knowledge apart. Nevertheless, rival technologies of equal merit did not constitute the general picture. Rather, an extremely talented and highly educated people was forced by a malfunctioning political and economic system to scramble even to maintain contact with the technologically dominant countries of the West. By contrast, what is in prospect now is the talents of all these people being available to everyone.

In short, the conditions for the discovery of knowledge are so transformed that in today's world, knowledge and ideas do not simply descend into our economy randomly. As Joseph Stiglitz puts it, we can now think of knowledge as capable of being *produced*, almost mass-produced. We can produce knowledge the way that 100 years ago we used to produce steel. Modern society can be a knowledge factory. With regard to thinking and discovering, comparing modern society with pre-industrial society is like comparing a production line with a cottage industry.

A Technological Illusion?

Throughout economic history, the really important technological developments have been "general-purpose technologies" that transformed the economic, social, and political structures of societies.[44] The main ones have been the domestication of crops, the domestication of animals, writing, bronze, iron, the waterwheel and windmill, the three-masted sailing ship, the movable-type printing press, automated textile machinery, the steam engine, electricity, and the internal combustion engine. Could the computer and the associated information and communications technologies soon rank alongside these revolutionary advances of the past?

The positive case has to overcome at least one very powerful argument. Computers have been with us for some years and yet there is no evidence that they have produced a great leap forward so far. Indeed, when it comes to the growth rates of productivity the record is not very impressive; except, perhaps, in the United States in the late 1990s.

Even this apparently strong performance is open to critical attack. For a start, it was strong growth of labor productivity made possible by large amounts of capital, rather than total productivity for labor and capital combined. Moreover, it may be explicable by three basic factors: improved *measurement* of inflation (which has reduced our recorded estimate of inflation and thereby boosted output and productivity); the normal response of productivity to rapid increases in demand and output; and the explosion of output and productivity in the production of computers themselves.[45] Nevertheless, in 2001 and 2002 US productivity performance was notably impressive for a downturn and in

2004 productivity growth topped 3 percent.

Outside the United States it is a more disappointing story. In the UK in the first quarter of 2005 the rate of productivity growth *slipped back* to about 1 percent, compared with an average of 2 percent over the previous 30 years. In the eurozone also productivity growth has been below the long-term average. As for Japan, what can one say? The "new economy" was like a hangover after a serious party. Bring back the old economy.

It does seem rather surprising that, if the impact of computers and telecommunications technology is so revolutionary, with the possible exception of the United States there is virtually nothing discernible in the data. In the words of Robert Solow: "We see the computer age everywhere except in the productivity statistics."[46] What could be the reason?

All reasons great and small

One explanation, of course, is that the impact is genuinely small. "Computers" are simply the most recent in a long line of incremental technological improvements, most of which, it can be argued, were of much greater importance.[47]

Moreover, whatever productivity gain is achieved has to be weighed against the losses, for example from staff sending social emails to one another or wasting time chasing amusing, or pornographic, material on the internet. Furthermore, for all the hype about massive IT investment, we should not forget that it remains a tiny part of the overall capital stock. One could argue that it would be surprising if the effect were not small.

Another explanation for the small impact of IT fits with the emphasis on demographic factors in the early part of this chapter. New technology is most easily adapted and transmitted through society by the young. Yet most of the industrial economies have rapidly aging populations who may readily tend to resist technological change. In this vein, the fact that the US has a faster rate of population growth may help to explain why it has been more dynamic in the widescale implementation of new technology.[48]

But I have two other explanations of a very different hue for why the economic impact of computers and ICT has not been greater. First, the numbers are wrong. By their very nature, recent technological changes tend to result in improvements that our widget-counting ways of measuring economic output find difficult to pick up. They may result in improvements in the quality of a service or in the timeliness of its delivery, rather than the sheer quantity, which make the good or service more valuable. Better information brings improvements of precisely that sort. Because the same information now reaches its consumers more quickly, it is often more valuable. In the age of the intangible, much of what brings value is also intangible, even in the delivery of ordinary goods and services, and is therefore difficult to measure.[49]

Furthermore, some of the impact occurs outside the nexus of money, in aspects like making it *easier* for people to get their bank balances over the phone or online rather than having to make a trip to the bank. Even if it could be measured, this would not appear in the GDP statistics because they have nothing to say about the alternative uses of leisure time. This does not mean, however, that the improvement is worthless.

The second, and more powerful, explanation is that we are looking in the wrong place and at the wrong time. The time lags between a technological advance and its coming to full fruition are always much longer than the techies fondly imagine. It took 40 years to build the canals and 50 years to build the railroads. As Arthur C. Clarke said, people usually overestimate the impact of technological change in the short run and underestimate it in the long run.

It is perfectly normal for technological developments, once they have overcome the initial skepticism, to generate a wave of investor enthusiasm, leading to a bubble that then brings a financial disaster for all those who invested in the new technology—only for the technology itself to prove a stonking success. This happened with railways, radio, automobiles, and air travel.[50]

The time lags are long because in order for there to be real economic benefit there have to be major organizational changes, and these often take far longer than the mere purchase and installation of new technology. Outside the United States, even the computer, never mind its interconnection through the internet, still has not penetrated very deep into the economy.

It is striking, for instance, that in the 1990s the rate of growth of productivity was so much lower in Europe than in the United States. Only part of the explanation lies with the US over-recording productivity growth. A significant part of the reason is probably the relatively low European investment in ICT, but this is bullish for the future. Much of Europe is roughly where the US was in the early 1990s. Given a period of strong aggregate demand, which would provide European companies with the incentive to invest, European productivity performance could pick up significantly in the next ten years.

Moreover, with new technologies there is usually a large initial displacement effect, so that the gains are at first offset by redundant workers, plant, equipment, industries, and regions. Only once these resources have been fully absorbed will the true benefits of the initial technological change come through.

There is some empirical support for the idea that modern business has not fully exploited the technology currently available, never mind what is in the process of development. Umpteen companies in North America and beyond have reported that when confronted by cost increases that, in a competitive environment, they cannot recoup by increasing prices, they are able to offset those increased costs, apparently at will, by installing new technologies.[51] (Quite why they didn't install these before does not gel with profit-maximizing behavior, but business is often like that. It needs a catalyst.)

Improvements still Required

Just as with earlier technological breakthroughs, information technology needs some further developments in order to reveal its true importance. In particular, the full potential of e-commerce must await further technological advances over and above the development of a convenient and fully functioning means of e-payment, which I discuss in Chapter 7. For all the hype, most people find using the internet an extremely slow and frustrating process and "surfing the net" is one of the greatest time-wasters known to man.

Even in advanced countries computers have not spread throughout society and until they do it is difficult for computer-based methods of commerce to become standard. By contrast, the television is a piece of technological equipment that is not only ubiquitous but easy to use—and widely regarded as such. A fully interactive, smart TV, available round the world, would do wonders for the global spread of e-commerce.

Additionally, computer systems must not only be safe but must be believed to be safe. Events over the last few years have diminished public confidence. First there was the devastation caused worldwide by the "lovebug" virus. Then there was the revelation that Microsoft's offices had been broken into and the vital codes governing the whole system stolen. More prosaically, there have been a host of security failures at internet banks.

It is not only the technology that needs to develop further. Most people do not make anywhere near full use of their computers. The reasons are a mixture of lack of awareness and familiarity and the fact that computers usually have many functions for which the potential demand is bound to be small. As computers become more user-friendly, the gap between their potential and their active use should become smaller.

So although the computer has been with us now for many years, its full impact may lie in the future. As the following examples show, this would be fully in line with historical experience.

The Victorian comparison

The nineteenth century provides several examples of the tortuous progress of technology. The received wisdom about the Industrial Revolution is that productivity was driven forward in a series of great leaps as new discoveries were made and new inventions applied. But it seems that even then technological progress took a very different form. Innovation proceeded through small, incremental changes made by many largely anonymous individuals, not some brilliant leap forward by a great hero. The bulk of technological improvement seemed to come from the application of *old* knowledge, made valuable by a series of subsequent discoveries or inventions.

The story of the long-distance telegraph, for example, was tortuous in the extreme. It was not a single miracle technology that appeared overnight but rather required many subsequent inventions and improvements, which took decades to complete. Submarine cables were subject to intolerable wear and tear. Of the 17,700 kilometers of cable laid before 1861, only 4,800 kilometers were operational in that year. The rest were lost. In August 1858, Queen Victoria and President James Buchanan made history by exchanging messages via a transatlantic cable, but three months later it was out of action.

The economic history of ice is another fascinating example. People used ice in the eighteenth century, indeed they had *ice cream*, but without mechanical refrigeration there were limits to how far ice could be used. It was preserved in special icehouses. Even in the early nineteenth century, although there was an international market in ice, in the warm seasons the price was so high that only the rich could afford it. Mechanical refrigeration was gradually developed and in 1861 the first frozen beef plant was set up in Sydney, Australia. By 1870, through the use of chilling, beef could be transported from the United States to England. By the 1880s, fully refrigerated ships were supplying Europe with beef, mutton, and lamb from South America and Australia. The result was a big drop in food prices and an increase in consumer living standards.

The development of electricity may be a particularly striking historical parallel for the computer. The economic potential of electricity had been suspected since the beginning of the nineteenth century. Humphrey Davy had demonstrated its lighting capabilities as early as 1808, and the electric motor was invented in 1821 and the dynamo in 1831. Yet there was still no electric revolution. As long as batteries remained the source of electric power, it cost 20 times as much as steam power. Indeed (internet enthusiasts should take note), from the mid-1840s enthusiasm about electricity as a source of cheap energy declined. Its full potential had to wait until the twentieth century.[52]

Both the computer and the dynamo are the key constituents of a widely spread set of physical, technical, and social arrangements, all of which need to be changed to bring full results. At the beginning of the twentieth century engineers could foresee the profound changes that electrification could bring to homes, factories, and businesses. Nevertheless, it took ages for the benefits to appear. In the US in 1899, electric lighting was used in a mere 3 percent of homes and electric power contributed less than 5 percent of the mechanical drive in factories. In fact, electric power did not have an impact on manufacturing productivity growth until the early 1920s.[53]

I am not suggesting that the full effects of ICT will take as long to come to fruition. There are good reasons to believe that the impact of developments in ICT should be much quicker, not least because of the extraordinary speed of their spread. While it took 36 years to achieve 50 million users for radio, 13 years for TV, and 16 years for PCs, the internet took less than 5.[54] Even so, the impact will not be as quick as the near-instantaneous effect that many commentators—and perhaps most investors—have assumed.

The next stage
There is another and potentially more powerful reason for delay in realizing the full economic impact of computers. If you like, the computer is to future

technology as Newton's "giants" were to him. It is the "shoulder" for future discoveries to stand on. Modern information and communications technology should make it possible for future improvements in techniques and advances in knowledge to be more quickly and widely disseminated. In brief, it should increase the learning capacity of society. In this way, it may raise the growth rate of the economy not merely fleetingly, or for a decade or two, but permanently.

Accordingly, a large part of the effect of computers and the internet will only be seen once the next big technological advance comes on the scene. Because of the impact of the communications and information revolution, *its* effects will be quicker and more widespread. So the major part of the gains even from the existing technology are not here now but are there to be realized in the economy of the future.[55]

And there are important new technologies on the horizon. Eventually, nanotechnology and biotechnology will probably be more revolutionary than advances in ICT. Nano- or molecular technology builds individual atoms and molecules into aggregates precisely specified, which may be two or three molecules or a large object. It is already being used to produce medical machines the size of a few hundred atoms and it will be employed to reduce the size of computers sharply to molecular proportions. It is not fanciful to imagine rooms filled with airborne nano-machines the size of a molecule of air but possessed of substantial computing power. As Minsky puts it:

> *Nanotechnology could have more effect on our material existence than those last two great inventions in the domain—the replacement of sticks and stones by metals and cements and the harnessing of electricity.*[56]

By contrast with nanotechnology, in a sense biotechnology is nothing new. We have been using it since we domesticated crops and animals some 10,000 years ago. What may more appropriately be called the "new biotechnology," however, is about the use of cellular and molecular processes to solve problems and make products. Already more than 350 million people have been helped by more than 130 drugs and vaccines developed through biotechnology. Of the biotech medicines on the market, 70 percent have been approved in the last six years. There are more than 350 biotech vaccines and drug products currently in clinical trials, targeting over 200 dis-

eases, including heart disease, diabetes, Alzheimer's disease, multiple scle-
rosis, AIDS, and arthritis.

Outside the sphere of medicine, environmental products deriving from
the advances of biotechnology make it possible to clean up hazardous waste
more efficiently by harnessing pollution-eating microbes. Industrial applications have led to cleaner and less wasteful processes, with lower use of energy
and water in sectors such as chemicals, pulp, textiles, and paper production.

Already the biotech industry has reached a substantial size. It currently
includes about 1,500 companies employing about 180,000 people in the
United States alone. Its growth rate is impressive. In 1992 its revenues were
about $8 billion, but by 2001 the figure had grown to almost $28 billion.
This industry is right at the center of the intangible economy. In 2001 it
spent $15.6 billion on research and development, more than half its total
revenues. In 2000 the top five biotech companies spent almost $90,000 per
employee on research and development.[57] This research and development,
and indeed the growth of the whole biotech industry, would not have been
possible on anything like this scale without the prior advance of information
and communications technology.

Trade and communications

Communications technology will also surely be of prime importance in realizing gains from a most ancient source of economic benefit: international
trade. The communications revolution is the handmaiden of globalization
and, as I shall argue in the next chapter, globalization holds the key to realizing the full benefits from expanding knowledge.

In this respect modern ICT will be following a well-worn path. In the late
Renaissance and early modern period, the most important arena for technological progress was naval technology—the internet of its day. In 1000 AD,
European ships and navigation were probably no better than they had been
under the Roman Empire. Thanks to improvements by the Venetians,
Portuguese, Dutch, and British, by the end of the eighteenth century ships
could carry ten times the cargo of a fourteenth-century Venetian galley,
despite using a smaller crew.[58] As a result of these improvements and the voy-
ages of discovery by the great maritime explorers, by 1750, for the first time
in human history, all of the world's oceans were unified into a single whole,
capable of constituting a world sea highway for commerce. In Peter Jay's
memorable phrase, the scene was set for globalization by "boats not bytes."[59]

Again in the nineteenth century, as before in the age of sail, there was close interaction between changes in naval technology and increased trade. While ships could only be made of wood there was a serious restriction on size, but iron ships could be made to more or less any size. Whereas most costs increased with the square of the dimensions, carrying capacity increased with the cube. So fuel costs and crew size increased at a rate less than proportional to displacement. Accordingly, larger ships meant lower shipping costs and this vastly increased the possibilities of economic growth through commercial expansion. Similar improvements have carried on in the modern world with developments such as containerization.

The internet is achieving something similar in increasing the spread of information flow and thereby reducing the cost of globally dispersed goods production, international trade in goods, and internationally traded services. Because of the computer and modern ICT, the world is now set for globalization by boats *and* bytes.

The Intangible Revolution

There is a stage beyond the accumulation of knowledge about how to build machines able to produce more and better goods or deliver more and better services, or about how to improve the production process, or even how to transmit knowledge more easily and cheaply. The increasing importance of the mental over the physical has gone much further. More and more of what we choose to spend our money on is itself some form of knowledge. More and more of the things we wish to buy are not "things" at all. They are intangible; that is to say, strictly speaking, they are neither a good nor a service. They are "nonthings," products of the human mind, not *manu*factures but *mente*factures. Examples include computer software, medical treatments, recorded music, or films.

So in our modern world we have reached the stage where knowledge produces knowledge. The capital that produces the flow of consumption is knowledge and increasingly the consumption "good" itself is also knowledge: knowledge in and knowledge out.

The knowledge components of consumption goods possess some striking characteristics—the same characteristics as knowledge applied to the production process. They occupy no physical space and have no weight.

Consequently, they themselves take up no real resources whatsoever. They all possess, from an economist's standpoint, a remarkable quality, namely that if I consume more I do not reduce the quantity available for you to consume.

This quality has been dubbed by the economist Danny Quah "infinite expansibility."[60] Whether a film is seen by 200, 2 million, or 200 million people has no effect on its cost of production. A cure for cancer, when it comes, will cost no more or less to develop, however many people are treated with it. (The treatment itself, of course, will be paid for on a per capita basis.)

But let us get one thing straight. Although the economic qualities of tangibles and intangibles are radically different, in the practical world there can usually be no rigid division between the two. There are no sectoral boundaries, and no signs announcing to visitors "You are now entering the intangible zone." In practice the old physical world makes plenty use of intangibles, while the delivery of intangibles at least brushes with the material world, if nothing else, through the necessary presence of the computer, without which little of this would be possible.

For many intangibles, the connection with the material world goes further: to embodiment. Take cures for medical ailments, for instance. The essence of a medical product, and hence its value, lies in the knowledge that it will cure a complaint, and perhaps also in the knowledge of how to embed the curative qualities in a particular form. That knowledge is quintessentially intangible. Yet for as far as we can see, such knowledge will have to be communicated to the patient, and literally swallowed by him, in the form of a pill.

In the realm of entertainment, think of the Harry Potter phenomenon. What gave rise to this in the first place was something quintessentially intangible: J.K. Rowling's amazing flight of imagination. Thereafter, bringing the creation to market required turning the idea into books and then films and videos—not to mention the Harry Potter merchandise of various sorts—all of which required some real resources.

The convergence between tangibles and intangibles is also being driven from the opposite direction. Increasingly, even items that one might regard as irredeemably *things*, such as cars, have a significant intangible component. As Danny Quah puts it, "A machine can be considered as heavy metal wrapped round an idea."[61] Alternatively, you could say that many manufactured products were simply ideas in a box.

The knowledge or intangible economy stretches into surprising places. You wouldn't think that Coca-Cola was an obvious beneficiary of the knowledge economy, but it is. As John Kay says:

> *The value of Coca-Cola lies not in the fizzy sticky water it produces, it doesn't even lie in the secret formula that is locked up somewhere in the Atlanta safe. The value of Coca-Cola and its products rests in the international brand which it has created and all the distribution and attributes that follow.*[62]

So although the different characteristics of tangibles and intangibles mean that they behave differently, these differences are often likely to be seen within a process, good, service, business, or industry that has both tangible and intangible components. The intangible parts are typically becoming increasingly important. In 1975 the number of microcontrollers used outside computers was just about equal to the number used in computers. Today about nine times as many are used outside computers as inside them. They include some nine billion microchips in cars, phones, pagers, modems, and consumer electronic products. What is more, as such familiar items as electric toasters become more sophisticated, they take on more of the characteristics of intangible software. In the end, the software effectively takes over the host object. And the industries producing such objects will increasingly come to resemble software operations.[63]

Mind you, some sorts of knowledge that become incorporated in what we want to buy are not so much the result of calculated effort and industry, incurring cost, as of creativity, often random and uncontrolled. A Beethoven symphony is an intangible idea created (or discovered?) by Beethoven at next to no direct cost. Nevertheless, the same point applies. This near-zero cost does not become any greater no matter how many millions of people derive delight from the symphony.

Some creative output may fall in between these two extremes. The effort that goes into a Spielberg film or a Disney cartoon is creative, although it is definitely not achieved at zero cost. But again the point applies. Once the creative effort has been made and the expenses for this effort incurred, they do not have to be incurred again. The film has to be distributed and copies of the discs have to be made and sent out. These costs will obviously vary with the number of people who enjoy the films or cartoons, but the part of the cost corresponding to the original creative effort does not rise.

Nothing could be further from the Malthusian world of trying to scratch a little more output from a limited amount of land. The benefits from intangibles just carry on and on and on. The Intangible Revolution is the route to money for nothing.

Dynamic forces are at work that are transforming the balance between the tangible and the intangible. The natural growth of demand for intangible products in the sphere of health, education, information, communication, and entertainment far exceeds the growth in the demand for food, cars, or washing-up liquid. So even without any further structural changes, the balance between tangibles and intangibles will have changed radically in ten or fifteen years.

Such a shift in economic structure would be far from unprecedented. Just look at the size of agriculture, fishing, and mining in today's economy. They are tiny; yet at one time they accounted for the lion's share of all economic output. Car manufacturing and retailing could one day be just as insignificant in relative terms, even though, as with food production, they will have become no less vital in absolute terms.

Losing weight

One consequence of the increasing importance of these intangibles is the extension of a trend that has been going on for some time, namely the diminishing importance in our economy of heavy physical things such as steel or oil. The average weight of a dollar's worth of real American exports has halved since 1970. Admittedly, some of this fall is due to the fact that America now imports a good deal of its heavy physical things. But similar trends are evident in the exports of other countries too—and in overall production. In the advanced countries of western Europe and North America, in terms of output recorded as GDP people today are about 20 times better off than they were 100 years ago. Yet GDP weighs about the same today as it did then. It is as though the world's production system has been on an extended diet.

The weight loss is partly because of the move toward the use of lighter materials in industrial goods. New architectural and materials technologies allow buildings to be constructed enclosing the same space as 100 years ago but using a fraction of the physical material.

It is also partly because of a move toward the miniaturization of goods themselves. Whereas once the aim was to produce things bigger and bigger, now for most electrical goods, such as mobile phones or computers, the drive is to produce them smaller and smaller. Technical progress has reduced components from the size of a car to a notebook. Meanwhile, the electronics in a car cost more than the steel.

But matters have gone a stage further than miniaturization. As I discussed above, much of our GDP has dematerialized altogether. It falls into the category known as weightless goods. Even for many familiar goods, the aspects that give value are increasingly the intangible, "weightless" things like design or styling. So the weight to value ratio falls further.

You can see the same trend toward weightlessness in a comparison of the world's richest people at the beginning of the twentieth century and the beginning of the twenty-first. Most of them, then as now, were American. Not that I am suggesting that the weight of the average American has fallen sharply, but if you look at the sources of great personal wealth they, if not their beneficiaries, have been on the most effective weight-watching program known to humankind. A list of the ten richest Americans in 1920 would reveal the sources of their wealth as predominantly heavy: oil, steel, cars, railroads. The equivalent list today is super-light and many components of it are nearly completely weightless: telecommunications, pharmaceuticals, media. The richest of them all, Bill Gates, made his money from something completely weightless, namely software.

The characteristic of infinite expansibility, which ideas have, has a major effect on the way in which costs behave. The more important intangibles are, the less average costs will rise with rising output, and the greater the chance that they will fall.

Once the research and development has been done to introduce a new anticancer drug, for instance, it does not have to be done again no matter how many doses of the drug are dispensed. That is it: a once-and-for-all cost. The greater the number of doses, the lower the average cost of production. Similarly with the design for a new airplane. The cost of design is irrespective of the number of the planes made, which gives the manufacturers of the plane a strong interest in maximizing the size of the market.

As such things as knowledge, entertainment, and health become more important in the basket of things we wish to buy, the potential additions to human welfare are enormous, being unlimited by restrictions of material substance or distance. Unlike the gains from an increase in food production or car production, the increase in wealth produced by the discovery or construction of an intangible is there for everyone to enjoy at virtually no extra cost—money for nothing.

The cynic's riposte

It is easy to be cynical about the significance of the transition to an economy of intangibles. Most tellingly, you could imagine that whatever benefit emerges from their capacity to generate increasing returns is swallowed up by expenditure on other intangibles such as marketing, advertising, and branding. In that case it would be true that we are moving into an intangible economy, but so what? It would not itself be a source of economic advance. Nevertheless, as I argue in Chapter 8, there are good reasons to believe that in the economy of the future these intangible costs will *not* swell to absorb all the gains from the greater production of intangibles.

On a completely different tack, you could reasonably argue that production has *always* involved a substantial "knowledge" input. So what's the big deal now? Even the very basic economic activity of gathering food, or hunting, requires knowledge of where to look and how best to transfer Nature's gifts to the human stomach.

And it wasn't that intangible consumables did not exist in the daily world of the great fathers of economics such as Smith, Malthus, and Ricardo. The urban masses in cities such as London and Edinburgh would pay something to enjoy live entertainment in the popular theater, or to listen to music.

So why the fuss about what is going on today? The answer is that it is all a matter of degree. Although when Adam Smith visited the theater the essence of what was being enjoyed was immaterial—the structure of the play, or the juxtaposition of actors and actresses, the quality of voice and expression, or the music of Handel or Haydn—the economist did not feel at all challenged by such activities in his view of the material nature of wealth. They were regarded merely as ways of redistributing wealth between different people, the wealth itself corresponding to the amount of valuable "things," either food, extracted materials such as metals or stone, or manufactured goods.

Interestingly, although Marx foresaw in the communist future a period of superabundance in which material scarcity would be overcome, it was the power of accumulated capital to deliver material goods of which he was thinking and not the unlimited capacity of intangibles such as films, computer programs, or chemical compounds. Marx thoroughly accepted the classical attitude to services, with the result that the national accounting methods of communist countries regarded services merely as inputs to the productive process, rather than as a source of value in and of themselves. This may well have contributed to the appalling standard of most consumer services in those countries, even as myriad factories belched out more output, "fulfilling" and "overfulfilling" successive five-year plans.

The failure of the great economists to see that intangibles could be a form and source of wealth and to recognize their different qualities was simply due to the fact that at that stage of development, ruggedly material things such as food, clothing, buildings, or furniture were overwhelmingly important in the economy, and the knowledge component in these things was relatively low. For those of us who live in developed economies, this is no longer true.

Revolution in one country doesn't work

Just like the Industrial Revolution before it, the Intangible Revolution is the result of a combination of build-up and breakthrough: the gradually increasing importance of knowledge and knowledge products and the surge as a result of the computer and information and communications technology. Economic history is the story of the increasing predominance of mind over matter. Now we are at the tipping point.

But just like the Industrial Revolution, to realize its true potential the Intangible Revolution needs markets—and not merely on a national scale. It needs a global stage on which to play out its drama. Fortunately, it is going to get it.

5
The Wealth Spiral

The greatest improvement in the productive powers of labour, and the greater part of the skill, dexterity and judgement with which it is any-where directed, or applied, seem to have been the effects of the division of labour.

Adam Smith, *The Wealth of Nations*, 1776[1]

It is a hen-and-egg question whether historically it was the growth of commerce which continually enlarged "the size of the market" and thereby enabled increasing returns to be realised, or whether it was the improvement in techniques of production and the improvement in communications which led to the growth of commerce. In the process of the development of capitalism the two operated side by side.

Nicholas Kaldor[2]

Of all the men who have contemplated the sources of prosperity, none has contributed more to our understanding than Adam Smith. Smith was what we might call a swot—not the sort of person to set the world alight. Born in the small town of Kirkcaldy in Scotland, which in our own time was also home to the British Chancellor of the Exchequer Gordon Brown, Smith entered Glasgow University at the age of 14 and thence went to Balliol College, Oxford. At the age of 28 he was appointed professor of logic at Glasgow University, and then professor of moral philosophy. So you could say he was a spectacular early developer.

In matters financial, however, Smith was pretty unspectacular. He didn't make a fortune on the stock market; he didn't lose one either. But he was one of the early beneficiaries of a good pension. He left academia to travel Europe in the service of the young Duke of Buccleuch, and this was his route to financial assurance, if not largesse. The reward for this service was a life's pension, which Smith used to finance his "retirement," living back in Kirkcaldy where he wrote *The Wealth of Nations*.

Intellectually, Adam Smith was a firebrand and *The Wealth of Nations* was his torch. He was a master observer of the world as it appeared to him in the eighteenth century, but his observations were of such acuity that they uncovered truths that ring out down the centuries. He came up with many insights that apply directly to our modern world—and light the way ahead to the economy of the future.

Smith had the essence of a theory of economic growth that would generate self-sustaining expansion. It held the clue to why the increasing importance of mind over matter should make so much difference to man's estate and it explained why trade was so important.

The theory was pitifully simple—and beautifully profound. One of the most widely quoted parts of *The Wealth of Nations* concerns the description of a pin factory where umpteen men are employed, each performing some tiny task as a part of the overall process of pin production. The result of such specialization is a drastic increase in the production of pins compared to what would be possible if each man had to make his own pins. Another expression for specialization, the one used by Smith himself, is the *division of labor*. Specialization meant that the same quantity of inputs could produce a higher quantity of outputs—money for nothing.

Smith's understanding of the importance of specialization was insight enough, you might think, but he went on to add something truly monumental in its implications. The extent of the division of labor is limited, he said, "by the extent of the market." Allyn Young called this "one of the most illuminating and fruitful generalisations which can be found anywhere in the whole literature of economics."[3] The bigger the market, the more the production of a good can be subdivided into sections, and the lower the average cost of production can be.

Smith's insight might seem a little esoteric in today's world, but with a little imagination you can see that it is extremely powerful. Forget pin factories. Think machine tools—or pharmaceuticals. If the market for a particular good is small it may not be worth investing in a specialized piece of equipment—or piece of research—to perform a single part of the process extremely efficiently. The machine—or the research—is so expensive that it is not worthwhile. Something similar even applies to skilled labor. What is the reward for investing in acquiring a specialized skill or knowledge if the demand for the good in question is tiny?

Once the market expands, however, the whole mode of operation can be transformed, with the result that the average cost of production can be lowered. Output can rise by more than the increase in inputs. In other words, the economic system is subject to *increasing returns*.[4] This is the economist's version of a free lunch—or, if you like, money for nothing.

Smith's insight about increasing returns was intimately bound up with the importance of the human factor. Admittedly, there are some examples of increasing returns that emerge solely out of the characteristics of the physical world, such as the fact that whereas the cost of the metal used to build a pipeline rises with the square of its size, the capacity of the pipeline rises with the cube. (As we saw in the last chapter, this same principle applies to the carrying capacity of ships.)

But these cases are not prevalent, whereas the human sources of increasing returns are. Smith's pin factory example embodies three critical human attributes that are at the center of economic growth: specialist knowledge embodied in skills; the capacity for "learning by doing" so that the capabilities of workers increase with experience; and coordination, or management. It is only with coordination that the cooperative efforts of the workers can exceed the cumulated efforts of all of them working individually.

This is where Smith's insight connects with the great driver of economic advance during our ascent from poverty, discussed in the last chapter: the accumulation of knowledge. Admittedly Smith's pin factory example, although it has much to say about the accumulation of practical knowledge and by implication about human capital, appears to have little to say about the accumulation of pure knowledge. Nevertheless, there is a connection; a connection that, as I shall show in a moment, has major relevance to Malthus and his unjustified pessimism about humanity.

Lost Wisdom

Smith's insight about specialization and increasing returns may seem trite now, yet somehow in the development of economic thought it got lost in the thickets of theory. As the subject was formalized, the idea of decreasing returns lingered on as the dominant view, even with regard to the conditions in which manufacturing activity took place. It is as though economists were blinded by the characteristics of agricultural production that dominated the economy when the subject first grew up and that so concerned Malthus, and ceased to ask questions about the fundamental economics of production. Rather, the old, simplistic, good-for-all-purposes model of the world was patched up, restored, repaired, and life-extended. Exceptions were recognized and qualifications allowed, but the central vision was retained.[5]

So it was assumed that firms in manufacturing faced rising cost curves; that is to say, the marginal cost of producing an extra unit rose with increasing amounts of output. This led economists to be able to draw their famous supply curves, which, intersecting with the demand curves that sloped the other way, neatly determined the price and quantity produced.[6]

There are, of course, many activities where marginal, and even average, costs do rise as the level of production increases. However, in manufacturing, the dominant experience seems to be of falling average costs as fixed costs are spread over a larger volume of output, while even marginal costs may fall if the employment of extra workers enables greater specialization.

Nevertheless, economists persevered with the concept that constant or decreasing returns were a reasonable working assumption. It was vital for this assumption to be retained, because increasing returns played havoc with the established view of the way the economy worked. In particular, with increasing returns it was impossible to establish the time-honored central tenet of orthodox economics that a freely functioning competitive economy tended toward a full-employment equilibrium, which gave its citizens the best of all possible worlds in the circumstances of the time. So increasing returns had to be kept to the margins of the subject, away from prying eyes lest outsiders should be unsettled by what they saw.[7]

Economists were helped in this regard by the changing structure of the economy. Increasing returns, it was thought, occurred mainly in manufacturing, and they arose from the technological necessity to have substantial machines arrayed in a large plant. These costs were fixed come what may, and hence average costs would fall with increasing levels of output.

In the service sector the large fixed plant that characterized manufacturing hardly figured. After the war, in North America and western Europe the service sector came to be increasingly important. Restaurants, hairdressers, dry cleaners, mortgage advisers: these were the new growth areas and in these activities, it could be thought, there was little or no scope for increasing returns. So the view of the world that had been fashioned for agriculture, having survived a difficult time during the era of mass manufacturing, was out of the clouds and into the sunlit uplands. Economists could breathe a sigh of relief.

But today's new economic activities have features that radically depart from this characterization, and in the future will do so still more. Because of the increasing importance of intangibles in both the production process and the type of goods produced, more businesses will now find themselves in the falling cost category for wider sections of their output. In the case of so-called weightless goods, there may be no increase at all in total costs with increasing use of the "thing" in question. With the growing prominence of "weightless" production, economic activities that we still tend to characterize as services will increasingly exhibit increasing returns.

The new communications media are themselves subject to increasing returns through "network effects." It is well known that when you add another member or subscriber to a network the benefit to society exceeds the benefit to the additional member, since all those already signed up can contact one extra member. The size of this extra gain rises with the number of members. Examples of economically important networks include telephones, faxes, email, and access to the internet.[8]

Economic growth and trade

But the real message of Smith's insight goes beyond the confines of what is possible within a single firm or even industry. The theorem encased in Smith's example of the pin factory was the essence of his theory of economic growth.[9] The efficiency of production depended on the division of labor. But the extent of the division of labor depended on the number of units of the thing you were making, what Smith called the extent of the market. If the market were enlarged for some reason, this would permit greater specialization, which would bring more efficiency and greater prosperity. As people got richer they would, of course, have more money to spend, which would enlarge the size of the market still further, and so on and so forth.

But how could the "extent of the market" be enlarged? Through trade, of course. Without the finding and creation of markets even the boldest of inventions would not lead to money-making industrial products. This explains the emphasis that Smith and other contemporary writers placed on *commerce* in the development of industry. Indeed from Smith onwards, the policy thrust of classical political economy was to promote the freedom of trade and exchange.[10]

Moreover, in Smith's worldview the benefit from increased trade is not a static improvement but a dynamic process. This is particularly important for the interaction today between the developed and developing countries. When the developed countries trade with the developing countries they enrich them, helping them along the development path, thereby enabling them to buy more goods and services from the developed countries, thereby making the developing countries richer, unleashing more increasing returns, leading to increased demands for imports from the developing countries and so on, bringing increased wealth to both sides. This is the wealth spiral: a mechanism for mutual enrichment through trade and specialization that has operated throughout history.

The implications of the wealth spiral are the complete opposite of those that most people in western Europe, North America, and Japan draw when contemplating the further advance of the developing world. What they see is a *threat*: competition for *their* companies and *their* jobs. Implicitly, they think, their and their countries' interests would be better served by shutting out imports from the developing world. It would be even better, many think, if somehow the development process could be stopped in its tracks. It's the same old story. Exports are "good" and imports are "bad." But the opponents of development have it completely wrong. Exports are not an end in themselves. They are the price we have to pay in order to be able to enjoy the benefits from imports.

Even on their own terms the developed-economy opponents of development have it wrong. Why do they not see the great opportunity from much-expanded markets? The development of previously underdeveloped countries provides the developed world with two sorts of gain: cheaper imports of goods and services than the home-produced versions they enjoyed before, *and* expanded markets for their exports. Once you grasp the importance of increasing returns and the workings of the wealth spiral, the gains are greater than they seem. Larger markets for the things (and nonthings) that the developed countries produce lower the average cost of production, even for the things (and nonthings) that they produce for their own consumption.

Think of this apposite historical comparison. In its early years, America consisted of a group of colonies that were less developed than, and subservient to, their European motherland. Now, though, America easily outshines not merely Britain but just about every country in Europe in terms of per capita income and overall GDP. However, can it be seriously argued that the people of Europe would be better off if America had never been discovered, or if discovered never developed? Surely without American know-how and technology, without American markets, and without the supply of American goods and services, the standard of living in Europe would be much lower. For America then read China now—and multiply the impact severalfold.

In short, the world is a giant pin factory. Everyone gains from increased specialization. The upshot is that the developed countries have a strong self-interest in seeing the advance of the developing countries. Even if other countries forgo the opportunity for specialization by imposing trade restrictions, it will still usually be in their interest to impose no restrictions themselves.

The interaction between intangibles and trade

The gains from specialization, which have been around since the beginning of time, interact particularly favorably with a key aspect of the modern economy that was discussed in the last chapter. As a higher proportion of our expenditure comes to fall on things with a high intangibles content, a higher proportion of the economy will be subject to increasing returns. This will create its own growth machine—just as Adam Smith envisaged. Increased consumption at little extra resource cost will make it possible to extend the market still further, permitting further specialization and further growth in consumption—money for nothing.

The conditions of the modern economy are set to increase the potential gains still more. Consider what the emergence of new markets in Asia and elsewhere does for the economies of the western world. As the newer economies become richer, they start to want, and to be able to afford to buy, many of the goods and services produced in the advanced countries, including those that are "intangibles heavy" such as medical care, entertainment, and software. To supply these new demands costs western economies next to nothing, as the marginal costs are so low. But it is only when China is both developed and open to trade that it has something to exchange. In return, the developing countries must send the West a stream of other goods and services.

So the increasing importance of intangibles and their role in international trade constitutes a gearing effect.[11] If you like, it gives the wealth spiral another twist. This is where Adam Smith meets the modern world.

There is a further twist. The intangible is digitizable. This means that it is capable of being stored, accessed, transported, and traded in electronic form. As intangibles come to be more important, more and more economic activity will be digitized. What is digitized is tradable *par excellence*, without the costs and time delays that the transport of physical goods incurs. (I discuss which parts of the economy are readily digitizable in Chapter 8.)

Initially, the shape of trade is likely to be the developed countries exchanging "ideas for things," in accordance with the comparative advantage of the developed and developing countries. Some of the developed countries' exports may be intangible-heavy things, some pure intangibles. However, there will always be marked exceptions to the regional pattern of trade and advantage, as with the Asian Silicon Valley in Bangalore and the emerging software industry in Russia.

Once the developing countries have reached full maturity, there is no reason why things and ideas should not be produced in equal measure in the formerly developing and developed countries. Nevertheless, there will still be extensive trade, albeit more balanced in tangibles and intangibles. No matter: the gains will still be there, the gains from specialization and exchange, laid out so clearly by Adam Smith more than two centuries ago.

Trading Places

The scope for increased trade to bring enrichment has been amply illustrated throughout history. There are numerous examples of economic success built on trade, even without industry, and of industry being successful only through the expansion of international trade.

Of all the states that have grown rich on the fruits of commerce Venice is the most spectacular example, although Genoa was for a time a close rival. In its heyday, Venetian ships plied the Mediterranean and the Black Sea far and wide, and its merchants extended their tentacles far inland from distant ports. Famously, Marco Polo trekked all the way to China, for a time worked in the service of the Emperor, and then returned home with tales of eastern wonders. In a pattern repeated throughout history, commercial predominance brought Venice mastery of finance as well. On the Rialto its merchants and bankers would trade in currencies and interest rates, hedging and speculating, risking and venturing.[12]

Venice's trade not only brought the benefits of high-value oriental spices and silks to Europe, but also facilitated the transfer of technology from Asia, Egypt, and Byzantium, including glassblowing, rice cultivation, and textile production. Moreover, Venice played a major role in European intellectual development, making Greek works known in the West, creating manuscript libraries, and blazing a trail in book publishing. The former wealth of Venice is still visible to the visitor today in wonderful *palazzi*, gorgeous public monuments, and magnificent churches—all financed, along with a large maritime empire, a huge navy, and the burden of countless military *imbroglios*, from the profits of international trade.

Going Dutch

Centuries after Venice's heyday, seventeenth-century Holland provided another example of enrichment through trade. Here was a small, unprepossessing country with next to no natural resources, except its people, and considerable natural disadvantages in the form of the constant danger of flooding by the sea.

In 1500 Holland's level of development was far below that of the southern part of the Low Countries (which we call Belgium), never mind the then economic leader, northern Italy.[13] Yet it rose from being a relatively insignificant outpost of the realm of Charles V of Spain to become a far-flung trading empire, with the highest standard of living in Europe, a thriving commercial and financial center of extraordinary sophistication, and a lively hub of political activity and the arts. By 1700 Dutch income per head was 50 percent higher than England's, its nearest rival. Moreover, the Dutch economy was less dependent on agriculture and more urbanized than England's.[14]

Trade was the driving force. What enabled the Dutch to achieve such success was that Dutch institutions were modern and favorable to capitalist enterprise and the prevailing state of mind favored it too. Because Holland was a country of recent settlement on land reclaimed from the sea and marshes, the Dutch mind naturally accepted the possibilities for altering material circumstances. In David Landes' words, the Dutch had a "Faustian sense of mastery over man and nature."[15] Recent settlement and the absence of a feudal past in most of the country also helped to make Dutch society tolerant and to accept large numbers of both Protestant and Jewish immigrants, who proved to be economically successful.

However, Holland was not particularly technologically dynamic. The only aspect of technology that was important to its success was naval technology.

The Industrial Revolution reconsidered

It is all too easy to believe that the success of states like Venice and Holland, based on trade, is a feature of the pre-industrial world and that when it comes to *the* seminal economic "event" of the modern era, the Industrial Revolution, the role of trade falls back to bit-part status. But nothing could be further from the truth. Britain's commercial pre-eminence in the nineteenth century was both cause and effect of the Industrial Revolution.

Its industrial expansion was greatly aided by its extensive commerce across the world, not least with its colonies—and this continued to play a huge role throughout the nineteenth century. In 1846 tariffs on agricultural imports were abolished and by 1860 all trade and tariff restrictions had been removed unilaterally. Britain was able to impose free trade on India and its other colonies, but it was also able to insist on a low-tariff regime in its extended sphere of influence—including China, Persia, Thailand, and the Ottoman Empire. British trade policy, and particularly the country's preparedness to import a substantial part of its food, had a significant beneficial effect on the world economy.

Indeed, a large part of the gains from the Industrial Revolution were only realizable because of the expanded opportunities for international trade in which Britain played a dominant role. Throughout the nineteenth century commerce was the handmaiden of industry, operating under the Pax Britannica. The century began with trade severely constrained by the British blockade of Napoleonic Europe, but after the end of the Napoleonic wars trade picked up sharply as Britain adopted a policy of free trade. Later in the century there was a substantial reduction in tariff barriers as a result of a series of important treaties. Trade was greatly favored by the sharp drop in freight costs through the improvements in naval technology alluded to in the last chapter. From 1820 to 1913 world trade grew by about 4 percent a year in real terms, far faster than GDP.[16]

The Golden Age

It was a similar story during the first 25 years after the Second World War, the fastest-ever sustained expansion of the world economy, often referred to as the Golden Age. The growth rate of real GDP in Europe during the years from 1950 to 1973 was out of line with anything experienced in Europe before or since: 4.6 percent a year (and 3.8 percent per capita), compared with 1.4 percent from 1913 to 1950, and 2.6 percent from 1890 to 1913. Even the UK, the worst-performing of 16 European countries, experienced a rate of growth of 2.4 percent, which was the fastest growth (for a sustained period) it had ever experienced, including during the Industrial Revolution.[17] Interestingly, this was a period when western Europe (and Japan) was catching up with the leading economy, the United States, while that country was itself expanding rapidly.

The extraordinary success of this period was due to a combination of reasons, but surely prime among them was the period's enormous expansion in international trade.[18] After the war, the world's leading countries were determined that the retrograde movement of the 1930s should be reversed. They set up the General Agreement on Tariffs and Trade (GATT), which from 1948 to 1994 initiated and oversaw an enormous reduction in tariff and other barriers to trade. (GATT was superseded by the World Trade Organization—WTO—which pursued a similar agenda.)

The result was a massive upsurge in international trade. In the US, imports soared to 14 percent of GDP. In the UK, imports as a percentage of GDP rose from the lows of about 10 percent reached in the war years to around 25 percent. In France, Germany, and Italy they rose from about 10 percent to over 20 percent, and in Canada they rose from about 15 percent in the early postwar years to over 30 percent.[19]

Between 1950 and 1973, for the world's six largest trading countries, average trade volume (exports plus imports) increased by 9.4 percent a year, compared with growth of less than half a percent in the years between 1913 and 1950. The growth in international trade effectively brought the advantages of a large domestic market, which previously only the United States had enjoyed, to all the major trading countries of the world. Yet again, commerce was the handmaiden of industry.

The Scope for Increased Trade

Today we face an opportunity for expanded international trade of staggering proportions. If Adam Smith were alive now, imbued with knowledge of the importance of commerce to the development of industry in the eighteenth century, I am sure he would believe that the single most important force for economic progress in the world was the advance of the developing economies and their incorporation into the international trading system.

For what I call the developed countries are but a fraction of the world. The group of prosperous countries in western Europe, North America, Japan, and Australasia are home to about 800 million people, some 13 percent of the world total; within this, the elite club of countries we refer to as the G7 accounts for about 700 million people, or about 11 percent of the world total. The countries of the G7 account for almost 70 percent of world GDP, with the United States alone accounting for over 30 percent. As you might expect, the countries of the G7 conduct the lion's share of world trade, about half of it with each other.

This hallowed circle excludes about 2.2 billion people in India and China, another billion in the rest of Asia, some 300 million in the Middle East, some 800 million in Africa, and 350 million in Latin America. Meanwhile on Europe's doorstep, in eastern Europe and the former Soviet Union, stands a population of some 400 million people living in a sort of limbo, neither rich nor poor, neither advanced nor underdeveloped, but assuredly living well below their potential and contributing much less than their potential to the world economy.

The scale of the current discrepancies in development between different countries is remarkable. In terms of 2000 prices at market exchange rates, the citizens of the United States have a per capita annual income of $36,154, compared to just $856 for the citizens of China. Even when comparison is made using exchange rates that give a fair picture of relative purchasing power (i.e., at Purchasing Power Parity, or PPP, exchange rates), Chinese GDP per capita rises to just over $3,500, with the US figure coming in at just over $32,000.

In these terms, the figures for the average inhabitant of this planet come out at just over $6,600 per annum. The inhabitants of the poorest areas in both Central Asia and Sub-Saharan Africa have incomes of about $500 per annum, measured at market exchange, and well under $2,000 even when measured at PPP rates. Poor Sierra Leone clocks up a mere $420. At least that is a huge improvement over the $116 that it enjoys when valued at market exchange rates.

So even when properly measured, the citizens of the world's largest economy, the United States, enjoy on average an income some five times the average for the world as a whole, about 20 times the average for inhabitants of Sub-Saharan Africa, and nearly 80 times the average for one of its poorest states, Sierra Leone.

These international comparisons of GDP, particularly GDP per head, will readily excite feelings of outrage—in both "East" and "West." But they are not referred to here in order to excite, still less to incite. My concern is not how great the inequalities now are—even though they, and the concomitant injustices, may reasonably be thought to be enormous—but rather to illustrate just how different the world would be if these differences were substantially eliminated, as they could be.

For all the depressing facts about the world's poor and the exclusion of so many millions, humankind has a remarkable opportunity to deal with poverty—a historic opportunity. The tantalizing possibility before us is of the developing countries catching up with the developed world, both contributing and enjoying their due share of a now much increased world GDP, and taking their due part in international trade. In short, the opportunity is to close the gap that first opened up like a chasm between rich and poor countries with the onset of the Industrial Revolution some 250 years ago. Then the ratio between richest and poorest countries was perhaps 5 to 1 and that between Europe and China 1.5 or perhaps 2 to 1. Today the ratio between income per head in the richest industrial country, Switzerland, and the poorest nonindustrial country, say Mozambique, is more like 400 to 1.[20]

A world transformed

The size of developing-country populations tells us how large their economies will become once they have caught up. The population of China alone is about five times the population of the United States, and India's population is not far behind.

This is not to say, of course, that the transition can be immediate or trouble free. (I discuss the requirements for successful catch-up in the next chapter.) There are considerable differences between the developing countries with regard to the size of the gap to be closed and the difficulties that may be encountered. China seems to offer the most potential, but has a huge gap to close in terms not only of GDP per capita but also institutional development. It has some massive difficulties to overcome, most notably a weak banking sector, high public debt, rising unemployment, and a significant level of corruption.[21]

However, the recent performance of the economy is remarkable. Since the transition to a market-based economy, China has grown at an average annual rate of 9 percent. The share of exports in GDP has risen from about 15 percent in 1990 to 35 percent in 2004. Nike, for instance, now produces about 40 percent of its footwear in China, while China is responsible for more than a quarter of all the world's population of color televisions.[22] Still the zones of rapid development represent a relatively small part of the country. China started experimenting with market reforms in the Pearl River Delta in the early 1980s, but now this area feels strong competition from the Yangtze River Delta, centered on Shanghai. China is rapidly becoming the workshop of the world. Already it has usurped the US as the biggest exporter to Japan, while also usurping Japan as the biggest exporter to the US.

Rising unemployment is a problem because China probably needs to grow by at least 8 percent per annum, perhaps 10 percent, to absorb surplus labor. About half of China's rural population of 800 million are expected to become surplus to requirements in the coming decades as its agriculture approaches western efficiency levels. Because of this seemingly infinite army of reserve labor, China has massive scope for industrial expansion without running out of workers or pricing itself out of world markets through rising real wages. Indeed, despite phenomenal economic success, in the Pearl River Delta wages have not risen substantially in 15 years.[23]

The impact of China's development is not all in one direction. With China's full accession to the WTO its markets will be open to foreign firms and exporters. It is striking that while so many western firms and individual members of the public see its development only as a threat, most Chinese firms and ordinary people are fearful of the impact of foreign competition on their formerly protected domestic markets. The development of China alone potentially dwarfs the discovery and development of new markets that Smith thought was so important in the eighteenth century.

A long historical view may put current developments in perspective. For 18 of the past 20 centuries, China has had the largest economy in the world. The last 200 years of underdevelopment and colonial occupation can be seen as an aberration. China could readily reoccupy top-dog position within 20 to 30 years, although its GDP per capita would still be well below that of the United States.

The notion of China being the world's largest economy fills many people in the West with dread. They see this as inevitably bad news, both economically and politically. There certainly will be huge political ramifications that may indeed not be all good news, but from an economic standpoint China's progress can only enrich the developed countries. Those who cannot accept this either subscribe to the erroneous zero-sum-game view of trade or are confusing relative movements with absolute. Of course, if China progresses on the scale described above people in the developed countries will be *relatively* worse off. However, that is quite consistent with their becoming better off in absolute terms.

By comparison with China, India has been disappointing. Even so, its growth has been pretty impressive. In the ten years since the balance of payments crisis of 1991, growth has averaged 6 percent per annum and 4 percent per capita. This means that over ten years average incomes, and hence living standards, have risen by a half. In 2004, GDP growth was 7 percent. Admittedly, India has far greater potential. The current five-year plan has a growth goal of 8 percent per annum.

Interestingly, there are signs that Indian development is starting to accelerate. In 2001 foreign direct investment (FDI) into India was about $3 billion, up by 50 percent from the previous year. From its plant in south India Ford is already exporting 28,000 assembly kits a year, and other car manufacturers such as Toyota and Honda are sourcing imports from India's car components industry. White-goods manufacturers such as Whirlpool, LG, and Samsung are using Indian suppliers for their component requirements.[24]

The Indian IT industry is a spectacular success story. In 2001 it grew by 25 percent to reach almost $10 billion in revenues, of which more than $8 billion was accounted for by exports. Roughly half of the world's largest companies and many government agencies use India for contracted-out IT and business-processing work. And recently insurer Prudential and global bank HSBC announced plans to move thousands of contact-center jobs (which provide telephone and IT support) from the UK to India.[25]

India possesses a number of advantages over China, including the use of the English language, a democratic political system, and the established rule of law. Its growth potential is widely underestimated. If India could become another China, which is certainly possible, the world would really feel the effects.

The forgotten Europe
At the other end of the spectrum from China and India comes much of eastern Europe and the former Soviet Union. The Czech Republic, Slovakia, Poland, the Baltic States, Hungary, and parts of the former Yugoslavia are by history, geography, and culture an integral part of main-stream Europe. They are now set on a path of convergence toward western Europe.

They bring a massive reservoir of labor, intelligence, education, and skills. Their integration into the European economy is going to be of far greater importance for western Europe than the development of the Asian Tigers has been. In many ways these countries of "New Europe" are more vibrant, more market focused, and more against bureaucratic ways of ordering soci-ety than the countries of "Old Europe." These countries constitute a whole zoo full of tigers on western Europe's doorstep. Their integration in the European mainstream, and their competition, may yet invigorate the economies of Old Europe.

Further east there are countries—Bulgaria, Romania, Ukraine, Belarus, and other parts of the former Yugoslavia—which have not been so fully part of the European mainstream in the past and are further behind in develop-ment now. However, they are capable of approaching western European lev-els of development within a couple of decades.

Further east still lies Turkey, not fully European and yet closely con-nected to Europe by history and geography. This is a country of almost 70 million people, a large proportion of whom, unlike the members of the European Union, are young. Turkey has been plagued by bad government yet its people are industrious and talented. When the country gets its act together it will be a major force to be reckoned with.

Then there is Russia, not capable of easy categorization—part European and part Asian, in some ways highly developed but in others just like an ordi-nary developing country. On the eve of the First World War it was the most rapidly industrializing and most rapidly growing country in the world, the emerging market *par excellence*. Today, its troubled history and the scale of the institutional changes necessary to reach western levels of development are bound to instill caution. However, its people are well educated and supremely talented. It is clear that Russia has the capacity to make a huge difference, not just to the European economy but to the world.

There are real signs that the Russian economy is starting to motor as it passes through the trauma of postcommunism and begins to see some of the benefits of capitalism. Over the years 2000–2004 its growth rate averaged 7 percent. While it is true that some of this is due to a bounce back from crisis, the benefits of devaluation, and high energy prices (Russia being a substantial net exporter), this is by no means the whole story. There has recently been a strong increase in productivity.[26] Before long, Russia will be surging forward as one of the leading "Tigers" and contributors to the world economy, just as it was in the years before 1914. Moreover, its continued development will give an important boost to those countries that have historically been bound to it but, since the demise of the Soviet Union, have struggled—both the countries of eastern Europe and the Caucasian and central Asian republics.

Only at the beginning

Of course, not all the poorer countries of the world look to be on the brink of a leap forward. Even in Asia, there are many countries whose growth rates are pitiful. And Africa, as we all know, is a sorry story. Much of the Middle East is mired in poverty. By and large, the countries of Latin America have not fulfilled their potential. To call many of these countries "developing" would be a sad joke. I put them into a separate category: "underdeveloped." I discuss why these countries have failed to make substantial progress, and what they can do to make things better, in the next chapter.

Even if these underdeveloped parts of the world continue to languish in poverty, the impact of those that are developing fast will be enormous. The upshot is that although in much of the developed world workers and bosses are already unsettled by competition from the developing countries, they haven't seen anything yet. Globalization has hardly begun. All the forces that have been so troublesome (and so enriching), involving the relocation of traditional industries to other countries and the hollowing out of manufacturing in western Europe, North America, and Japan, are set to intensify.

There is another development afoot. Even at the beginning of the twenty-first century international trade is still primarily about the movement of goods rather than services. Although there are large parts of the economy that are bound to be fairly immune from international competition, there are also major parts of the service sector that are still primarily local but will become increasingly subject to international competition and may even become thoroughly globalized. Examples include education, health (both diagnosis and treatment) research, clerical and office work, IT, and financial services. (How trade in these services will develop in the future is discussed in Chapter 8.) So globalization is set to thrust its effects both wider and deeper into the societies of the developed world.

This process needs to be seen in its proper historical context. Primitive humans operated in a society that was the opposite of Adam Smith's pin factory. Either hunting alone or in a small group, each man would know virtually everything there was to be known and do everything there was to be done. As societies became more sophisticated specialization grew, but even in the eighteenth century, in the mainly agricultural economies of Europe, peasant farmers did most things for themselves.

With further economic development and urbanization, people became more specialized but still operated largely within a national or even regional setting. As international trade grew specialization increased, but still these were predominantly national economies operating in an international setting. Now globalization promises to bring specialization to a new pitch, moving from an international economy to a truly global one. Globalization may seem new, but it is simply a continuation of the process that has been operating throughout history, leading to greater prosperity. Globalization brings specialization to a world scale, and the parable of the pin factory is its leitmotif.

Arguments against Free Trade

By no means everyone is as enamored of the attractions of globalization as I am. Indeed, the combination of the prospect of constant and unsettling change and the presence of key interest groups who appear to lose from it ensures that the antiglobalizers have great political force. They could yet carry the day, shutting down the wealth spiral before it has really got going. In part, the ideas and concerns of the antiglobalizers are merely a rehash of all the old arguments about protectionism. These are no more valid now than they ever were, but they may be more influential.

One of the most beguiling anti-free-trade arguments is for protection of so-called infant industries. This holds that given underdeveloped or myopic capital markets, *some industries* in their early stages may be nurtured toward competitiveness under a regime of protection. There are several cases where the infant industry argument is justified. But the numbers are nothing like so large as the protectionists allege. And it is extremely difficult to restrict protection to the few justifiable cases. The world is full of sickly infants who, judged by the sheer lapse of time (and expenditure of money), should already be well into their dotage, but struggle on equipped with nappies and dummies. The developing countries have wasted countless billions, for instance, nursing infant steel industries on just those arguments.

Sometimes whole countries appear to have done well out of protectionist policies. Frequently cited examples include the UK in the 1930s and Japan in the 1950s and 1960s. Even if these examples stand up to scrutiny, however, in today's conditions they offer scant consolation for the world as a whole, only the prospect of one country stealing a march on another. That is even more self-defeating now because our economic prospects are so inter-related.

Despite the overwhelming benefits of trade, protection remains a potent threat because, for large numbers of people adversely affected by international competition and even for large numbers of others, it apparently offers an obvious gain—a no-brainer, if you like, money for nothing. Shutting out foreigners from "our" markets is obviously good for "us," although it is bad for "them." It creates jobs for us, so it is bound to be good. People typically see themselves as being patriotic in supporting "their industry" against the opposition, as though they were cheering for Real Madrid playing soccer against AC Milan. In this way of thinking, the only reason to allow foreign access to our markets is if they will agree to do the same: "reciprocity."

At the root of this attitude is a complete misunderstanding. Trade is often viewed by the man in the street as a competition in which there can be only one winner, whose winnings are exactly balanced by the losses of the losers, or as economists would put it, as though it were a zero-sum game. But it isn't. We all win. More than that, how much *we* can gain from trade depends on what *they* have to exchange and how much they can pay for what we have to exchange. In other words, *we* have a stake in *their* success. For example, Africa is no competitor for the developed countries of the world in almost any industry or service, but that does the developed countries no good because Africa is not successful enough to supply the West with very much of value, or rich enough to constitute much of a market for the West's output.

But that is not how the supporters of the so-called Fair Trade movement see it. They seem to believe that trade is a zero-sum game in which the developed countries hold all the cards so the developing countries inevitably "lose." Many of their adherents advocate a move toward localization; that is to say, local self-sufficiency. It is difficult to reply to this idea in measured tones. While it is possible that the terms of trade are skewed against developing countries and that more should be done to enhance their development, the notion that they lose by international trade is just drivel.

Usually the proponents of such notions have not even got the first idea of the basic economics of trade. The "morality" of trade is all very well, but it usually helps to get the economics straight first of all. Moral concern is no substitute for thought. The simple facts are that, whatever the potential for redressing bargaining power, the developed countries could easily do without the developing but the developing countries could not easily do without the developed.

Although some of the more thoughtful members of the group, such as George Monbiot,[27] have finally begun to acknowledge that trade is enriching for the developing countries, the advocates of trade still face a barrage of ignorance and prejudice, masquerading as outraged concern for the underdog. By all means flirt with the idea of the "localization" of economic activity as attractive for romantic reasons, if you so wish. But you should be in no doubt that there will be a price to pay for your romantic indulgence. Localization spells loss of income and spending power. In the rich countries this, though regrettable, will be tolerable. In the poor countries, it means impoverishment, which is unforgivable.

What will the developed countries manage to sell?
Interestingly, in complete contrast to the ideas of the Fair Trade movement, there is a widespread fear in the developed countries that "they" will become so competitive that there will be nothing that "we" can sell. After all, how can the countries of Europe and America compete with super-low wages? Hence development for "them" means impoverishment for "us."

Again, this fear is seriously misplaced. The developed countries' ability to have something to sell does not depend on their being absolutely more efficient in the production of anything, but rather on the idea that they will be *comparatively* more efficient at some things than others such that it is in the interests of other countries to trade.[28]

All of this was set out long ago by the famous economist David Ricardo, who is credited with having originated the theory of international trade.[29] He used the example of trade between England and Portugal in wine and cloth. England exported cloth to Portugal and Portugal exported wine to England because this is where the comparative advantage lay. Trade was beneficial to both countries even if one of them was absolutely more efficient than the other in production of both commodities, because trade allowed it to specialize in one and exchange its surplus for foreign-produced supplies of the other on better terms than if it were to produce both commodities itself.[30]

This idea of relative efficiency or comparative advantage is absolutely fundamental, but old though it is, it is still not widely understood even today. Ricardo certainly does not reach first-grade high school and he rarely reaches top-grade boardroom. The business mind is obsessed by absolutes. That wretched word "competitiveness" captures the mind and spirit of the body business as well as the body politic. Accordingly, it is necessary to engage the fears of developed-country impoverishment through developing-country competition and suggest the things that the developed countries will be able to sell to the developing, even when the latter have become a good deal more developed and, dare I say it, competitive. (I do this in Chapter 8.)

Protection as reflation
But suppose that a country has unused resources of labor and capital that can be employed as a result of stronger demand. In that case protection will cause a net increase in output as domestic suppliers supplant foreign ones and thereby, surely, *we* do gain at *their* expense.

There are serious problems with this apparently seductive argument. Why are there unused resources of labor and capital? If such resources exist, the obvious policy is to exploit them by relaxing monetary and fiscal policy. If there is a problem of competitiveness manifested in a trade deficit with other countries, the appropriate policy is a lower exchange rate that affects all industries equally, and affects exports as well as imports. Only if these policies cannot work for some reason should a country contemplate trying to escape from a recession by protection.

Arguably, something like this is occasionally true for some countries looking at their own position individually, but again, all countries cannot gain by
such a policy. Any gain in demand and output by one country is a gain
secured explicitly through a loss by some other country. As regards aggregate
demand, this *is* a zero-sum game. For each country taking action to shut out
imports or promote exports, there are others doing the same in relation to
their markets. The result is a race to the bottom. You shut out their exports
but they shut out yours. Clearly, this can do no good for the world as a
whole. The result is simply reduced trade. Since reduced trade means
reduced specialization and higher costs, as regards *real incomes* it amounts
to a negative-sum game.

Globalizers of the World Unite!

The old arguments about free trade and protection have reached a new
pitch over the concept of globalization. Globalization is in many quarters a
hate word, and in this word there are several layers of meaning: not just the
increase of international trade, but the spread of materialism, homogenization, the overwhelming of state power by the impersonal power of the markets, exploitation, and Americanization. In short, antiglobalization is a
cause that can serve as a rallying cry for every source of malcontent about
modern life, capitalism, and even the human condition in general. But do
the antiglobalizers have a point? Is it possible that the gains I have outlined
from increased international trade are illusory? Even if they are real, could
they be overwhelmed by other negative factors?

Some antiglobalizers fear and abhor damage to the environment, even
though it is difficult to see how *globalization*—as opposed to economic
growth—can pose an environmental threat. With regard to growth, as I
argue in Chapter 8, their fears for the environment are likely to prove
unfounded, not least because, thanks to the Intangible Revolution, we now
use fewer materials for each additional unit of GDP. Moreover, technological improvements and environmental awareness combine to reduce the
amount of pollutants and environmental damage at a given level of GDP.[31]

Part of the focus of the antiglobalizers' hatred is beyond the reach of economics. There is a feeling on the part of many people that for globalization
you should read homogenization—and homogenization *down* to an inferior

level of boring sameness. On the purely economic plane, there is something in this. In particular, convergence of living standards is bound to bring a certain convergence in the way people earn their living and spend their money: fewer quaint fishing villages and charming subsistence farms to delight the senses of jaded residents of rich northern cities.

Nevertheless, this point can easily be overdone. As I have repeatedly explained in this book, the benefits of trade come largely from specialization and globalization raises specialization to a new pitch. If you think about it, specialization implies difference, not sameness. This effect is clearly visible in the distribution of many of the world's most globalized industries. International financial services are provided in the City of London, films are made in Hollywood, mobile phones are manufactured in Finland. Precisely because of globalization, large cities, and even whole countries, can be very different in the way they earn their living.

By contrast, a world without trade would be largely homogenous as every country or economic area would have to provide more or less the same things (and nonthings) for itself. The so-called death of distance does not imply the irrelevance of location. On the contrary, as specialized production increases, locational differences, and the importance of many (though not all) workers and suppliers being in the right location, increases.

The alarm over boring, degraded homogenization is probably greater with regard to *culture*. Supposedly, we are all McDonald's eaters now. In the process of becoming richer we are losing our national and cultural identities and with them our sense of community. To many people in the developed countries, never mind the developing, these are more important issues than whether we are 20 percent, or even 200 percent, richer.

To this objection there is little that economists can offer in direct rebuttal. Yet they can say something. It would be regrettable if all cultural and national differences were eradicated by the spread of a single global culture. But is this actually going to happen? For a start, the apparent Americanization of the world is now largely a result of America's overwhelming economic might. If the forces of globalization are allowed to do their work, as I argue in this book, the result will be huge increases in wealth in the developing countries that will give many of them much increased weight and power in the world. In particular, China may rival the United States within 20 years. This will surely mean that there is no longer a single culture dominating the world.

The extent of American cultural domination is already exaggerated, particularly in Europe. France is especially sensitive over the apparent hegemony of Hollywood. In fact Bollywood (the Indian film industry based in Bombay) makes more films than Hollywood. I suppose the problem is that not many of them make it to the cinemas of the Champs Elysées.

Even without this grand-scale cultural rivalry, resistance to Americanization may build up as people get richer and they rediscover their own cultural roots and express different preferences. This could be rather like what has happened to eating habits in the developed countries over the last 30 years. The emergence of industrial-style food manufacture reduced the cost and increased the convenience of many foods at the expense of the taste, smell, and texture of "the real thing." This clearly applied to bread, meat, coffee, and beer. So great were the attractions of lower prices and greater convenience that at one point it seemed that the "real" versions might disappear altogether.

Now, as people are richer still, there is a move away from mass-produced, ersatz food and back toward the real stuff—even though it costs more. This may be partly to do with a realization of what has been lost, but the main reason is surely economic: people can afford it.

There is also a radical reply to those who fear homogenization. If homogenization means more equal access to decent levels of food, shelter, healthcare, and security, isn't it better that we are becoming more homogenized? However western *bien pensants* might live their lives, there is plenty of abject poverty in the world, some of it close to home. Although most of the footsoldiers in the armies of postindustrial workers in Europe and America can hardly be called poor by world standards, they still lack many a material comfort, not to mention rewarding leisure, that increased productive potential could supply.

Profiting from exploitation

A powerful strand of thinking in the antiglobalization movement is that globalization brings massive profits for multinational companies by exploiting cheap labor in the underdeveloped countries. It is up to governments to regulate, restrain, and tax them. Yet if governments impose added costs on businesses they will pass those on to consumers, who respond by reducing what they buy, thus hurting the very people the measures were supposed to help.

In this respect (and many others) the antiglobalization movement shows a deep-seated ignorance of basic economic principles. No one *likes* the idea of sweatshops or child labor, nor the very low wages being paid to workers in developing countries. However, what makes people vulnerable to these things is not trade but poverty. Yet many a well-meaning antiglobalizer thinks that expressing common humanity with poor people in developing countries means effectively outlawing goods produced by their labor through trade barriers and the like. Paradoxically, this is often very good news for the profits of companies operating in the developed countries, but terrible news for all those workers in the developing world who may now lose their jobs.

In particular, it is naive and arrogant to assume that differences in the amount of child labor employed in the rich and poor countries are the result of differences in the degree of parents' concern for their offspring. In many countries the alternatives to child labor are enforced early marriage or prostitution, starvation or begging on the streets. It is plain stupid to think that shutting off the opportunities for employing child labor somehow makes these children, or their families, better off. It simply provides false comfort for the consciences of well-meaning but misguided people living a comfortable life in the rich societies of the developed world.[32]

Meanwhile, those selfsame rich countries, whose governments and populace regularly opine about the dire plight of many people in the developing countries and the need to help them, blithely operate trade rules that discriminate heavily against developing countries, particularly in agriculture and textiles.

Security and political power

Then there are those in the developed countries who lament the increased insecurity implied by the unfettered power of market forces on a global scale. In the 50 years after the Second World War people were able to indulge the idea that life was now safe as the state was there to protect them. With living standards at first relatively low but work relatively secure, they were able to build a security and identity for themselves that revolved around their place of work. For many people in the developed countries, that is now no more than a fantasy world.

Yet we should not overdo the point about diminished security. As people get richer they should be able to provide more of their own financial security. Meanwhile, less of their identity should be bound up with their place of work, particularly if they end up having more leisure time. There is scope for different communities to emerge, no longer centered on the static place of work. As we progressively escape more and more from the material, there is less need for our identity to be shaped by the location of lumps of physical capital owned by someone else.

It is true that a more globalized world implies a weakening in the power of national governments. The implication is that the forces of government will have to become more globalized as well, with increased power for international bodies and greater cooperation between national governments. To some degree this has already happened with the emergence of regional trade and political entities and the treatment of global issues such as the environment on a global basis.

According to the United Nations Conference on Trade and Development (UNCTAD), 29 of the world's 100 largest economic entities are multinational companies. The largest of them all is US energy group Exxon, which is larger than all but 44 national economies. According to the UNCTAD report, based on value added, in 2000 the 100 largest companies accounted for 4.3 percent of world GDP. Exxon's estimated value added, at some $63 billion, put it about the same size as the economy of Pakistan.[33]

Mind you, this comparison of size is not a true reflection of power because these multinational companies operate in a market, whereas national governments do not. Indeed, unless they are subject to the ballot box, which many are not, governments are not subject to *any* direct restraints. Neither Exxon nor Microsoft has the power to conscript, fine, imprison, or physically harm people. Governments do. Thus governments of small and poor states around the world, notably in Africa, have regularly been able to cock a snook at the interests of huge multinationals.

This gives a completely different picture of relative power. If governments were pitifully weak in the face of all-powerful multinational business, wouldn't you expect to find the multinationals investing heavily in Africa, despite the governments? Instead, apart from the extraction of raw materials, they have largely given the countries of that continent a wide berth, for fear of what incompetent or malevolent governments might do.

Again, there is a more radical reply. Those who lament the reduced economic power of governments in the face of economic forces and large multinational enterprises seem to presume that government power has been exercised for the economic good of the world. Although, as I argue in the next chapter, *good governance* is vital for economic success, that is not the same as *big government*. There is plenty of evidence that in the twentieth century the large economic role of governments has done extensive damage. Being God and Tsar in their own economic areas, governments were able to levy ridiculously burdensome levels of taxation that greatly inhibited effort, administer inefficient and disincentivizing social security systems, and intervene in industrial ownership, management, and control in a way that wasted countless billions of dollars. The economic growth of the last 100 years was achieved largely *despite* the economic power of governments, not because of it. Its reduction would probably be a major source of enrichment, even in the developed countries.

The serious case to answer

There are nevertheless some telling points that the antiglobalizers can make. The most powerful cannon they can drag up in their support is none other than Joseph Stiglitz, Nobel prize winner and former chief economist of the World Bank. With a pedigree like that, when Stiglitz pronounces we should all sit up and listen, and when what he says has a title like that of his recent book, *Globalization and its Discontents*,[34] it surely appears that the antiglobalizers must have a point.

But Stiglitz is not against globalization. On the contrary, he is a great believer in it, or rather in the benefits that trade can bring to the developing countries and in its role in bringing forward their rapid advancement to the standards of the developed world.

What Stiglitz is against is "bad globalization." Yet in the spirit of *1066 and All That*, aren't we all? Moreover, what particularly irks him is not so much the globalization of production and exchange, but the globalization of policies. His ire is directed mainly at the "Washington consensus"—the set of views apparently espoused by the US Treasury, the International Monetary Fund (IMF), and the world's investment banks—that there is only one way to run an economy and that is the American way. So, this consensus has it, markets must be liberalized as soon as possible, foreign firms given free access to the domestic market, including the ability to buy up domestic firms, and international flows of capital must be given free rein. As and when a financial crisis occurs—which will always and everywhere be the fault of the country concerned and never the fault of the financial markets—the appropriate policy is to deflate the domestic economy through higher interest rates, cuts in government spending, and higher taxes.

Stiglitz scores many good points against this "one-size-fits-all" economic policy. After the debacle of the Asian crisis of 1997–98, it is difficult to resist the conclusion that the managers of internationally mobile capital display herd-like behavior, and when small countries are exposed to large capital flows these can potentially disrupt their whole economies and societies.

So what's new? As I argued in Chapter 1, there is a constitutional weakness in financial markets that makes them prone to such behavior, whether the asset in which they are dealing is equities or foreign exchange. Stiglitz is right to point out that we should not regard the valuations of financial markets as though they were the gospel truth. There may well be a case for controls on capital for developing countries. What they need to do is to control capital *inflows* and thereby be able to control the amount that can flow *out* when perceptions change.

Stiglitz is also right that on a number of occasions the IMF's policy of deflation through higher interest rates and fiscal tightening in the face of recession has been not only insensitive and inhumane, but also pre-Keynesian in its thinking and counterproductive in its effects. Mind you, the anti-IMF case can easily be overstated. As Kenneth Rogoff, chief economist of the IMF, puts it: "Saying the IMF causes austerity is like saying doctors cause plagues because you often find them around sick people."[35]

Stiglitz is also right that the benefits of globalization have been spread unevenly across the world. There are umpteen countries, particularly in Africa, that have hardly seemed to gain anything from the expansion of international trade over the last two decades. Many are still heavily dependent on the vagaries of commodity prices. Of 47 African countries, 39 depend on a mere two primary commodities for over 50 percent of export earnings.[36]

However, are these countries poor because *trade* has been impoverishing? Have the Americans bled them dry? Surely, so many of these countries are poor because they have hardly had a chance to take part in wealth generation through international trade. In some cases this is because they produce very little that anyone else would want to buy. The interesting question is why. The problems of Africa are not about overmighty markets or overmighty multinational corporations, but primarily about *bad* government. (I take up this theme in the next chapter.)

For all the defects in the role of markets in such countries, we have to look at the alternatives. The perfect policy designed by economist/philosopher-kings such as Joseph Stiglitz would doubtless on occasion be better than what we have—but the world is not overly supplied with economist/philosopher-kings, and certainly not in the governments of developing countries.[37]

Look at the Evidence

The best endorsement of the benefits of international trade for developing countries is the record. There *is* a major division in the world, but it is not so much between developed and developing countries, or North and South, or East and West, but between those countries that are taking part in the global economy and those that are not—between what I call the developed and developing countries on the one hand and the underdeveloped countries on the other.

According to the World Bank, developing countries that have increased their participation in global trade and investment, comprising some 24 countries with about three billion people, have doubled their ratio of trade to income over the past two decades. Their per capita rate of growth has risen from 1 percent in the 1960s, to 3 percent in the 1970s, 4 percent in the 1980s, and 5 percent in the 1990s. These rates are higher than those found in the developed world. In other words, they have been catching up. By contrast the nonglobalizing countries, which I call underdeveloped, with a population of about two billion, trade less now than they did 20 years ago. Their average per capita growth rate in the 1990s was negative. In other words, they are falling further behind.[38]

Moreover, for the developing countries that have taken part in the globalization process, the structure of their trade bears the clear marks of economic development. Whereas 20 years ago most exports from these developing countries were primary commodities, now they are predominantly manufactures and services. According to the World Bank, during the 1990s 120 million people in these countries escaped from poverty.[39] Furthermore, for these countries that have succeeded in integrating with world markets, there has typically been no increase in inequality.

Most strikingly, there is not a single example of a country achieving a high rate of growth through "autarky" or even near-autarky; that is, shutting out foreign trade and foreign influences. North Korea is about the clearest example of that policy and the results have been appalling. From 1990 to 2000 its GDP *contracted* at an average annual rate of 2.5 percent. Over this period, by contrast, South Korea's GDP grew at an annual average rate of 6.5 percent. North Korea's per capita GDP is just over $700 per annum, compared to America's $36,000 and South Korea's $9,000.

Cuba is an example of a rather different sort, since it is shut off from trade not because it wishes to be, but because the United States imposes trade restrictions on it. Nevertheless, the results are clear testament to the impoverishing power of the suppression of international trade, combined with an overbearing state and communist economic policy. Over the 1990s Cuba managed a real rate of GDP *contraction* of some 1.3 percent.[40] Admittedly, at market exchange rates its GDP per capita is some $2,500, way above North Korean levels, but it is still extremely low by world standards.

The openness of a country to foreign trade seems to have a greater effect on its relative economic expansion than conventional models of the benefits from trade would lead us to suspect. The reason seems to be that openness to trade is accompanied by the transfer of knowledge.[41] As one distinguished economist has pointed out, it is no accident that of the former socialist countries Slovenia had the most open borders and it is now the richest of the group. Albania had the least open borders and it is now the poorest. The identity of the distinguished economist? None other than Joseph Stiglitz.[42]

Trade relations

The ability and willingness to trade are central to the story of our escape from poverty, and central to our hopes for future prosperity. Trade's relationship with technological progress is symbiotic. Technological progress promotes trade and trade promotes technological progress.

If trade brings such benefits, it is striking that throughout history some countries have chosen to shut it out—and some still do. It is evident that in the ascent of economic man there has been another player besides trade and technology, something that when it was strongly at work underpinned, supported, and allowed these forces free rein, and when it wasn't undermined and suppressed them. Accordingly, as much as on the scope for increased trade and technological progress, it is on this third force that our hopes for the future must rest: good governance.

6
Good Governance

The inhabitant of London could order by telephone, sipping his morn-
ing tea in bed, various products of the whole earth, in such quantity as
he might see fit, and reasonably expect their early delivery upon his
doorstep; he could at the same moment and by the same means adven-
ture his wealth in the natural resources and new enterprises of any quar-
ter of the world, and share, without exertion or even trouble, in their
prospective fruits and advantages; or he could decide to couple the secu-
rity of his fortunes with the good faith of the townspeople of any sub-
stantial municipality in any continent that fancy or information might
recommend. He could secure forthwith, if he wished it, cheap and com-
fortable means of transit to any country or climate without passport or
other formality, could despatch his servant to the neighbouring office of
a bank for such supply of the precious metals as might seem convenient,
and could then proceed abroad to foreign quarters, without knowledge
of their religion, language or customs, bearing coined wealth upon his
person, and would consider himself greatly aggrieved and much sur-
prised at the least interference. But, most important of all, he regarded
this state of affairs as normal, certain, and permanent, except in the
direction of further improvement, and any deviation from it as aberrant,
scandalous, and avoidable. The projects and politics of militarism and
imperialism, of racial and cultural rivalries, of monopolies, restrictions,
and exclusion, which were to play the serpent to this paradise, were lit-
tle more than the amusements of his daily newspaper, and appeared to
exercise almost no influence at all on the ordinary course of social and
economic life, the internationalisation of which was nearly complete in
practice.

John Maynard Keynes, 1920[1]

Johnnn Maynard Keynes—man of affairs extraordinaire, civil servant, patron of the arts, and the greatest economist of the twentieth century—was very nearly wiped out twice in his investing career. At the end of 1927 Keynes' net assets totaled £44,000, the equivalent of £1.2 million (roughly $1.8 million) in 2003 prices. But in 1928 he was long on several commodities—rubber, corn, cotton, and tin—when the markets turned sharply downwards. To cover his losses he was forced to sell securities in a falling market. By the end of 1929 his net worth was down to just under £8,000, or £220,000 ($330,000) in 2003 prices.[2]

Despite these losses, Keynes died a rich man. Overall, he was a sophisticated and successful investor and speculator, on his own and King's College, Cambridge's account. He is said once to have been spied measuring up the nave of King's College Chapel to see if it would be big enough to accommodate a large amount of grain, which he might have to accept for delivery if his bull position in the futures market could not be closed out before expiry.

Keynes took over the running of the King's College fund in 1928, which was not, with hindsight, the best time to begin any investment enterprise. In the first three years he did far worse than the market. While the market was down 36 percent, the King's fund was down by a half. However, in the next five years Keynes achieved returns of between 33 and 56 percent per annum, easily outdoing the stock market. On the whole it was a fantastic performance.[3] Interestingly, had Keynes been a professional fund manager operating under today's conditions he would surely have been sacked after a year or two; in fact, probably just as the market was about to turn.

But Keynes was no crude capitalist believing in unfettered markets, content simply to take advantage of them for personal gain. He saw the dependence of the capitalist system on social and political institutions. The opening quote of this chapter is Keynes' description of the Pax Britannica enjoyed by most developed countries before the world order was shattered in 1914. What is so striking about these words is not only their description of globalized trade and investment, but their depiction of a state of mind: open, free, secure, and confident. In the background, supporting this state of mind, was a set of institutions: the rule of law and the sanctity of contract; stable, incorrupt, and nonrapacious government; the Gold Standard; and, protecting all this, the Royal Navy.

Although he was a member of the Bloomsbury Group—famed for its bohemian attitudes and behavior, many aspects of which he shared and exhibited—in other ways Keynes can easily be caricatured as the quint-essence of the English gentleman of his day, relishing the privileges of his caste and exercising a concern for the dregs of society only from a lofty and disdainful height. Although he is now renowned for his radical views on economics, his radicalism did *not* extend to questioning the then conventional views on Empire, race, and rank.

Nevertheless, Keynes' radical insight went far beyond the narrow confines of technical economics. He understood that if capitalism could not cure itself of the ills that produced the Great Depression, Europe, and perhaps the whole of western civilization, would fall under the sway of communism. In that case the foundations not just of prosperity but also of liberty would be knocked away.

Keynes' answer was an idea—and a set of institutions. The idea was managed capitalism, with the central government taking responsibility not merely for financial probity but for economic stability as well. And at the international level, the International Monetary Fund and the World Bank, which he helped to shape and which were in many ways his children, backed up by the progressive liberalization of trade that he favored, underpinned the phenomenal success of the quarter century after the Second World War, a period frequently referred to by economists as the "Golden Age."

Not long ago Keynes was profoundly out of fashion, but the events of the last few years, particularly in Japan, have brought about a marked revival of interest in his ideas about both theory and policy. His vision of the importance of institutions and values in society is also overdue for a revival.

I have emphasized that technological progress and increased international trade have been the prime drivers of economic progress through the ages—and they still are. Nevertheless, these two forces do not exist in a vacuum. Anyone reading about our economic history must be struck by the role of something much more fundamentally human. When she was Prime Minister, Lady Thatcher once said, "There is no such thing as Society. There are individual men and women, and there are families." She could not have been more wrong. There *is* such a thing as society and its nature has a profound effect on how individuals and families lead their lives, including their economic lives. The institutions and values necessary to make individual efforts combine into a successful collective outcome are, if you like, the social equivalent of the management component of Adam Smith's pin factory.

All the material resources in the world will not make people rich if those people are not motivated and organized to make proper use of them. In the worst cases, the fields can go unplanted and the crops unharvested while people starve, and buildings and capital equipment can be left empty and unused while people go unemployed and homeless. Equally, technological progress will not spring up in a society that is ideologically and institutionally unsuited to it. Nor can markets flourish in a system where governments are rapacious and incompetent. And trade can easily be restricted or even shut down altogether if governments so wish.

From the beginning of recorded history right up to the present, ideas, values, social structures, and institutions have played a critical role in deciding the fate of civilizations and cultures, including their rate of economic progress. And they hold the clue now to our progress toward the economy of the future. The whole world is set on a path to a system that will embrace both competitive markets and good governance.

Ideological Developments

Why is it that the world is on the brink of a surge of development and prosperity *now*? Why not 25 years ago, or in 25 years' time? Of course, development *was* proceeding rapidly in some countries 25 years ago. And development is a continuous process that is no respecter of dates or deadlines. Yet the hopes and prospects are genuinely greater now. Part of the reason is technological. The huge improvements in communications made possible by ICT are for the first time creating a truly global market and an extended global economic organization.

However, this does not go to the root of it. The underlying factor that opens up the opportunity for rapid advance is not technological but human. The big change is in the world of ideas—ideas about how we are motivated and how our efforts can be coordinated to produce the best results for society as a whole. These ideas about motivation and organization lead on to ideas about institutions and the structure of society. Amid all the late 1990s hype about new technology and the internet, businesspeople, markets, and politicians grossly underestimated the seismic event occurring in front of their very noses in the sphere of ideology: the breakup of the Soviet Union and the end of the Cold War.

There have been three key ideological developments:

- The effective collapse of communism as an alternative economic system, virtually throughout the world.
- The general acceptance within western societies of competitive markets as the best way of organizing the bulk of the economy.
- The rediscovery of the importance of effective social institutions for sustaining effective markets, enabling economic development in previously underdeveloped countries, and facilitating the transition of post-communist societies to capitalist democracies.

These three ideological developments are linked. While many communist countries appeared to be doing well economically in the first few decades after the Second World War, this served to bolster support in the nominally capitalist countries for substantial government involvement in the economy through state ownership and the suppression of market forces. In many of these countries, including the UK, the economic role of the state was very large indeed. Nevertheless, as it subsequently became obvious that the communist countries were struggling, this support was weakened.

Moreover, once it became obvious in the 1980s that the wider embrace of markets in the capitalist countries was enabling them to draw further ahead of the Soviet Union and its satellites, this served to undermine support for communism there. Equally, it was only after the fall of communism that the importance of social and civic institutions to capitalism was discovered—and only then that it became possible for the champions of capitalism to recognize and admit the limits to markets.

This ideological conversion marked the end of a long period of destruction and waste originating in the disputation of ideas about the state and society, involving two world wars interspersed with the Great Depression, and culminating in the Cold War. During this period two forms of totalitarianism, communism and fascism, infused the minds of millions and became the guiding force behind several great states. At times it seemed that one or other of these ideologies would take over the world, but eventually both were defeated.

History plays strange games with us. How fitting it is that the Berlin Wall was torn down in 1989, paving the way to the reunification of Europe, exactly 200 years after the French Revolution upset the established order and set the continent ablaze in 1789.

There are still differences between developed and developing countries over the role of free elections, within the developed countries disputes about precisely how large a role to ascribe to the state in the ownership of assets and the management of economic activity, arguments about how interventionist the state should be with regard to the protection of domestic industries and, dare I say it, about how to regulate the behavior of the financial markets. However, as far as the really big issue is concerned, the battle is over—capitalism has won. Now the debates are all about how best to govern it for mutual advantage.

Support from History

There is a temptation to believe that such changes in the world of ideas, and the concomitant developments with regard to institutions and government, are insignificant bit-part players beside the hard sources of wealth—technological progress and trade—analyzed in earlier chapters. Nothing could be further from the truth.

History is full of examples of failures of social organization and government outweighing the benefits of technological progress. The period after the fall of Rome, right up to the beginnings of the Renaissance, clearly illustrates this phenomenon. In the popular imagination, this period is a long expanse of wasted time. Not for nothing are the centuries after the Roman implosion known as the Dark Ages. So it comes as no surprise that in such economic records as we are able to piece together, the economic growth rate of this period was pitiful. Living standards in western Europe reached their nadir in about 1000 AD, when they were probably lower than they had been in the first century AD and lower than they were contemporaneously in Asia.[4]

In terms of practical technological progress, however, far more was achieved in the years from 700 AD to 1400 AD than from 300 BC to 400 AD.[5] Unlike classical technology, medieval technology was not grandiose or extravagant. It was small scale, practical, and located mainly in the private sector. The technical knowledge was held by peasants, wheelwrights, masons, silversmiths, miners, and monks.[6]

Yet whatever technological advances were achieved over Roman times, there was also a major loss. After the fall of Rome, in western Europe at least, most of the social and cultural foundations of the prosperity of the ancient world crumbled: literacy declined, law and order disintegrated, the transport system collapsed, and petty kingdoms proliferated. If you like, society lost the social capital necessary to bring about economic growth. Without it, technological progress was not enough.

The Industrial Revolution illustrates the flip side. It was made possible by the combination of technological advances and changes in ideas and institutions.

The critical supportive factor for Britain to develop first was that it was the most open society in terms of ideas. Most importantly, it was a nation of individual citizens, not mere subjects of an arbitrary power. As Adam Smith put it: "In Great Britain, industry is perfectly secure; and though it is far from being perfectly free, it is as free or freer than in any other part of Europe."[7] It was also relatively free of the religious intolerance that dogged its continental competitors and sent waves of immigrants to its shores.

Moreover, Britain's institutions made it the right country to lead the Industrial Revolution. Arguably it was another nonrevolution, the "Glorious Revolution" of 1688, that was critical in that it established a balance of power between king and parliament and thus helped to limit the danger of excessive taxation and abuses of state power in a way that could blunt economic incentives. In addition there was a "financial revolution" as Britain adopted Dutch financial expertise and even improved on it. The establishment of the Bank of England in 1694 and the fixing of the value of the pound (in which Sir Isaac Newton played a key role) were key developments underpinning not only Britain's growing commercial strength but also its ability to finance wars against the French, hence laying the foundations for its global hegemony.

Accordingly, this era of economic advance that is so clearly associated in the public mind with things—new machines, lumps of capital, and Blake's dark satanic mills—had many of its roots completely outside the material world: in the world of ideas, institutions, and culture. So you could say that even the fruits of the Industrial Revolution were essentially money for nothing.

The breakpoint

The ideological and institutional changes of the last 20 years, on their own, are not what really excite. It is the present interaction of forces that promises to be so fruitful. In the societies of the developed world there is a remarkable combination of the driving forces of economic progress—namely technological advance combined with expanding international trade—operating in the context of an organizational framework, that is best suited to promoting economic advance.

This golden triad is rare in history. One without the others is not enough to sustain economic progress. Equally, on the few occasions that they have come together, the results have been spectacular.

Meanwhile, without communism and with the rediscovered wisdom about the importance of social institutions, it is possible for the developing countries to catch up with the developed, and for the underdeveloped countries to begin the long haul out of poverty.

This is the sense in which the world is truly at a breakpoint in history. The prospect that lies before us is the achievement for the whole globe of what the Roman Empire once achieved for the Mediterranean world alone: a single, integrated civilization and a shared prosperity, albeit with a diversity of customs, religions, practices, and peoples.

Threats and Dangers

Although the ideological and political conditions are in place for the developed countries to take advantage of the opportunities that technological advance and growing international trade afford and to enjoy enhanced growth for many years to come, nevertheless it is not all plain sailing. There are a number of features of society in both North America and western Europe that threaten the existing order and that, in decades to come, could yet lead to a set of institutional arrangements that are highly antithetical to economic advance.

Most worryingly, the "war on terrorism" could lead to a society that not only spends large amounts of money on protection against terrorism but restricts people's movements, leading to more rigid controls on all sorts of activity, including economic activity, even reducing people's freedom of thought and expression, and slowing down decision taking. These threatened aspects of a liberal, open society may not be essential to enable a developing country like China to catch up with the leader, but they are the essential features enabling the leading country, the United States, to continue to be so innovative.

More prosaically, there are four other trends in American society in particular that, even without the war on terrorism, could lead in the same direction:

- Increased litigiousness.
- Increased regulation.
- The growth of political correctness.
- The rise of environmentalism.

Of these, the rise of environmentalism probably presents the greatest threat. The modern environmental movement exhibits shades of the extreme respect for inanimate nature that was one of the features that held back the economy of the Roman empire. Greco-Roman religion was animistic and anthropomorphic.

> *Religions that regarded nature as a personal force implied that tinkering with its rules was dangerous and sinful ... If every stream, every tree, every patch of land is populated by spirits, the environment remains capricious, unpredictable and uncontrollable. Any attempt to alter it may raise the awesome ire not only of Zeus but of small-time local deities as well.*[8]

Not that particular parts of nature are today thought to have personal identities, but rather Nature itself has become the god in whose name anything can be justified, and to the protection of which every other value is subordinated.

These four features of modern American society threaten to tie business up in a web of restrictions and paralyze it with fear. The danger has become more acute after the bursting of the stock-market bubble, since senior corporate executives are blamed for so much of what went on in the boom years—and are also castigated for taking such huge personal rewards.

Pre-eminence lost?

It may seem fanciful to imagine American enterprise and technological dynamism snarled up, never mind grinding to a complete halt. Nevertheless, in Chapter 4 I gave three major historical examples of great civilizations—Rome, China and the Islamic world—that experienced significant decline, mainly for ideological and institutional reasons. They sound a cautionary note.

There is no doubt in my mind that the ideological, cultural, and institutional threats to American dynamism are profound and could eventually weaken American performance. However, not all factors point in that direction. Much good can come out of the present wave of revulsion against corporate America. In the 1990s the "greed is good" culture went much too far. It not only caused some gross misalignments of relative rewards and some terrible injustices, but also wasted billions of dollars through the culture of short-termism and concentration on immediate financial rewards.

Contrary to some of the crass libertarianism dominant in America in the 1980s and 1990s, rampant individualism without any regard to community is out of line with basic human interests, and indeed basic human nature. Adam Smith may have stressed the selfish, rather than altruistic, motives of butchers, bakers, and candlestick makers in effectively and efficiently producing and delivering what we want, but even he was acutely conscious that competitive, self-seeking behavior needs to operate within an appropriate set of laws, moral constraints, and social context. David Hume went further when he wrote: "There is some benevolence, however small ... some particle of the dove kneaded into our frame, along with the elements of the wolf and the serpent."[9]

Moreover, as the British economist John Kay puts it, "the countries where systems most resemble the prescriptions of the American Business Model—unbridled individualism under weak government—are Nigeria and Haiti, which are among the poorest on the planet."[10]

But in the late 1990s parts of America came closer to this baleful state. The bubble years bred a sophisticated form of "gangster capitalism" akin to what went on in Russia after the collapse of communism. The weapons may have been bonuses and share options rather than guns and knives, but the selfishness and rapaciousness were just the same.

Modern capitalist societies require a balance between self-seeking and competitive behavior on the one hand and the forces of community and solidarity on the other. After the excesses of the bubble years, there will now be something of a swing back toward the latter, as there was in the 1930s after the 1929 Wall Street Crash and the onset of the Great Depression. What emerged from that counterpoint was the institutional structure and ideological climate that produced the Golden Age. Something similar can happen now. Provided that it does not go too far, the renewed appreciation of community values will be a boon, helping to rebalance capitalist societies toward the pursuit of the public weal.

Communism and Capitalism

So the developed capitalist countries now have their moment of historical destiny, when their system of government and economic organization permits and encourages the maximum advantage to be taken from the opportunities afforded by technological progress and international trade. But what of the still-communist China and the large number of developing countries that cannot be called liberal or democratic by any stretch of the imagination? Their institutions, values, and political culture are light years away from their counterparts in western Europe and North America. Does this condemn them to slow growth? Do they have to ape America in order to share in the spoils of globalization?

In China the Communist Party remains firmly in control and communist ideology still plays a role in society that would be extraordinary in a western country. Nevertheless, the changes underneath the surface are enormous. China's private sector now generates 33 percent of GDP compared to 37 percent from the state sector, with the remainder coming from companies of mixed ownership.

Not only has China moved to open markets and increased the sphere of private production, but it has recently undergone an important ideological change. It is encouraging rich entrepreneurs into the Communist Party, calling them "red capitalists." One of these—Mr. Jiang Xipei, chairman of the Jiangsu Fareast Group, which makes electrical cables—was recently invited to attend one of the Party's five-yearly congresses. Jiang Xipei reads Jack Welch on management and aspires to surpass Bill Gates in fame, if not wealth; not exactly the traditional image of a loyal Communist Party member.[11]

Recently China has made protection of private property and wealth a pillar of its economic policy, thereby removing the preferential status given to state assets since the 1949 communist revolution. Moreover, at the most recent five-yearly Communist Party congress, President Jiang Zemin said that citizens should be judged on their contribution to society and not penalized as a result of their property holdings.[12]

China is even embarking on limited political reform. It has announced an experiment for the southern boom town of Shenzhen that will impose strict limitations on the powers of the ruling Communist Party and implement a series of checks and balances, mimicking western democracy.[13]

Although Russian communism has collapsed, taking its main satellites around the world with it, officially Chinese communism survives. The truth, however, is somewhat different. Rather like Charlton Heston strapped to his steed at the end of the film *El Cid*, in order to encourage the masses there is a pretense that Chinese communism lives on. But in reality it is dead—and people like Mr. Jiang Xipei are living proof of it.

The fact is that the changes required in the formerly communist world and the authoritarian regimes of former colonies to bring them within the capitalist world's ambit were always much more mundane than the stormtroopers of the libertarian right would have us believe. Free prices, respect for profits, and orderly government get us 90 percent of the way. Huge swathes of the developing world have reached this point. They could not have done so without the ideological revolution that undermined communism and put markets at the center of economic life.

The result is that although a large number of developing countries, notably China, are not remotely free in a liberal, democratic sense, the sharp changes since the collapse of Soviet communism and the knock-on effects on economic policy around the globe have led to the opening up of large parts of the world to trade and commerce, thus bringing the opportunity to close the centuries-old divisions between West and East, rich and poor, privileged and excluded.

A blueprint for success?

Based on the experience of the capitalist countries and successful transition economies like China, what form of organization of society is most conducive to the accumulation of social capital and thence economic success? There can be no definitive answer to this question, not least because our experience is relatively short and historical accident may have played a large part in creating such evidence as we think we have. Still, there are some things that we have learned.

There is no single blueprint for the economic structure of society. In practice, there are fairly wide variations in the structure of societies that have been successful in ascending the development ladder. The rapidly growing Asian countries—China, Korea, Taiwan, Hong Kong, and Singapore—have each followed a different path to god, or rather to mammon, and only one of them, Hong Kong, can be said to be purest white from the standpoint of the Washington Consensus. (And even Hong Kong's halo has slipped.[14])

Furthermore, the ideal form may change as a society develops. Government-linked companies (GLCs) have played a prominent role in

Singapore's rapid development, but there are serious doubts about them as the island state moves away from manufacturing and into a knowledge-based economy.

Nevertheless, there are certain key requirements for a country to aid economic advance: clearly defined property rights[15]; a system of taxation that leaves individuals and companies with a clear incentive to create wealth; a system of corporate governance that ensures that the surplus of the business is not siphoned off by the companies' managers; and a system of government that fosters enterprise and trade, maintains law and order, and minimizes corruption.

Advocacy of these principles does not simply amount to trumpeting the virtues of liberal democracy. Indeed, within liberal democratic societies it isn't always easy to sustain all these requirements. Equally, a number of non-democratic or imperfectly democratic societies have been able to meet some or all of the criteria and deliver rapid economic growth.

It is striking, for instance, that most of those who have experienced the two countries find democratic India more bureaucratic than communist China. A recent survey sponsored by the World Bank found that in India, the executives of private-sector companies spend as much as 16 percent of their time dealing with government officers, compared with 11 percent in China.[16] Whereas it takes 10 permits and 90 days to set up a business in India, the equivalent figures for China are 6 and 30 days. In the *Global Competitiveness Report* for 2001, for restrictions on the hiring and firing of workers India ranked 73rd out of 75 countries, whereas communist China ranked 23rd. In India it takes an average of 10.6 days to clear goods at customs, compared to 7.8 in China.[17]

Nor, even if development depends on the embrace of the market and of globalization, does this mean that the whole world must become "westernized." Admittedly many eminent thinkers have believed so—as have the leaders of a fair few underdeveloped countries. This has been a leading reason why they have been fearful of globalization.

And one can see why. After all, the fundamental reason why Europe, rather than the Middle East or China or India, staged the Industrial Revolution *was* ideological and cultural. Moreover, ideology and culture continue to underpin the dynamism of American society, the technological leader. However, catch-up is not the same as driving the technological frontier forward. Japan managed an extraordinary burst of development without ceasing to be Japanese and it looks as though China will do the same. This is the lesson that India and the Islamic states of the Middle East have yet to learn.[18]

The key point for economic success is that the institutional structure should ensure that self-seeking behavior operates in the interest of the many rather than the few. "Political maneuvering is a zero-sum game at best, whereas technological change is a positive-sum game. It is the political sphere that determines which game attracts the best players."[19] Those societies work best where institutional arrangements encourage individuals to deliver results that foster the common weal, even though they are motivated by self-interest. This can clearly occur in states that fall a long way short of the liberal, democratic "ideal."[20]

The Development Ladder

Institutions and values may have been at the root of the success or failure of countries and civilizations throughout history and the effective collapse of communism has opened up economic opportunities in China, Russia, and many other countries. But what does this say about the position of all those countries in Africa, Asia, and Latin America that have never been communist yet have been, and still are, extremely poor? Is there any message of hope for them? Indeed there is.

The World Bank has estimated that a bus driver in Germany enjoys a standard of living 13 times as high as a bus driver in Kenya. Yet the skills required are more or less identical. The Kenyan bus driver is paid an income that is affordable given the overall productivity of that economy.[21] The effective functioning of institutions is at the root of a complex interaction of factors explaining that level of productivity—and the functioning of institutions can undoubtedly be made more effective.

Of course, a developing country aspiring to get richer needs to accumulate physical capital, not least because new techniques are almost always embodied in the latest machinery, rather than descending like manna on all men and machines alike. The "small" four east Asian fast-growing economies—Korea, Taiwan, Singapore, and Hong Kong—have all had high rates of capital accumulation. It seems likely that what made this accumulation possible, and made it deliver decent rates of economic growth, was the interaction between technological progress and an effective system of governance (albeit one with warts and all). Yet there has been a tendency in many underdeveloped countries to think that dollops of capital, particularly large infrastructure projects, have a magical quality. Many of their governments suffered from a particular form of thingism: the machinery fetish.

A whole generation of development economists once suffered from the same syndrome. The essential problem with poor countries, they thought, was lack of investment in physical capital, which was itself primarily due to low levels of development permitting very low rates of saving. The answer was to supply finance from outside in the form of foreign aid, thereby overcoming the financial constraint. Hey presto, fixed investment could boom and economic growth could take off in its wake.

A moment's reflection could have assured these economists that lack of machinery could be nowhere near the main problem, let alone the source of all the difference in productivity between developed and underdeveloped countries. US per capita income is about 15 times Indian per capita income. For machinery alone to explain this difference, American workers would have to have about 900 times the level of machinery of Indian workers. The true multiple is about 20 times.[22]

Similarly, given this discrepancy in machinery per capita, the rate of return on capital employed in machines in India should have been 58 times larger. Accordingly, capital should have flowed from America to India, and indeed to all underdeveloped and developing countries held back by a lack of machinery. In practice the opposite has happened. Rich countries have received the bulk of internationally mobile fixed investment.

Economists have been astonishingly naive about something that you would think was right up their street, namely the sources of economic growth. The reason is partly to do with the excessively mechanistic nature of the subject for most of the last 50 years, which led them to see the answer as some sort of mechanical process. They latched on to a series of failed panaceas: foreign aid, investment in machinery, and investment in human capital.

They were also influenced by something highly political. They were blinded by the development success of Soviet Russia in the 1930s, which had managed to transform itself into an industrial giant. Moreover, the Cold War played a key part in propelling large-scale and often indiscriminate aid to the Third World. Given the Soviet Union's apparent success, it was easy to see much of Africa and Asia quickly turning communist. Aid was intended to forestall this.

Interestingly, something both deeply human and, as I argue below, of supreme importance in holding back underdeveloped countries, namely corruption, hardly featured at all in the concerns of the early development economists. It was as though development was all about machines and impersonal processes, with no role for the human factor. *The Handbook of Development Economics*, a prestigious four-volume work, does not mention corruption anywhere in 3,047 pages of text.[23]

But there has recently been a step-change in recognition of the importance of social capital. Whereas in the World Bank for decades the focus was on the "weighty" economy of infrastructure and factories, things that one could show visiting dignitaries or feature on postage stamps, the focus has shifted to what the bank now regards as the more important part, namely building up the intangible infrastructure of knowledge, institutions, and culture. So much so that Joseph Stiglitz, then the Bank's chief economist, once said that the World Bank wants to be seen as a Knowledge Bank.[24]

Moreover, because of the initial failure of some of the countries that tried to make the transition from communism to capitalism, we have also discovered the *limits* to markets and the importance of the institutions and ideas necessary to make capitalism work. In particular, we now know more about what needs to be done to make a capitalist system work properly in transition economies.

Disappointing results

These lessons have not been learned before time. The returns to aid-financed fixed investment in developing countries have been pitiful over a long period. It has been extremely difficult to make foreign aid translate into increased fixed investment, not least because huge amounts of funds were typically siphoned off by corrupt governments and their officials. Even when there was some fixed asset to show for the donor's money, the fruits tended to be disappointing.

In 1952, for instance, there were very high hopes for the newly independent state of Ghana. Typical of this optimism was the grandiose project to build a dam across the Volta River providing electricity for an aluminum smelter, kick-starting a Ghanaian aluminum industry, along with a north–south water transport link, a fishing industry on the gigantic, artificial Lake Volta, and large-scale irrigation to boost agricultural production. In 1967, the head of the World Bank's Economics Department thought that

Figure 6.1 Zambian per capita income, 1960–1996 (1985 dollars)

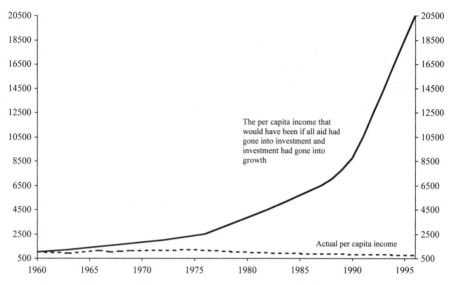

Source: W. Easterly, *The Elusive Quest for Growth*, MIT Press, 2002. © 2001 Massachusetts Institute of Technology. Reproduced with kind permission of MIT Press

the Volta project gave Ghana the potential to reach 7 percent per annum economic growth. In reality, economic performance has been starkly different. Ghanaians today are still about as poor as they were in the early 1950s.

Guyana was another spectacular example. Between 1980 and 1990 investment as a percentage of GDP increased from 30 to 42 percent, and foreign aid ran at 8 percent of GDP. During this period, however, Guyanan GDP actually fell.

Or take Zambia. If all of its foreign aid had gone into investment and this investment had produced the returns predicted by the development experts in the World Bank, Zambian per capita income would have quadrupled in just over 30 years. The reality, as shown in Figure 6.1, is pathetically different.

There are some startling comparisons between countries. Between 1960 and 1985, both Nigeria and Hong Kong increased their physical capital stock by over 250 percent. In Hong Kong output per worker rose by 328 percent. In Nigeria, however, it rose by only 12 percent. Over the same period, the increases in capital per worker were over 500 percent in both Japan and the Gambia. The increases in output per worker were 260 percent in Japan and 2 percent in the Gambia.[25]

Why is it that in so many underdeveloped countries the returns to investment in physical capital have been so disappointing? There is both a proximate and an underlying answer. The proximate answer comprises a rag-bag of reasons, including such simple factors as the newly installed machines producing things no one wants, or critical inputs being unavailable, or the transport and distribution infrastructure breaking down. The underlying reason is more controversial—and more illuminating.

Human Capital

One possible answer is that more investment in machines will not do much good without the requisite skills in the labor force. Or, to put the matter in economese, investment in physical capital needs to be complemented by investment in *human* capital. If you measure the returns to physical capital alone you are measuring the returns to only a part of the capital stock.

Basic education is clearly a necessary requirement to build up human capital. The spread of the technology underlying modern economic growth depends to a considerable degree on acquisition of the appropriate traits and motivation through formal schooling.[26] South Korea is a good example. Starting in the late 1960s, it made primary education universal and secondary education increased from 25 to 100 percent participation, while university enrollment rates trebled.

On this basis, the shift to mass education across large parts of the developing world gives cause for optimism.[27] Even so, enabling large numbers of individuals to acquire human capital is not sufficient for success. It is essential that they are able to interact productively with others, transmit their skills to others, and hand them down across the generations. Many of the societies of the old communist bloc were rich in human capital. The former Soviet Union and eastern Europe compared very favorably with the United States and western Europe in the average number of years of schooling attained. Yet these countries were by and large hugely unsuccessful as economies.

The same can be said of Egypt, where between 1970 and 1998, although primary school enrollment rates increased to more than 90 percent, secondary schooling levels went from 32 to 75 percent, and university education doubled, the country made no progress in the ranking of economies. Equally, it is noteworthy that Zimbabwe, a country currently in the throes

Figure 6.2 Education capital and GDP per capita growth, 1960–1985
(% per annum)

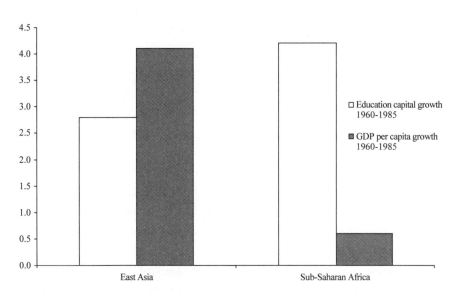

Source: W. Easterly, *The Elusive Quest for Growth*, MIT Press, 2002. © 2001 Massachusetts Institute of Technology. Reproduced with kind permission of MIT Press

of an economic disaster, has an 85 percent literacy rate, the highest in Sub-Saharan Africa.

In fact, the results from getting underdeveloped countries to invest in human capital through increased participation in formal schooling are very similar to the results for investment in physical capital. Merely cranking up the educational "machine" without attending to the surrounding social structure of institutions, mores, and motivations delivers similar results to forced investment in real machines—next to nothing. One study could find no positive association between growth in "education" and growth of output per worker.[28]

Most striking is the comparison between the growth in "educational capital" and GDP per capita in East Asia and Sub-Saharan Africa, as Figure 6.2 shows.[29] Over the period 1960–85, Sub-Saharan Africa enjoyed a faster growth in educational capital than east Asia, but the growth of per capita GDP was pitiful by comparison.

African queens
Thus as with machines, high skill levels and high levels of education are not much good in themselves. They need to be combined not only with each

other, but also with the missing, magic ingredient to produce the goods (and services) for the economy: social capital. Otherwise, you get the phenomenon so widely observed in communist and underdeveloped countries of skills going to waste—highly educated taxi drivers or, as in Cuba, trained doctors becoming tourist guides.

The really striking aspect of Africa, the source of its poverty and hence the key to its future prosperity, is not so much the low levels of human capital as the *collapse* of this social capital. Many African countries have a lower GDP per head now than they had at independence. This is primarily due to a malfunctioning political system and the absence of the key set of beliefs necessary to support a well-functioning economy.[30]

Rampant corruption and government incompetence figure high in the list of reasons why African growth performance has been so miserable. One frequent source of government destruction of the economy is through the systematic operation of a policy of negative real interest rates as a result of the combination of fixed interest rates and rampant inflation created by deliberate government money printing. This acts as a tax on bank depositors and thereby severely inhibits the banking system. A healthy banking system is critical for economic growth. One can think of money as one of the inputs into the productive system of the economy. In so many poor countries of the world this input is systematically destroyed by the government through inflationary monetary policy.[31]

Moreover, bad government has been sustained and even inadvertently encouraged by the international aid agencies. According to the *International Credit Risk Guide*, in the 1980s and early 1990s the most corrupt developing countries in the world were Zaire, Bangladesh, Liberia, Haiti, Paraguay, Guyana, and Indonesia. Nevertheless, these countries collectively received 46 "adjustment loans" from the World Bank and IMF. Zaire received nine such loans. Not unrelatedly, the personal wealth of Zairi President Mobutu Sese Seko was measured in billions.

The case of Côte d'Ivoire is one of the most scandalous. In 1997 it received 1,276 times more in per capita aid than India despite an appalling record of government incompetence and corruption. It has twice created lavish new national capitals in the home towns of successive national leaders. Between 1979 and 1994, the income of the average Ivorian halved. Meanwhile, some of the country's citizens became outrageously rich. In 1999 the EU suspended aid to Côte d'Ivoire after a history of gross embezzlement including such stinkers as billing a $15 stethoscope at $318 and a $40 baby scale at $2,445.[32]

The Nigerian government has been another spectacular failure that can hardly be blamed on the country's lack of export capacity. It has failed to provide basic public services despite receiving $280 billion in oil revenues since the late 1950s. Where has the money gone? Some $8 billion went on building a steel complex (the machinery fetish again) that is yet to produce any steel; goodness knows how much went on building a new national capital from scratch; and countless billions went—you've guessed it—into the pockets of the rulers. Talk about money for nothing.

Even where funds are not directly siphoned off into the rulers' pockets, the poor functioning of the political system often leads to a gross misallocation of government funds. It is common for funds to find their way to someone—the workers employed—rather than into spending on equipment or material. For instance, Guinea spends only 3 percent of its health budget on drugs for its clinics, compared to 34 percent on health workers' wages.[33]

Interestingly, the damage done by corruption seems to be much greater when government is weak than when it is strong. The reason will be familiar to economists. A "monopoly provider of corruption" will take account of the effects of his actions on the overall health of the system and hence the ability of the goose to keep laying the golden egg.

By contrast, with decentralized ("competitive") corruption, each agent is too small to take account of his actions on the overall system and consequently the "theft rate" is set at a much higher level. This explains why corruption was more damaging in Zaire than in Indonesia. It also explains why the collapse of so many former communist regimes has led to an apparent increase in corruption. In the past, the centralized party dictatorship exercised considerable monopoly powers as a "supplier of corruption." Consequently, it had some interest in keeping the rate of corruption in check.

Luck or Judgment?

What makes the prevalence of bad government so devastating is that government has a vital role to play in the development process. Development has much of the virtuous circle about it. This has led some economists to say that one of the most important determinants of development is luck. A burst of good luck, for example a high price for a country's staple export, can set it on the right path. Similarly, a run of bad luck can set it on a downward spiral.

Clearly these effects are present to some degree, but they are surely not fundamental. The key is how you try to break into the virtuous circle. It is difficult to break into it through the fixed investment or even the human capital link. But good government is, after all, within the capacity of government to deliver. When instead it delivers bad government this turns the virtuous circle into a vicious one. The key point about good government and strong institutions is that they are able to draw full benefit from good luck and withstand the blows from bad luck. By contrast, poor government and weak institutions leave a country fully exposed to "bad luck" and unable to make use of its "good luck."

The world is full of countries that have had runs of good luck with commodity prices or discoveries of oil, but have nothing to show for it because the government has squandered the money. Indeed, resource-poor or "unlucky" countries have in general had better economic performance than those with abundant natural resources.[34] The reason is surely that in giving rise to rewards without effort—money for nothing—these resources have depressed incentives, politicized the economy, and inhibited the growth of the institutions and social attitudes that produce growth.

Think of the fate of Argentina, whose territory is not only huge but also blessed with every sort of natural advantage. So much so that at the beginning of the twentieth century it was the seventh largest economy in the world. Now it is down with the also-rans. We are accustomed to the idea that it is extremely difficult for third-world countries to develop and reach the standards of living of the first world. Argentina must be the only country that has successfully transformed itself from the first world to the third. Whatever the reasons for its regress, and they are complex, they have nothing whatever to do with shortage of land or raw materials, and everything to do with the malfunctioning of the country's institutions.[35]

This point can be generalized. Why has the economic development of North and South America been so different despite similar resource endowments? Surely a good deal of the answer lies in their different political and cultural heritage, with the North molded by sixteenth-century England and the South by sixteenth-century Spain and Portugal.

Rescuing the laggards

So social capital is at the root of economic success and needs to be nurtured for countries to climb the development ladder. Among economists, development agencies, and the governments of many developing countries, this lesson has been learned. However, is it feasible for the countries of the developing world to advance so fast that they catch up with the developed world?

Being behind in economic development confers both advantages and disadvantages. When one country, or a group of countries, has a substantial lead in technology and living standards over the rest, there is no necessary reason why the gap should be closed.[36] Rich countries can be locked into a path of rapid advance just as poor countries can be locked into stagnation or slow growth. In some ways being backward confers some advantages, in that a country can leapfrog the stages of development by borrowing best practice from the leaders. For instance, the advent of mobile phones has enabled many developing countries to overcome the barriers posed by having to depend on inadequate and badly maintained landline systems—barriers created by hopelessly inefficient and often corrupt state-owned telephone companies. More than a third of underdeveloped and developing countries have a waiting time for a telephone line of six years or more. In Guinea, the waiting time is 95 years.[37]

When there is an established technology to borrow or emulate, it should be much easier to progress than when a country is at the cutting edge of technology.[38] Developing countries do not have to have their own version of Bill Gates. Nor do they have to produce their own PCs; they can import them. Mind you, being able to pay for them requires having something to export, and being able to use them efficiently requires having a population that is both PC literate and of a certain general educational standard. In some cases, though, governments have constructed barriers of their own. At one point, Brazil banned PC imports in an attempt to stimulate a domestic PC industry.

The achievement of South Korea once again shows what can be done. In 1955, its economic prospects seemed to be so poor that American officials predicted more or less indefinite dependence on foreign (mainly US) aid. Between 1971 and 2000, it managed an average annual real growth rate of 7.5 percent. That meant that at the end of 30 years, its GDP was eight times the starting level. That truly is a transformation within a generation.

The Korean experience, wonderful though it is, is not a one-off. Something similar happened earlier in Japan. In 1960, Japanese income per capita was a third the level of American income per capita. Over the next 25 years Japanese income per capita grew by 5.8 percent per annum, while the equivalent American figure was 2.1 percent. Japan caught up fast. By contrast, over the same period India, starting with per capita income at one-fifteenth the American level, grew by only 1.5 percent per annum. Consequently, India fell further behind.

The American Challenge

Yet large parts of the world will not be able to ascend the development ladder without outside help, and that help will mostly have to come from America. This is not simply a matter of handouts. What is needed is for America to exercise leadership in shaping the governance of the world.

This means that the challenge facing America is immense. It sees itself as free, open, fair, and generous. Others see it as blind, prejudiced, dictatorial, and selfish. It sees the rest of the world as an extension of the United States. Others see their societies and their values under assault from Americanization. And there is no doubt that this clash could lead to a very ugly result indeed.

I have already referred to the tendency for the US to succumb to domestic pressure for trade protection. The danger goes further. America has never fully adopted the position of the previous world leader, Great Britain, which was a unilateral free trader. In Martin Wolf's words, it is "a multi-lateral liberaliser."[39] But this means that if other countries cut up rough the US could readily decide to shut up shop. Moreover, there are prominent voices on the neoconservative right who wish to halt and even reverse globalization. They see it as a threat to both national sovereignty and national security. The free, unfettered movement of goods about the globe does not sit easily with the perceived need to prevent attacks by chemical, biological, or nuclear weapons.

And in a sense, if all America is interested in is relative prosperity and American power, it may be right to resist globalization. For this force, which the anticapitalist protesters see as a way of extending American power, is actually the way that America *can* be tamed. Vast though its economy is, it does not dominate the world. But America easily dominates any individual country that might be up against it on a bilateral basis. Only the combined weight of the EU can match it, and that grouping of countries is seldom able to speak with a single voice.

One often-heard complaint about America is that it does not behave as though other countries are equal. But this criticism completely misses the mark. How can America treat other countries as equal? They are not equal and there is no point in pretending otherwise. What the world needs is not for America to disguise its power or to dissemble, but rather to exercise leadership in a spirit of enlightened self-interest, and effectively to run the world in what the conservative writers, William Kristol and Robert Kagan, described as "benevolent global hegemony."[40]

But given the obvious problems and the signs all around us, not of American leadership but of American exceptionalism and triumphalism, what grounds are there for hoping that America will meet this challenge and behave in an enlightened way to enhance the prosperity of the whole world? First, its security is manifestly deeply connected with the prosperity of the whole world. Indeed, in this regard we have just lived through an event that will reshape the world to come as surely as a much earlier event shaped the twentieth century.

American hegemony

The assassination in Sarajevo, the capital of Bosnia, of Archduke Franz Ferdinand on June 28, 1914 set in train events that transformed the world. In the carnage of the First World War there perished not just millions of men but also the whole international order. The age of empires was over.

In the slaughter of the innocents in New York and Washington on September 11, 2001 another world order perished. The age of petty national-ism, created by the end of empire, was finished, and a new sort of imperialism was about to begin. What these events brought home was that the world's only superpower was not safe in its own backyard. Accordingly, the traditional response of America to the horrors of the outside world, isolationism, was no longer an option. To be truly safe America had to reorder the outside world and make sure that "failed states" did not harbor and support terrorists.

This doctrine soon led to the invasion of Afghanistan, but it was surely only with the attack on Iraq in 2003 that the full implications became clear. The United States was now prepared to undermine the established inter-national order based on sovereign states, underpinned by the United Nations, and to substitute the Pax Americana.

The immediate reason, of course, was perceived self-interest, namely ensuring America's security. However, the underlying moral justification was broader, and was similar to the factor that drove and motivated America's former opposition to the European empires: the international order had lost legitimacy. Brutal, corrupt, and rapacious governments, although they might be sovereign, had no right to respect. As I write, it looks to me as though it will soon be believed that they have no right to sovereignty either.

America is on the road to creating a new sort of empire. It will not look the same as the British Empire. It won't consist of colonies but of protectorates. Yet like the British before it, its tentacles will extend well beyond its apparent boundaries to encompass most of the world.

While the immediate driver of these developments is to do with security, there is a marked economic aspect, not least because impoverished countries are more likely to be breeding grounds for extremism and fundamentalism. Reducing the supply of terrorists requires the world's impoverished millions to share in the new prosperity of the economy of the future.

Moreover, once the concept of sovereignty has been undermined on security grounds, it is undermined on economic grounds also. In the future, how is America going to react to the idea of a blatantly corrupt African dictator continuing to impoverish his people because he rules over a sovereign country? If I am right about the logic underlying future American international economic policy, then there is a powerful reason why the underdeveloped countries will not now languish in poverty: the rest of the world— or, more particularly, the United States—will not let them.

Interestingly, this logic seems to have been accepted not only on the right but also on the left of the American political spectrum. American Democratic Presidential candidates John Kerry and Joe Lieberman urge not withdrawal from Afghanistan and Iraq, but greater involvement. Whatever other politicians may currently say and whatever masses of US voters currently think, the post-September 11 logic is irresistible. Isolation and withdrawal make America intensely vulnerable. Only engagement and involvement can bring security.

The reasons for hope

There are already signs of new thinking on these issues in the White House. Most particularly, President Bush has announced the objective of forming a US–Middle East free-trade zone by 2013. The economic potential is huge. The only county in the region to have signed a free-trade agreement with America so far is Jordan and its exports to America rose from $7 million in 1987 to $420 million in 2002.[41]

The gap between potential and reality is not confined to the Middle East. American trade policy can play a key role in Latin America. Brazil faces high American trade barriers on its exports in many activities where it has a strong competitive advantage, including steel, shoes, ethanol, citrus products, and sugar.[42]

Clearly, though, good intentions are not enough. The countries of the Middle East are among the most protected in the world. And while the Arab–Israeli conflict continues and the Arab world sees America as hopelessly biased toward Israel, then success in dismantling trade barriers and thereby allowing in American (and Israeli) goods will probably remain elusive.

Equally, America's objective is to introduce not only economic but also political liberalization. Institutional reform is sorely needed. In 2000, a survey of Arab companies revealed that weak legal systems that fail to enforce contracts are considered the single biggest obstacle to commerce.[43] But it remains to be seen how attempts at reform driven by America will be received.

Moreover, it is still to be decided whether it is possible to marry a modern secular state with Islam; if you like, whether it is possible to have an Islamic enlightenment that effectively secularizes the religion. The only state that can reasonably be regarded as having done this is Turkey, but it is hardly a raging economic success and it has managed to keep religious fundamentalism at bay only through repeated interventions by the fanatically secular armed forces.

There is no doubt that the barriers are huge. Yet not all of the evidence of the past is negative. America has shown enlightened self-interest on a massive scale in the past. After all, it turned its back on the protectionism of the 1930s when fashioning the multilateral trading system that brought such prosperity in the 50 years after the Second World War. And it was America that both gave aid and brought institutional reform to its defeated enemy, Japan, and pumped huge amounts of money into Europe under the Marshall Plan.

The upshot, I believe, is that America is set to embark on a program designed to bring all the countries of the world into a single economic system, divided by all sorts of differences but united in the pursuit of prosperity, under American hegemony.

There may be aspects of this regime that you do not like—indeed, that I do not like—but all the evidence of history suggests that the consequences of such a framework will enhance global prosperity. Anyway, like it or loathe it, this is the inevitable consequence of the forces unleashed on September 11, 2001.

The Take-off Point

Since the Industrial Revolution there have been two examples of a long boom: between 1870 and 1913 and between 1950 and 1973, the Golden Age. They, and the Industrial Revolution before them, were each driven forward by the interaction between the exploitation of new technology and substantially increased international trade, underpinned by an institutional structure that favored economic progress. In the present conjuncture we have the makings of another long boom.

There are eight key factors that favor enhanced prosperity:

- A backlog of underexploited technology.
- Exciting, transforming technologies appearing on the horizon.
- Scope for faster knowledge discovery and application.
- Massive potential for expanded international trade.
- An institutional structure in the developed countries that fosters and encourages economic progress.
- The effective end of an impoverishing ideology.
- A new-found understanding of the institutional and social foundations of successful development.
- A fresh determination on the part of the global leader, the United States, to see good government and competitive markets prevail across the whole world.

The combination of these factors produces a unique conjuncture. There has never been a fully interconnected world. Until the Middle Ages the leader, China, was relatively isolated. By the time Europe was better connected to the East through sea travel, China was already in decline and substantially cut itself off. After the Industrial Revolution, Europe pulled away and achieved a level of prosperity that set it, and soon North America, apart from the rest of the world.

In the twentieth century a further division was created by the split between communism and capitalism, which cut across the geographical divisions of East and West and the division between developed and under-developed countries. The result was a fractured world, only a relatively small part of which was able to enjoy a high level of prosperity and a rapid rate of advancement while the rest was consigned to backwardness. This was even true during the much vaunted Golden Age. Large parts of the world were mainly excluded from this wave of prosperity: not only the communist countries, including China and Russia, but also the Asian Tigers, many of which were under colonial rule and progressed only slowly in the 1950s and 1960s.

There is now a chance for economic history to speed up and for much of humankind to jump the stages of economic development. We are at the take-off point into a future of untold wealth and prosperity. This vision is no pipedream. Its essential features are already taking shape. On the horizon we can begin to discern the form of what is heading ineluctably toward us—the economy of the future.

Part III

The Economy of the Future

Introduction

Assuming that we manage to navigate our way through the shark-infested waters of the immediate present that I described in Part I (and quite how that can be done is a subject I take up in the Finale), the forces analyzed in Part II will be free to work a transformation in the world economy.

The scene is set for the economy of the future, a time of promise and prosperity, when we can not only enjoy increased material wealth but could also realize our full human potential. In what follows here in Part III, I describe how matters will develop over a wide time horizon. Some of what I have to say refers to the next one or two years, while some applies to the decade ahead—and beyond. The timing should be obvious from the context, but whenever I can I try to make it clear.

My vision of the economy of the future comprises four parts:

- The future of finance, and all those employed in it.
- The world of business, the winners and losers, and how companies will change.
- What life will be like for people: how they will earn their living, spend their money, and find their fulfillment.
- A question of values—what it is all about. The purpose of work, effort, and money in a world of superabundance.

7

The Finance of the Future

I used to think if there was reincarnation, I wanted to come back as the President or the Pope or a .400 baseball hitter. But now I want to come back as the bond market. You can intimidate everybody.
James Carville, adviser to Bill Clinton in the 1992 Presidential election campaign[1]

There is no anguish like the anguish of the man who is trying to extract cash from a fellow human being and suddenly finds the fellow human being trying to extract it from him.
P.G. Wodehouse, *Money for Nothing*[2]

At the beginning of the twenty-first century, there is nothing unusual about someone having their life reshaped by the poor performance of the financial markets. The developed countries are full of such people, especially in America. Often the consequence of financial loss is the enforced deferment of plans for retirement. In the case of one 70-year-old man, however, the consequence was exactly the reverse. In 2000, after a couple of bad years in the markets, he retired. Mind you, his position was a bit out of the ordinary. His net worth? About $5 billion—having already given $2.8 billion to charity.[3] What makes this so remarkable is that all this wealth had been amassed through speculating in the financial markets.

Nevertheless, even George Soros got his fingers burnt at the end of the 1990s. He lost $2 billion in the Russian default in 1998. The following year he lost $700 million betting that internet stocks would fall. (Right idea; wrong timing.) He then rushed to buy tech stocks just before the NASDAQ plunged in the spring of 2000, taking his losses to $3 billion. So it was time to fold his tents.

What had Soros achieved? His greatest claim to lasting credit is having forced the British pound out of the ERM in 1992, thereby facilitating a decade of good economic performance in the UK. His reward? A cool $2 billion. Talk about money for nothing!

It was financial markets that not only brought Soros his billions but also brought the world economy to the current pretty pass, so it is appropriate that we should begin thinking about the wealth of the future by considering how the end of the wealth illusion and the strengthening of the forces of real wealth creation will affect them. The behavior of financial markets and the returns offered by investments, which formed the substance of the problems discussed in Part I, will be transformed. In particular, as low inflation and even deflation alter the investment scene radically, investors will have to learn not to expect anything like Soros-type returns in the years ahead. Meanwhile, two of the forces that I argued in Part II will bring enrichment to the world, the Intangible Revolution and globalization, will have major effects on the financial services industry, bringing benefits to all those who use them; although not necessarily for those people working there.

In the high finance of the future, economic policy will also be transformed by the end of the wealth illusion and the shift into the economy of the future. (I briefly discuss policy in the Finale.)

In short, all those whose future depends on financial markets, including the millions who work in them, are going to be in for a major shock.

Continued Illusions

What sort of return can investors reasonably expect from their wealth in the economy of the future? Not what they received in years gone by. The realized returns of equity investors over the last 20 years are unrepeatable. Still, the prevailing view in some quarters is that even if these juicy returns prove unreasonable for the immediate future, once the market has returned to "normal" they will be back on the menu again.

Who can blame people for clinging on to these absurd expectations? After all, that is the way the investment industry has led them to think about the future, by looking at past performance.[4] What is more, investors continue to have to run the gauntlet of "advisers" and "experts" who are predicting another great bull surge in the stock market. Incredibly after the massive price falls of 2001–2003, the snake-oil salesmen remain in business. Typically they peddle some overwhelming force that will override normal considerations of value.

A favorite source of such forces is "demographics." The argument usually involves American baby-boomers now saving for retirement or European firms and governments wanting to turn unfunded pension liabilities into funded ones. The result is that, in the argot, there is a "wall of money" set to go into stocks, come what may. In that case, the stock-market weakness of 2001 and 2002 will be a flash in the pan and the prices ruling in 2005 represent a wonderful opportunity. So you had better get in quick, right?

This argument is so misguided that it is difficult to know where to begin. For a start, even if this demographic view is appropriate as a short-term *explanation* of high stock-market values, it would be no sort of justification. It depends on investors being blind to the poor value that shares offered, or carrying on regardless, investing in them like automata, as though there were no alternative. Of course there is an alternative, namely cash. If investors were convinced that stocks offered very bad value, to the point that they were likely to fall, surely they would prefer to hold their money in cash. In practice, it would only take a small proportion of investors to see this blinding light for the whole edifice to come crashing down.[5]

So much for the wall-of-money argument. Nevertheless, watch out. This argument has such remarkable robustness, and pays such scant regard to the facts, that in the economy of the future it is bound to crop up again in some other form and tantalize more gullible investors. Coming soon, to an investment adviser near you…

Investment without Fantasies

The key to protecting and growing your wealth in the economy of the future is to go back to first principles. Isn't it still right to presume that equities will in the long run give a higher return than bonds? Yes, or rather yes but. It is true that over long time horizons in the past stocks have come out well. For periods of 20 years and over, there is not a single year in the twentieth century when an investment in US stocks, taking account of both capital gains and dividend income, would have yielded less than zero in real terms. As I noted in Chapter 2, even if you had bought on the eve of the Great Crash of 1929, and completely forgetting about dividends, you would have got your money back in the end. Mind you, you would have needed to wait until 1954, 25 years later.[6] These holding periods are much too long for many investors.

Moreover, even over protracted periods the prospective return on equities is not as spectacular as many investors seem to think. *Provided that equities start from a reasonable basis of valuation*, equity investors should expect to receive the risk-free rate of return available on government bonds plus a risk premium. Few analysts have argued that the risk premium that equities should earn over risk-free bonds should be any less than 1 percent or greater than 5 percent. So if the risk-free real rate of interest were 3 percent, *once the market has returned to a reasonable basis of valuation*, this puts the range of reasonable real rates of return on equities between 4 and 8 percent; and I think that the lower end is much more plausible.[7] With inflation rates very low, sometimes zero and perhaps even negative, the nominal returns will not be much different.

Thus I am suggesting that 4–5 percent, a rate of return at which not so long ago most investors would have turned their noses up, may be a perfectly reasonable expectation, once stocks have settled to a reasonable price in relation to the economic fundamentals.

Another way to think about this is to see equities as giving the holder a stake in the real growth of the economy. *Once they are at a reasonable starting point*, the price of equities should rise in line with the value of the economy's total output. If the economy is growing at 3 percent real and the inflation rate is 2 percent, meaning that the money value of GDP is growing at 5 percent, then 5 percent is the warranted rate of increase of equity prices. If the rate of inflation is zero and real growth is still 3 percent, then the warranted rate of increase of equity prices will be only 3 percent.

Both these approaches to the market are predicated on market prices being in line with the fundamentals to start with. If they are well above them, warranted equity returns will be lower than the formula suggests. If they are well below them, warranted equity returns will be higher. It was precisely because this proviso was ignored in the great bull market that so many people thought that equities were guaranteed to return so much above government bonds, regardless.

These prospective returns may seem particularly low given the forces making for strong real growth in the economy that I analyzed in Part II. If real growth rates are higher than in the recent past, then real returns on equities may well be somewhat higher. But investors should beware. As I argue in Chapter 8, in the economy of the future there will be powerful competitive forces acting to distribute the fruits of real growth to consumers rather than companies. Moreover, even if the prospect of higher growth does justify some increase in share prices now, the size of the boost will be very small compared to the apparent multiplication of wealth that occurred during the bubble. Furthermore, investors must bear in mind that a large part of future real profits will accrue to companies that are not yet in existence, or, if they are, do not issue publicly quoted shares.

To buy or not to buy?

Although I firmly believe that the above approach will give you a sound way of evaluating investment in equities, I fully recognize that you may not find it very helpful. What you want to know is whether you should buy or sell stocks! But I cannot begin to tell you whether you should buy or sell stocks when you read this. How could I possibly do that? I do not know what the price of stocks is for you "now." As I write, I do not even know what the price "was" when this book was published.

Nevertheless, I do have a few suspicions about the shape of the market over the next few years. Even though, beginning from the situation in mid-2005, stocks look as though they will prove a moderate investment, I believe there are likely to be good buying opportunities in the years ahead. As a result of the history of desperate disappointment with the market and severe pressures on the corporate sector over the next few years, many investors will turn away from equities altogether. They will conclude that there is something wrong with this whole asset class; or, at the very least, that it simply isn't for them. In the process they will be making a similar mistake to the one they made in the bull market of the late 1990s; that is to say, latching on to an investment idea without due regard to the central thing that makes investments tick—the price.

For some very large investors, however, there may not be much choice. In the heady days of the bubble, British insurance companies and pension funds held extraordinarily high proportions of their assets in equities. Now they will be restrained by law, market pressure, or a sense of self-preservation to hold much smaller proportions. In particular, it is coming to be realized that the pension funds of companies should not be taking large bets on the equity market and thereby endangering the viability of their sponsoring companies. Their pension liabilities are much more appropriately matched by holding bonds. Moreover, as the British retailer Boots discovered when it shifted its pension fund assets wholly into bonds, the costs of running the fund can be sharply reduced as well. The consequence will be that as more pension funds switch money from equities into bonds, the natural constituency for holding equities will be much reduced.

As a result of the shunning of equities, I suspect that the stock market will be driven *below* fair value, just as in the euphoric period it was driven well above it. In other words, although from the market values holding as I write this in mid-2005 equities do not look outstandingly good value, I would not give up on them as an asset class.

Interestingly, over the last 100 years, for holding periods of 20 years all the bad years to have bought US stocks bar one come from the late 1920s and the late 1960s to early 1970s. In both periods, according to Smithers and Wright, there was near-universal agreement "that things were going swimmingly, with the economy in excellent shape." By contrast, the best year to have bought stocks was 1932, which was widely regarded, and still is, as being one of the most disastrous for the United States in the whole of the twentieth century.[8] So perhaps if the next couple of years match my direst fears about the world economy, at the very least there will be some outstanding opportunities to buy stock.

Dividends and interest

During the stock-market mania, as I stressed in Chapter 1, it was customary for investors not to be too fussed about dividends.[9] In the economy of the future, this is going to change. Income will again be a significant component of the expected returns on stock. It could even be the main part.[10]

Then surely the investments that hold out the prospect of income alone, namely bonds and deposits, should be center stage. But what sort of return will they give investors? "Not much" is going to be the answer. The aftermath of the bubble is so severe that escaping from the threats I described in Part I may well require in the immediate future a long period of very low interest rates; perhaps even zero rates. Accordingly, the returns to depositors will be pretty low. If official rates have to fall to zero, deposit rates cannot be much above zero and may even be marginally below it.

In that case bond yields may fall further from the already low levels experienced in mid-2005, thereby conferring capital gains on the present holders of such bonds.[11] After all, in the 1930s long bond yields fell below 3 percent in America. The US long bond yield reached a low of $2\frac{1}{4}$ percent just after the war. Moreover, recent Japanese experience illustrates that given very low short rates, bond yields can come very low indeed, under the pressure of deflation. Japanese 10-year yields have recently been as low as 0.7 percent.[12]

While rates at 3 percent may seem fantastical, they were the norm for the bulk of the nineteenth century and the attractions of a holding in government bonds, yielding what to 1990s investors would have seemed a pittance, is a recurring feature of nineteenth-century literature. In Trollope's novel *Dr Thorne*, for instance, published in 1858, the eponymous hero fails to secure his future by investing £3–4,000 (about £300,000 or $450,000 now) in the "Three Per Cents."[13]

The emergence of deflation could make a significant difference to yields. Without the possibility of deflation, the inflation risk for bond holders is asymmetric. The downside risk of an upsurge of inflation is unbounded, but the upside risk of a fall in inflation is bounded at zero. With deflation that zero barrier is breached and the risk becomes more balanced. I suspect that the first experience of deflation may cause investors to see falling prices as a part of a new regime rather than a flash in the pan. (As I have repeatedly argued, they may be right.) Moreover, short-term interest rates may have to stay very low for a protracted period and the expectation of this will drag long rates down. Accordingly, long bond yields may stand much closer to short rates than you might ordinarily expect and the yield curve should in normal circumstances be fairly flat.

Once the immediate problems of deficient demand are over, however, in the economy of the future both short-term interest rates and bond yields can be rather higher. Indeed, if I am right in thinking that the sustainable growth rates of the developed world can speed up, the real rate of interest (and bond yields) should be higher than in the recent past. (See the Finale.) Unfortunately, that should not make all *prospective* holders of bonds and deposits crack open the champagne. If economic growth (and therefore real interest rates) were to be 1 percent higher that would be a fantastic result for the economy, but a 1 percent increase in the real return per annum doesn't exactly set the pulse racing (even though it properly should). Of course, for existing holders of bonds a rise in the market yield would land them with capital losses.

How all this translates into the interest rates and bond yields that are eventually received by investors obviously depends on the transition from real to nominal; that is to say, on the rate of inflation. You will already know my views on that score. An inflation rate of about 2 percent is widely taken for granted, but I believe that the major risks to this scenario are on the downside. There is a good chance that the rate may come to average out at somewhere close to zero. On this basis nominal interest rates may be not that much higher than real rates, if at all. While deflation is occurring, nominal rates will be *lower* than real rates.

The upshot is that in the economy of the future, once the immediate period of super-low or even near-zero interest rates is over, for both short-term interest rates and bond yields the *normal* range may be 2–6 percent, with 4 or even 3 percent a perfectly reasonable level.

Pensions and Annuities

In Anglo-Saxon countries this will come as a shock and a considerable disappointment to many prospective pensioners, because it implies that the "low" annuity[14] rates of recent years are set to continue, or even to fall further. I have some sympathy with their plight; but only some. I have more sympathy for prospective pensioners in the UK, because there anyone who has a money-purchase pension scheme is *obliged* to take an annuity at retirement, which is a distinct infringement of their freedom. In other countries you are not obliged to take an annuity and there is therefore a choice and an escape, if annuities are for some reason unreasonably expensive.[15]

However, my sympathy runs out when people complain about how low the annuity rates are without distinguishing between real and nominal rates. The overwhelming bulk of the fall in annuity rates over the last 20 years has been a reflection of the fall in inflation. Annuitants are not significantly worse off in real terms than they were in the old days of 15 percent annuity rates and high inflation.[16]

Many a pensioner has difficulty recognizing this because they pay insufficient attention to what happens to the real value of a pension over time. Compared to a regime of low annuity rates and low inflation, a regime of high annuity rates and high inflation redistributes real income across the pensioner's life, toward the early years and away from the later years of retirement. In the past, many a pensioner retired on what seemed to be a good income only to end their days in penury. This is conveniently forgotten by many who complain about today's low annuity rates. What pensioners naturally want is high annuity rates and low inflation, but that is wanting to have your cake and eat it—and that particular form of money for nothing is not on offer.

Pensioners can expect no relief in the economy of the future. While annuity rates will be "low" in nominal terms, so will inflation and the two will be broadly offsetting. There will be no cause for pensioner anguish on that score—although there may be on others.

The pension system of the future

In Chapter 2 I stressed how the developed countries faced a pensions crisis that imperiled the corporate sector and could destabilize the whole economic system. Once the immediate crisis is over it might be possible for things to carry on much as before, although I seriously doubt that this will happen. Rather, after the shattering of the illusions that have shielded companies, pensioners, and governments from the truth, there is likely to be a reworking of the whole pensions system.

The Anglo-Saxon countries plus the Netherlands have tended to congratulate themselves on having provided satisfactorily for pensions by running pension schemes that are largely funded, as opposed to the pay-as-you-go systems predominating on the continent. But this is largely an illusion. The only way a society can build up assets to finance consumption in the future is to lay down extra capital or to build up financial claims on other countries, which are run down in the future. Widespread saving through pension funds principally bids up the price of existing assets, with little if any effect on the level of real investment in the economy. Indeed, the investment rate of the US and the UK has tended to be low compared to those countries with unfunded schemes, such as France and Germany.

Meanwhile, although the buildup of foreign assets is a plausible scenario for any one country individually, clearly it is a complete nonstarter for all countries taken together. Net overseas investment for the world as a whole must equal zero.

The basic reality of all pension systems is that those who have stopped working have to be provided for by those who are still working. This is as true for a funded pension system as for an unfunded one. The pensioner's hot lunch has to be cooked today, and if she wants to spruce herself up her hair has to be cut today, even if the money to pay for these services was saved 30 years ago.

Funded private-sector systems do have certain advantages. First, with designated financial claims it is not easy for the younger generation to renege on the commitment to support the older generation without disavowing the whole institution of private property. Second, the flow of funds into pension schemes may stimulate higher investment in the economy (although, as I argued above, the evidence is far from compelling that this has happened much in practice). Third, having pensions privately funded rather than provided by the state out of general taxation avoids the distortions and disincentives created by taxation.

The disadvantages of this system, however, are plain for all to see. Most particularly, companies can be endangered by the scale of their pension obligations. (Admittedly, unfunded private-sector pension schemes, such as those proliferating on the European continent, also potentially endanger the viability of the sponsoring companies.) The result is going to be widespread cutbacks in company pension provision through the progressive closure of final-salary schemes and their replacement by much cheaper and less risky money-purchase schemes, which offer less protection to employees.

Meanwhile, in Britain certainly but also to some extent in most other developed countries, in the public sector pensions are both secure and generous, being determined by final salary, index linked, and guaranteed by the state. The worth of these pension entitlements is only now coming to be appreciated as the scale of the private-sector pension crisis becomes apparent.

There is now a serious risk that the economy of the future will be marred by a striking inequality in pension treatment as society is divided into three tiers: the top tier consisting of public-sector pensioners and lucky members of surviving and solvent private final-salary schemes; a middle tier of those with a mixture of various barely adequate private schemes, both final salary and money purchase; and a huge underclass of those with next to no provision, who have to rely on the state.

What is the way out of this unattractive prospect? The logic of the situation points to a solution involving compulsory saving, deducted from income by the government but with the money amassed in a designated investment fund. One model of such an arrangement is the system used in Singapore. Its Central Provident Fund (CPF), established in 1955, requires total contributions of 40 percent of covered pay up to a maximum of $45,800 a year, half of which comes from employers and the other half from employees. Subject to certain limits, members can draw on their funds for designated purposes such as financing a house purchase, paying for health insurance, or providing funds for education. However, the Singaporean scheme has come in for heavy criticism on the grounds that it is too statist and allows no scope for variety and competition. Furthermore, historically the returns to savers have been poor because although the savings have been largely invested abroad, the excess returns have gone to the government.

A more attractive solution may be to adopt something like the Chilean model. Again, contributions are compulsory but there are many institutions that can receive and invest the savings and individual savers can choose which one to put their money in. Several countries either have or are about to install versions of the Chilean system, including Argentina, Hong Kong, Mexico, Poland, and Uruguay.[17]

Housing as an Investment

A common reaction to the disastrous performance of many pension funds has been for people to turn away from both the stock market and all organized saving and instead put money into residential property. Once the present housing bubble has burst and house prices have stabilized, there is no reason why holdings of residential property should not form a significant part of people's wealth portfolios and even constitute a large part of their individual pension funds—provided that their expectations of return are not founded on the financial fantasies of the past.

Nevertheless, there are several cautionary factors to be borne in mind. For a start, in many countries the overwhelming bulk of the investment returns to residential property ownership in the past have come from inflation. That is to say, although property ownership has given the owners protection against inflation, the real capital gains have been comparatively small. In the new era of low or no inflation, the returns on housing will be more or less totally dependent on real increases in value. In conditions of deflation, house prices may readily fall.

Moreover, there is a world of difference between the returns enjoyed by householders occupying their own property and those earned on a property let out to tenants, not least because in most countries there are significant tax advantages applying to owner occupation but not to letting property out to tenants. And although this point has been obscured by often high increases in house prices, the property *does* have to be let out for it to register a decent return. Merely leaving a property to lie idle and relying on capital appreciation is most unlikely to be a profitable strategy, particularly not in an era when deflation is an ever-present danger. But getting and keeping tenants may also not be easy. By contrast, when you occupy your own property you are always assured a tenant: yourself.

Furthermore, there are substantial expenses involved in owning and maintaining a property that do not apply to shares and bonds. These may readily amount to 1–2 percent per annum. And for tenanted properties the expenses are usually much higher than for owner-occupied ones.

The property of the future

Nevertheless, over the coming decades as we get richer, property is one thing of real economic substance that will be scarce, and its price, once the current housing bubble is over, may be expected to rise relative to basic goods and services.

Fly into any large city today and you see substantial blocks of apartments housing people in cramped conditions. It is only money that keeps them there; or rather the lack of it. As they get richer they will seek to spend a good proportion of the increase on better accommodation and that means more space. More space means more demand for land. Land is what they don't make any more, which means its price should rise. In some countries in western Europe this pressure will be tempered, or even more than offset, by the projected fall in population levels, but elsewhere population is set to rise for some considerable time to come, thereby adding fuel to the fire.

Even so, compared to the current property bonanza the rates of increase of prices will be modest. The real price of property may be able to rise at something like 2–4 percent per annum. In an age of near-zero inflation, of course, that will mean that nominal prices increase at about that rate too. That is not a bad return—even though it has to be set against the expenses I discussed above—but it is well short of the rates of increase achieved in many European countries over the last decade and will hardly set the property speculator's pulse racing.

There is an added complication—and risk. In the economy of the future, it will not be any old property that the newly affluent masses will want to buy. They will all want something better. Ironically in a world that supposedly spells the death of distance, polarization may sharply affect the price of property with regard to both quality and location. If you are connected to the internet, supposedly you can work almost anywhere. This could be thought to equalize prices as one place is now considered to be as good as any other. Nevertheless, the continuing need for personal contact that I discuss in Chapter 9, and the tendency toward specialization and agglomeration discussed in Chapter 5, mean that for the foreseeable future one place will *not* be thought to be as good as any other.

And whatever is necessary for the world of work, one place will never be as *pleasant* as any other. Given that we will still exist somewhere other than in cyberspace, there will surely be an increased desire to live in the places, and in the sorts of accommodation, judged to be the most desirable. So the result of increasing wealth created by the intangible will be the increasing desirability of just about the most tangible thing imaginable: land. This may be one of the primary ways in which people, newly enriched, seek to improve their lives and distinguish themselves from their contemporaries, by paying good money not so much for some*thing* as for some*where*.

The upshot is that if you want to jump on to the property bandwagon you will have to be sure to choose the right vehicle. Apartments in blocks near the world's airports may easily fall in value and before too long be so undesirable that they are demolished in huge numbers. At the other extreme, apartments with a prized view of Central Park or Hyde Park will probably appreciate sharply. This is a prime example of the irresistible force of increasing demand meeting the immovable object of fixed supply.

Mind you, we cannot all get rich by letting out apartments to each other. Similarly, even though the appreciation in value for trophy properties will confer capital gains on their owners, this in no way connotes an increase in wealth for society as a whole. All that is happening is a transfer of wealth to those who own such properties from those who don't. In the economy of the future, when property values start to rise again, this will be the result of the scarcity of land and good location, not the result of any "productivity" revolution in the output of the services that property provides. So for society as a whole, rising property prices most certainly do *not* offer the prospect of money for nothing.

Managing the Wealth of the Future

In that case, where is the investor of the future to go for super returns? Where is the asset that will bring easy money? It doesn't exist. Investors will have to get used to the idea that sometimes there is no asset that can yield the 15 or 20 percent to which they have become used. There will always be assets that are driven up on speculative waves and the canny and the quick may be able to ride the bubble and get out in time. This is hardly a contradiction, because again it is simply a recipe for one investor to get rich at the expense of others. Quite apart from the ethics of the issue, clearly all investors will not be able to avail themselves of this opportunity. Most would be best advised not even to try.

Instead, if you are to manage your wealth successfully in the future, you would do well to abide by four simple principles, outlined below.

- *Think real.* Changes in the value of money itself have caused gross distortions to investment performance in the past through inflation and they could do so again, especially if we undergo periods of deflation. The way to avoid these distortions is to think, and to calculate, real; that is to say, in this context to think in the money values of a single year, say 2005, and be alive to the possibility that disturbances to the price level may cause substantial real capital gains and losses, in the way I outlined in Chapter 3.
- *Think long term.* In the economy, as opposed to the fantasy world of the financial markets, real investments do not bear fruit in a matter of weeks or even months. Rather, they take many years and sometimes even decades. Financial markets enable financial investments to be separated from this real investment and thereby serve the essential purpose of providing liquidity for the individual investor that is not available to society as a whole. Nevertheless, it is important not to be misled by this liquidity. Trading cannot be the source of profit for investors overall. This simple fact has been obscured by the long bull market that has convinced millions of people that they are expert traders, adept at getting their timing right, whereas in fact they have been merely riding the upwave.
- *Minimize expenses.* Again, this ties in with not trading a great deal. In the long bull market it was common for investors not to think too much about the expenses of dealing—commissions, price spreads, and taxes—but these eat into the overall profits of investment considerably, without collectively raising the return one little bit.
- *Match up your investment to the fruitfulness of the real economy.* This principle really brings the other three together. The key is to ask where the prospective profit from an investment derives from. Is it a company's superior management team? Does the company have excellent products that competitors will not be able to match? Are the attractions you see equally obvious to other investors, so that they are already reflected in the market price? If an investment seems to be too good to be true, it probably is. This

principle may help investors to avoid being caught up in scams and frauds, and to draw a clear distinction between investment and gambling:

Margins under Pressure

If the behavior of the markets will be different in the economy of the future, the financial sector is set to undergo radical changes brought about by the combination of a regime of prolonged low inflation, the technological advances of the Intangible Revolution, and the reaction to the bursting of the bubble.

Inflation has been the great deceiver, confusing people about real values as they became befuddled by the rapid increase in prices and found it difficult to compare prices over time. The world started to undergo the transition to a regime of low inflation in the early 1980s, but different parts of the economy fell into line at different times. Company pricing behavior was forced to adapt pretty quickly. The setting of wage and salary rates was slower; the setting of interest rates and bond yields in financial markets slower still, but the structure and practices of the financial services industry did not adjust at all.

The reason was simply the illusion spawned by the great bull market. This meant that the returns on financial assets continued at rates recalling the earlier inflationary period even while, in the world of nonfinancial business, companies were having to grapple with disinflationary and even deflationary forces.[18]

But now things have changed. Interest rates and bond yields are very low and the stock market looks set to deliver pedestrian returns, or worse. Think about what this transition does for all those businesses supplying some sort of intermediary financial service and taking a cut out of the investor's overall return. When the overall return to investors is 15 percent, the odd 1 or 2 percent might not go amiss. But when the return is 4 percent, the odd 1 or 2 percent sticks out like a sore thumb. And what about when the return is zero, or even *minus* 15 percent?

This pressure on margins will apply across the financial system, from banking to investment management. Official interest rates could not be negative but they could be stuck at low levels for a considerable time (see the Finale). Suppose they are zero. It is not going to be easy for banks to charge customers 1 or 2 percent for the privilege of entrusting their savings to them. But with official interest rates at zero, competitive pressures will mean that borrowers will expect some mouth-wateringly low borrowing rates. The result is bound to be a squeeze on margins.

In investment management it is a similar story. Who will want to be paying 1 or 2 percent per annum for the privilege of having their wealth managed down? Again, competitive stresses will intensify and this sector, where staff levels and remuneration boomed in the bubble years, will be under sharp downward pressure. This is bound to fan out into all those other businesses in financial markets linked to the money managers: the brokers and investment banks, the analysts and tipsters, and the shoals of other fish that swim in their wake and feed off their scraps.

Putting your money where your mouse is

If these demands were not enough, the financial services industry is also going to be under stress from the Intangible Revolution. The whole of its business is essentially intangible and large swathes of it can be digitized. At the wholesale level, the trading of bonds, shares, foreign exchange, and deposits over the internet is rapidly catching on, reducing the need for human intervention and putting sharp downward pressure on costs (and therefore on the *salaries* of people working) in the financial services industry. The result is that the level of employment in the wholesale financial markets is set to fall.

As far as retail services are concerned, in the US shares are already widely dealt over the internet, and deposits, loans, and mortgages can be set up online. The European experience with online share dealing is mixed. In the UK large numbers of online stockbrokers are having to fight for business in a demanding market.[19]

Already, even in the short life of e-commerce, a pattern is beginning to emerge. Clearly, with large-scale financial products such as a mortgage or a pension, even more than with an important consumer good such as a new car or a holiday, trust is absolutely essential. The very intangibility of the financial contract may mean that people place even more value on signs of substance and reality on the part of the provider. In the nineteenth century banks placed great store by having elegant marble entrance halls because this was a sign to the public that they were sound; it may be that customers need similar reassurance now.[20]

Nevertheless, in the economy of the future the greater tendency for consumers to do financial business and compare prices over the internet will put increased pressure on the employment of people as the mere executors of financial transactions. To have a continuing role they will have to offer an additional service. Many, perhaps most, will not be able to. The financial sector is about to go through the scale of revolutionary change and thinning out that earlier beset industries such as shipbuilding and car manufacturing.

Clearing out the Augean stables

There will also be some major changes to the financial services industry as a direct result of the bubble—and its bursting. If the behavior of corporate executives during this episode is an area of concern, then the behavior of the Wall Street investment community, and its London satellite, is just as serious. From beginning to end, this is an industry in dire need of reform. Its role in the stock-market boom is nothing short of scandalous.

In the UK there is particular anguish over what has happened to so-called split capital investment trusts. Many investors evidently took these out as low-risk investments, but in fact some of them were highly geared plays on the level of the equity market. Some of the managers of such trusts have defended themselves on the premise that when the trusts were launched they were rightly described as low risk because no one had anticipated the scale of the subsequent falls in share prices, and in particular that the market could fall for three years in succession.

But what about the string of academic and market commentators who warned of the severe overvaluation of the markets and in particular the comparison with the 1930s? And isn't thinking about risk supposed to encompass things that you don't believe *will* happen but just *might*?

Much of the financial services industry has been peopled by individuals who have no knowledge of history or of economics, whose pretense to wisdom is a rough familiarity with what has happened over recent years and a touching faith that the immediate future will be exactly like the immediate past. At one level, the financial services industry has a greater concentration of top talent than any other industry in the modern world. At another, it displays a unique combination of blatant incompetence and unbridled greed. For thousands of people in London and New York this remarkable industry really has been a source of money for nothing. For millions of ordinary investors it has been a case of nothing for their money. In the economy of the future this has got to change.

Again, fund management is in for a big shock. It has always struck me as bizarre that firms in the investment management industry should compete largely on the basis of their performance figures over some past period. The notion is, apparently, that if you could deliver that sort of performance before, you can deliver it again. This fails to recognize the extent to which such performance was the product of luck or excessive risk taking, or the extent to which external circumstances have changed to make the achievement of similar returns nigh-on impossible.[21] It is rather as though having successfully backed the winner of the 2.30 horse race at Newmarket, you are presumed to have the answer to life, the universe, and everything.

It has seemed equally bizarre that the industry should employ so many people, many of them highly paid, judging whether the XYZ fund and thousands of others like it should go marginally "long or short of the indices," or marginally long or short of whatever stock or sector that takes their fancy, particularly when we know that most fund managers do not even match the performance of the stock-market indices, let alone beat them. Where is the value created to justify their enormous salaries? The long bull market obscured their poor performance and obscured the costs. Now all will be laid bare.

Admittedly, even in the economy of the future there will be a role for speculative selection of stocks and active asset management. Indeed, as I argued in Chapter 1, without it the efficient markets theory cannot be remotely right and market values are left without an anchor. The health of the market probably requires that *more* money be managed on this basis. However, what we currently have is large numbers of institutions that are closet index trackers, continually looking over their shoulder to see how they stand in relation to each other, yet staffed and paid as though they were star asset managers.

The way this industry should be structured in the economy of the future is for a large chunk of investment fund managers to be making no decisions at all about fund allocation, and therefore incurring very low costs and imposing very low charges.[22] Essentially their role is to act as postboxes, and the rewards of the people who perform this function should have more in common with the rewards of ordinary postmen than with popstars. Meanwhile, the role of assessing market value, and thereby determining market prices, should fall to a number of managers of speculative funds, probably structured along the hedge fund model. Their rewards should be greater, and in some cases may reasonably reach superstar proportions. The rub is that, as in any other activity, the number of superstars will be small.

Naturally, for the swollen ranks of traders, analysts, stock pickers, administrators, and, dare I say it, economists employed under the current regime, demotion to the rank of postman does not appeal—let alone facing the exit. Nevertheless, it is high time that the also-rans of the investment world stopped running off with rich prizes.

All change for the analysts

Structural change is going to be particularly sharp and painful in the world of the research analyst. There is far too much stock-market research, much of it duplicatory, lacking insight, originality, or judgment, and there is a distinct lack of responsiveness to clients.[23] Most importantly, a large part of investment research is produced by analysts employed by major investment banks with large corporate finance departments. It has been observed on numerous occasions that analysts seem to find it extremely difficult to issue sell notices on stocks, and in the internet and dotcom frenzy there were hardly any major "bear pieces" issued by the big houses. This shouldn't be very surprising: the analysts were handsomely paid to produce this puff material.

Yet many clients rely on such research, not purely for information but also to help form their view of the economic fundamentals and the outlook for the markets. It is surely both distinctly odd and thoroughly unhealthy that the whole financial services industry should rely for its investment research on the same institutions that make money by dealing in stocks and securities, and also advise companies on mergers, takeovers, and corporate restructuring.

In late 2002, several large American investment banks were falling over themselves to separate their research departments from corporate finance in order to forestall action by the regulatory authorities; in 2003 it became clear that they faced large fines for past misdemeanors and in the future would indeed need to separate their research functions. By 2005, this had become common practice among investment banks. But I cannot believe that this is the ultimate solution. If research departments are going to be hermetically sealed off from a bank's activities, what is the point of having them there in the first place?

In this regard I must declare an interest. I am the founder and managing director of an independent research company, Capital Economics, so you may want to dismiss what I am about to say on the grounds that I am biased. On the other hand, you may be inclined to believe that my views carry more weight because I have put my money where my mouth is. In the financial markets of the future, there should be three guiding principles for how the provision of research should be organized. First, there should be transparency about who is paying for what. Second, there should be the opportunity not to take something and not to pay for it, while still being able to take other services from a provider. Third, a good proportion of the research available should be independent.[24]

How appropriate it will be when in the economy of the future the bloated financial services industry is cut down to size. At least then the pain of the post-bubble years will have had a purpose. Not only will charges for financial services for both individuals and businesses be lower, but the ridiculously large number of individuals, both untalented and talented, dedicated to the principle of getting rich quick regardless of the social consequences, will be released for more *profitable* (if not more remunerative) employment elsewhere in the economy.

Electronic Money[25]

At the heart of all parts of the financial system is something, or rather a *non-thing*, that could itself be transformed by the Intangible Revolution: money. Money may be fixed in the mind as solid, and not so long ago in our history it was precious metal, but it is in essence thoroughly immaterial. If there is one aspect of the modern economy that above all others should have been transformed by the development of advanced communications technology, and so far hasn't been, it is money.

But it will be. Technological change is creating new methods of transferring value, bringing a radical transformation of the payments system that could render it unrecognizable within a few years. Cash, checks, direct debits, and the rest could be replaced with a new system of immediate value transfer involving smartcards, mobile phones, and PCs. Within the next decade, we could see the emergence of a multitude of different payment mechanisms as the remnants of the old system, heavily based on paper and plastic, compete with new instruments more suited to the electronic age.

As a result of technological progress and the threat of competition, even the existing old-fashioned payment mechanisms will become faster and cheaper, and will adapt to the changing needs of online business. This is one area where the wonders of the computer and the internet can make a huge difference, by both reducing costs and increasing the quality of service.

The costs and charges that consumers and businesses currently pay for money-transmission and payment services, some of them open and some of them hidden, add up to a huge total for the economy as a whole. In

America, according to one estimate, about 5 percent of the value of an average consumer's purchase is eaten up in payment costs. In the UK, the costs to banks and building societies of providing money-transmission services to their customers amount to some 0.7 percent of GDP.[26]

It *could* all be very different. Technological change promises to sweep away many of the practices, institutions, and conventions that we have accepted without question, but that should be viewed as mere relics of our monetary history, including the settlement day, the payment of interest by the day, delay in receiving value, and dealing for "spot" in the wholesale money markets.

In the economy of the future, making payments and transferring money may be so cheap that they will be regarded as virtually free. Anyone will be able to make payments to whomever they like, whenever they like, and in whichever way they like. There will be no settlement delays, mountains of paper, or ludicrous charges. Money will pass between people and businesses as seamlessly as electricity passes along wires. This could work as well for foreign currencies as for domestic money. Whether someone needs to be paid in dollars, euros, or pounds, payment will be instantaneous and cost no more than in domestic money.

This is not mere fantasy. Although there are serious vested interests to overcome and several institutional obstacles remain, it is the way the payments system is already heading. Radical changes could happen sooner than you think. One system that has been operating for a few years in Finland allows consumers at Coke-vending machines to use their mobile phone to call a number advertised on the outside of the vending machine. The cost of a Coke is then added to their phone bill, and they are given a code number to get the drink out of the machine. The system is unsophisticated and clunky, but it has been implemented successfully with the minimum of glitches. In the economy of the future, more and more payments will be made by mobile phone.

Will banks survive?

Some thinkers have even suggested that technological changes could lead to the end of money itself, although my money is on money outlasting the lot of us, including our successors—whatever happens to computer technology.[27] However, if money—like the people who don't have it, the poor—will always be with us, the same is not necessarily true of the institutions that make their living by dealing in it, namely the banks. After all, intermediaries exist as a result of information asymmetries and transaction costs. Information technology can eliminate the asymmetries and sharply reduce the costs.

In the economy of the future, borrowers could fill in (electronically) standardized forms and their loan requests could be aggregated and securitized, and sold by computer to people and companies who have positive cash flows. In this way, banks and other financial institutions would be *disintermediated*, that is, to you and me, done away with. To some extent this is already happening. In the US, securitized mortgages and consumer loans are very common. Nevertheless, intermediaries are surely likely to retain some advantages as "wholesalers," so the disintermediation process will tend to have a limit.

Even if technological change does not lead to the complete extinction of banks, it will surely threaten some of their functions, and may cause those parts that remain to lose their power and importance to other players in the system. Mobile phone operators are the most likely winners. It is interesting that the phone companies already come into direct competition with the credit card companies. For example, if you renew a subscription on mcafee.com you are offered the choice of paying by credit card or with a charge to your telephone account via e-charge.

But there's still life in them there banks. There could be a striking parallel with the challenge posed for the cross-Channel ferry operators by the opening of the Channel Tunnel. Forecasters expected that the increased competition would lead to declining passenger numbers and yields on ferries, and the eventual disappearance of ferry services as the tunnel became dominant.[28] Instead, the ferry companies provided an improved service at a competitive price. In the economy of the future, the banks could readily do something similar and thereby hang on to a substantial part of the money-transmission business. In that case, consumers would be the gainers.[29]

The Insurance of the Future

Advances in information technology will also make possible significant developments in insurance. Conventional types of insurance are already being revolutionized by the availability and analysis of better information about risks with regard to both property and lives. In America, for instance, improvements in credit scoring have led to a sharp reduction in the cost of refinancing a mortgage.

More importantly, there is the potential for insurance to move into whole new areas of risk that are currently uninsurable, thereby ending the gratuitous economic inequality and injustice that occur because particular individuals strike it unlucky in some of the big gambles of life, such as which profession to follow or where to live. For instance, livelihood insurance would be able to protect against long-term risks to individuals' income from economic factors that alter their absolute and relative rewards in those activities.

This idea has been developed and promoted by the American economist Robert Shiller.[30] He gives the example of a young woman who would like to be a violinist but is worried about the risk to her future income. New financial technology will enable her to borrow money to fund the training and her early professional career, money that will not need to be repaid if an index of the earnings of violinists falls below some designated level. The application surely goes much wider to the very substance of this book, namely to the insecurities created by the waves of creative destruction unleashed by international competition and technological change.

Similarly, home equity insurance would provide protection for the economic value of your home—not protection against specific risk such as fire, but against the economic risks arising from factors such as the decline of a local industry. Shiller also thinks that there could be macro markets dealing in such things as the GDP of countries, enabling investors to hedge liabilities and real economic risks and allowing countries themselves to hedge.

These ideas may sound fanciful, but they simply follow a well-worn path in the development of financial markets. Today we take futures markets for granted, but the first did not appear until the 1600s, near Osaka in Japan. We also take life insurance for granted, but it only really emerged in the nineteenth century. The information revolution will bring further financial innovations that will help us to take the risk and uncertainty out of life.

Globalized Finance?

The combination of globalization and the intangibility of financial services would, you might think, have potentially profound effects on the location of financial market activity—and it will, but the process will not be straightforward.

At first sight the financial world is already intensely globalized, with massive amounts of capital flowing across the world, banks and financial companies cross-located in many countries, and the whole international financial system working as an integrated global entity. But when you look at it more closely, it is not quite so globalized.

For a start, although the financial *markets* may seem globalized, financial *services* are clearly not. The overwhelming bulk of banking business, both personal and commercial, is done with domestic banks. For those few people who readily do their banking business with a foreign bank located in their country, this business is usually done in their home currency. Moreover, for long-term financial contracts such as pensions and insurance policies, the financial system is still less globalized. American pensioners draw their pensions from American pension funds and Germans insure their property with German insurance companies. Here the barriers to globalization are not easy to surmount, because they involve differences of law and fear of political instability disrupting long-term financial contracts made with entities across borders.

Even in the European Union, it has been difficult to create a single market in financial services, although one has to assume that in due course it will happen. An integrated market in financial services between Europe, America, and Japan remains a pipedream.

Still, globalization may be able to make a good deal of difference to the process by which financial services are delivered. There is no reason why this could not increasingly include the support functions for the financial markets. Already large numbers of firms have outsourced clerical and call-center work to India and, according to a recent report by Deloitte Consulting, the world's top 100 financial institutions expect to transfer another $350 billion of their cost bases abroad, putting at risk about two million jobs in the developed countries. In this regard, India has a definite advantage over China because of its use of the English language and the infrastructure of laws and institutions on which financial business relies to function effectively. The Deloitte study identified India as likely to be the major offshore hub because of its combination of low cost and high technological expertise.[31]

The center of activity

Even as far as financial markets are concerned, the existing level of globalization really represents only the linkage of the members of the hallowed circle of the developed countries, which deals with but a fraction of the potential financial business of the world as a whole. Is financial market activity one of the areas in which the developed countries are set to retain a comparative advantage, or, like manufacturing, will a good deal of this activity migrate to the developing world?

I think the evidence is clear. For a considerable time to come, financial activity is going to remain concentrated in the existing major financial centers, London and New York, with Asian cities competing to fill the role of minor counterpart in the Asian time zone. You might have thought that the advent of modern communications technology might have led to a dispersion of financial market employment as business sought the lower costs made possible by diversifying away from the major international cities that have hitherto been dominant. In fact there is little evidence of this happening. The investment management business in the United States is well spread out, but other financial market activities, especially those conducted by investment banks, remain heavily concentrated in New York.

London's position is even more striking. Within the UK, many financial businesses have moved operations *away* from provincial centers such as Glasgow, Perth, Exeter, and Norwich to London. For international business London has also gained market share as the advent of the euro has put pressure on the smaller continental financial centers. Europe is probably moving toward having one continental financial center, which will probably be Frankfurt, and one offshore global giant, which will definitely be London.

The reasons for the endurance of established financial centers such as London are not difficult to find. Financial markets are subject to major agglomeration effects, not least because of the continued significance of face-to-face contact. For all the talk of virtual meetings, it is still important for business to be able to meet people. And the more people there are together in one place, the easier it is to meet more people. That gives established centers such as London a head start.

Something similar applies to employers seeking to maximize their pool of suitably qualified labor and the vast network of support services that need to be used for financial business, including lawyers, accountants, printers, clerks, and computer programmers. If an employer locates in a small city its pool of suitably qualified people will be restricted and this will cause it to experience increased business costs.

Prospective recruits who might be tempted to work for such a company will feel the same way; they will be worried about moving out of the mainstream. Since the professionals working in financial markets are by and large highly paid, sophisticated people, they have definite preferences as to where they would like to live and some degree of freedom about realizing those preferences. Most of them would not regard Frankfurt as preferable to London. When it comes to Bucharest or Riga, or whatever putative location you might imagine, the new options are not in the same league.

Nevertheless, despite the enduring advantages of the great financial centers of the developed countries, as Asian business becomes ever more important in the world the Asian financial centers will gain in relative strength and at some point one of them could replace London and New York as the global leader. At the moment the leading Asian financial centers are Tokyo, Hong Kong, and Singapore, but in due course Shanghai may be the leading candidate to become an Asian financial powerhouse.

In any case, London, New York, and even Tokyo will have to rebalance the thrust of their activities. They will need to move away from concentration on the provision of ever more sophisticated forms of liquidity for trading in developed-country financial instruments and the redesign of developed-country corporate structures, and toward playing a key role in financing the growth of the developing countries. In other words, London, New York, and Tokyo have to return to the sort of role that London fulfilled for the rest of the world for much of the nineteenth century: supplying capital from the old world to the new.

For the role of the financial system is not to provide the raw material for financial fantasies, but to enable the creation of real wealth. This means facilitating the workings of business and its expansion. And in the economy of the future, the combined forces of globalization and the Intangible Revolution are going to transform the business world and open up new areas of business growth.

8
Doing the Business

This "telephone" has too many shortcomings to be seriously considered as a means of communication. The device is inherently of no value to us.
Western Union internal memo, 1876

One could reasonably expect the chairman of AT&T to know what his corporation will be in ten years from now. He doesn't. One could, within reason, expect the chairman of AT&T to be able to predict how technology will transform his business a decade hence. He can't. At least, he should know who his major competitors will be in 2005. Stumped again. But here is what he does know: something startling, intriguing and profound is afoot.
Robert Allen, chairman of AT&T, 1995[1]

The Austro-Hungarian Empire has much to answer for, both good and ill. Yet another of its famous sons had a life that mixed high finance and academic economics: Joseph Schumpeter. But Schumpeter had the balance of the mixture the other way round from George Soros. He was one of the few academic economists to enjoy high political office. In 1919 he was Minister of Finance in the Austrian Republic. I say "enjoy," although he presided over Austria's hyperinflation and was sacked in the same year.

Schumpeter soon sought refuge in academia as a professor at Graz. A year later he was back in business, so to speak. In 1921 he was appointed president of Biedermann Bank. However, in the economic crisis of 1926 he was sacked from that position too, with large personal debts that he wasn't able to settle until over a decade later.

Failed politician and failed banker, Schumpeter was nevertheless a great success as a thinker. Some judges, not least Schumpeter himself, put him on a par with Keynes—or above. He saw the capitalist system operating in a maelstrom of what he called "creative destruction."[2] Entrepreneurs were the great heroes responsible for innovation, and innovation was the source of growth.

However, growth was not a smooth, easy, or painless process. As Schumpeter put it:

> *The proper role of a healthily functioning economy is to destroy jobs and to put labor to better use elsewhere. Despite this simple truth, layoffs and firings will still always sting, as if the invisible hand of free enterprise has slapped workers in the face.*[3]

This process, he said, was bound to be cyclical. Booms and busts were endemic, and were to be welcomed as the result of the economy's life force. Similarly, he excoriated the orthodox economist's emphasis on the benefits of perfect competition and even thought that monopoly could be beneficial as a spur to innovation.

In many ways Schumpeter is the economist whose thoughts and theories most closely match the events of the 1990s—and anticipate the shape and substance of the economy of the future. Mind you, he did get one big thing very wrong. "Can capitalism survive? No. I do not think so." That is how he began one of his great books.[4] His idea was that capitalism would be undermined by its very success. It would harbor and support an increasing number of people who were steadfastly opposed to it. The greatest villains in the piece were the intellectuals. Funny that: what was Schumpeter?

Gales of Creative Destruction

So far I have spoken of the economic forces at work in the economy of the future as though they were disembodied, descending on all people and institutions in society alike. That is no more than a convenient shorthand. In practice these forces will work almost entirely through the medium of an institution that has been at the center of the economic achievements of the last two centuries and will be at the center of the enrichment yet to come: the company.

As I argued in Part II, globalization is a force through which people and activities in different countries are brought together for common profit. When the subject of globalization arises the talk is almost always of countries, governments, and cultures, but the agency for achieving this coming together is usually companies, in particular that much vilified entity the multinational enterprise. Companies trading internationally do more than merely exchange goods or services: they spread business culture, values, knowledge, and skills. If the countries of the underdeveloped world are to be brought within prosperity's embrace, it is likely to be companies and not governments that do the job.

Equally, companies are at the center of the drive toward economic growth from expanded output and greater economies of scale, and from the increase in productivity stemming from innovation and knowledge creation.

Nevertheless, there is a paradox. What companies do overall matters enormously, and within individual companies it is natural that people should identify such good things with the survival and prosperity of *their* company. Yet society's interests are often best advanced by the continual *death* of individual companies and the re-creation of new ones, rather than by the perpetuation of old companies long past their sell-by date. This produces an acute tension. While society needs a healthy corporate sector in order to flourish, in order for this health to be preserved the identity of the corporate sector needs to undergo constant change.

In the economy of the future, it will certainly get that. There will be gales of creative destruction deriving from two key forces highlighted in Part II: the shift to globalized markets for most tangible goods and intangible services; and the increasing importance of intangibles in what people want to buy. These gales will produce a more competitive and fluid business climate in which consumers are empowered and corporate identity is in a state of flux.

The Shape of Trade

The gale of creative destruction unleashed by the increased specialization of production between countries and the relocation of many industries and processes to the developing countries will cause carnage among many of the established businesses of the developed countries, which will no longer be able to compete with much lower-cost production in the developing countries. Doubtless many will go bust. Many *should* go bust in order to facilitate the shift of resources into other areas where they can be better employed.

There should be no mystery about the sort of things and nonthings that the developing countries will sell to the developed, and therefore the sectors in which the developed countries will lose market share, and perhaps even

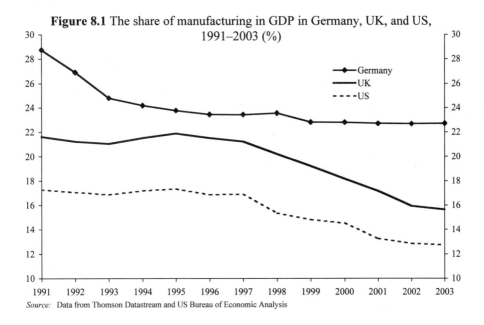

Figure 8.1 The share of manufacturing in GDP in Germany, UK, and US, 1991–2003 (%)

Source: Data from Thomson Datastream and US Bureau of Economic Analysis

lose capacity altogether. Much of existing manufacturing activity will continue to migrate to the developing world. Initially, as before, this migration will be concentrated on relatively low-skill, low-value-added manufacture. In November 2002, for example, Black & Decker announced that it was transferring most of the production it had undertaken at Durham, in the North-East of England, to the Czech Republic. This followed an announcement earlier in the year that it planned to open low-cost sites in China and Mexico.[5] There is much more of this sort of production transfer to come, but as the developing countries become more sophisticated the movement will include higher-value-added things, and more and more nonthings as well.

The transformation will be particularly great in Germany, where the share of manufacturing in GDP, although declining, remains large, as Figure 8.1 shows. Deeply thingist though its people and businesses still are, Germany cannot escape the logic of comparative costs. It is not even as though German industry necessarily has to relocate or lose business to places far a field in Asia. A good deal of its manufacturing will migrate to the super-growth zone on its doorstep, namely the former eastern bloc. Already there has been a significant migration of German production to the Czech Republic, Hungary, and Poland, but this is set to go much deeper in these countries—and to spread wider now that most of the countries of "New

Europe" have joined those of "Old Europe" in an expanded European Union.

The loss of so much economic activity, particularly since it is so obviously *real*, raises the question—and the acute fear in many people's minds—of what the developed countries, including the likes of Germany, will be left with as sources of income and employment. These fears are misplaced. As I point out in the Finale, the worry is based on a misconception at the macro level.

It also reflects a misunderstanding of the micro makeup of economies. The economic activities sucked into the area of globalized competition are the production of tangible goods and the delivery of intangible services. This still leaves a great deal of economic activity that will *not* be subject to international competition, including the host of things demanding personal interaction between a single consumer and the service provider, for example meals in restaurants, haircuts, theater visits, gym sessions, and a host of other activities that, as I argue in Chapter 9, are set not only to survive but to increase in relative importance.

Even so, it is true that if the developed countries lose substantial parts of their current industrial base, and even whole swathes of their service sector, to the developing countries, they will have to be able to step up sales of something else to the developing countries in order to be able to pay for what they import—as well as to generate income and employment for all those whose industries and jobs have migrated. What will these things be?

In the economy of the future, the comparative advantage of the developed countries will lie in the higher-value-added end of manufacturing, higher-value-added services, and a range of intangibles that depend for their creation on skill, education, and innovation. The list of things and non-things they will be able to sell is endless, but it may help the reader to envisage the economy of the future if I give some examples.

Ownership, software, and business services

One significant source of income will be the ultimate intangible: ownership. Even when the production of a good migrates to a developing country, often the developed-country originator will own the overseas production facility, giving rise to a stream of profits. If it does not own the production facility it will usually still own the brand, giving rise to a stream of royalty payments. When Germany relocates much of its car manufacture to lower-cost countries, for instance, the production facilities will frequently be German owned, the brands will often still be Volkswagen, Mercedes, and BMW—and the profits will still flow to those companies.

Already a significant part of US and UK overseas earnings comes not from the sale of things, but rather from the ownership of such nonthings as rights, royalties, license payments, and brands, as well as straightforward investment income. In 2002 royalties and license fees accounted for some 6 percent of total service exports for the UK. In the US the proportion was even higher: 15 percent, amounting to $43 billion. Moreover, these receipts have been growing fast. Whereas between 1986 and 2002 service exports as a whole grew by some 230 percent, earnings from fees and licenses grew by 430 percent.

Similarly, for the two leading overseas investors, the US and the UK, the profits on direct investment abroad are huge, accounting for more than 10 percent of all overseas income accruing to both countries. Again this source of income has been growing fast, reflecting the expansion of overseas investment. For the US, whereas overseas income of all sorts (including exports of goods) grew by 200 percent between 1986 and 2002, receipts of profits from direct investment abroad grew by 470 percent. In the economy of the future, these sources of income are set to increase still further.

The growth of more conventional intangibles is also set to soar. One area of great growth potential is computer software.[6] PC ownership is growing twice as fast in developing countries as in developed countries. Since 1992 China has increased its ICT expenditure by 30 percent a year, going from 0.6 percent of worldwide ICT spending to 2.2 percent in 1999.

Although a good deal of the computer hardware will be sourced from developing Asia, for as far as the eye can see the leading software companies in the world will be American, albeit employing substantial amounts of highly skilled labor from the developing countries. As the developing countries continue to grow rapidly, the demand for software will grow by leaps and bounds.

This is also true of business services, including accounting, legal, and business advisory work. Here the US and the UK have a deep-seated competitive advantage.

Health and education

As levels of prosperity rise, the demand for higher standards of healthcare will rise more than proportionately.[7] This will create an upsurge in demand for pharmaceuticals. There is not the remotest prospect for a good while yet of the developing countries being able to compete in the development of such products. Moreover, the demand for medical hardware, private healthcare involving treatment in overseas medical centers, and the building of new hospitals will increase sharply and all these will be largely supplied from North America and western Europe, principally the US and the UK.

Similarly, throughout the developing countries economic growth will both require and lead to a substantial increase in spending on education. In the first instance there will be an increase in demand for educational services and infrastructure *within* the countries themselves. Expenditure on new buildings, teacher training, and textbooks will provide opportunities for foreign construction companies and education providers. An expanding middle class will more actively consider overseas education, particularly in the US, Canada, and the UK, because of their high educational standards and their use of the English language.[8]

Up, up, and away

Although much manufacturing activity will migrate to the developing countries, large areas of high-tech, high-skilled manufacture will remain, including telecommunications kit, optical and medical equipment, advanced machine tools, and precision-engineered goods of all types. Here the growth potential is huge.

A prime example is aircraft. Despite the current difficulties facing both airlines and aircraft manufacturers in both the developed and developing world, the number of commercial flights continues to grow at an extraordinary rate. Even in an apparently mature market such as the United States, analysts predict that regional airline traffic will increase by 8 percent annually up to 2020. Aircraft engine manufacturer Rolls-Royce predicts that the growth of passenger and cargo traffic will expand at double the rate of growth of the world economy. This will involve a huge expansion of the global passenger fleet, while the number of freight aircraft will grow from today's figure of 1,700 to 3,400 in 2020.[9]

In China, with over four times as many people as the United States, the potential for new planes to be supplied by Boeing and Airbus is enormous. A recent forecast by the Civil Aviation Administration of China (CAAC) expects that the country will need 400 more planes over the next five years.[10] In Russia and Central Asia, over the next 20 years passenger air travel is forecast to grow by over 6 percent per annum, requiring 1,080 new aircraft.[11]

Commercial aircraft makers are not the only likely beneficiaries of rapid economic growth in the developing countries. Much of the international arms business, including military aircraft, consists of sales by the developed countries to the governments of developing countries. This business is likely to expand as the developing countries grow richer.[12]

Consumer goods

Market opportunities for the developed countries will also include many consumer goods. The mobile telecommunications industry is currently suffering from sluggish sales in Europe and North America, but the falling cost and rising demand for mobile phones seen there over the last ten years are already being replicated in the developing countries. By the end of July 2001 China had 120.6 million mobile phone users compared to America's 120.1 million. Once market penetration rises to 70 percent, the "saturation rate" reached in the Scandinavian states, there would be a billion Chinese users.[13] This would present enormous opportunities for western companies such as Nokia, Motorola, and Ericsson.

As the developing countries grow more affluent, the demand for leisure goods such as luxury cars, jewelry, haute couture, furniture, and imported foodstuffs will intensify, and most of them will be supplied by the developed countries. For the young—and developing countries are overwhelmingly young—it is not so much luxury goods that are important as "lifestyle" goods. In the economy of the future the demand for western fashion will grow, along with all the other artefacts of western popular culture including the western diet.

Cigarettes are an example of a lifestyle "good" that is in strong demand across all developing countries. As smoking becomes less popular in the mature markets of Europe and North America, the large cigarette manufacturers are seeking new opportunities. In recent years cigarette consumption has increased noticeably in Indonesia, Russia, Turkey, India, Brazil, South Korea, and Poland. The 1.1 billion smokers in the world today are forecast to grow to 1.64 billion by 2025. China is already the largest consumer of cigarettes, with over 300 million smokers. Accession to the WTO will create opportunities for western exporters as this market is liberalized.

Movements to regulate the global tobacco industry under the auspices of the World Health Organization (WHO) could restrict the promotion and advertising of cigarettes in developing countries.[14] It is perhaps more likely, though, that the health problems caused by cigarette smoking will lead to increased demand for western medical services, just as the producers' drive to increase smoking will lead to increased demand for the services of western advertising agencies. In this case it may not quite be money for nothing, but you could say that much of the benefit of increased prosperity will have gone up in smoke.

There's Life after all in E-commerce

The second source of creative destruction will come from the internet and the development of e-commerce. At the height of the internet mania the visionaries made it sound as though we were about to enter a world of science fiction where just about everything would dematerialize and all contact with our old and familiar lives would be lost. The executives of e-business startups appeared to believe that they only had to put a service on the web and encourage a high "hit rate" to build a successful business for the future. Right from the beginning there was an astonishingly naive attitude to the relationship between technology and customers. Imagine a retailer saying to customers "Come to my store because I'm connected up to electricity" or "Use us because we have telephones."

Perhaps it was this aspect of what I call the Intangible Revolution that made so many people uneasy, both because they did not *want* to lose contact with their existing way of life and because they did not quite believe this was possible. Hence it led to a strange mixture of feelings of dread and disbelief.

Following the failure of so many internet businesses we have gone to the other extreme. There are plenty of business leaders who, after the events of the early Naughties, breathed a sigh of relief. They thought that the internet would pass them by.

Their reaction was unjustified. E-commerce is on the way back. In mid-2005 internet flea market eBay was valued on the stock market at almost twice the value of Sears, and the online travel service Expedia was worth roughly the same as four of the biggest American airlines put together.

In a sense, both the visionaries and the skeptics were right. In the economy of the future some economic activities, such as the production and consumption of food, will still be deeply rooted in the old material world and will be left relatively unaffected by the internet revolution. But, as I shall show in a moment, other parts of the economy are essentially intangible and are destined for radical change. They have been trapped in the world of physical form and location by what you might call an accident of history. Like Sleeping Beauty they have lain there dormant, awaiting the prince's kiss. In this case, if the handsome prince has any physical form at all, it is likely to be Bill Gates.

Adding together apples and *Pears' Encyclopedia*

In the early development of e-commerce for consumers tangibles were in the forefront: books, CDs, groceries—although it was the intangible elements of these that was deliverable by the internet, specifically the ordering.

At first sight ordering seems to constitute only a small part of the value created by the production and sale of a book. Attempts have been made to build up the importance of the intangible element, or to use it to create value in other ways. So Amazon.com tells you how other readers have reacted to the book you are considering and, if you decide to take a particular book, tells you which other books you might like on the same or similar subjects. It makes the paying easier by inviting you to input your credit card details so that once you choose to take a book, your click automatically activates your standard payment instructions. It also boosts sales by running its Associates program, under which merchants selling something else are automatically paid a commission for book sales resulting from automatic online referrals to Amazon's website.[15]

This is all good stuff, but the essence of the book business remains the same. Amazon has to acquire the stock, hold it in warehouses somewhere, employ someone to pick out the book you ordered, package it, and transport it to you. Although Amazon may be thought of as the paragon of the new intangibles-dominated e-commerce sector, it is so rooted in the tangible world that it has become the world's largest individual investor in warehouse space.[16]

What Amazon is offering may be portrayed as revolutionary, but in reality it is nothing of the sort. It is glorified mail order. Provided that the glorification does not cost much—or if it does, it at least creates benefits for which customers are willing to pay—there is no reason why in the economy of the future e-commerce should not take over more or less the whole mail-order market. The website is merely a glorified catalog. But contrary to the initial forecasts of complete domination when the mail-order idea first emerged, the mail-order business was only ever a relatively small part of the whole retail market.

On your bike

The use of the internet quickly spread into areas where the catalog never reached, most notably into groceries. From companies like Peapod in the US or Tesco Direct in the UK, people are able to order the week's food shopping by the click of a mouse and, without even having to stir from their seat, the stuff is delivered. Is this the way of the future?[17]

No. Unless some means is found to reduce the cost of delivery or to reengineer the process to add value in some other way, once the full costs of delivery are passed on, even in the economy of the future the online ordering and delivery of groceries will be restricted to the once-in-a-while option, or the preserve of enclaves like Kensington in London or the rich and fashionable parts of Manhattan, populated by people with oodles of money and little time. Anything that depends for its rationale on a large discrepancy in income between the purchasers and providers of a service cannot ever find a mass market.[18]

Ideas, not things

Given that the future lies with the movement of intangibles, the radical possibilities lie not with the ordering of CDs over the net, but rather with the downloading of the music that would otherwise be on the CD. This has already caused the recording companies serious headaches, particularly given the spectacular early success of Napster, the internet group that pioneered the sharing of music files. Napster brought together 20 million users in a year, thereby proving that the potential market for online music is huge.

The problems of the music industry are all too obvious from its sales figures. In 2002 global music sales fell by 7 percent, the third successive annual decline. Each of the world's big "record" companies—BMG, the music division of Bertelsmann, Warner Music, Sony, and EMI—announced plans for limited digital downloading of music. The reason for the limits was simple. Although they could all see that this was the way of the future, they were yet to work out how they could make it pay for them. In October 2002 the British music business offered music fans £5 ($7.50) worth of free downloads from legitimate internet sites in a bid to lure them away from illicit online music services.[19]

And in the month of May 2003, 43 million Americans—that is, half of those who connected to the internet—used file-sharing software that allows people to listen to music without paying for it.

Some concluded that if you cannot beat 'em you should join 'em. In April 2003, EMI announced plans to release singles exclusively to internet users, after sales of singles fell by 16 percent in the previous year. And the intention was to develop an official online chart to replace the traditional

Top 40, based on retail sales.[20]

But things have recently gone much further. At one point, Napster was closed down following a legal judgment, but it re-emerged.[21] Now in both the US and the UK consumers can legally buy from Napster an "all you can eat" subscription for a monthly fee of $9.95 (£9.95 in the UK). And there is a Napster Light service that allows you legally to buy individual tracks or albums online.

Perhaps books will go the same way as CDs, through the downloading of the written word that would otherwise be contained in a book. Already a limited number of e-books have been published, but the mainstream publishers are dragging their heels until there is a proven method of preventing people from copying and distributing them indiscriminately.[22]

In a similar vein, given sufficient bandwidth films could be downloaded rather than rented or purchased in physical form on videotape or DVD, and visits to a shop to have camera film developed are already being replaced by home printing of photographs from your digital camera.

All sorts of entertainment that happen outside the home also have a component that is readily digitizable, namely the search for alternative attractions, the choice between alternative providers, and the booking and ticketing of such events. So holidays, hotel bookings, concerts, and theater visits—all of them set to remain irremediably tangible—are commonly chosen, secured, and paid for over the internet, and the penetration of e-commerce in these areas is set to increase markedly.

Interestingly, one of the few e-companies established over the last few years to do well financially is Ebookers.com, an online travel-booking firm. Again, this is a company dealing in the purely intangible element, the *booking* of something that is most definitely tangible, namely the transport of people from A to B.

Estate agency is another industry where the net could eventually have a big impact. After all, what do real-estate agents do? They are essentially information exchangers. They bring together potential buyers and sellers and exchange information between them. Their jaundiced clients might well want to say that they are another group who have long been on to money for nothing.

Surely in the economy of the future this will be done better. In the United States over 80 percent of all buyers already look for property online and this sort of figure could soon be replicated in Europe. The two biggest property websites in the US, Homestore and Move.com, are combining and are set on a path of international expansion, with the UK targeted first and France and Spain set to follow.[23]

Intangible manufacturing

Even in the world of the apparently tangible, there is more of the intangible involved than one would think at first blush. Manufacturing sounds irreducibly tangible, but large parts of the associated processes are in fact intangible: procurement, stock control, invoicing, cash management. The internet will help manufacturers reduce the cost of these functions.[24] The electronic medium offers the possibility of checking that an order is internally consistent and that an order, receipt, and invoice match. Although this may sound trivial, General Electric and Cisco report that one-quarter of orders have to be reworked because of errors. E-commerce has reduced Cisco's errors to 2 percent.

Nick Scheele, chairman of Ford's European operations, has said that the online purchasing of automotive components through new internet auction procedures would reduce production costs by $1,000 per vehicle—with the benefits largely going to consumers.[25] Even parts of the manufacturing process itself can be digitized: design, and the making of the good exactly to customers' requirements; that is, customization.

Whatever benefits the internet can bring to manufacturing will increase as time goes on, since more of the value in a conventional manufactured good will be represented by intangibles. Again, the motor car is in the forefront of this change. Developers are working on models that replace the traditional instrument panel with a computer screen. The installation of so-called telematics will provide voice-activated access to the internet, emails, and real-time data, including traffic information, news, stock prices, and weather. (Let's hope that drivers still keep their eyes on the road.)

Ford's former chief executive, Jac Nasser, enthused: "This is not about new economy versus old economy. This is about shifting competitive advantage from hard assets to intangible intellectual assets." But will consumers be prepared to pay what this stuff costs the manufacturers to install? If not, this development will merely be another dent in car manufacturers' profits.[26]

Nevertheless, the essential principle stands. In the economy of the future features like design, customization, and smart add-ons will be incorporated into goods and account for a higher and higher proportion of their value. Manufactured goods will increasingly come to resemble ideas in a box.

Business efficiency

There are three general forces that the internet will unleash throughout the economy, and that will strongly affect even those businesses that remain steadfastly in the realm of the material. First, there is the elimination of waste and empty space. In any modern economy spare capacity is endemic because of the effects of uncertainty and variability. Capacity has to be built to allow for the fact that demand varies over time. In order to be able to meet peak demand, you have to plan to have spare capacity when demand is lower. Spare capacity is not restricted to manufacturers. It is a serious problem for airlines left with empty seats or restaurants with unoccupied tables for most of the week, although they are overflowing on Fridays and Saturdays. Some service providers, such as cab drivers, spend time and money literally *searching* for customers.

The technological and communications revolution is having a dramatic impact on this waste of capacity by transmitting information about the avail-ability of services and the potential demand for them. Taxis can be made more efficient by the use of computers that tell them where they may pick up the next fare, and increasingly they are equipped with information sys-tems telling the driver the best route to the destination and updating him or her on any traffic congestion en route. Airlines now ask customers to bid online for empty seats. There is a website allowing companies to trade in empty lorry space. In the economy of the future there will be scope for much more, and businesses that do not use ICT to eliminate empty space will find themselves becoming uncompetitive and will be driven out of business.

Second, the explosion of information about alternative sources of supply, prices, and different qualities and the availability of sophisticated software to help consumers make their choice increase consumers' responsiveness. In economists' jargon, they increase the elasticity of demand. The result is to force suppliers to operate with lower margins and to seek to maintain or increase profitability through higher volumes.[27]

Third, the much greater availability of information can improve effi-ciency by helping customers to make better-informed choices. Take booking a hotel, for instance. How large is the room you will be allocated? What is the view? What does the restaurant look like? Many hotels enable prospec-tive customers to view such things online. In the economy of the future such access to information, and hence better-informed choices, will become standard and much more comprehensive and sophisticated.[28]

Perfection on Earth

So far I have discussed the pressures on businesses originating from the forces unveiled in Part II and analyzed what they imply for businesses in the economy of the future. But what about the business of doing business? Here too companies are set to face gales of creative destruction, and are set to come up against the encroachment of government.

During the internet craze many economists thought that the economy of the future could see the realization of the economist's dream (and the businessperson's nightmare): perfect competition. You can readily understand what excited them. The foundation of perfect competition is the availability of information and that is what the internet is all about. Moreover, the internet makes possible the open-market determination of prices through bidding. Several effective internet operators—such as eBay, offering online auctions for almost anything, and Priceline, especially well known for auctions of airline tickets—have made this possibility a fully functioning commercial reality.

At the same time, because of its universal reach and instantaneous transmission, the internet overcomes spatial barriers, which are the source of nearly all local monopolies. In addition, the cost of setting up a web-based distribution channel is comparatively low, so this should ensure that barriers to entry are low and that any excess profits are quickly competed away.

Putting these together, you reach the conclusion that over the internet there should effectively be one price for the same product and the responsiveness of consumers to price changes should be extremely high. Because of price transparency and rampant price competition, this should deal a massive blow to the viability of advertising and all the usual attempts at product differentiation. In summary, the internet should help to achieve just about the best allocation of resources humanly possible, albeit with devastating implications for the current structure of business. The message to government would be loud and clear: keep out of business.

As web-enthusiastic economists pondered these possibilities, it was rather like a biologist discovering a unicorn alive and well. A model long thought of as a fictional beast, having its existence only in textbooks, was now not only a fully functioning commercial reality, but seemed to be the template for the economy of the future taking shape before our eyes.

The current reality looks rather different. Having too much information can leave you in much the same position as having none. The very qualities

that make e-commerce attractive—openness, global reach, and lack of physical contact—also make it particularly vulnerable to fraud. That means that
trust and security may be even more significant than before, which implies
that product differentiation, branding, and advertising are back in the
frame. Of course, we should never forget that companies will do their
damnedest to make competition as imperfect as they can.

Furthermore, at least until e-commerce becomes better established, it
seems that successful branding is achieved in conventional business rather
than on the web. For those companies that in the economy of the future
wish to establish a presence on the web alone, heavy advertising expenditure
will become necessary. Nonprice factors, not the least of which are effective
delivery and aftersales service, will be even more important.[29]

Going, going, gone

As for the auction model pioneered by Priceline, it is highly unlikely that
this will figure large in the economy of the future. The original idea was that
customers would simply name their own price for anything from airline tickets to bananas. Naturally, suppliers would take the highest prices bid. In
1999 Jay Walker, Priceline's chief executive, boasted that there was no category into which this model would not extend, and at first money poured in
from backers such as George Soros and Goldman Sachs. However, in
October 2000 Mr. Walker had to admit to at least a serious reverse, if not
defeat. He announced the closure of WebHouse Club and Perfect Yardsale,
two affiliates of Priceline that invited customers to bid for small-ticket items
such as groceries and gasoline.[30]

Even in its core airline-ticket business, Priceline has encountered some
serious problems. Customers have to bid blind for their goods and services,
including air travel, so they do not know what time of day their flight will
leave, what airline they will be flying on, or what transfers they may have to
make. This leaves Priceline wide open to customer complaints and
disappointment over quality. In September 2000 the Connecticut Attorney
General opened an investigation into Priceline after receiving more than 100
customer complaints.

This should not be regarded as merely the result of teething troubles but
is, rather, fundamental to the concept. The group of people for whom price
is more important than convenience is limited.[31] Although Priceline targets
a mass market, according to Peter Fader of Wharton Business School "its

true market may only be the niche group of price-sensitive consumers who doggedly clip out supermarket coupons week after week."[32]

So e-commerce turns out to be a far cry from the incarnation of perfect competition. Economists will have to carry on grappling with the messy practicalities of an imperfect world, poor souls.

Branding and the height of imperfection

The continued, and even enhanced, importance of branding in the globalized, internet-connected economy of the future raises an intriguing possibility. Could all the gains made by the selling of intangibles on a much larger world market made possible by global development be eaten up by the extra costs of branding and distribution? The answer is that in principle they could be. When you look at the sums laid out on advertising by companies producing everything from cars and washing powder to financial services, it is easy to envisage such an outcome.

But appearances can be deceptive. These industries' vast expenditure on advertising has *not* eaten up all the advantages of technological progress in the production process. You can see this by looking at the relative price movements of heavily branded and extensively advertised goods compared to average components of a consumer's shopping basket. Over recent decades cars and washing powder, for instance, have been becoming steadily cheaper compared to most services, and most service-intensive components of what consumers buy. In other words a large part, probably the overwhelming majority, of the benefits of lower costs of production have not been eaten up by the costs of branding and have been passed on to consumers in the form of lower (relative) prices.

Similarly, as the market for intangibles such as recorded entertainment and medical cures expands with the enrichment of the developing countries, although distribution costs will rise along with the increased numbers of people, there is no reason to presume that additional branding expenditure will eat up all the extra revenue, or anywhere near it.

This does not mean, however, that as the international market expands, the price of intangibles and intangibles-heavy goods such as pharmaceuticals and CDs will necessarily fall. That will depend on a number of factors, including the state of competition and the regulatory system, as well as the extent of protection of intellectual property through patents and the like. At one extreme the protection will be total and there will be no reason for the price to fall. In that case, without large branding expenditure profits will soar with increasing volumes. At the other extreme it will be impossible to prevent competitors from moving in and the price will plummet. Indeed, it could be difficult for the originators of the knowledge underpinning the very existence of the good, such as a cure for cancer, to get an adequate return on their initial investment before the genie, if not the treatment, is out of the bottle.

But as long as branding and distribution costs have not grown like crazy, the price does not have to fall for the expansion in the size of the market to bring great benefit. If prices do not fall, this simply means that the benefits go to profits rather than to consumers. Shareholders are people too—or institutions such as pension funds acting for people. A benefit to shareholders is still a gain for society. Whether they will be able to hold on to those gains is another matter.

The Business of Deflation

The death of inflation has already had consequences aplenty for business managers and in the economy of the future, as deflation looms, these will go further. However, we must distinguish between the immediate and the more distant future. For the immediate future, as I made clear in Chapter 3, deflation could be devastating for business and indeed for the whole of society. In the more distant future, though, when the system has adjusted and the immediate problems of deficient demand have been overcome, and occasional bursts of deflation are normal as part of a regime of fluctuating prices, the consequences may be minor. Just as with inflation, if everything is adjusted to the changed monetary environment, there need be no difference to the corporate sector in *real* terms.

But will everything adjust? Part of that depends on businesspeople themselves. Everything that business used to regard as fixed must now be regarded as variable, and this will require managing. Pay is the most important example. As I stressed in Chapter 3, serious consequences follow if selling prices are under downward pressure while costs are constant or keep going up. In the economy of the future managers will have to ensure that a higher proportion of pay is in variable form, and that those parts of it that are supposedly fixed, namely wages and salaries, are more readily capable of being reduced as well as increased.

Clearly, if the environment is deflationary businesspeople will have to face acute issues of pricing policy. They will have to get the rate of *decrease* of their prices right, just as in inflationary times they have to get the rate of increase right, in keeping with the demand and supply in the sector. But this may not be as straightforward as it sounds.

Pricing power

There will be marked differences between sectors, and even between different products within the same sector, in the way they respond to the deflationary process. Businesses that produce inputs for other businesses will usually find it difficult to resist the downward pressure on prices as their customers will be well up with deflationary trends and will beat their prices down. It will be similar with businesses selling simple products to consumers where there are several alternatives that are all very much alike.

The more nearly a product is commoditized, the more difficult it will be to resist deflationary pressures—as companies producing raw materials such as rubber, tin, and bauxite, or foodstuffs such as grain, coffee, and tea know only too well. Prices are determined on a market by the swings of demand and supply, pure and simple. The market sets the price and you take it or leave it.

At the other end of the spectrum are products that have a single producer who has to set the price, making a judgment about market conditions and about its own strategic objectives with regard to the positioning of the product. Microsoft is in this position.

In between there are producers of goods and services that are individual because they are differentiated from the competitors but are substitutable with those of competitors. The car producers are in this position, as is your neighborhood Italian restaurant. These businesses may all think that they have control over their prices because they set them, but in reality they are more at the mercy of market forces than they imagine—and therefore more at the mercy of deflationary pressures.

What distinguishes these different sorts of businesses is pricing power. The more a company has it, the more it will be able to resist the trend toward falling prices. But the importance of this factor can easily be overdone. In general it does not provide a way of escaping from all the consequences of deflation, but rather gives companies the power to choose how to react. After all, a company with pricing power is not able to determine everything: it cannot set both the price and the quantity sold, even though it can try to achieve something like this by expenditure on advertising. If it chooses to use its pricing power to set a high price, then it will have to accept that it will sell less than if it set a lower price.

Deflation does not change this logic. If a firm had chosen the right combination of price and quantity in its own interests and then experienced the onset of general deflationary conditions, it could, of course, choose to maintain the price, but if it did so it would tend to lose sales as its products would start to become more expensive in relative terms. It has the ability to decide how to react, and it has the luxury of time to decide, but it does not have the ability to avoid suffering any consequences at all from deflation. And if the original combination of price and quantity that it chose for itself was the right combination for its immediate profitability and strategic interests, then the right thing to do as deflation proceeds may well be to cut its prices in line with general deflationary trends.

Nevertheless, in industries where there are a small number of producers, the barriers to entry are high, and the responsiveness of customers to price changes is not great, the appropriate strategy may be for each of the competitors to defend the existing price structure—while taking full advantage of the falls in costs that occur in the deflationary process. Provided that they can escape the clutches of the regulators for anticompetitive behavior, their profit margins will rise.

Producers of branded goods that are in close competition with unbranded products have a degree of pricing power, but it does not constitute a license to print money. In deflationary conditions, they would face a tricky dilemma. Think of foodstuffs like instant coffee and baked beans, where well-known brands compete on supermarket shelves with the supermarket's own brands. Or, at the other end of the spectrum, think of Gucci shoes and Prada handbags. As deflation proceeds, it may be tempting for their producers to leave the price of the branded products the same and allow the margin over their unbranded competitors to rise, if they succumb to the general deflation. But of course, this means that the branded product is becoming more expensive in relative terms. The simplest thing to do is to cut the price of the branded product along with general deflationary trends. The danger here, though, is that the brand loses its cachet and is perceived as going down market, thereby undermining its ability to command any sort of premium over the unbranded alternatives.

One part of the economic system stands out as having the power to resist deflationary pressures: the public sector. All sorts of public-sector charges as well as social benefits would lag the deflationary process, as there would be next to no competitive pressure to drag them down. Indeed, the government might well regard it as a bulwark against generalized deflation if the public sector held out, just as in inflationary times many governments used restrictions on public-sector pay as an anti-inflationary weapon.

So the upshot is that not all of the economic system will succumb equally to deflationary pressure. But this is not wholly good. It is precisely the tendency for modern companies producing differentiated products to try to resist falls in prices, along with the resistance of workers to wage cuts, that translates the deflation of prices into a slump in output. In the nineteenth century when more output was commoditized, prices fell readily. In the 1930s they did not—and the Great Depression was the result.

In today's conditions plenty of companies, if faced with deflationary pressures, would try to hold their prices, but competition is now so acute and consumer sensitivity so great that few would be able, in the end, to resist the forces of deflation. But the process would be far from smooth and even. Some producers would hang on, some would give in, some would resist at first but would be forced to cave in later. The result is that, as with inflation, deflation may play havoc with the structure of relative prices.

Ups and downs of the price structure

Quite apart from the instability of the structure of relative prices brought about by the deflationary process, in the economy of the future relative prices will undergo more permanent, and more important, shifts as a result of the real economic forces that I analyzed in Part II. Although the aggregate movement of all prices on average will be described by an inflation rate that is very low, and from time to time negative, there will be some huge variations within the average.

The economy into which we are moving could readily be presumed to be a deflationary economy because we commonly experience falls in the price of high-tech goods. According to Moore's Law the computing power of a microchip doubles roughly every 18 months, and the cost of computing power has fallen roughly as fast. A $1,000 PC today contains about as much computing power as a big mainframe ten years ago. Meanwhile, the cost of telephone calls has plummeted. A call costing $1 today would have cost, in today's money, $1,000 fifty years ago.

In the economy of the future, however, not everything that is produced will be high-tech. Moreover, what happens to the overall level of prices will be determined primarily by the *monetary* factors discussed in Part I. So if the overall price level is stable and high-tech prices are falling relentlessly, not merely in relative terms but absolutely, the implication must be that other prices are rising. Indeed, in the economy of the future some prices will rise, some will fall, some will do next to nothing, and some will fluctuate.

The outcome will not be random, but will be a reflection of the profound economic forces battering our society, which I have analyzed in this book. In the UK over the last 30 years the general level of prices has increased by about 600 percent. But the price of audiovisual equipment has increased by only 44 percent, cars by 300 percent, and clothing and footwear by only 130 percent. Whereas the price of food has risen by 430 percent, the price of restaurant meals has risen by over 900 percent.

In general, you should expect the pattern shown over the past few years to continue in the economy of the future. Goods and services whose prices are likely to fall in the future, or rise only marginally, are those whose providers benefit from strong productivity gains or can switch to cheaper sources of supply in Asia and elsewhere. Most basic goods like food and clothing fall into this category, as do relatively sophisticated goods such as audio and telecommunications equipment and computers. So do important household services such as telephone calls.

Most of the things that assuredly do *not* fall into this category are consumer services, such as taxi rides, restaurant meals, theater tickets, legal advice, visits to the dentist or doctor, and school fees. Here there will be some shocking increases in prices. Suppose that a restaurant meal for two currently costs $100. Within 15 years, even if the general rate of inflation is next to zero, the price will be more like $200. If you currently pay $5,000 in school fees, within 15 years the bill will be nearer $10,000.

These are things where the primary input is labor and the scope for productivity increases is limited. How do you wring extra output out of a waiter or a teacher? Or an actor? You could perhaps get an additional matinee performance of *King Lear* out of him or her once in a while, but there is a limit to the number of possible matinee performances (as well as a limit to the size of the audience for *King Lear*).

The extensive parts of the average consumer's expenditure where prices are under relentless upward pressure explain why even in an era of low inflation large numbers of people still complain about the constant upward march of prices. But in the economy of the future there will be no need to be completely passive about this. If you want to manage your personal inflation rate down, you will be able to. You will even be able to install a computer program to monitor your spending and advise you on what to do to reduce your own inflation rate.

This is what it will say: you should stay indoors, enjoying music, making phone calls, putting on CD-Roms, sending emails—and eating (but careful with the heating!). You may also accompany any of these activities with copious amounts of alcoholic drink; except in Scandinavia, where it would bankrupt you after only a few sessions. You may venture out to buy clothes, if you must, but do not take a taxi to the shops. Reconcile yourself to wearing your new clothes only at home (or on shopping trips). Donning them for visits to sports clubs, restaurants, or places of live entertainment will involve forking out more and more. Above all, stay healthy and don't have children.

Alternatively, you could pay up and stop complaining. After all, what makes these services more expensive is the increased cost of the labor that produces them, or, in other words, the increased *incomes* received by the people employed in those jobs, matching the increased incomes received by people throughout society. So the factor that will make these things more expensive will also make you able to afford them.

The raw material of business

These same forces also have implications for the prices of things that businesses use as inputs. As GDP is carried forward on a continually rising tide of knowledge, the demand for raw materials may hardly rise at all. It may even fall, particularly as some of the knowledge will relate to the more economical use or replacement of materials. In the economy of the future the relative price of raw materials will fall and, if I am right about the overall rate of inflation staying low or even negative, that means that the absolute price of raw materials may fall as well. The qualification to this prospect is that as the developing countries, notably China, become richer *their* demand for raw materials is increasing, putting upward pressure on prices. High prices for oil and other commodoties may persist for some years beyond 2005, but it would be unwise to extrapolate these trends forward. Despite rapid Chinese growth, the growth of the overall world economy is no faster now than it was in the 1950s when commodity prices were low and falling.

History indicates that in the years ahead, a surge of supply combined with a moderation of demand, encourage by higher prices, may cause the price of oil and other commodities to subside.

This sanguine prospect will strike many a reader, brought up under the influence of modern environmentalism, as bizarre. Concern about a coming shortage of raw materials is deep-rooted. Although, as I pointed out in Chapter 4, the weight of evidence long ago led to a subsidence of Malthusian worries about the supply of food, concern about shortages of other materials has readily taken its place, with similar results. In 1865 the economist Jevons predicted that a shortage of coal would bring growth to a halt within a century. He completely failed to foresee the extent to which oil would replace it.

In the 1950s the economist Colin Clark was concerned about water resources running out and in 1972 the Club of Rome created a scare by predicting acute shortages of every essential commodity. These warnings seemed to be particularly apposite after OPEC sharply increased the price of oil in 1973–74, precipitating the era of stagflation, and there were many forecasts of oil quickly running out. In the event more and more oil was discovered, techniques of recovery were improved, and the world became more efficient in its use of energy. There is a widespread perception that the oil price is now very high. As Figure 8.2 shows, in 2005 the price was well above the record peak reached in 1979, and was way above the levels of the previous 100 years. But once again inflation has disguised the truth. In real terms the price of oil is now much *lower* than it was in 1979–80. In fact, measured in terms of the consumer prices of 2005, as an annual average the oil price peaked at $85 in 1979 (and in monthly terms it peaked at $90 in November that year), compared to $65 in the middle of 2005.

Moreover, there is now something more fundamental at work than oil discovery and economy. What people increasingly want to spend their additional income on is services rather than goods, and these typically have a much lower resource content. Even with regard to purchases of goods, an increasing proportion of the value of the good is accounted for by intangibles, such as the software or the design, which have a nil resource content.

Accordingly, the total energy requirements per dollar of GDP have been falling. In the century after 1890 they more than halved. As Figure 8.3 shows, due to a combination of increased energy efficiency (itself the result of higher oil prices) and the increasing importance of parts of the economy

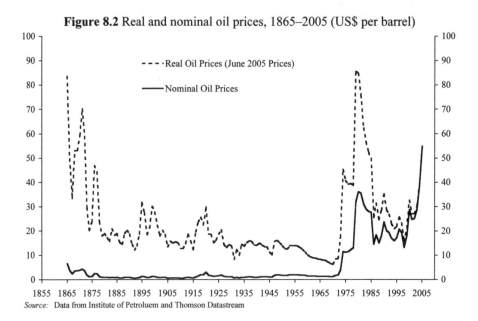

Figure 8.2 Real and nominal oil prices, 1865–2005 (US$ per barrel)

Source: Data from Institute of Petroluem and Thomson Datastream

that are not very energy intensive, in the OECD area the ratio of oil consumption to GDP has collapsed. In the economy of the future these trends will continue. The world is set on a path of enrichment that is less energy intensive for a given unit of additional GDP.

Business and the environment

For the developed countries the reduced importance of things and therefore of physical materials in the production process implies proportionately less pollution and damage to the environment, fewer health-threatening processes, and, because of the decline of heavy industry, less dangerous work. Admittedly the developing countries will at first suffer more of these ills as their GDP increases and as they take over much of the "dirty" production from the developed countries. Nevertheless, all the evidence suggests that, as they get richer, they will succumb to the same "clean" forces that are already affecting the developed countries.

There is a well-worn path along which, up to a certain stage, development increases pollution, and beyond that further development reduces it. Moreover, this relationship is improving all the time as the amount of pollution at any level of development falls, thanks to continued technological improvement.[33]

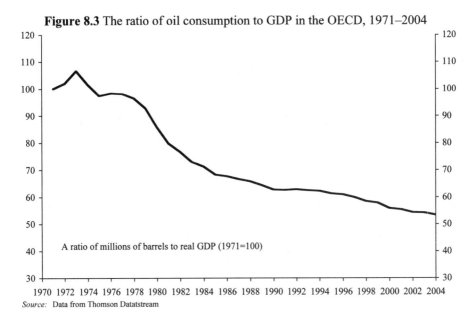

Figure 8.3 The ratio of oil consumption to GDP in the OECD, 1971–2004

A ratio of millions of barrels to real GDP (1971=100)

Source: Data from Thomson Datatstream

The coming decline in pollution, first in the developed countries and eventually worldwide, might be taken to imply that all those employed in environmental regulation and improvement are working in a declining industry. In fact I draw the opposite conclusion, but not because I believe that the world is set to become a dirtier or more unsafe place. Rather, it is because all the values that such environmental and safety work seeks to protect and promote are the sorts of things that as people get richer they esteem more highly and for which they are prepared to pay more.

When you are starving you do not stop to wonder whether the sandwich in front of you contains genetically modified food. When you are dirt poor with no alternative work you do not refuse to work down a mine because of the health risks. When you are unemployed with few prospects you are not particularly concerned about the pollution created by the aluminum smelter that might offer you a job. These are issues that become more and more important as people get richer. Accordingly, although we can have even faster rates of economic growth with less pollution and greater safety in our homes and workplaces, such lack of safety, health hazards, and environmental damage as remain are going to be viewed as even more important—and be less tolerated.

The "environment industry" is set to grow like Topsy. What is more, in the economy of the future more and more of companies' time will be taken up on environmental issues. This is one area where it is possible to imagine government encroaching severely on the realm of business. Nevertheless, this need not turn out negatively, either for business or for society. After all, when society cares about the environment and the environment is severely damaged by some "economic" activity, it is absurd to count the output as a "good" and the environmental damage as an irrelevance.

The key requirement for a successful adaptation to environmental concerns is that they should be capable of being measured and costed and not treated as absolutes. Already the world is clearly moving in this direction with the permitted trading of greenhouse gas emissions. By putting a price on pollution, the green agenda can be married with commercial enterprise. I expect that in the economy of the future fully incorporating such concerns into financial statements will become mandatory. The objectives of business will move outside the narrow confines of money to embrace many of the concerns currently regarded as the preserve of the green fringe.

Transport and information technology
A similar outcome will emerge in an area that is the blight of modern life for an increasing number of people: traffic congestion. In the economy of the future as we grow more prosperous, the number of motor vehicles on our already overcrowded roads could grow dramatically, yet in western Europe and many other parts of the world the scope to meet this by building more roads is limited. The result could be, despite much greater incomes, a life lived in frustration: ever greater periods of the day infuriatingly wasted sitting in traffic jams or waiting for public transport. The costs could be enormous—economically, environmentally, and, for the stressed individual, physically. Forget money for nothing, this sounds like a nightmare vision of the future. Most people, including the businesses and individual motorists who contribute to the congestion, apparently believe that this nightmare is more or less bound to become a reality.

Yet information technology offers a solution.[34] The essence of the transport problem is that road access is free even though road space is scarce. When individuals think about whether or not to make a journey, although they consider the stress and cost caused to them by making that journey, they do not consider the extra stress and cost they cause to others by increasing congestion.

This is a classic economic problem that is open to an easy solution: charge for road access. This option is not popular with voters, which makes it difficult for politicians to countenance, but it would work. Apart from the political problem, the difficulty up to now has been how to design a system that was flexible and foolproof enough and where charges were easy to collect. This is in essence an issue of information technology and in the economy of the future it will be overcome.

In Singapore the introduction of the Electronic Road Pricing (ERP) system in 1998 reduced peak traffic levels by 15 percent and raised the average speed to between 50 and 60 kilometers per hour.[35] This compares to an average speed in Central London of 15 kilometers per hour, the same as a century ago.[36] There are stirrings of radical reform there too, with the introduction of a congestion charge paid by people taking their cars into central London.

There is also a possible stage much beyond road pricing when cars on motorways are controlled and remotely steered by computer, with the "drivers" sitting there passively as a passenger until they have to leave the motorway for an ordinary road and resume control. The whole operation would be masterminded and controlled by the ground equivalent of air traffic control. This would give roads some of the characteristics of railways, with greater intensity of use, faster average speeds, greater predictability of journey times, and almost certainly a better safety performance than currently.

Well before we get to this stage, Singapore has shown the way forward with existing technology. In the economy of the future we will *not* be plagued by huge traffic jams and unnecessary delays. Despite more people and more wealth, travel by car will be easier than it is today and the need of business for predictable travel and transport times will be met. Of course we will have to pay for it—but we will be able to afford to do so.

Corporate Insecurity

Early exponents of the importance of the knowledge economy were so taken with the extent of economies of scale that they argued that in each product or sector the world was going to fall prey to a giant and unassailable monopolist. The process would involve a period of cut-throat competition since marginal costs were low or in some cases zero, but once the winner was established it would be able to act as monopolists always have. This naturally led on to a presumption that knowledge-based industries would need to be heavily regulated, and accordingly that in the economy of the future the role of government was set to increase markedly.

With a few years of the knowledge economy under our belts, things do not seem quite so extreme any more. Technology is changing so fast that even if a firm is in a quasi-monopoly position with regard to its existing products and markets, this is by no means a reason to rest on its laurels. If it fails to innovate it could soon be history. So although the economy of the future will not be perfectly competitive, it will be competitive in the Schumpeterian sense; probably more so than today.

The very idea of what a company is and what it does will be under assault from several directions. First, there is the question of how much of the company's functions should continue to be done in-house rather than outsourced. Many large corporate entities have already responded to the tensions by inventing their own internal market, complete with transfer prices and rewards in return for objectives met. In the economy of the future there is likely to be an increasing rejection of in-house providers of ancillary services and instead more reliance on outside providers whose services are bought in on a contract basis.[37]

Second, the boundaries between sectors will become increasingly blurred. Supermarkets have already become petrol retailers and petrol retailers have become supermarkets. In the UK, the interesting new kids on the block in retail financial services have their origins outside the financial sector: Virgin, Marks & Spencer, and Tesco. Former nationalized monopolies in gas distribution face competition from electricity companies selling gas; and gas companies sell electricity. The very words "gas company" start to ring untrue. These are companies whose business is becoming the management of retail distribution of utility services and the billing thereof. Gas simply happens to be where they started. In the economy of the future, who knows where they will end up?

At least gas companies do not have to cope with "star" gasmen—not yet anyway. But that is the third challenge to the modern company: from within, from the very people who make it work. In large sectors of the economy the value added from an activity depends critically on very few people. So in a competitive world, where individuals can transfer to another firm or set up their own quite easily, how does a business stop the "rent," the "surplus," the excess returns from accruing to a handful of these stars rather than to the shareholders? This is already a major problem in investment banking, advertising, and the media, and in the economy of the future it is set to spread into other sectors of the economy as human capital becomes more important. At the smaller end, particularly in the creative trades, employees will in the future see themselves more as self-employed and be prepared to have portfolio careers or come together in temporary groups, rather like actors.[38]

These three challenges to the modern company amount to a wholesale questioning and redrawing of corporate identity. In the economy of the future business will be in a state of permanent revolution. The result will be a mood of acute corporate insecurity.

One man's insecurity is another's security

This insecurity will bring advantages for society. The corporate sector's *unease* will be the consumer's *assurance*. Because the degree of competition will be sharper, and because it can come from unseen sources, you do not need so many competitors in the field at any one time to achieve a given degree of competition. The unrelenting pressure on companies is one of the main forces ensuring that in the economy of the future the benefits of the Intangible Revolution will go to consumers rather than being lost through inefficient pricing and production strategy, or being wasted on corporate indulgence and comfort.

The combination of strong global competition, more efficient distribution systems, and a welter of information available to consumers about alternative suppliers and their prices will mean that profits will be held in check by consumer power. The benefits of faster productivity growth—which back in the days of the new economy visionaries thought would boost profits, and which they thought could be anticipated and drawn down for themselves in the here and now in the form of higher share prices—will instead be spread far and wide across society. Companies will be engaged in a perpetual struggle to raise profits, but although some will succeed from time to time the corporate sector overall faces inevitable failure. Companies' strenuous efforts in pursuit of their own ends will have the effect of boosting the real incomes of ordinary consumers. Adam Smith would not have been surprised.

The economy of the future will therefore be the age of mass affluence. It remains to be seen, however, what the affluent masses will do with all that wealth. Even in the economy of the future, money will not buy you love. But will it at least buy you abundance, contentment, comfort, and repose?

9
Life in the Time of Plenty

If we were to prophesy that in the year 1930 a population of fifty millions, better fed, clad and lodged than the English of our time, will cover these islands, that Sussex and Huntingdonshire will be wealthier than the wealthiest parts of the west Riding of Yorkshire now are ... that machines constructed on principles yet undiscovered will be in every house ... many people would think us insane.

Thomas Babington Macaulay, historian, in 1830[1]

There is nothing so disturbing to one's sense of well-being and judgement as to see a friend get rich.

Charles Kindleberger[2]

If there was one man who epitomized the 1990s American spirit of radical change and unbounded technological promise, mixed with unbridled wealth, it was Bill Gates—no physicist, economist, or, to the best of my knowledge, any expert on stock-market investment, but much, much, more: computer geek, founder of Microsoft, squillionaire, and visionary.

There is a story (which may or may not be apocryphal) that when Bill Gates was courting the woman who is now his wife, they had to overcome the problem of spatial separation. This was not the sort of distance that could be construed as advantageous on the "absence makes the heart grow fonder" principle: he was on the west coast of America and she was on the east, which makes dating a little tricky. Not to be deterred, they developed what is termed the virtual date. They would see the same movie, eat the same type of pizza, and then discuss it all by email. Distance, where is thy sting?

Some of us would find certain aspects of this kind of dating more than a little unsatisfactory. Still, help may be at hand to make the virtual experience even more like the real thing. One of the problems with buying fruit over the web, for instance, is that it does not give any sense of texture. A gadget has been developed to give the user just that. A sort of glove-like appliance is added to the PC and when a hand is inserted into this, the texture of objects shown on the screen can be felt. I suppose some other appliance can also emit smells that correspond digitally to their real counterparts. In this way, just about any real experience can be reproduced digitally. Presumably, once a way is found of attaching the mouth to the PC, even the sense of taste will be reproducible.

Is this a template for the future as we all get richer and technology impinges more and more on our lives: hard work, money, and alienation from ourselves and other people as virtual reality takes over? Or will most of us not work at all—and still be alienated? What will *life* be like in the economy of the future?

The forces analyzed in this book are the forces of enrichment. Dramatic changes to our lives may occur simply as a result of having more money. But the particular factors bringing enrichment will have a special impact on our lives: increasing trade and interdependence and the rapid advance of technology. The impact is going to be felt on our spending patterns, our leisure pursuits, our jobs, and our personal relationships.

How Rich Will We Become?

Before we analyze these effects, we need some idea of how rich most of us will be in the economy of the future. Not as rich as Bill Gates, of course, but richer than you might imagine. Most people think of their material advancement as deriving from their own efforts: working hard and saving, climbing the career ladder, dealing well in property, investing well in the stock market—or perhaps being lucky with inheritance. Naturally these aspects are important and the economic forces rampaging through society affect them too, as we shall see. But without overall economic progress these sources of improvement represent either a temporary phase in a person's life, or their personal success counterbalanced by someone else's failure.

What makes improvement possible for everyone is economic growth. The simple onward march of productivity, year after year, can raise the standard of living of the ordinary person to amazing heights without any extra effort, or luck—money for nothing. Just being there is all it takes.

Then everything depends on how fast our economies will grow. Will they grow faster in the future than in the past? In real terms—that is, stripping away the illusions created by inflation and adjusting for the growth of population—over the last 30 years the per capita growth rate of the developed countries has been about 2.5 percent per annum. A growth rate of income per head of 2.5 percent a year may not sound much, and it will sound particularly paltry to those readers who have been used to the large inflationary pay increases of the 1970s and 1980s. But, of course, they were an illusion.

Real rates of growth, no matter how paltry, deal in realities. Under the influence of compound interest over extended periods of time, even 2.5 percent per annum works wonders. This apparently meager rate of growth results in an increase in real incomes of some 60 percent in 20 years and a doubling in 28 years. At the very least, that is what should lie before people in the developed countries.

Raise the growth rate a mere 0.5 percent to 3 percent per annum and the increase over 20 years goes up to 80 percent and the doubling of income occurs in less than 24 years. Raise the growth rate to 4 percent per annum and the 20-year increase is 120 percent and income doubles in just under 18 years. At this rate, the average parents of a newborn child will see their income double by the time the child goes to college. At the growth rates achieved from time to time by the Asian Tigers (and the Celtic Leprechaun), living standards can double while the children are at school. At a growth rate of 7 percent they double in ten years. At 10 percent they double in seven years.

You can easily work out how long it will take income to double by dividing a magic number by the growth rate. Some of you may remember a book a few years back entitled *The Hitch Hikers' Guide to the Galaxy*. In it two philosophers were searching for the ultimate answer to the universe. In the end it turned out to be not quite what they expected: 42. In this case the answer is not 42 but 72. Just divide 72 by the annual growth rate in income and the answer will tell you how many years it will take for income to double.

So unless I have seriously underestimated the appeal of my writing to the over-eighties, in the developed countries a doubling of general living standards looks highly likely within the lifetime of most readers of this book. And if I am right in my optimism about the pace of economic growth, it will come remarkably soon. In the developing countries, doublings could occur much more quickly.

Moreover, because of the power of compound interest, even moderate rates of economic growth would bring some enormous increases in wealth over extended periods. For example, 2 percent growth per annum sustained for 100 years would make people's incomes in 2103 seven times those of people living in 2003. And 3 percent growth per annum would raise their incomes to 19 times the 2003 level; 4 percent per annum would raise them to 50 times the 2003 level.

The scale of these increases makes one shudder at the possible transformation to the lives of our children, not to mention their children and grandchildren. But what will life be like?

There is less mystery about what economic life will be like for people in the developing countries. The progress of technology and the increasing importance of trade will obviously make a difference, but in terms of the overall standard of living they will be treading the path already trodden by millions of people in the developed countries. Modes of work and patterns of consumption will converge on what is already experienced as normal in developed countries.

In many of the developing countries there is even scope for living standards to be improved by the availability of more food, and certainly by better food. Bigger and better homes and more consumer durables will follow fast behind: cars, fridges, washing machines and dishwashers, televisions, telephones, and mobile phones. Soon the various consumer services that have long been central to the American or European consumer's expenditure will also arrive.

Meanwhile, as they develop these countries will gradually come to experience the same shifts that at the moment still lie in the future for the people of the developed countries. Thus it is on these shifts that our attention should fall.

In the developed countries, certain individuals will have previously enjoyed the material riches that will become commonplace for all, but society as a whole will not have. Consequently, how the economy and society will function in this world of riches is unknown. It is a world waiting to be discovered.

The End of Work?

Every now and then people in the developed countries undergo a scare about the impending end of work—and thereby of prosperity. This anxiety can latch itself to any one of several crackpot economic ideas, but the combination of rapid technological advance and intensified competition from the developing countries, the forces that I have analyzed in this book, is bound to bring anxiety about jobs to a new pitch. Whatever jobs there are will supposedly be taken by workers in Asia, Latin America, and wherever else labor is cheap.

This anxiety is misplaced. I bow to no one in acknowledging how powerful an influence competition from the developing countries will be. It is a major theme of this book. However, to see only the competition is to miss half the whole. As I have argued throughout, developing-country success means that developing-country workers and companies have more income with which to buy developed-country products and services—and that means job opportunities. There will, of course, be massive changes in the job market and reduced security for individual jobs, but no loss of jobs overall. We can all get rich together through the wealth spiral and still be employed.

In the last chapter I gave some examples of the areas where the developed countries will be at a competitive advantage against the developing countries and these will generate significant job opportunities. Even in our more globalized world, most jobs in the developed countries will not originate in the direct provision of goods or services to other countries but rather in catering for demands within the domestic economy, about which I shall say more in a moment.

However, even if there is sufficient aggregate demand for goods and services in the developed countries, the job gloomsters fear that the resulting jobs will be filled not by men but by machines. This is an age-old worry, but it has apparently become more serious because of the advent of the computer and the robot. In the really extreme versions of this paranoia people find themselves not only redundant and devoid of purpose but poor to boot.

The fear of widespread unemployment because of technological progress is utterly unconvincing. The redundancy of particular skills and the loss of particular jobs have been going on since the invention of the wheel. At each stage it has been possible to ask where the new jobs are going to come from. In the event, all sorts of new goods and services on which to spend money, usually completely undreamed-of beforehand, have appeared and all sorts of new sources of employment have arisen.

What has happened to all those people who used to find employment in the business of equipping, caring for, and supplying the huge army of horses that used to provide both personal transport and dragging power in agriculture and commerce? When horses were on the way out no one could have foreseen the enormous numbers of people who would eventually be employed in motor transport, not only making cars but designing, selling, servicing, and advertising them.

And just think of what has happened in the last 30 years. In the countries of western Europe and North America, employment in the mines, shipbuilding yards, factories, and fields has plummeted. Yet the majority of people—including most of those who used to work in the mines, shipbuilding yards, factories, and fields—are incomparably better off.

The upsurge of employment in the information services that has absorbed so many people released from declining industries was largely unforecast. Over the decades to come employment opportunities will doubtless arise in all sorts of unexpected places, although I try to anticipate some of them in what follows.

The threat from robots

It is widely believed, however, that the advent of robots marks something completely different. Supposedly, they potentially render *all* human skills redundant, with next to no scope for the creation of new jobs. At the limit, the robots are created and repaired by other robots. Poor old *Homo sapiens* has reached the end of the road. He is on the scrapheap. Apparently the Sermon on the Mount was wrong: it is the robots who will inherit the earth. (In that case, I ask myself, couldn't we end up working for *them*? That may not be nirvana, but at least there would be jobs.)

This particular nightmare vision of impoverishment by machines is decidedly odd. After all, someone must *own* the robots—and their output. So even if there were no jobs as such, this would hardly be an impoverished world.

More importantly, there *will* be jobs even in the age of the robot. The widespread view that the scope for human activity is narrowing as machines take over is understandable, but mistaken. It is another manifestation of our obsession with the material as a source of both income and employment. What will surely happen is that the realm of the personal and human will rise to replace the worlds of drudgery into which human beings have been condemned for so long. In the economy of the future these will become the preserve of machines, including robots.

It is strange that so many special-interest groups in our society should fret and protest over the preservation of jobs that are surely the modern equivalent of the worst sort of mass industrial employment, often in establishments that could readily pass for dark Satanic mills. The computers and the robots are welcome to them. Many jobs that are being fought over today by trade unions may, within the lifetimes of most people reading this book, be outlawed as inhumane, as child chimney sweeps and women working in the mines were once outlawed.

About time too. Just as industrial machinery made our ability to pull a heavy load almost redundant, so the computer is making redundant certain of our mental powers, the bits to do with pure computation and repetition. This leaves other and, dare I say it, *better* parts of people, the more *human* parts: our capacity for innovation, imagination, caring, personal relationships, and spirituality. In the age of the robot, people will still want interaction with other people—and that will include the provision of services by people, not robots.

Satiation

All of this assumes that there will still be things that people want produced for them or served to them. According to some of the jobs doomsayers, though, there won't be. Supposedly, people in the developed countries are victims of their own success. They have reached the point of satiation where there is a lack of things on which they can spend their money. Producers keep turning the stuff out, but people simply don't need or want it. The economic system has satisfied all economic human needs. The result is that people are left with diminishing opportunities to work.

This is complete poppycock, but it is influential poppycock nevertheless and therefore demands to be taken seriously. There is no shortage of work to be done. As long as there are unsatisfied human wants there will be work. The discussion below, concerning what people will want to spend their money on, clearly indicates the wide variety of sources of income and employment.

Even so, the idea of satiation is difficult to dislodge. Whenever the world experiences a severe economic downturn leading to job losses, it appears as a putative explanation. It even did the rounds in the 1930s, and that ought to demonstrate what nonsense it is. From our current perspective of much greater wealth and consumption, we can clearly see that the millions of desperate people reduced to the dole queue and the soup kitchen by the Great Depression were not there because either they, or society as a whole, had no more unsatisfied wants. Rather, they were there because of a malfunctioning of the economic system meaning that their very real wants for food, warmth, shelter, and myriad other basic things could not be satisfied, even though there they all were, willing to work and thereby collectively able to satisfy these wants. The causes of this malfunctioning were monetary and institutional. This is equally true of the tendency toward deflation in the world today, discussed in Chapter 3.

It is theoretically possible that human wants *could* eventually be satisfied—or at least the sort that can be met by someone else providing some good or service. This could happen either because of generalized superabundance or because of a shift in values against further enrichment, or some combination of the two. In that case opportunities for work would diminish, but this would hardly be a source of impoverishment! On the contrary, it sounds like some economic version of utopia, a cross between Marx's vision of communism and the Buddhist nirvana. (To what extent we will *choose* to work less and take more time for leisure is a different matter from enforced unemployment, and I turn to it in Chapter 10.)

The Fruits of Success

But what will be the object of our employment? From the beginning of time, we have striven to improve our material lot. More food, more shelter, more clothes. Then better food, better shelter, and better clothes. Then more mobility. Then more comfortable mobility. Then more choice. Then more pleasure. Then greater pleasure. Then what? As the world gets richer beyond our forefathers' wildest dreams, what will there be to strive for? In the economy of the future what will the mass affluent spend all their money on?

Even in the developed countries, there is room for more improvement in regard to basic material necessities. Certainly for large parts of the population there is room for *better* food, even if the obesity statistics suggest that there is no room for more of it.

There is also room for more consumer durables; although not, please, on the roads. Yet it is difficult to escape the conclusion that we are coming close to the limit for this phase of our development and that as people get richer there will be a shift in the pattern of consumption.

Sharp changes in the pattern of consumption are nothing new. Since the engine of economic growth really started to change the standard of living of ordinary people some time in the early nineteenth century, patterns of expenditure have been continually changing. In 1820, for instance, food and clothing represented about two-thirds of private consumption. By the late 1980s this share had fallen to only a quarter.[3]

It is not that in the economy of the future we shall stop wanting more and better, but rather that what we want more of, and what we consider to be better, will change; indeed, it is already changing. Take eating, for instance. We may not want to eat much more, but we do want to eat *out* much more. Eating out has become more common, not because people have suddenly discovered a taste for it but because they are now able to afford to indulge their taste more often. In the process, they have created a large number of new jobs in the restaurant and catering trades. As the wealth spiral works its wonders, this trend is set to go much further. And it will be people, not robots, who will be doing the eating—and the serving.

More generally, what we will be wanting more of is entertainment, service, space, comfort, health and health products, status goods, travel, education, plastic surgery, personal development, and, in America at least, litigation. Within all these categories, and even in the mundane parts of consumer expenditure such as food and groceries, greater wealth will mean greater preparedness to pay for something a bit special, a little different, or of higher quality.

In the world of the superabundant, a world of *virtual* reality, a world where basic goods and services are copied to the point of becoming almost free, people will search out the things that will mark them out from others. For the really rich these will be unique, original, and creative. For others they may be branded, styled versions of plain and ordinary goods and services, such as cars, suits, handbags, restaurant meals, and personal training regimes. In a world of superabundance, scarcity has to be artificially created.

Convenience and value

And we will want more *convenience*. The value of things, and even some nonthings, will be dictated by how they fit into the pattern of our preferences and requirements, and these will differ sharply from one individual to another and from one time to another. This developing tendency is already playing havoc with our traditional ideas of what something is worth.

This was brought home to me when someone I knew was persuaded by an aggressive salesperson to buy a booklet of vouchers for admittance to assorted attractions, including hotels, theaters, restaurants, and theme parks. The total face value of the vouchers was $3,000 and they were available to the hapless purchaser for a mere $200. What could be easier? Someone was effectively giving you all that value. This was a clear case of money for nothing. So my friend bought the booklet of vouchers, thinking that it represented incredibly good value.

The trouble was that the restaurant vouchers were all for a meal for one, on a Monday night, with a restricted choice. Another person would have to pay full price, and the prices were extortionate. The theme park was located 200 miles away, the hotel room was 200 miles the other way (available one night of the year, and needing to be booked four months in advance), while the theater ticket only applied to the matinee performance on the pier— and it wasn't *King Lear*.

Far from being a bargain, not a single voucher was used. It was $200 down the drain. It was money for nothing all right, but not quite in the way my friend had imagined. In the end it would have been better to pay $200, or even more, for just one of the attractions, and to forgo everything else, provided that it was available at a time and place that suited.

This is merely a foretaste of what is to come. In the economy of the future, because of increased wealth, convenience and individual preferences will count for much more—and because of increased wealth people will be able to pay for them.

Personal services

There will be an upsurge in demand for the services of the caring professions: nurses, people caring for the old, and those caring for the young. There will also be an upsurge in numbers supplying what is intriguingly described in the British national income statistics as "personal services."

Take hairdressing, for instance. How many times did the average person go to a professional hairdresser 100 years ago? The answer is probably "never." Now the answer, in western Europe at least, is eight or nine times a year.[4]

Why don't they go more often? For some the answer might be lack of time or lack of inclination, but for many the answer will be cost. A trip to the hairdressers is not cheap. It is not uncommon for the full works, including cutting and coloring, to set a woman back the equivalent of half a week's gross average earnings.

Although presumably even the most fastidious of women, or men for that matter, will have some natural limit to the number of times they would wish to visit their hairdresser, nevertheless it would surely be much higher than the average number of eight or nine ruling today. When she was Prime Minister, for instance, Lady Thatcher used to see her hairdresser every day. If hairdressers were free, how many times would the average woman want to go? Once a day probably is the limit, but quite a few would want to go more than once a week. I say "go," but the ultimate luxury is to have them come to you. This is exactly what British Prime Minister's wife Cherie Blair did in 1999 when she flew her personal hairdresser to Durban in South Africa to ensure that her hair looked tip-top for the Commonwealth summit.[5]

Not that I am suggesting that hairdressing will ever become free. (Unless, that is, it is distributed on a system rather like the British National Health Service.) Instead, as people get richer it is one of the things on which they will probably choose to spend more money—and they will have a lot more money to spend. This means that hairdressers, unlike manual workers in factories, will be in increasing demand. What is more, Mrs Jones in Sidcup, or Frau Schmidt in Dortmund, is not going to be flying off to Bangalore to have her hair done. So the increased demand for this service will translate into jobs in the domestic economy.

Hairdressing is the thin end of the wedge. Over the last 20 years personal services have extended to include all aspects of beauty, health, and fitness. In the economy of the future there will be even more pedicures, leg waxing, face cleansing, and training; more health farms, sports tuition, beauty salons, and gyms. As far as status is concerned, personal trainers are the new mobile phones. In the economy of the future they will be joined by beauty advisers and clothing and fashion advisers: some the sort you go and see in their salons and some the sort who come to see you; some whose services you employ on an "industrial" basis, some who are dedicated to you.

Such attention to the person need not stop at the body beautiful. Personal development in all its aspects is ripe for similar treatment: lessons in languages, music appreciation, good speech and conversation, cooking, entertaining, flower arranging, house management, carpentry, DIY, and even spiritual development. The list goes on and on.

Help wanted

There is something much more mundane that will generate job opportunities. Most middle-class people in Europe and America are crying out for help—in the home. Their need is for personal help, help with the children most particularly, but also help with the cleaning, cooking, gardening, shopping, collecting the dry cleaning—all sorts of things that people *can* do themselves but that take up too much time, or are too boring or troublesome to *want* to do them. The home is the new economic frontier.

What suppresses their demand is largely lack of money. It is too expensive for even the moderately successful middle-class professional to contemplate having domestic help extending much beyond a few hours' cleaning or, for those with young families, the part-time, unprofessional services of a young woman mainly interested in learning the language.[6]

We must be the first society in human history where successful people have not been accompanied by a retinue. Successful sportspeople and film stars have staff who arrange their lives, even down to their love lives, but the ultra-successful financial market trader or lawyer does not typically have a personal assistant, apart from in the office where the costs of employing them are set against tax—for their employer. In the economy of the future large numbers of people will be employed directly serving other people, some in a general professional capacity, some in their homes, some on a part-time basis, some full-time.

As people get richer they will readily contemplate paying other people to perform simple tasks that they do not have either the time or the inclination to do. A hundred years ago only the rich with servants would pay someone else to bake a cake for them, yet now virtually everyone pays someone else to do so through the intermediation of the supermarket. This tendency will go a lot further, once the finances allow. Whether or not it makes sense depends, of course, on how much the service costs—and on how much your time is worth. If you value time according to how much you earn per hour in your job, you can easily work out whether or not it is worth your while to pay someone else to perform mundane tasks for you.

Buying a jar of pre-chopped garlic, for instance, saves roughly 20 minutes of slicing and dicing. Anyone who makes more than $10,000 a year can afford it, but freshly chopped garlic tastes better. At the other extreme, hiring a professional to tidy up your messy desk—believe it or not, such professionals exist—although the service costs a mere $85 an hour, would probably only be worth it if you were earning over $500,000 a year, because in order for the professional to do a good job you have to be on hand to tell them what to do. But as people get richer, more and more will contemplate hiring such apparently esoteric service professionals.

So much for the idea of a fixed number of jobs to go round. The truth is exactly the opposite. In the economy of the future jobs will spring from nowhere to meet the apparently unquenchable desire of human beings for things, nonthings, ease, service, comfort, and status.

Fear of McJobs

But will the jobs of the future be *real* jobs? There is a widespread suspicion of the world of restaurants, coffee shops, and beauty salons that we already inhabit, never mind the wilder shores I believe we shall soon visit, including pampering to every whim for personal attention, beautification, development, and entertainment. Incredulity and bafflement are the reactions I encounter most commonly when I address groups of people employed in manufacturing, whether "workers" or managers. "Never mind all the basket weaving and learning to play the harp," they say, "who is going to pay for it all? And who is going to be doing the *real* work?"

By implication, they, the manufacturers, are currently doing the real work, producing the real things, and all the other stuff is peripheral or parasitic. The parasites are becoming so many and so large that they are endangering the very body that gives them sustenance. It cannot go on like this. In the economy of the future, they say, we can't all be advertising executives and cappuccino makers, can we? And even if advertising and cappuccino bars are all very well when you are young, how are we going to support all those retired advertising executives and cappuccino makers?

I have never understood why we can't all be advertising executives and cappuccino makers in *my* country (or yours)—as long as someone, somewhere else, is producing the things that we want to buy and that need to be advertised; and getting the coffee beans, of course. Admittedly, this does raise security concerns for countries that are dependent on others for vital supplies. A world where countries accept such dependence can only really emerge in stable conditions of open trading relations and considerable global security. Yet, as I argued in Chapter 6, that is the position in which countries will find themselves in the economy of the future.

In our only recently de-industrialized world, many find the notion of very few people employed in producing "things" difficult to accept, not for security reasons but because they have a warped sense of where value comes from. Part of their problem is that they do not see things (and nonthings) in the round. Of course, a country of advertising firms and cappuccino bars has to sell something to the outside world in order to be able to pay for the coffee, as well as the foreign-made cars to transport us, the foreign-made cups to drink out of, not to mention the host of other manufactured goods that people want to buy. Yet countries like the US or the UK, which have de-industrialized a good deal, already manage to do that pretty easily. One of the reasons is that their advertising executives sell their skills abroad to those who are good at producing cars or even coffee beans, but are not much good at advertising. They have even had a certain amount of success at persuading foreigners to drink cappuccino.

Developed countries can readily afford to employ a far smaller proportion of their population in manufacturing because of the greater scope for importing things from cheaper countries, the tendency for people, as they get richer, to spend their increased income on nonthings, and the ability to produce "things" with fewer and fewer workers.

The atavistic belief that to be "really productive" means being employed in the production of things is particularly amusing because at the beginning of the Industrial Revolution there was a similar dislocation of values. At that time large parts of society, not least the land-owning classes, thought that true wealth lay in the land and manufacturing wealth was a sort of parasite or second-order form. Now manufacturing has apparently eased itself into the established position threatened by the upstart.

Retiring Gracefully?

Interestingly, just as anxiety about the impending end of work has been stoked up, so anxiety about the need for work has also mounted: the need to keep on working until we drop because of the appalling position of most people's pensions, which I discussed in Chapter 2. At the beginning of the twenty-first century the financial world is abuzz with scare stories about impending doom with regard to pensions. Continental countries have aging populations and unfunded pension schemes. Anglo-Saxon countries may have predominantly funded schemes, but they still have to face the prospect of much lower returns on pension investments than in the past.

Moreover, as I emphasized in Part I, not only are many pension funds under-funded but they are in the front line to receive a battering from a weak world economy and the threat of deflation. Meanwhile, advances in medical science and healthcare are threatening to produce a very large increase in longevity at just the time that more people are retiring "early." The combination could lead to large numbers of people with inadequate provision for their old age.

The big insurance companies are using this as an excuse to launch lavish marketing campaigns to get prospective pensioners not yet out of nappies to make provision for their future. On top of that, pension actuaries are leading a campaign to try to persuade us that we have to think about retiring *later.* Mr. Peter Thomson, chairman of the UK's National Association of Pension Funds (NAPF), has said that pension promises made by companies to millions of workers are in danger of becoming "increasingly unaffordable." He went on:

> *I don't think we can carry on—indefinitely—promising ourselves an ear-lier and earlier retirement and a longer and longer life. It doesn't stack up. If people retire at 55, their 30 or 35 years of work could be followed by 30 years of retirement.*[7]

So will the economy of the future see most of us having to work well into what would have been considered old age, merely to keep body and soul together? Something seems not quite right. The scare stories about impending penury in old age hardly gel with the prospect of prosperity unbound heralded in this book. As well as all the other benefits it will bring us, could rapid economic growth save us from the prospect of either having to scrimp like Scrooge or work until we drop?

I don't know about you, but I am always skeptical about a consensus of experts. I cannot suppress an inherent tendency to believe that it will be proved wrong. (Or is it simply that I *want* it to be proved wrong?) I suppose that if this expert consensus is grossly wrong it is likely to be because some ghastly disease or natural disaster overcomes the advances of medical science and halts the improvements in life expectancy.

However, the economic prospects discussed in this book do provide another possible way in which it could founder. In the developed countries it would not be at all remarkable if real incomes per head were to grow at 2.5 percent a year. This gives rise to the possibility of people saving more in the years ahead without reducing what they spend. They have the option of devoting some or even all of their increased income in future years to saving.

Imagine that the developed countries were able to grow at 4 percent rather than 2.5 percent. Over a working lifetime that makes quite a difference to the prospective flow of income from employment, even if it produces no extra income from investment (because all of the boost to profits is competed away, thereby transferring it to workers). After 20 years average annual incomes would have increased by another 50 percent, over and above the increase generated by 2.5 percent annual growth. This means that we might well feel justified in postponing saving on the grounds that we will be much richer later in life—exactly the opposite of what all the experts are saying.

If the objective is to sustain an income in retirement *in the same proportion* to the income earned during the years of work, I'm afraid that the increased rate of growth of incomes does nothing to alleviate the imperative to save. We may well have a larger income out of which to save in the future, but we will also have a greater standard to live up to. The two effects are exactly offsetting.

That means that we are back with the over-riding influence of inadequate past provision and increased longevity, leading to the need to save more and/or work longer. Regrettably, it seems as though the pensions actuaries may be right after all. But there is one important proviso. If the objective is to sustain a given *absolute* standard of living in retirement, the effect of increased prosperity in the years ahead *is* to allow us to enjoy a longer period of retirement. Greater longevity implies a longer working life, but greater prosperity makes possible the opposite. Surely we might well be prepared to take the benefit of increased prosperity not in the form of increased consumption throughout our life, but rather in the form of an extended period of retirement at the same sort of standard of living as before.

Economic growth is like that. It gives us choices. But it is up to us, and not the actuaries, to make them.

Winners and Losers

Granted that I am right that there is no shortage of work in the aggregate, but that we will not all have to work until we drop, there will be enormous *distributional* implications of the sweeping changes affecting the economy and the world of work described in this book. Average incomes are one thing, but what people really care about is their own incomes, and the general advance in incomes will pass many people by. The flip side of this, of course, must be that there will be others whose incomes will increase by more than the average. In the economy of the future, who will the winners and losers be?

Frankly, no one knows for sure whose incomes will rise relative to the rest, but I am prepared to hazard a guess. The forces described in this book can be summarized as a progressive lessening in importance of both physical labor and repetitive mental effort and, where the need for them remains, the increasing supply of those human faculties in the developed countries by people living in the developing countries. So down go the unskilled and people without the creative or personal skills now in demand. This represents a continuation of recent trends against manual and low-skilled labor in most developed countries.

It is tempting to see this switch against the unskilled also as a switch against the uneducated. At the extremes this will doubtless be true. That is to say, the highly educated are likely to enjoy a rise in relative income and those with next to no educational qualifications to suffer a fall. But in between there is scope for much mischief. The decent secondary education that used to ensure hordes of school leavers clerical jobs in banks, insurance companies, and large corporations will no longer cut much ice in the jobs market. It will be similar with the majority of degrees churned out by universities.

Not only has the demand for clerical and simple administrative work sharply diminished, but its successors in various computer applications and telephone answering will, as I pointed out in Chapter 8, increasingly be performed by people in India, who cost a fraction of their western counterparts and are often better educated to boot.

So who will be on the way up in the economy of the future? Paradoxically certain manual skills, for which the traditional liberal education will *not* equip you, may increase in value. A clear example is plumbing, where already someone can earn a very decent middle-class income without needing much by way of formal educational qualifications.

Professional skills will continue to be in demand and will not be replaced (although they will be aided) by technological gizmos or robots. Doctors and lawyers will experience increases in their real incomes. The foundation for these rises will be the growing real value placed on their skills by consumers, the continuing need and desire to have these services delivered personally rather than by a robot or a computer program, and the limited (albeit increasing) ability to have them supplied from the developing countries, combined with the increasing demand for them from those countries. Even so, increased incomes will not accrue to the weakest members of the professions, as I argue below.

Star incomes?

As I suggest above, the demand for the services of the "less intellectual" professionals such as hairdressers and beauty technicians will also increase. Alas for these people, this will not necessarily mean that they will do particularly well in income terms. They will enjoy the general increase in incomes generated by the forces of prosperity and will do better than the unskilled, but they will not experience a bonanza. For in the economy of the future, the supply of those offering personal services will rise to meet the increase in demand. The thousands of bank clerks, ticket issuers, and call-center operators released by the combination of modern technology and developing-country competition will be transformed into hairdressers—among other things. (One has to hope, for all our sakes, that they will have had some training in between.)

There is one source of hope, though, for much greater incomes. Where the consumer's desire for extra quality translates directly to the demand for skilled staff in short supply, the result will affect relative incomes. Often the supply of a particular sort of labor is limited in the short run, but over time the supply of skills will tend to rise to meet the demand. Accordingly, the forces that at first might lead to increased incomes for the lucky few will, over time, become the forces creating more jobs in the favored areas of expenditure.

Even so, there are some things whose supply cannot respond to increasing demand. The top providers of all sorts of personal services, whether it be hairdressing, cooking, legal advice, design, teaching, or research, will always by definition be in short supply. Because the extra skill they bring becomes even more highly prized as people get richer, *their* rewards are likely to increase relative to the rest of the population.

There is a technological aspect to this that will become even stronger in the economy of the future. In a localized world, the local practitioner of almost anything is largely immune from competition from other locales even though standards there may be higher. His or her customers probably do not know how much better others are, and even if they do know, it is probably not worth their while to travel in order to benefit from improvement. This applies to legal advice, estate agents, travel agents, teachers, and entertainers.

Globalization and the internet undermine all this. Why listen to a third-rate lecturer in Scunthorpe when you can log on to hear the greatest expert on the subject speak at Harvard? Why go to your local doctor for advice when you can have access via the internet to the best medical knowledge there is? Globalization and the internet thus give a decided boost to what may be termed the "star system," thereby increasing the earnings of a very few practitioners against the many. The result across all spheres of sport, entertainment, education, and professional advice will be to undermine market demand for the second and third rate and increase it for the really excellent—the "winner-takes-all" society.

What stands against this, nevertheless, is the continuing and even increased desire for personal contact. In some professions it is difficult to imagine expert practice at a distance replacing less expert practice in the here and now. Hairdressing surely falls into this category.

Even so, hairdressing is already swept up in the star system. As people get richer, so star hairdressers will command even greater premiums over run-of-the-mill hairdressers. Every hairdresser will aspire to make his or her fortune through becoming a "star." But although many will aspire, few will be chosen. It cannot be otherwise. After all, if it could, they wouldn't be stars, would they?

Adjusting to Change

One overwhelming aspect of the changes to the economic landscape described in the last chapter leaps out at us: change itself. How companies cope with the instability is one thing, but in the economy of the future how will individuals cope and what effect will it have on our lives?

In a world where technological shifts and the continual march of international competitive forces regularly undermine companies and sources of employment, it is unreasonable to expect the same degree of work security as existed in more stable times. That means that if people still have the same hunger for stability and security, either the economy of the future is set on a collision course with the happiness of ordinary people or they will have to find other ways of deriving security. I think the increased prosperity thrown up by the economy of the future will ensure that the answer predominantly lies with the latter, but it will require some adjustments.

The first sort of adjustment is financial. If sources of employment are going to be more unstable, it makes sense for people to carry large savings to act as a cushion against difficult times. The development of new forms of insurance to protect against economic risks, discussed in the last chapter, will also provide an important means of combating insecurity.

The second adjustment needs to be in education. It is extraordinary that the educational system seems to be moving more in the direction of training for specific jobs and yet the logic of the insecurity of employment is that what people will require is skills *flexibility*. This means not only being prepared and able to retrain and redevelop skills when you are older, but also having the general educational skills to be able to do that. In other words, what young people need most of all is not some particular sort of skill or learning but the learning that teaches you how to learn other things.

The third adjustment is surely more important than the other two. With people much richer and arguably not working as hard or as long (see Chapter 10), the variability and insecurity of employment should imply that people see less of themselves and their identity as bound up with their "fixed" place of work. It should seem more and more extraordinary that people define themselves in relation to the location of various pieces of fixed capital. Mind you, for people to be able to achieve this degree of separation and distancing from their place and even type of work, their personal relationships, and relationships with the communities in which they live, will have to be stronger than has typically been the case in most of the industrial West for the last 50 years.

In one sense, recent developments in communications technology make that seem feasible. The Industrial Revolution took work out of the home. The Intangible Revolution could put it back. Yet I am skeptical that working from home will ever broadly replace full-time work in a place outside the home. The reason is simple: personal contact matters. It matters for personal relationships, and it matters for effective communication in business. For all the supposed attractions of working from home, I suspect that a large proportion of the work force would rather leave the home to earn their living and go to a place of work where they can interact with colleagues.

But could globalization alter the location of both home and work? The development of the global economy as a single entity is bound to have significant implications for where people live and work. At the very least, there will be more international exchange of people as business arranges itself on multinational lines. This means more international postings: more Americans and Europeans being sent to China and more Chinese being sent to Europe and North America, for example.

Within the developed countries themselves there will also probably be a continued move of population away from the old manufacturing centers whose rationale for existence, never mind prosperity, is often lost in the mists of the Industrial Revolution, and which cannot easily prosper in the new service- and intangible-dominated economy. So the population may continue to leech from Britain's industrial north, for instance, from the old towns of northern France and Belgium, and from the industrial heartland of western Germany.

That said, increased global involvement need not imply massive movement of population. That is the point about the efficiency of communication and the possibility of coordinating globally dispersed production. Globalization will imply greater interdependence, but this does not mean that we will all gradually become homogenized citizens of the world, without ties to a particular country. We can become more interdependent staying just where we are.

Enjoying Our Leisure

Enough of work and its implications. What will we do when we are not working? We will be trying to enjoy ourselves, of course. As I explained above, one of the things we will be wanting more of as we get richer is entertainment, in all its guises. But it will not simply be a matter of quantity. The combination of greater wealth, globalization, and the Intangible Revolution will bring some major changes of type.

Globalization is of particular relevance to the travel industry. Already there has been an upsurge of demand for travel to "exotic" locations, and the recently exotic quickly becomes the commonplace. As the developing world continues to advance, new destinations will come to prominence in China, India, the former Soviet Union, Africa, and Latin America.

Meanwhile, consumer preferences with regard to the mode and comfort of travel will alter. It is extraordinary that for mass-market holidays air travel is no more comfortable or enjoyable than it was when the package tour first took off half a century ago. By contrast, in relation to car travel much has changed to make the driver more comfortable and the experience more enjoyable.

For mass air travel the accent has been on packing as many people into planes as possible. The revolution of the last five years has been the emergence of budget airlines that have competed away the huge gross margins of the bloated national carriers. This competition has been welcome, but there is a limit to how far the minimal-frills ethos can go. Once the current cost-cutting binge has run its course, in the economy of the future since travelers will be much richer, one of the things on which they will want to spend their money is comfort during the journey, and that will include the amount of space they have.

Rising expectations leading to higher standards will also apply at the other end of the journey. There will probably be increased demand for activity and risk holidays where the hotel standards are not what will matter, but for more conventional travel people will expect bigger and better-equipped hotel rooms and more and better entertainment facilities.

This pattern of rising standards following a period when the accent was purely on cost is fully in line with other experiences during the mass-production era. Cost and efficiency considerations led to the proliferation of mass-produced instant coffee, beer, bread, meat, and vegetables. Production costs have been reduced to pretty much rock bottom and now that people have more money to spend, the "real thing" is re-emerging and standards are rising. The same will happen with mass-produced air travel and the holiday business. We will demand and expect higher standards—and we will get them.

Virtual leisure?

Important though these developments will be, it is likely that the changes to our leisure hours brought about by globalization will be dwarfed by the changes wrought by technology. We will be swamped by cheap digital entertainment. Films constantly on tap; music downloadable instantaneously at negligible cost; complete digital experiences of travel, danger, sex, being in love, anything you like, available at the click of a mouse to envelop you in all-around sound and pictures. I don't know why we don't simply go for implanting a chip in the brain and have the images transmitted directly.

The sheer ubiquity and virtual costlessness of all this stuff could kill off the real thing. Take soccer, for instance. Why go and see your local Hopeless

FC struggle to play when wherever you are in the world you can watch Manchester United play the best football there is? At the moment there might be some sort of rationale, as Hopeless FC still commands local loyalty and provides a reasonable day's entertainment. But the difficulties of Hopeless FC, and all providers of less than top-class sport and entertainment, are set to increase. The possibility of global distribution of sports coverage, in opening up a huge audience, dramatically improves the finance available to those soccer clubs like Manchester United that are able to command a world following.

This not only means that the gap between their ability to attract and retain the best players and Hopeless FC's ability to attract them increases, but also, partly because of this, the facilities for those people who turn up to watch the game in person improve. By contrast, Hopeless FC gets none of this money and progressively the facilities and entertainment afforded to its fans will seem more and more inadequate.

Classical orchestral concerts are another activity where digital technology is having a significant impact on the market. Attendances at classical concerts are falling. Some observers think this is due to a change in cultural values, yet this hardly seems credible when classical radio stations attract significant audiences and singers like Luciano Pavarotti have a huge following, with their personal popularity reaching parts of society that no previous classical artist ever managed to penetrate.

The main reason is staring the concert promoters in the face, if only they would recognize it. There was next to no recorded music 100 years ago. If you wanted to listen to classical music you had to go to a concert. This restricted the audience because even among those who might be interested, not many were close to places where concerts were performed and many of those who were would not be able to afford to go. Nevertheless, there was no competition from recorded music. Eventually the radio, the gramophone, and then the record player made classical music widely available, but the sound quality was so poor that the listener was just getting an impression of the "real" sound.

Modern recording and reproduction techniques mean that the sound experience of recorded or broadcast music is remarkably close to the real thing. Moreover, for your CD, or your internet download, you can choose the all-time great performance of, say, Beethoven's *Ninth Symphony* by the Vienna Philharmonic. Why would you be interested in paying to go to hear one of the all-time pedestrian performances by the Croydon Philharmonic?

This is particularly so when you consider the cost. The relative price of CDs has already dropped dramatically in relation to the price of concert tickets and is set to fall much more. To download from the internet—even legally—you pay next to nothing. A typical concert ticket costs about $25. For that you could buy two CDs; in America, probably three. That is before you have taken into account the other costs of going to a concert. Your $25 will buy you perhaps one and a half, or at most two hours of music. Is it any wonder that concert audiences are in decline?

It's the atmosphere, stupid

So do the fate of Hopeless FC and the Croydon Philharmonic spell a disaster for all sorts of live entertainment? No. When television first arrived it was soon predicted that it would kill all sorts of live entertainment—except the stuff that was broadcast live on television. Nothing of the sort has happened. Rather, performers often make a name for themselves on television and can then charge a small fortune to appear live in front of people at shows, clubs, conferences, or business functions. For a time television and video certainly threatened the cinema, but now even cinema audiences are recovering.

Human beings are social creatures. Scientists still do not fully understand much of what drives and motivates us, what we enjoy and fear, but the ordinary man and woman has more than a decent grasp of it. Why do we still go to live events like a football match or to a concert or to the opera, rather than watching it virtually, on screens, in the comfort of our own homes? You might try to explain it by reference to the width of vision given to the live viewer on the spot as opposed to the prison of the screen; or the free choice of what to look at rather than being a slave to the cameraman's penchant for gravitating to the third clarinet, even though she happens to be devastatingly beautiful.

If you put this question to live audiences for sport, music, theater, opera, anything at all, they will all come back with the same reply: the atmosphere. They are telling you that their pleasure is intimately connected with being there in the presence of others and sharing the experience of the sport, or music, or whatever. You may regard this as a sort of frippery or optional extra and consider that the aficionados are paying good money for nothing, but they most assuredly are not. "The atmosphere" is part of the very essence of these things. What is more, I reckon that before too long physicists will be able to identify what it is that causes this reaction. It is surely some sort of emotional energy passing between people like a form of electricity. (Identifying and understanding this energy could be a worthy task for the modern Isaac Newton, whoever that may be.)

Atmosphere is closely related to the question of why it still seems important to meet people even in these days of instant digital communication, and why it is better to discuss difficult issues, or try to form bonds and engender feelings of trust with business partners, face to face rather than modem to modem.

The importance of personal contact and atmosphere is even true for an activity like gambling that, because it is so quintessentially intangible, you might think would gravitate almost entirely to the world of the virtual. There already is a market for purely screen-based gambling but it seems unlikely that it will ever draw the high-rollers or replace the real thing. It hasn't got the atmosphere. Casinos and race courses will survive, even prosper in the internet age. Indeed, the growth of the virtual market will help the real thing by broadening the audience, supplying more revenue with which to fund the real thing, and providing a comparator against which that can be judged.

This view is put most forcefully by a British on-course bookmaker called Barry Dennis. His job is to stand at race courses calling and changing the odds on different horses. Despite the challenge of the internet, Dennis feels that his future is secure.

> In my lifetime, I'm not going to worry about these anoraks staring at screens inches from their nose for hours on end. People having a tenner with me, 2–1 chance, getting their grubby hands round 30 quid—it's far more exciting than waiting for a statement to come through, a month later, saying they've been credited with twenny pand. You don't go out and buy a bottle of champagne with that, do you? Bet on-course, and the readies are there, in your hand. That Internet, I tell you, it's soulless.[8]

Nevertheless, there will have to be some adaptation from the providers of entertainment to adjust to the changes in the marketplace made by the digital revolution: to provide a real experience, with atmosphere that, given the costs, can compete with the digital alternatives. Granted sufficient development of the product, maybe even Hopeless FC can survive.

Live concerts will continue, but not on the scale of the postwar years. There are currently too many orchestras performing too many concerts. Like the shipbuilders and miners before them, the orchestral ranks will have to be thinned out. Yet precisely because of the wider spread of the appreciation of classical music throughout the populace—partly brought about by the spread of excellent recorded, broadcast, and downloaded music—the market for the top performers will probably *increase*.

Global Relationships

Economic circumstances and technological development will also have a profound impact on even the most human part of our life, our relationships with each other. Some commentators allege that they will transform them.

Globalization will open up the possibility of more relationships with people from wider afield than previously seemed possible. More people posted to work abroad and more frequent and more distant travel for both work and pleasure are bound to have this result.

Admittedly this does have its potential downside, namely the loosening of ties with a community and the increasing superficiality of friendships that are constantly subject to the breaks associated with frequent relocation and the strains of distance.

Increased prosperity will also give people the wherewithal to maintain these relationships by seeing people separated by large distances, while keeping in touch through email and the telephone is already both easy and cheap and will eventually become even more so, not least through commonplace videophone links.

These changes to the field of human relationships will be a continuation of a development that has been proceeding since the Industrial Revolution, and even before, whereby improved transport and social and economic change have released people from the tyranny of their own locale and widened the field of people with whom they could have relationships. This point applied as much to friendships and sexual relationships as to business. Before the nineteenth century it was the norm for people in Britain and continental Europe to marry someone who lived in their own village, simply because they did not get much opportunity to meet people from elsewhere.

Today we regard this as unthinkably restrictive, as we have become used to the idea of the field of our possible relationships extending more or less across the country. In the economy of the future, we will come to see *this* as unthinkably restrictive as well.

Virtual relationships

Does the combination of globalization and the communications revolution mean that many of our relationships—even our intimate ones—could shift to the world of the virtual? Some people think so and there are signs pointing that way. More than 30,000 Japanese men have struck up relationships with virtual girlfriends through an online service called Love by Mail, which they can access on their internet-capable mobile phones.[9] The men can choose between different women, including a flight attendant, a school teacher, and a bar hostess. The girls write back to their "mail friends," while quite *how* they respond depends on how the men behave. For example, men who talk incessantly about sport during a romantic encounter, or who pledge undying love too soon in the relationship, are given the cold shoulder. Just like the real thing, right?

This is not as much tosh as it sounds. As computer technology becomes more and more capable, there will doubtless be more and more experiences that can be imitated or insinuated over the net, including seeing and touching people in their full glory. These services will have their takers.

At one level, as with the family that cannot be together on an important occasion like a child's birthday, being able to get virtually close will be a big improvement over the current situation, where voice contact by telephone has to suffice. And that, of course, is a huge leap forward from the days before the telephone, when there was nothing.

At the other extreme, nerds of all types will be able to make up for the inadequacies of their lives by enjoying the virtual equivalents: meals, friendships, sexual relationships. This will not make such encounters the real thing, or even anything close. In the realm of the truly intangible, the digital will supplant the physical as not only the norm but also the standard. Nevertheless, in the realm of the truly human the digital will be known as the ersatz, the second rate, what you put up with if you cannot get, or cannot afford, the real thing.

Mind you, in Silicon Valley you could be forgiven for thinking that personal relationships had already been almost extinguished in favor of computers. A team of anthropologists from San Jose State University spent two years studying families in California's Palo Alto–San Jose area.[10] What they uncovered makes anthropological field studies in the South Seas seem pretty tame by comparison. Employers commonly refer to families as "drag units" because they restrict the time staff can spend at work. But it does not seem as though staff need much encouragement to see their families as subsidiary to their work. Parents develop "mission statements" for their families and talk about having "value-added" romances. It is common for all family members to send emails during dinner.

Somehow I don't think that this behavior is going to catch on outside the narrow confines of the digitally certifiable. In the economy of the future I don't see computerspeak ever becoming the universal language of romance, or gourmets asking for emails to accompany their foie gras.

Because so much of the new world will be virtual, far from the importance of real contact with real people diminishing in the economy of the future, it will increase. Precisely because you can have a virtual meeting with almost anyone on the planet, meeting someone in person and shaking their hand, reacting to their body language, absorbing the messages coming from their *presence*, will become more important in business, not less. As for romance, what can I say?

Although virtual meetings will proliferate, whether for business or romantic liaison, they will never be regarded as the real thing. And in the end, for human relationships only the real thing will do.

The Ultimate Destination?

This is the culmination of all the wrenching changes that, gathering pace with the Industrial Revolution, have transformed our daily reality over hundreds of years: a life of abundance for all, in which the basic material needs are easily satisfied but we have now moved on to want, and receive, even the basic necessities in a more sophisticated, comfortable, differentiated, and individual form, and new wants appear relentlessly as if from nowhere; the proliferation of more and more sophisticated forms of entertainment; the continuation of work, even with the presence of millions of robots to minister to these various desires; and the widening of both the business and the personal locale to encompass the whole world.

However, there is surely a major question that will nag at all of us in the economy of the future, and already occurs to many people today. Is this what it is all about? Having conquered the economic problem that has been man's estate from the beginning of time, is this it?

If it is, many people will wonder whether all the effort has been worthwhile. The search for wealth may have met with enormous and unprecedented success and therefore reached some sort of conclusion, but the quest for meaning goes on.

10
Money for Nothing?

No man can practice virtue who is living the life of a mechanic or a laborer.

Aristotle[1]

I would predict that the standard of life in the progressive countries one hundred years hence will be between four and eight times as high as it is today ... this means that the economic problem is not—if we look into the future—the permanent problem of the human race.

John Maynard Keynes, 1930[2]

This book began with an episode from the life of the most famous victim of the lust for money for nothing and it is fitting that it should end by continuing his story, not least because it has a further message for us today. Sir Isaac Newton not only survived the South Sea Bubble but died a rich man, thanks to lucrative public appointments such as Master of The Royal Mint. And as a result of his remarkable scientific and mathematical achievements, he died famous, with a standing among men that was beyond compare. As Alexander Pope put it:

> *Nature and nature's laws lay hid in night;*
> *God said, "Let Newton be!" and all was light.*[3]

Yet Newton was by no means all pure scientist, "one who taught us to think on the lines of cold and untinctured reason." The range of interests over which his genius extended its extraordinary powers of concentration and enquiry is intriguing. Nor by this do I refer to his role as a public servant, figure of fame, or survivor of financial misfortune. There is something else, something much more important. For a large part of his life this apparently most inhuman of men was frantically and exhaustively seeking the answer to the ultimate human question, the meaning of life itself. According to one of his later admirers:

> He looked upon the whole universe and all that is in it as a riddle, as a secret which could be read by applying pure thought to certain evidence, certain mystic clues which God had laid about the world to allow a sort of philosopher's treasure hunt to the esoteric brotherhood.

And a large part of his writings was concerned with the apocalyptic: "writings from which he sought to deduce the secret truths of the Universe—the measurements of Solomon's Temple, the book of Daniel, the Book of Revelations." Another large section of his writings was about alchemy: transmutation, the philosopher's stone, and the elixir of life.

In the nineteenth and early twentieth centuries, the nature of these papers was hushed up by all those who saw them. For what they reveal is that Cambridge's most famous son, the discoverer of gravity, calculus, and much else besides, was a "magician." No wonder Roger W. Babson was so taken with him.

We might not ask exactly Newton's questions, or expect his answers, but we should join him in the intensity and boldness of his quest. As we stand on the brink of great wealth, we too should reflect on the ultimate question. For economic activity that question is surely: What is the point of it all? Will the continued enrichment of the human race that lies before us make us happier? And if not, why are we so frantically engaged in pursuing it?

The Keynes connection

The man who brought Newton's mystical and magical sides out into the open and who was responsible for the above-quoted descriptions was another of Cambridge's famous sons, none other than John Maynard Keynes. Keynes was fascinated by Newton,[4] and he had something in common with him. Keynes was no physicist, nor was he a mystic, alchemist, or theologian. But on top of his technical and policy work he was also seriously concerned with the ultimate question. He too was seeking the meaning of life, but in a different sense. He was seeking an answer to what I have suggested should be our question: the point of economic activity. And for an economist he came up with a radical answer.

Despite his expertise in matters financial and his evident enjoyment of material comforts, Keynes was no materialist. What he valued above all was the nonmaterial; intellectual inquiry certainly, but also art and human relationships. And this was his vision for the rest of humankind, once the economic problem had been overcome.

Because of the fecundity of the economic system, he envisaged a time when everyone could enjoy a life not only of material comfort, but also of leisure, with their attentions devoted to the really important, human things. And most significantly, people's values would be the essential, eternal, moral ones. As he put it:

> I see us free, therefore, to return to some of the most sure and certain principles of religion and traditional virtue—that avarice is a vice, that the exaction of usury is a misdemeanour, and the love of money is detestable, that those walk most truly in the paths of virtue and sane wisdom who take least thought for the morrow. We shall once more value ends above means and prefer the good to the useful. We shall honour those who can teach us how to pluck the hour and the day virtuously and well, the delightful people who are capable of taking direct enjoyment in things, the lilies of the field who toil not, neither do they spin.

Forecast good or bad?

The grandchildren have grown up, so Keynes' vision should have been realized, or at least be within sight. Is it?

In the underdeveloped and developing countries, it is not even remotely on the horizon. Despite some improvement in living standards over recent decades even in poor countries, countless millions of people continue to live with the daily reality of hunger and millions more with the fear of it. Even where food is regularly available, hundreds of millions of people have a standard of living hardly removed from the Malthusian concept of subsistence. In Pakistan, for instance, 85 percent of people live on less than $2 a day and 31 percent live on less than $1 per day.

This poverty is not merely a matter of bald GDP or income statistics but goes to the roots of human misery. In this age that people in the developed countries are accustomed to think of as affluent, the poor remain afflicted by the old horrors that have traditionally accompanied poverty: disease and untimely death. Many of the diseases that have virtually disappeared from the developed world are still rife in poor countries, including tuberculosis, syphilis, polio, and leprosy; now joined by AIDS. In the richest fifth of countries the typical rate of infant mortality is 4 out of every 1,000 births, but in the poorest countries the rate is 200 out of every 1,000 births. Two million children die annually of dehydration from diarrhoea alone.

Nor is there much doubt about the link between poverty and the rate of child death. One study has concluded that in 1990 the death of half a million children would have been averted if Africa's growth in the 1990s had been 1.5 percent higher.[5]

In view of the continuing presence of real poverty and deprivation, there is no doubt that if the underdeveloped and developing countries enjoy good economic growth in the years ahead, the money will be spent on providing the bare necessities of life for decades to come, with Keynes' vision of a life of leisure and the higher good a mere pipedream. The good news is that over the approaching decades the wealth spiral can lift them out of poverty, thereby bringing not merely increased GDP figures but also a palpable improvement in the quality of life and a reduction in the sources of misery and affliction for hundreds of millions of people.

Work, rest, and play

What about the developed countries or, as Keynes put it, "the progressive countries"? Some observers apparently believe that his vision of leisure in the ascendant has already been realized. According to the newspaper columnist Christina Odone, work has been debunked and leisure has taken its place. Whereas work used to consume almost all our lives between cradle and grave, it is now fitted in between umpteen other activities that are more important: sex and shopping, children, exercise. Society now operates on what she calls the unwork ethic. Our business, she says, is hedonism.

Compared with the position 100 years ago, she has a fair point. From 1870 to 1990, in both Europe and North America, incomes soared and the average number of hours worked per annum fell from 3,000 to 1,600.[6] In some countries the fall in average hours worked has continued since 1990, albeit at a much slower pace.

A fair proportion of people in the developed countries do exercise their preference for more leisure over more money. Some do it by opting voluntarily for early retirement; some by choosing less time-consuming and less stressful jobs; some by choosing to work part-time; some by spending an extended period studying at a relaxed pace rather than working hard to earn money. Equally, the intensity, sophistication, and expense of many leisure activities are much greater. But that is exactly what you would expect given the huge increase in average incomes over the period. It is natural and inevitable that a large part of people's expenditure goes on leisure goods and leisure pursuits.

Yet I do not think it is fair to say that society as a whole operates on the unwork ethic. Even with regard to hours worked, if you look at trends over the last 20 years you see a rather different pattern, at least in the Anglo-Saxon countries. Designated hours of work in manual jobs may have fallen, but actual hours of work in office, professional, and managerial jobs have actually risen. And whatever the average hours of work may be per head, it should never be forgotten that more heads are working as married women increasingly stay in full-time work. In short, work plays a larger, not a smaller, part in our lives.

Admittedly, things look rather different in France. In 2001, to widespread consternation in French business circles and amazement in the Anglo-Saxon countries, the French government introduced a 35-hour week. This could be construed as another major shift away from work and toward leisure, a shift that other countries will soon follow. But the measure was designed not so much to shift the work–life balance as to share out work "more equitably." If people are not allowed to work so many hours, the argument ran, more people will have to be employed, thereby reducing France's chronic unemployment rate.

Even if it is sensible to be moving in the direction of more leisure, this notion of creating jobs through restricting working hours is an abomination. It assumes that there is a fixed amount of work to go round, a misguided idea that has been around for hundreds of years and economists know as "the lump of labor fallacy." In the event, the 35-hour week caused minimal adverse effects on productivity because employers were allowed to interpret it extremely flexibly, even managing to annualize it, thereby diluting it by including holidays.

In America matters are definitely starker. In the 20 years to 1992 the working hours of the average employee in the US *increased* by the equivalent of one month per year.[7] Americans seemed to be choosing money over time. In America especially, but also in some other Anglo-Saxon countries, if there is one "thing" that most working men and women are really short of it is time. The more successful you are, the more short of time you tend to be. This is the exact opposite of how things used to be in the old days, good or bad, when wealth conferred leisure. Nowadays, the only people with oodles of time are the retired and the permanently unemployed—the underclass. In general, however, they have little or no money with which to enjoy their "leisure."

In the Anglo-Saxon countries certainly, and spreading into the countries of continental Europe, the work culture has become more intense and more demanding, with a concomitant increase in feelings of stress and pressure. Although some people undoubtedly do enjoy work, all the evidence is that large numbers do not—and they certainly do not enjoy the excessive pressure, stress, and sheer input of hours. Even in France, although people work fewer hours than the British, over recent decades the pace of life has increased and such customary practices of yore as the three-hour lunch are on the wane.

Accordingly, I think we must count Keynes' vision of a mass switch away from work and toward leisure as largely unfulfilled.

Higher values

What about Keynes' idea that without the incessant struggle for money in order to meet our material needs we could revert to a more *moral* life, following a different set of values? Is there any sign of this? There is not much altruism to be seen in the burgeoning levels of crime experienced in most developed countries—or at least those in the West—and it appears that basic civility and neighborliness are in decline.

Perhaps it can be argued that there is an increase in concern for others on a grand scale, as manifested in widespread anxiety, and occasional generosity of spirit and money, in Europe and North America about recurrent starvation and natural disasters in parts of Africa and Asia. Yet I think it would be more accurate to see this as a fringe concern. Most people in the developed countries are suffering from compassion fatigue.

In western societies there is currently an upsurge of interest in religions and philosophies outside the western mainstream—including so-called new-age thinking, paganism, Islam, and various eastern religions—which results from a disillusion not only with Christianity and Judaism, but also with secularism and materialism. A good part of the appeal of environmentalism and the antiglobalization movement arises from the same source. So perhaps there are signs of the emergence of a different set of values, just as Keynes suggested.

Yet the thoughts, values, and aspirations of the majority of people in the developed countries are just as dominated by the selfish pursuit of money as they ever were. After all, what was the bubble all about if not rampant greed on the part of millions? Nor was this for everybody merely the lower-order selfishness of pursuing one's own interests without thinking of others. For some, the higher orders, involving the knowledge that someone else was suffering from your gain, were also actively involved. The gross frauds that took place in corporate America and the misrepresentation and bending of the truth by the investment banks in order to mislead clients to their own advantage, as well as the absurd levels of personal wealth sought after and received by senior executives, all fell into this category.

Far from a widespread shift to higher values, the lives of hundreds of millions of people in the developed countries are degraded not by abject poverty but by rampant consumerism, which has caused them to lose sight of both common human feeling and spirituality. Admittedly, this is not quite the same as base materialism. The relative decline of bare material things has altered the status pecking order. As I argued in the last chapter, consumption of "designer" goods, differentiated services, and "lifestyle" are more the focus of "achievement" than the amassing of more and more things. But is this really all that different? Is it any better?

A flawed vision?

Is Keynes' vision unfulfilled because it was fundamentally flawed? Is it simply another aspect of his intellectual "Edwardianism," out of place anywhere outside his own particular, comfortable corner of western Europe, and now completely out of time everywhere?

Some people argue that the present intensity of work and never-ending pursuit of money are caused by necessity. This supposedly explains, for instance, why both husband and wife typically have to work, and often work themselves into a frazzle. These days, they will say, things are so tough that you simply have to work this hard merely to keep afloat.

This is nonsense. How can the richest society in the whole of human history *require* people to work harder? The economic system has turned out to be no less productive than Keynes envisaged. The average rate of economic growth since he wrote the essay has been faster than in the interwar period in Britain, and faster also than the rate of growth in the heyday of Britain's industrial supremacy in the nineteenth century. No, people today pursue money as avidly as before despite, in Keynes' terms, not having to.

Or was Keynes' vision flawed in its concept of work? Work is one of our deepest needs and a life without it, no matter how rich you are, is often a life unfulfilled and unhappy.[8] There is no doubt that plenty of people actively enjoy their work, including some of those who seem to work every hour God sends—in the financial markets, at the law, in the corporate world, or running their own business. For some of those people, their work is their life. And work can be part of the pursuit of the higher virtues of which Keynes wrote.

To my mind, though, this criticism misses the mark. I do not think Keynes' vision was one in which *work* disappeared. It is all a matter of what work is—and what it is for. When saying that we need to work, what is really meant is that we need "purposive activity." That need not be sitting at a loom for 14 hours a day in one of Blake's dark Satanic mills, or sitting at the modern-day (much more highly paid) equivalent, a desk in a cavernous dealing room at one of the investment banks.

What Keynes was surely arguing is that as we get richer, the nature of our purposive activity should move progressively away from the pursuit of money in order to be able to satisfy basic material needs, simply because these needs would be more nearly satisfied.

Of course, it could be argued that spiritual development has nothing at all to do with levels of material comfort. Some of the world's greatest religious thinkers and moralists have lived at times of general poverty and many have themselves led lives of particular material deprivation. Some would argue that there is even a *positive* link between material deprivation and religious devotion. Accordingly, you could say that we are spiritually impoverished, not despite our material wellbeing but because of it.

However valid such thinking may be for a few religious fanatics, I cannot accept this as the general truth about humanity. As Douglas McGregor put it:

> *Man lives by bread alone, when there is no bread. Unless the circumstances are unusual, his needs for love, for status, for recognition are inoperative when his stomach has been empty for a while. But when he eats regularly and adequately, hunger ceases to be an important need.*[9]

In similar vein, with hard work having produced so many much-needed material goods, we should be freer: freer to pursue, develop, and express our emotional, moral, and spiritual side. Yet that is a freedom most people don't exercise. Despite continued enrichment, they continue in the old, money-obsessed ways.

Happiness and the Economy

That would be all very well if the pursuit of money made people happier. But when you look at the evidence, one depressing thing leaps out at you. In the developed countries, despite the enormous increase in wealth and the improvement in living standards, by and large people seem to be no happier than they were 50 years ago.

As Professor Richard Layard has pointed out, this is what emerges conclusively from surveys asking people how happy they are.[10] Since the early 1970s the General Social Survey has asked people in the US this question. Before then Gallup asked a similar question going back to 1946. Although the proportion who said that they were very happy rose in the 1950s, it subsequently fell back and since the 1960s has been fairly stable. Other countries, including Japan and most of Europe, similarly reveal no increase in happiness despite enormous increases in income. (Denmark and Italy are the exceptions.)

Moreover, when you measure levels of reported happiness *across countries* you encounter a startling result. Up to an average per capita annual income of about $15,000 a year, GDP and happiness rise together. Up to this point, therefore, it is reasonable to suppose that increased income brings increases in happiness. But after that, higher incomes are *not* noticeably associated with higher levels of happiness.

The average citizen of the US is no happier than the average citizen of Puerto Rico, even though his income is about three times as high. People living in rich countries such as Britain, Italy, and Canada are not appreciably happier than those living in much poorer countries such as Columbia, Taiwan, and South Korea. Japan registers about the same level of happiness as the Philippines, even though its citizens are about 10 times as rich. Indeed, according to Gavin McCormack, "nowhere is the emptiness of affluence more deeply felt" than in Japan.

Before you dismiss such evidence as meaningless because it is hopelessly subjective, it should be noted that neuroscience is starting to be able to measure feelings of happiness and it produces results that broadly accord with those of the surveys.

So, according to the evidence, once countries reach the sort of affluence that Britain reached in the 1950s, the "never had it so good" years, further accretions of wealth do not seem to bring happiness. Although economic growth has seen living standards rise several times over the last 50 years, people are no more satisfied than they were before. If growth is supposed to make us happier, or at least more satisfied, the verdict is staring us in the face: it has failed.

GDP won't buy you love

Why? In the words of Polly Toynbee, "When God died, GDP took over and economists became the new high priests."[11] It has long been recognized that GDP is a flawed measure of wellbeing, but perhaps its flaws are so serious that it can continue to rise headily while human wellbeing stagnates or even declines.[12]

There are certainly many quirks of national income accounting that can cause GDP to rise or fall without any corresponding real change in human wellbeing. For instance, much of what contributes to our wellbeing are services that are performed by family members in the home, but because these do not get paid they do not enter our measures of national income. It is only when activities move into the money nexus that they get picked up by the national accounts.

If, for example, two women who previously looked after their own children employed each other to do the job for them, the national income would go up, even though exactly the same amount and type of activity is taking place and no one is any better off. In a different vein, expenditure on dealing with crime and pollution is recorded as part of GDP, whereas the crime and the pollution giving rise to this expenditure are not recorded as reducing it. Rising divorce rates contribute to GDP because of divorce lawyers, counseling, and multiple households—and money spent on antidepressants.

There is another more technologically based explanation for the disjunction between GDP and wellbeing. According to Richard Tomkins, there have been no increases in wellbeing simply because whatever the GDP figures say about the amount of goods or services being pumped out by our economy, we haven't recently come up with any new products or processes that truly revolutionize our lives. That is because we have progressed so far down the line that there are no really major improvements left to be made. As Tomkins puts it: "More than 40 years have passed since the introduction of the last blockbuster product: disposable nappies, or diapers as they are known in the US."[13]

Tomkins is clearly skeptical about the claims of information technology to be such another life-enhancing advance:

A copy of the Financial Times already contains more information than someone in the 17th century would have been exposed to in their lifetime. How much more are we capable of absorbing?

The technology is not always right
There is even a chance that the changes of the Intangible Revolution, which I have argued will bring so many benefits, will also cause significant losses that reduce the quality of our lives in ways that are not recorded in the GDP statistics. This would come as a great surprise to all the digitally certifiable techies whose natural inclination is to think that whatever is technologically feasible is both desirable and economically viable.[14]

According to one frequently espoused argument, our GDP statistics *underestimate* the growth in real income because they give insufficient weight to the relentless improvement in the quality of goods. But what about services? There is a good deal of evidence that the quality of many services has deteriorated. What is more, technological "improvements" are often at the heart of what has gone wrong.

Technological advances in the field of communication, for example, are rather like advances in warfare. Each advance in offensive techniques is quickly followed by advances in defensive techniques. Voicemail, properly used, is wonderful. But how often is it properly used? I know several business organizations where it is routine for staff to have voicemail on all the time, inviting the caller to leave a message or alternatively to contact the secretary on extension 6421. And these are organizations where even the secretaries have secretaries—and they are all on voicemail too. Doubtless this is supposed to save the organization costs somewhere along the line, but where is the allowance for the wasted time and frustration on the part of callers, who might be existing or potential customers?

Even worse than this is the routine deployment of voice messages inviting you to choose from a list of options, each with a number attached. You are supposed to press the number corresponding to the nature of your call, and then you will be put through to the appropriate department. If you're lucky. If you're like me, though, none of the options quite corresponds to what you want, or several do, so you have to listen to the message again and again. If you do finally venture a number, when you eventually get through to the appropriate department there is a message saying in a computerized voice that sounds like a cross between an "I speak your weight" machine and

Stephen Hawking: "I am sorry. The person on extension 6–4–2–1 is on the phone. Please try later." It's enough to make you want to spit blood.

In some cases that is what you might be doing anyway, because doctors' surgeries use the same system. "If you are ill, press 1. If you are seriously ill, press 2. If you are at death's door, you shouldn't be able to press anything at all."

We were not made for technology. Technology was made for us. (What is more, it was made *by* us.) Awkward things, people. We keep on insisting on convenience, familiarity, and simplicity. What is more, we want things to be *enjoyable*. Precisely what we think is convenient, familiar, simple, and enjoyable may pay no heed whatsoever to what the techies tell us is an "advance." We just don't know what's good for us, that's our trouble. And long may it remain so, well into the economy of the future.

Only when technological advance is based on an understanding of human nature and human needs will technology's promise be realized.[15] This is something that passes most techies by—and it passes the GDP statisticians by as well.

Health and GDP

Yet I do not accept that the apparent disjunct between the GDP statistics and wellbeing is fundamentally due to any or all of these functions: the quirkiness of GDP as a measure; the end of real improvements; or the creation of large offsetting losses that are not recorded in GDP. In particular, the balance sheet on the accuracy of GDP is not completely lopsided. There are areas where the GDP statistics do not record real improvements in human wellbeing that originate from advances in knowledge. These include things where current improvements are going to have a significant effect on people's lives in the economy of the future.

The provision of healthcare services is probably the most important. What could be more important than health? Nevertheless, except when it prevents people from producing, the state of their health does not figure in the GDP statistics. Yet throughout the last 200 years of rising GDP, by and large, health standards have improved and the pain associated with both ill-health and its treatment has sharply diminished. In 1836 the richest man in the world, Nathan Rothschild, died from a form of routine blood poisoning, originating from an abscess.[16] Today *anyone* living in the developed countries could be easily cured of this condition provided that they could find their way to a doctor, or even a pharmacy. This aspect of our economic advance is surely one of the greatest instances of progress in the human condition, and yet it is not picked up by the GDP statistics.

Similarly, consider the countless millions of women over the ages who endured agony and even died giving birth to children, many of whom did not survive. The transformation of childbirth into a relatively safe and less painful experience must be one of the greatest advances of the last 100 years.

Or think of the pain and discomfort that people regularly endured from toothache—and the often greater pain endured in its treatment by tooth extraction. As a young boy, whenever I complained about the horrors of having to visit the dentist, my father would regale me with tales of what had happened to him some 50 years before. Despite the lapse of all this time, the pain and horror of the event were still vivid in his memory. While serving in the trenches during the First World War, he had a tooth extracted by a fellow soldier using a pair of pliers. The only anaesthetic was a few swigs of whisky. He had to be held down by four other soldiers.

Indeed, for the overwhelming bulk of our history such barbarities were normal in peacetime, never mind in war. One of Newton's contemporaries, Sir Samuel Pepys, for instance, whose life is familiar to us through his famous diary, was in his early years afflicted by great pain caused by a stone in his bladder. In the end he decided to have the stone removed by a surgeon. This was no easy choice, because it was a hideously unpleasant procedure and a huge gamble. But he took this course as his only hope of escaping from "a condition of constant and dangerous and most painful sickness and low condition and poverty."[17]

The operation involved inserting a silver instrument through the penis into the bladder in order to position the stone before an incision was made and the stone removed with pincers. Given the agonies Pepys went through it does jar to describe him as one of the lucky ones, but he was lucky enough to survive the operation.

Of course, the comparative lack of pain is not exactly the same as greater happiness, but you would think that it would contribute to human well-being. Perhaps when people reply to the happiness surveys they put the lack of pain into a completely different category, or perhaps they simply do not register it as a factor, effectively taking it for granted. But they, and the GDP statistics, surely should register it as a significant improvement in our lives.

Computers and health

The trend of improving health and reduced pain from ill-health and medical treatment is set not only to continue in the future, but to accelerate. Medical knowledge is increasing rapidly and the range and efficacy of medical treatments are growing fast, thanks to the efforts of the pharmaceutical and biotechnology industries. However, even without more medical knowledge and better treatments, computer technology will have a major impact on healthcare, not least through the advent of personalized surgical planning. Imagine a situation where before a single incision is made, a customized computer-generated model of the patient is produced, to help in diagnosis, evaluate treatment options, and rehearse the chosen procedure. Before the operation begins, a computer will overlay a 3D surgical plan on the patient. Robotic tools guide the surgeon's hand to aid surgical precision using real-time imaging and sensors.[18]

Far-fetched? The scenario may appear futuristic, but surgeons in America have already pioneered the use of "hands-free" technology. Medical procedures can be performed using tools that respond to verbal commands issued through a headset. A computer passes on the instructions to remote-controlled keyhole surgical instruments. The system, called Hermes, can be employed for almost all types of surgery and the precise nature of the instruments is said to reduce tissue damage and cut the duration of operations by up to 15 percent.[19] Once diagnosis and surgery are digitized the possibility is opened up of remote surgery, perhaps even by a surgeon in another country or another continent.[20]

In addition, medical record keeping and diagnosis will also be transformed by computers. If you have something wrong with you, at the moment you visit your local doctor and recite your symptoms, which he (or she) probably writes down by hand on a buff card. He wracks his brain for what remains of his medical training, scours his experience, and then pronounces a diagnosis and a treatment—if you're lucky. If your condition is obscure, or there is something about your personal circumstances that makes a relatively mundane condition more dangerous, your case may readily pass him by. And there is a good chance that you will be prescribed the wrong drugs. It is estimated that 5 percent of all written prescriptions contain errors over the type of drug therapy selected. Indeed, it is said that a typical airline handles customers' baggage at a far lower error rate than health professionals administering drugs.[21]

In the economy of the future your symptoms and medical history, and your family's medical history, will be on computer and standard diagnosis and treatment programs will be applied.[22] Rare conditions that might go undiagnosed will be picked up, as will rare combinations of circumstances that might make your condition more serious. When it comes to treatment, through the medium of your doctor you will have access to the best medical brains in the world and the latest research. That research will surely have produced cures for umpteen conditions that currently cause severe pain and even death.

The result of the coming medical, technological, and economic advances will be a healthier, better-treated population, less plagued by unnecessary delays and poor diagnosis and therefore likely to live longer. (Mind you, this will make the problems for pension funds, described in Chapter 2, all the more serious.) Unless our techniques for recording real income immeasurably improve, however, little of the real worth of these advances will be picked up by the GDP statistics—nor, on present form, by the happiness surveys.

The roots of happiness

So the deficiencies of GDP as a measure of wellbeing point in both directions. Indeed, so great is the influence of the health, death, and pain factors that I would judge that on balance the GDP statistics *understate* the increases in human wellbeing.

This reinforces my suspicion that the quirks of GDP accounting cannot be responsible for the apparent irrelevance of income above a certain level. That must be due to something much deeper. That something is surely tied up with the fact that beyond the bare necessities, the things that make people happy are nonmaterial and cannot be directly secured by money.

Happiness is less to do with the pursuit of day-to-day gratification and more to do with the fulfillment of someone's potential. Aspects that have more bearing on happiness than money include personal psychological factors, life events such as divorce or the birth or death of a child, marriage, and social participation.

This should not be such a great surprise. Abraham Maslow, a behavioral psychologist, drew up a hierarchy of needs in 1943. At the bottom of the pyramid were the basics of life such as food, water, and material comforts. Next were safety and security needs. Then came love and belongingness, including the desire to feel accepted by the family, the community, and colleagues at work.

After that came esteem, both self-esteem and other people's respect and admiration. Then at the top came what Maslow called self-actualization, the happiness from becoming all that the person was capable of becoming.

Clearly, money is important at the bottom of all this. Yet as incomes increase the importance of income and economic factors falls. This was once described by Nobel Laureate in Economics Sir John Hicks as "the law of the diminishing significance of economics." The irony, and the tragedy, of our society is that we have become stuck on avidly pursuing income even as we should have moved on.

If the roots of happiness are predominantly social and not economic, you can easily see why in most developed countries increasing income has brought little or no increase in happiness. In nearly all developed countries there is clear evidence of social breakdown that, even if the phenomenon is not caused directly by the increasing wealth, has occurred simultaneously with it. These factors are sufficiently significant that they have evidently off-set any benefit from increased wealth. Virtually all western societies have experienced sharp increases in crime, marital breakdown, suicide, and depression; in fact depression has taken on epidemic proportions.

Human nature
So why do people continue with the same old pursuit of money when the evidence suggests that beyond a certain point it does not make us any happier? Part of the reason is that making a radical switch of values and priorities is beyond the easy control of individuals. The "system" is geared to a certain concept of work and is apparently oblivious of the fact that changing economic and social circumstances should bring changes to the workplace and to the balance between work and other aspects of life, the so-called work–life balance. It is frequently difficult for an *individual* to make a markedly different choice from the rest of society because we usually either have to take a job that conforms to the accepted social norms with regard to pressure and working hours, or we don't get the job at all.

Nowhere is this better illustrated than in the still rigid divisions between full-time work and retirement. Even if greater wealth should mean us opting, at the margin, for more leisure and less work, this does not mean that we should enjoy enforced full-time leisure at some arbitrary cutoff point, whether that be age 55, 60, or 65, particularly not when up to that age we are obliged to subject ourselves to full-time work, often with little time left over for other pursuits. Longer life could also imply a longer *working* life. The secret surely lies with greater flexibility about the needs of work and leisure throughout life.

However, I do not think that the inflexibility of "the system" is the main reason why people in today's rich societies still work so hard and are so obsessed with money. If enough individuals felt dissatisfied with the current norms, those norms would gradually change.

The fact is that people pursue more wealth—and work hard to achieve it—because they *think* it will make them happier, even though the evidence is that collectively it won't. The first reason is habituation: we get used to increased income and living standards and these no longer make us any happier than the lower levels used to. So we strive for incomes and spending that make us happy only fleetingly. Once there, we slip back to our old levels of happiness. Yet we could not easily go back to the old levels of income and spending without feeling deprived. Richard Layard says that people are on a hedonistic treadmill, which he likens to a case of addiction where "people's past standard of living affects in a negative way the happiness they get from their present living standard. In this way it is just like smoking."

The second reason for the continued dominance of money-driven work is probably more important. It is something Keynes himself envisaged as a major factor: the competition between people for status, as symbolized by wealth and "advancement." As soon as x reaches a certain standard of living that he (or she) thinks is acceptable and relaxes, works less hard, or whatever, he makes it possible for y to overtake him. As long as he keeps going he may keep ahead of y. And y is feeling something comparable about the prospects of catching up with x.

Rivalry need not take such a crude form in the contestants' minds. One way in which the competition between members of society may be driven is over the pursuit of what the late Fred Hirsch called positional goods, such things as Centre Court seats at Wimbledon, stalls seats at the opera, or the apartment with the best view of Central Park. Precisely because the supply of these things cannot be increased, they acquire social cachet. Plenty of people aspire to have them but only a few can ever be successful, no matter how materially rich the society becomes. So large numbers of people are motivated to try to acquire the things that, by definition, only a few of them can. This is a *perpetuum mobile*. When we define our needs and our success in relative terms then, collectively, they can never be satisfied. The "poor" will always be with us, no matter how rich they become.

The theory of relativity

This coincides with survey information about how people on different incomes judge their happiness. In complete contrast with the time series data revealing that many feel no happier as society as a whole gets richer, cross-section surveys questioning people on different incomes at the same point in time by and large reveal that richer people consider themselves to be happier. The implication is that they are happier because they can see that they have more money than other people.

And there is powerful supporting evidence for the importance of relativities. It is striking that although living standards in former East Germany have soared since reunification in 1990, east Germans' level of happiness has plummeted. The reason is surely that whereas they used to compare themselves with other people in the Soviet bloc, they now compare themselves with people in the former West Germany who, by and large, are still much better off.

Similarly, generations of young people have wondered at the way they are able to manage happily as students on incomes that were nugatory compared to their current incomes as thrusting young things in the financial markets. The reason, of course, is that in their student days they were accustomed to their financial status and everybody else was in the same position.

Nowhere is the importance of relativities better illustrated than in the mad, mad world of "compensation," pay to you and me, in the investment banks and other major financial institutions. For many people working in the financial markets, their whole year is dominated by "the bonus." When it arrives, no matter how large it is, it typically satisfies the recipient for a trice. Even though it is often a king's ransom by the standards of the outside world, the world from which the star traders and analysts will recently have come, its value and "fairness" will be judged with reference to what Smith on "the special derivatives desk" next door got, not with regard to what the millions of Smiths outside get.

Incidentally, in my experience these bonuses are a sort of drug, in just the way that Layard suggests. Whatever the amount, they only bring fleeting pleasure and satisfaction, and the recipients quickly become focused on the need to earn the next fix, in nearly a year's time.

The importance of relative position in society goes a long way to explaining why much-increased material wellbeing has not brought increased happiness. The freedom from the material exigency that has dogged humans throughout history should release us for higher things. Instead, we seem to be continually striving for more success in order to secure *relative* position, and this is a game that humanity as a whole can never win. Boundless wealth, at least when everyone has it, will not bring happiness.

A Radical Agenda?

The question is, what should we do from here? Layard believes that governments should embark on a policy of taxing high incomes punitively in a deliberate attempt to discourage the preference for work over leisure. Presumably, the funds thus raised could be spent on better healthcare, especially for the treatment of depression and mental illness, and on collective goods.

This would be a complete about-turn in the course of political economy over the last 30 years. The Thatcher/Reagan conservative revolution was driven by the desire to reduce the interventions of the state and sharply curtail the redistributive bias of the tax system. Layard's agenda would see all this reversed and a return to the ideology of the immediate postwar years.

I cannot see this as the answer. On grounds of freedom alone, the notion of the state taxing income so heavily is repulsive. If some people wish to work extremely hard to pursue financial advancement, it is best that they should be left to get on with it. Moreover, there are economic dangers in Layard's proposals. Heaven knows what misuses the state would put all the extra money to if it were free to tax extra income so heavily and was apparently unafraid of reducing economic performance as a consequence.

Layard admits that GDP would be reduced, but argues that this does not matter because it is such a hopeless measure of wellbeing. However, the policy of punitive taxation and redistribution might readily cause such waste of resources and reductions in income that it would take our national income well below the point at which further income gains yielded little extra happiness.

And what about all those people in today's society whom extra income *would* make happier? Designing a system that suppressed outrageous greed while not stifling those people's ability to improve their lot would be extremely difficult. The evidence of past attempts is not at all encouraging.

The way forward
There is a more fundamental critique of Layard's agenda that follows from the weakness of the evidence about happiness. The fact that happiness did

not increase at the time of a large increase in income does not necessarily mean that the extra income was of no worth. It may simply be that its benefit was offset by other adverse factors, such as marital breakdown, crime, and depression, which, as I mentioned above, have overwhelmed most developed countries but which, although they have occurred simultaneously with increased income, were not caused by it. It may well be that they have been caused by ideological developments within society, such as increased individualism, or by the characteristics of the technologies predominating at the time that incomes rose, rather than by the rise in incomes itself.

There is considerable evidence that television, for instance, may have played a major role. The small, isolated, Himalayan kingdom of Bhutan has given us a test case. This used to be a virtually crimeless state, steeped in the traditions and beliefs of Buddhism. Now it is undergoing a crime wave and an upsurge in marital breakdown that would be familiar to urban residents of North America or Europe. Plenty of Bhutanese think that the change is fundamentally due to television. In June 1999, the king lifted a ban on it and his Himalayan kingdom became the last country on earth to enter the television age—with all that brings in its train.[23]

If it is true that such factors have increased unhappiness, then if they ceased to increase any further, higher income might well see recorded levels of happiness rise. Certainly, the happiness evidence is still too vulnerable to the charge that it merely reflects rising expectations to overrule and suppress many people's fervent wishes for what they would see as self-advancement.

Even if the evidence on happiness is fully accepted, it should not turn us against the idea of economic progress. Pushing forward the limit of our productive potential is a good thing because it gives us choices. But we do not have to exercise those choices in the same way that we did 50 years ago. In particular, we do not need to pursue more material goods for ourselves as individuals. We could use our increased productive potential to improve many nonmaterial parts of our society that nevertheless have a financial cost: expenditure on healthcare and safety, and expenditure on beautifying the built environment.

Equally, we could take the fruits of our increased productivity in the form of reduced working hours. In that case, the increase in "income" would show itself as an increase in leisure, or in the period of our lives we spend in full-time education, or, as I argued in the last chapter, in retirement. Or we could devote more time and attention to our children who, after all, are the main sufferers from the working-all-hours culture. And the signs are that their suffering is great. The average North American child answering surveys in the 1980s reported as much anxiety as child psychiatric patients in the 1950s.[24]

The sensible choice would probably be to take the increase in prosperity in the form of a mixture of more income and more leisure. That way we would have both more money to spend and more time in which to spend it. Nor would such a shift toward leisure, whether whole or partial, lead to the economic catastrophe the doomsters allege. If we did decide to work fewer hours, there would be no excess supply of goods and services and no surplus of available workers. In choosing to spend less time at work, workers would reduce the supply of labor and thereby reduce the supply of goods and services. It is a straight choice between income and leisure, pecuniary and nonpecuniary values, that's all.

In the economy of the future, whether people end up working longer or shorter hours, taking shorter or longer holidays, and whether they continue to give primacy to the making and amassing of money are not mainly economic questions. It is all a matter of values. And a change of values is much better achieved from below than from above.

So if you lament the pressures, money obsession, and amoralism of modern society, don't blame it on the economics. Our economic system is more than capable of keeping us all in the manner to which our forefathers would have loved to become accustomed, while still affording us more time, more leisure, and more scope to practice the higher virtues. It is open to us to opt for even more leisure and decide to spend less time at work in order to "spend more time with our families," if that is what we would like, and up to us to conduct our lives with greater weight placed on nonpecuniary objectives, if that reflects our values. If fault there be it lies in ourselves—and it is a fault that cannot readily be overcome by social engineering through the tax system.

What Is the Point of It All?

So how should we regard the advance in material living standards that has transformed our lives since the Industrial Revolution but now, according to the surveys, makes us no happier? First, it is clear that large parts of the world are still in the phase where further advance in income *does* bring increased happiness, and will do so for some decades into the future.

Even in the developed countries, we should not regret the advances of the last 200 years. If it is true that more income overall does not now seem to bring more happiness, the reason is that the economic system has delivered the increases that *do* increase people's happiness. The absence of pain and deprivation in today's society would rank it very high, if not top, of a happiness index of any society across the ages. And surely today's happiness surveys are not giving due weight to the absence of pain, rather than the promotion of pleasure. This has been no wealth illusion—it is the real thing.

Nevertheless, it is right for us to ask the fundamental question about the point of human effort and the ends of economic activity. What is more, as we stand on the brink of the economy of the future, this is the moment to ask it. For the first time in our history the fecundity of the economic system, built up first through hard labor and more recently through the ample capabilities of the human mind, is making possible for millions of people, in the developed countries at least, a life lived outside and above the necessity of humdrum, money-driven work. We need to know what we should do with all the wealth that is about to fall into our laps. It potentially opens up a whole new epoch for humankind. There is a serious risk, though, that most people will remain stuck in the same old ways, following the same old values. If that were to happen, then although we had become incomparably richer, you could readily say that the result of so much human effort had turned out to be "money for nothing."

Introduction

The reader has now been taken on a long and varied journey. In Part I she was immersed in the evils and dangers that still confront us as a result of the end of the financial fantasies of the late 1990s; she was then uplifted by the forces of real wealth creation analyzed in Part II; and perhaps she is now intrigued by the shape of the economy of the future that I have depicted in Part III.

But there is still some unfinished business. As I said right at the beginning of the book, it is by no means obvious that the forces of progress will prevail. The clear and present dangers that I described in Part I *could* overwhelm us, sending the world into a slump, thereby stopping up the wellsprings of prosperity and leaving the economy of the future as another sort of fantasy, left permanently out of reach, over the rainbow.

How can that outcome be avoided? What steps must be taken to ensure that the economy of the future becomes our emerging reality? That is the subject of this Finale.

Finale
Skirting Catastrophe

We step upon the threshold ... facing a brighter dawn of civilization.
New York Times, January 1, 1900

The benefit which is derived from exchanging one commodity for another, arises in all cases, from the commodity received, not the commodity given.

James Mill, 1821[1]

Sir Winston Churchill is one of those historical characters who genuinely needs no introduction. Almost everyone is familiar with his heroic leadership in the Second World War, with his memorable appearance and his many unforgettable speeches and quotable sayings. However, there is one aspect of his life with which most people are not very familiar, not least because in relation to the struggle during the war it is of apparently little consequence. Yet it is of great moment for anyone thinking about economic policy and finance. Money was Churchill's weak spot—and in more ways than one.

Churchill cannot be said to have had a great deal in common with Sir Isaac Newton, but he did share one or two things financial with him, including the experience of devastating personal financial loss.[2] If Income and Expenditure did not meet then his usual approach was to endeavor, somehow, to increase Income.[3] This made him particularly susceptible to the lust for money for nothing. So it should come as no surprise that he naively piled into the American stock market—just before the Wall Street crash. After he was nearly wiped out he had to redouble his efforts at writing and speaking to restore his financial position.[4]

After the war, however, fame and the constant flow of royalties from his many books and articles more than restored his fortune. At last he was rich, beyond even his capacity for squandering. But this was despite, not because of, the stock market.

Churchill also shared with Sir Isaac Newton the experience of guardianship over the nation's finances. Indeed, in his case the responsibilities were much greater. Whereas Sir Isaac was Master of the Royal Mint, with responsibility for the coinage, in the mid-1920s Sir Winston Churchill was Chancellor of the Exchequer, with responsibility for everything economic and financial. By common consent, he made a mess of it. It was Churchill who, following the advice of the economic policy establishment, took sterling back to the Gold Standard in 1925 at the old pre-war parity, thereby ensuring a period of serious deflation. Among other things, this prompted the General Strike of 1926 and made sure that Britain endured a dire time of it even before the Wall Street Crash of 1929 and the Great Depression. It was only when Britain abandoned the Gold Standard in 1931, undoing Churchill's disastrous mistake, that the country was able to pursue the policies that would lead to recovery.[5]

Today's economic policy establishment whose ideas are so critical is the collection of central bankers, government officials, senior politicians, and even a smattering of economists, who decide economic policy for the world's largest economies. These are the eternal summiteers, the globetrotting glitterati, who move from one talking shop to the next.

It is vital that these policy makers recognize the full extent of the economic dangers confronting the world and shift from talk to action. The world needs from them the vision and quality of leadership that Churchill displayed during the war, allied to the highest degree of economic and financial surefootedness, which he evidently did *not* possess.

Bubble Transferred

In this book I have identified the key challenges facing policy makers as originating from the contrast between the real and illusory sources of wealth. Developments since the book was first published have heightened this contrast—and intensified the challenges.

Admittedly, one key part of the financial scene has proved robust: equity markets. In the two years after this book was published, the American, British, and German equity markets rose by between 20 and 30 percent, and the Japanese market by about 10 percent. This served to allay the fears of meltdown—and deflation—that prevailed only a few years ago.

Such success is not altogether surprising. In the wake of the bursting of the dotcom bubble and the events of 11 September 2001, the American authorities, helped by governments and central banks elsewhere, threw everything into staving off an economic disaster. The policy of 1 percent interest rates, big increases in government spending, and reductions in taxes did the trick.

Whether this policy has completely fended off the day of reckoning or merely shifted it into the future, though, is still a moot point. Ultra-low interest rates have had the effect of boosting asset prices—including those of equities. The result is that on some measures the US equity market still looks markedly overvalued. The chances are that it may put up a pretty sickly performance in the years to come.

But the biggest effects of the policy have been in the residential property market. As I pointed out in Chapter 2, the property boom has raged on— and on a world scale. According to *The Economist*, over the last five years the total market value of residential property in developed economies has risen by more than $30 trillion, equivalent to more than these countries' combined annual GDP. In proportion to GDP, this is a larger increase in asset values than occurred in the global equity market boom of the late 1990s or the American boom of the late 1920s. This bubble may have transferred from the equity market, but now it is bigger. It is simply the biggest bubble in financial history.[6]

There May Be Trouble Ahead

The signs of trouble brewing are blatant. By the late summer of 2005, in the UK and Australia the housing market appeared to have topped out. The bulls say that the market has stabilized at the current high level, yet all the traditional valuation measures indicate that it is heavily overvalued. In the US, there are some classic signs of market strain. It is notable that the incidence of variable-rate mortgages has soared—because they are cheaper—as has the incidence of interest-only mortgages. Indeed, nearly one in ten of recent US homebuyers has chosen a so-called "negative amortization mortgage," in which they do not even pay full interest. Whatever they do not pay is rolled up into the debt outstanding.[7]

What has driven the housing market, and what sustains the hopes of the bulls, is undoubtedly the policy of very low interest rates pursued worldwide. And although the signs of a turning point are clear, I have to acknowledge that this policy could yet mean that the housing bull market goes on some way further yet. After all, as I re-emphasize below, interest rates are going to stay low for a long time.

But low interest rates will not be enough to keep the boom going forever. As I argue below, interest rates are likely to remain very low because of incipient economic weakness. Across most of the developed world, housing markets have reacted to the medicine applied to counteract the ailment, but not yet to the ailment itself. I suppose you could say that was rational as long as it can be presumed that the treatment will work. In Europe conditions remain dire, while in the UK and the US there are dictinct signs of an impending slowdown in the rate of growth.

Moreover, housing markets and the economy enjoy a symbiotic relationship. In the UK, in the summer of 2005, it looked as though the slowdown of the housing market from increases of almost 20 percent to roughly zero had been enough to bring consumer spending shuddering to a halt.

The reason is clear. As I argued in Chapter 2, the housing market has been a money-making machine—the producer of money for nothing. Without a huge increase in the value of their properties, consumers have felt less wealthy and less confident, which implies less spending. And the same will surely happen soon in the US. Furthermore, because consumer spending is highly generative of jobs, there is a significant danger of a rise in unemployment, which would then serve to dent the housing market still further. What would happen if house prices were to *fall?*

In today's conditions, it may not be higher interest rates that burst the residential property bubble, but rather economic slowdown and the fears of higher unemployment that go with it. In the summer of 2005, fears of resurgent inflation abounded, particularly after the oil price topped $65 a barrel. Not for the first time, such fears will prove to be unfounded. Indeed, when the economy slows markedly the deflation threat that I discussed in Chapter 3, which, in most people's minds, is now consigned to the back burner, will re-emerge. The result is that the policy makers will have to maintain continued vigilance against deflation and be ready to deploy the full panoply of anti-deflationary policies.

Technological Progress

But if the factors that made me worry about the immediate future are still very much with us, then so my optimism about the forces making for strong economic growth in the years ahead has also been reinforced.

In the two years since this book was published, the judgments it made about the progress of technology and the perspective on the ICT revolution have been largely vindicated.

It is striking that many technology companies have prospered so much that there is now something of a second boom in technology stocks. The $23 billion float of Google in August 2004 was an iconic moment. Each year it is now generating cash of $2 billion and doubling in size. But the signs of increasing confidence in the IT revolution are widespread. Some of this is simply due to a catch-up between the hype about the internet and the reality. In the last five years internet usage has taken off, and much of it on high-speed broadband. There are now 700 million PCs in use around the world, seven times as many as a decade ago.

The internet has transformed shopping. It is not that the bulk of retail transactions is now done online—although the online total has been rising rapidly—but rather that people use the web more and more for research. This means that consumers are better informed than ever before and intensely price conscious. This even affects sales of cars. According to *The Economist*, over 80 percent of Ford's customers in the US have already researched their purchase over the internet by the time they reach the showroom.[8] This is surely a leading explanation for why businesses have found it so difficult to push up prices, even when their own costs have risen sharply.

And the internet is making a major contribution to "high" as well as "low" culture. In June 2005, the BBC made available online Beethoven's first five symphonies. The BBC website registered 657,399 individual downloads, a figure so large that it exceeds the annual sales of any classical record label. What's more, the evidence is that most of the downloaders are young—under 20—many of whom had previously known little or nothing about Beethoven.

Meanwhile, in biotech, although there has certainly not been a stock-market bonanza, the signs of significant real progress are palpable. Whereas a decade ago there were fewer than 10 oncology drugs in clinical trial, today there are over 400 biotech anticancer medicines in human clinical trials.

Governance Matters

On the issue of governance, which I argued was so important for economic success, recent developments have been a mixed bag. On the positive side it is increasingly appreciated how important this issue is. Moreover, although not everyone agrees with what America has done in the Middle East, it is now at least putting emphasis on the governance issue as a way forward, even pressuring Egypt, one of its leading allies in the region, to make moves toward democracy.

And Africa has moved to center stage, largely thanks to the efforts of the British under Tony Blair and Gordon Brown—and not before time. But agreeing to write off billions of dollars' worth of debt, which was agreed at the G8's Gleneagles summit in July 2005, does not seem to be in accordance with the argument made in this book. It effectively gives resources to governments rather than the private sector. And it rewards those who were profligate in the past at the expense of those who were circumspect. Moreover, it does nothing directly to aid the development of the institutions that underpin a successful modern economy. But the British Treasury would surely reply that debt writeoff has been made conditional on good behavior, and that is a step forward. Nevertheless, I remain skeptical that the G8 will be able to monitor such good behavior effectively, or find the political will to suspend the debt writeoff if they find that behavior has not come up to scratch. Still, this is a start.

Meanwhile, Zimbabwe goes from bad to worse. One recent bright spot in the news about Africa, though, was the sacking for alleged corruption of a senior minister by South African premier Thabo Mbeki.

Elsewhere, too, things are stirring. Once again, Brazil and Argentina are showing good growth rates. The perception is growing that East Asia has no monopoly on rapid growth.

And Russia has registered a period of strong growth. Indeed, I sometimes wonder whether Russia isn't the new China. Ten years ago, when I wrote *The Death of Inflation*, in which I placed so much emphasis on China as an emerging economic giant, the country was hardly taken seriously in discussion of the world economy and its outlook. Now, of course, China is everywhere—to the point where just about any economic ill in the west is supposedly due to "Chinese competition." However, Russia is still underplayed.

Making Way for Asian Strength

One of the simplest but most powerful messages of this book is the contrast between relative and absolute income. According to the conventional view, because "they" are going up, "we" must be going down. I have argued that although this is obviously true in a relative sense, it is not true in an absolute sense. People in the west can be better off because of the prosperity of China and India.[9]

There has been some sign that this message has hit home. More and more businesses have come to see the opportunities afforded by the Chinese market. Between 2000 and 2004, German exports to China rose by an annual average of 25 percent. And with Chinese retail sales growing by 12 percent year on year, in contrast to flat-as-a-pancake conditions in much of Europe, the opportunities are immense. Within five years China may account for 20 percent of the world's sales of luxury goods. Cartier, Prada, and Armani have already expanded faster in China than in any other part of the world.

In these conditions, in many western countries there is a growing understanding that to lose large parts of manufacturing to China and other emerging countries is not necessarily such a disaster. Indeed, a large proportion of Chinese exports are produced in China by companies with substantial western ownership. The impression has gained ground that they will sell cheap manufactured products to us and we will sell expensive high-tech kit, pharmaceuticals, luxury branded goods, and knowledge-intensive services to them.

But as signs of increasing economic sophistication in China and India have become established, so anxiety has returned. It is starting to sink in that, never mind the umpteen millions of low-skilled workers employed in thousands of factories producing toys, China now produces 2 million graduates a year, of which more than 600,000 have studied engineering and more than 100,000 medicine. In 2003/4 India produced 127,000 IT graduates alone. Meanwhile, it has announced plans to expand its biotech sector fivefold over the next five years. And this industry is expanding rapidly in China too. Take the example of Capital Bio. Based in a bioscience park outside Beijing, it is emerging as a world leader in the technology of biochips, devices that combine biotechnology and electronics for medical and biological testing.[10]

As a result, the fear is growing in the west that soon "they" will be able to outcompete "us," not only in basic manufacturing, but also in software, medicine, and countless other service areas as well. At that point, what will we be able to sell to them? This fear, although thoroughly understandable, is also misplaced. Even if China were to become more efficient than the west at producing absolutely everything, it would still pay it to buy many goods and services from the west. China's best interests would be served by concentrating on producing the things in which its advantage was greatest and importing the other things from the west. This is what economists call the law of comparative advantage, which I explained in Chapter 5.

In practice, it will be decades before China's overall productivity is even on a par with the west's, never mind in advance of it. Worry about the advantage conferred by ultra-low Chinese wages is overdone. Wages are low because overall Chinese productivity is low. As productivity rises, then either wages will rise or the exchange rate will rise, or both.

As China becomes more prosperous it would be nigh on impossible for it to rely on the west for all its business services, software engineers, medical and educational services, or pharmaceuticals. It will produce increasing amounts of these itself. But that should not induce panic in the west. It does not mean that it will pay China to be self-sufficient in everything. On the contrary, comparative advantage will still argue the case for imports.

After all, the biggest, most powerful, and, according to some measures, the most "competitive" country in the world is the United States. But it imports so much from the rest of the world that it runs a huge current account deficit! Even as China becomes more sophisticated and produces more high-tech goods and domestic services, the balance of its exports to the west will still be weighted toward basic manufactures and the west's exports will be weighted toward high-tech manufactures and services.

But there is an even higher level of western anxiety. As China develops it will become the technological leader in some fields. That will do nothing for western feelings of self-confidence, although again there should be no alarm. Chinese technological advance will help to promote western levels of prosperity. As I have argued in this book, potentially one of the largest sources of gain from the incorporation of India and China into the world economy is the potential for the faster growth of knowledge. As their output of scientists and engineers increases, for anyone interested in our absolute levels of prosperity this should be cause for joy, not anguish.

The Threat of War

Yet there is an aspect of all of this that is much less positive. It may be absolute prosperity that is what economics is about, but *power* depends on relative prosperity. As China becomes economically larger relative to the west, then there will be losers in a power sense. The most obvious loser is the world's current sole superpower, the United States. Will it be prepared to accept the loss of its hegemony?

The closest historical analogy is with Britain in the twentieth century. Will the US be prepared to retire gracefully, as Britain (just about) did, and if so, will it be prepared to forge a partnership with the new global leader? I am often asked what factors I think could upset the predominantly sunny outlook that I describe in this book. Sometimes I say "protectionism," but I have come to believe that this is too narrow an answer. The biggest threat is that America perceives China as a strategic challenger and decides to try to head that challenge off. Protectionism is one way it might go, seeking to cut off China's access to world markets and thereby slowing its manufacturing expansion and overall development. Moreover, in this enterprise America might readily acquire support, for once, from the EU. Worse, such a move could be part of a wholesale raising of trade barriers, including between the US and the EU.

But conflict could easily take a more straightforward form. As I emphasized in Chapter 6, the world was thoroughly globalized in 1914, in some ways to a greater extent than it is now, but war destroyed all that—and much else besides. The First World War was very much about the pressures unleashed by the emergence of a new power, namely Germany. Moreover, although in the west the Second World War could be regarded as merely part two of this same conflict, in Asia it was about the pressures unleashed by the emergence of yet another new power, namely Japan. It is a ghastly thought, but in my nightmares I sometimes imagine a repeat: a war between America and China that reduces all the hope and optimism of this book to nought.

Just to make my nightmares worse, in July 2005 the Chinese general Zhu Chenghu said: "If the Americans draw their missiles and position-guided ammunition on to the target zone on China's territory, I think we will have to respond with nuclear weapons." Making clear that the definition of territory included warships and aircraft, he went on to say: "We... will prepare ourselves for the destruction of all of the cities east of Xian. Of course the Americans will have to be prepared that hundreds... of cities will be destroyed by the Chinese."[11]

The Reasons for Weak Aggregate Demand

The danger of trade, and even military, conflict is all the greater the weaker economic performance is in the west. Overcoming the forces making for weak aggregate demand is the central challenge facing the world's economic policy makers. But the first requirement is to understand them, and that is easier said than done.

In complete contrast to the conventional wisdom, the fundamental problem of global imbalances does not originate in the United States. In 2005, the US came under more pressure to do something about its trade deficit. This pressure shows a complete lack of understanding about the reasons for the deficit—and about the consequences of its reduction. I have argued in this book that the deficit poses a long-term threat to the stability of the global economy and I stand by that. But it matters a great deal how the deficit is reduced. The deficit is not so much the result of overspending by the United States as of *under*spending by the rest of the world. Tackling the deficit by getting Americans to spend less or, as the protagonists usually put it, making it sound more palatable and even virtuous to save more, would reduce output in the US and the rest of the world.

But the United States economy is not operating above full capacity; rather the opposite. There is plenty of slack in the labor market and in capacity utilization. What's more, there is a similar picture in much of the rest of the world, including Japan and the eurozone.

Another way of looking at this issue is to examine the rate of growth of global output. In 2004, with growth of just over 5 percent, the world economy had its best year for almost 30 years. But the average for the first four years of the Noughties, 2001–4, was 3.7 percent. Considering the fantastic growth rates in China and India, this was a pretty feeble performance. Indeed, it was slower than the average growth rate registered in the 1950s and 1960s. This was not due to weak productivity growth. There have been clear signs that the prediction of this book that productivity growth will speed up is being vindicated. In the years 1995–2003, annual world produc-

tivity growth was almost double what had been achieved between 1990 and
1995.[12]

The problem is that although the world has experienced a surge in productive capacity, aggregate demand has not kept pace. In combination with
the intensification of competition, which I analyzed in *The Death of
Inflation*, that is, after all, why inflation is so low everywhere and why the
deflation danger has not gone away. I am often asked why I think that the
rise of India and China will not lead to an upsurge of inflation in the west,
and why, indeed, I believe that in the west, the contribution of these countries has on balance been to *reduce* inflation. A good part of the answer is
that the growth of productive potential has left an insufficiency of aggregate
demand.

This lack of adequate aggregate demand on a global scale has several
causes. First, there is the continued underperformance of Japan. Between
2000 and 2004, the average annual growth rate of domestic demand in the
world's second largest economy was just 0.9 percent. And in 2004, the
Japanese current account surplus was $172 billion, equivalent to roughly a
quarter of the US deficit.

Second, the eurozone continues to operate well below capacity.
Unemployment rates of about 10 percent in Germany and France, the
world's third and fifth largest economies, indicate underused potential. In
2004, the eurozone's growth rate was only 1.7 percent, having been 0.7 percent in the previous year. The eurozone as a whole ran a current account surplus of $36 billion, but its biggest individual member, Germany, ran a sur-
plus of $96 billion.

Third, the increase in the price of oil in 2004–5 transferred purchasing
power from a group of countries, namely the oil consumers with a high
propensity to spend, to a group, namely OPEC and the other oil-producing
countries, with a low propensity to spend. In 2004, the combined current
account surpluses of OPEC, Russia, and Norway amounted to $237 billion,
or 36 percent of the American deficit.

The fourth reason is what is happening in developing Asia. This is not
only about China. In 2004, the Chinese surplus was "only" $70 billion. From
an American perspective this figure seems unbelievably small. After all,
America's bilateral deficit with China was $162 billion. But the compara-
tively small Chinese surplus is because to supply its domestic needs and to
make its exports, China imports a great deal from the rest of Asia—

including Japan. In the end, bilateral deficits and surpluses don't count; the overall position does. The best way to look at this issue is to regard developing Asia as a single bloc. In 2004, Asia excluding Japan—comprising China, India, Korea, Singapore, Hong Kong, Malaysia, the Philippines, Thailand, Vietnam, and Taiwan—collectively ran a current account surplus of some $187 billion, equivalent to roughly 28 percent of the American deficit.

An analysis of *changes* in the current account position is even more telling. Between 1996 and 2004, when the US deficit increased by $546 billion, the developing countries changed their current account balance from a deficit of $90 billion to a surplus of $326 billion—a net change of $416 billion. Of this change, Asian countries (excluding Japan) accounted for $220 billion.[13]

The identification of the surplus countries—and the reasons for their surpluses—is vital. It is all very well saying that America must reduce its deficit, but it takes two to tango. If these surplus countries insist on operating policies that protect and promote their surpluses, then the rest of the world must be in deficit. For practical purposes, the rest of the world must mean the United States.

Exchange Rates

The widespread view of these surpluses in developing Asia, and also of the Japanese surplus, is that they represent the consequence of undervalued exchange rates. But this is only part of the answer. As I write in July 2005, China has just made a small adjustment to its currency regime, apparently involving both a slight revaluation against the dollar and a move toward pegging its currency to a basket of international currencies rather than just to the dollar. But these adjustments look cosmetic. Before too long, it seems likely that China will make some more substantive change to the currency regime, effectively revaluing more against the dollar.

If the Chinese renminbi were allowed to rise further, it would make it easier, and indeed likely, that other Asian countries would revalue and even that Japan would allow the yen to appreciate too. In this way, the currencies of the whole of East Asia could rise against the euro and the dollar, while leaving internal Asian relativities more or less unchanged.

In my view, this would be a welcome development all round—but it would not solve the problem of global imbalances and global under-performance. For a start, the Chinese authorities are unlikely to allow an appreciation large enough to make a serious dent in Chinese competitiveness. A rise of 10 percent might be tolerated, but this would not make a huge difference, and particularly not at a time when concerns about deflation are resurfacing in Beijing.

More importantly, higher exchange rates for developing Asia, and for Japan, would be an "expenditure-switching" policy. They would tend to switch expenditure away from the output of Asia toward the output of America and the rest of the dollar bloc. But, of course, that would do nothing to increase world output; it would simply redistribute it. And within Asia, growth would be lower.

That may not seem such a bad result given how high developing Asia's growth rates are by western standards. (Japan is obviously a very different case.) But they are not excessively high by local standards. Developing Asia needs rapid growth rates to keep its population fully employed. In China, for instance, millions of people leave the land each year to seek employment in the cities. Weaker growth of aggregate demand is the last thing that China needs.

So expenditure switching has to be accompanied by expenditure raising. Again, we come back to inadequate aggregate demand and the need for the policy makers to stimulate it. As and when expenditure is switched to the United States as a result of a lower dollar, whether US policy has to be tightened or not is unclear. It all depends on the size of the net increase in demand for American output compared to spare capacity. It could go either way.

In the eurozone, however, things are more clear cut. With or without a weaker euro against Asian currencies, interest rates need to be cut to 1 percemt and possibly even to zero to stimulate demand. There may even be a role for fiscal relaxation. In Japan, policy makers should refrain from the monetary and fiscal tightening that they seem itching to enact. In the UK, the Bank of England should be prepared to cut interest rates, if necessary to 3 percent or below, to prevent the bursting of the housing bubble from causing the economy to stagnate or decline.

But this will not be enough. What is really needed is action in the east, and particularly in China. It might readily be objected that surely China and the rest of rapidly developing Asia cannot grow any faster than they are already. This objection is wide of the mark. For a start, if aggregate demand were stimulated in China and other Asian countries, accompanied by higher exchange rates, much of the increased output would not occur in China and the rest of developing Asia but rather in the US, the eurozone, and Japan.

In any case, on a per capita basis, China's expansion over the last 25 years has actually been slower than Japan, Taiwan, and Korea all managed in their rapid development phases. Moreover, although China has recently been growing at 9 percent, India has "only" managed 6 percent. There is surely scope for this emerging giant to grow much faster.

The Asian Challenge

So what holds developing Asia back from faster growth of domestic demand? For a start, in many Asian countries there is a strong tendency toward high personal saving ratios, not least because systems of social security are nonexistent or inadequate. So the problem begins in the private sector. Nevertheless, in a western context you would expect the authorities to be able, and to want, to offset this through expansionary fiscal and monetary policies. Why doesn't this happen sufficiently in Asia?

Part of the reason is a fear that looser monetary policy could lead to bubbles, particularly in property, and could encourage ill-judged lending policies by a domestic banking system that is already weak, thereby increasing the risk of a financial crisis at some point that could easily result in yet weaker domestic demand. After all, Korea only recently underwent such a crisis. And in China's case there is also a fear that ill-judged spending decisions by the public sector could result in massively wasteful projects, which would continue to have a large deadweight financial cost.

Another perceived risk is higher inflation. But this really should be put to rest. The whole point of combining expenditure switching with expenditure-increasing policies is that it allows domestic demand to increase *without* bringing higher inflation. And a country growing as fast as China should expect its price level to rise relative to the already developed world, either through higher domestic inflation or through a stronger exchange rate. The inflation excuse is particularly lame in mid-2005 as the Chinese authorities are starting to worry again about the re-emergence of *deflation*.

A good part of the reason for Asian policy preferences is straight power politics rather than rational analysis of economic advantage. China, or rather the Chinese government, appears to be stronger in world politico/economic affairs by running a substantial surplus. (This does not necessarily mean, though, that the Chinese *economy* is stronger as a result.)

Moreover, many Asian governments cling on to mercantilist ways of thinking. Growth and success are measured in terms of exports and surpluses. As a piece of straightforward economics this view is nonsense, but in terms of recent international monetary history it is thoroughly understandable. In the Asian crisis of 1997–8, those countries whose currencies were heavily attacked tended to be those with significant current account deficits. What's more, this episode was one in a series of financial crises: Mexico in 1994, Russia in 1998, Brazil in 1999, and Argentina in 2002.

Many countries have drawn a lesson. Up to 1997–8, although some Asian countries, such as Hong Kong, were in congenital surplus, many were not. China's trade was more or less balanced over the previous 20 years. India, Malaysia, Korea, Thailand, Vietnam, and the Philippines all tended to run deficits. After 1997–8 they have all tended to run surpluses. From taking in capital from the rest of the world, after the 1997–8 crisis they became suppliers of capital to the world. In many ways, the western world is now paying a heavy price for the 1997–8 episode.

Financial Solutions

It seems ridiculous that the world's largest economy, the United States—fully mature and, despite the new-economy madness, not in line for a great development surge—should be running a huge current account deficit, thereby sucking in the world's savings, whereas the world's fastest-growing large economy, China—aided and abetted by several smaller Asian economies—still woefully underdeveloped but blessed with prospects of sustained high growth, should be running up significant current account surpluses, thereby contributing savings to the rest of the world. This apparently absurd position is at the root of the world's most severe economic problem: its deficiency of aggregate demand.

It also has a vital connection with the *financial* problems of the west. The investors of the developed countries were until recently used to super returns on their investments, including in their pension funds. After the illusions of dotcomery and the easy money of the late 1990s, it has become clear that investment in companies where activities are restricted to the developed countries offers at best modest returns. Yet in the developing countries the prospective returns are potentially large.

The trick must be to bring the two sides of the world together. The solution is that the developing countries of Asia, led by China, should allow their currencies to rise, thereby worsening their trade positions, but offset the adverse effects of this on domestic demand by spending more. If they ran current account deficits, funded by the savings of the developed world, this would solve both the economic and financial problems of the developed countries while assisting the growth of the developing countries.

This would parallel what happened in the nineteenth century. In the late decades of the century Britain directed about half of its savings abroad—principally to North America, Latin America, and Australasia—with the receiving countries running substantial current account deficits. The result was better returns for British investors than if they had been restricted to investment in Britain, as well as rapid development for the US and the other recipients. Surely this relationship should now exist between the developed and the developing countries in general, and between America and China in particular.

Nevertheless, getting from here to there will be extremely difficult, and not only for America. On this issue, a substantial part of the leadership burden falls on the Chinese authorities. Something that could help them is a radical reform of the international monetary architecture. In so far as monetary and economic policy is governed in some international forum, that forum is the G8, consisting of the G7 plus Russia. But if nothing is done, the composition of this body—Russia, North America, old Europe, the UK, and Japan—means that it will become less and less representative of the world economy. The time is ripe for the G8 countries to invite China and India to join them and to participate fully in the management of the international monetary system.

Equally, they should assist the authorities in China and the rest of developing Asia in improving the governance and stability of domestic financial structures and institutions, in order to make these countries feel more relaxed about accepting substantial inflows of western capital—and western investors happy about providing them.

The Connection between Economic Dynamism and Deficient Demand

In this account of the world there is a major puzzle. This book has highlighted tremendous growth potential coexisting with the dangers of slump and deflation. But why should the two go together? Why should the emergence of great dynamism in the east, surging international trade, and the rapid progress of technology in east and west alike have produced a world in which there is a tendency toward deficient demand?

Could it be just an accident? It could be, although it would be a pretty surprising accident. After all, you could much more readily imagine the opposite result as companies leapt at the opportunities afforded by eastern dynamism, rising trade, and technological developments and sharply increased their investment spending, while consumers sought to bring forward the enjoyment of future income by spending now. An acceleration of potential growth is much more likely, you would think, to lead to a boom than to a slump.

Some of the explanation for the paradox is that something of the expected bullish behavior did occur, on the part of both companies and consumers: during the dotcom bubble. And we are now undergoing the adverse consequences of its bursting. Equally, the continued slow growth of Japan is still in part due to the overhang from a previous period of irrational exuberance, namely the bubble of the late 1980s.

Arguably, the huge transfer of income to the oil-producing countries and their high propensity to save the benefits is *sui generis*. And so also, you could argue, is the collection of self-inflicted wounds that is responsible for much of the eurozone's underperformance.

But some of the factors that are contributing to the weakness of global aggregate demand are directly connected with the very forces that bring the prospect of prosperity. It is the very newness of Asian development and its speed that creates the problem. It is this that makes the economic and financial system in these countries vulnerable. Inadequate institutions and political instability—exacerbated in the Chinese case by the still so recent escape from rigid and antimarket communism—have meant that the authorities are fearful of allowing aggregate demand to grow as fast as it could. These countries' institutional development has lagged behind their economic potential.

This problem is made worse by the flipside of the Asian countries' rapid advance. Two large, mature economies, Japan and Germany, apparently face a future of steep relative decline and, as their populations fall, perhaps even absolute decline. So they are locked into saving mode, just as East Asia is reluctant to spend to its full potential.

With a bit of a push, you can even relate this analysis to the other group of countries that I identified as massive savers, namely the oil producers. The volatility of the oil price and the fact that oil wealth will at some point run out may predispose such countries toward the net accumulation of overseas assets through running persistent current account surpluses. Here again, though, the newness of the phenomenon in question is a major factor. The surge in Asian demand for oil has occurred before supply capacity has had a chance to catch up. When it does, and oil prices fall, this will reverse some of the transfer of real income, back to those who are more inclined to spend it. Equally, as oil producers get used to their new wealth they will be more inclined to spend it.

And there is another connection. Why have very low real interest rates and bond yields not prompted more spending in the west? Why has there not been an investment boom? The reason is partly related to the aftermath of the bursting of the bubble: weakened balance sheets and heightened corporate caution, as I discussed in Chapter 2. But globalization and the effects of competition from the east have also played an important part. What companies are now experiencing is continual revolution as more and more sectors are exposed to Asian competition. In these circumstances, why should they invest heavily? In order to do this they need to be confident of where production in the west will continue to have a comparative advantage and where they, as corporate entities, can best promote their survival.

Moreover, associated worries about employment prospects are also a contributing factor to depressed consumption in much of the eurozone. People can see the loss of jobs to the east, but they cannot yet see the growth of new sectors to take their place.

So there is a paradox. Fast growth of productive potential produces deficiency of aggregate demand in both the rapidly growing countries and the more sedate, older ones. This is the fundamental macro reason for the phenomenon of unused resources and the lingering threat of slump and deflation at a time of apparently boundless promise. The threats I explored in

Part I of this book are intimately bound up with the opportunities I discussed in Part II.

And this is the reason for the vision of the world economy over time that I have painted in this book, namely a continuing danger of recession and deflation in the short term, accompanied by very low interest rates, but succeeded by a period of much stronger growth. That growth can only be realized when the world has recovered from the after-effects of its recent bubbles and when it can adjust to the new structures and changed behavior demanded by the rapid advance of developing Asia.

When will that happen? No one can be sure. But I suspect that it is several years—though not decades—away.

The Conundrum

This analysis can help to unravel what experts from Fed Chairman Greenspan downward regard as a "conundrum," namely the fact that bond yields have fallen to very low levels when everyone—well, almost everyone—thought that they should, and would, rise. After all, from June 2003 to July 2005, US official short-term interest rates rose by 2.25 percent, and yet 30-year bond yields fell by 0.3 percent. In the UK in July 2005, official short rates were 1.25 percent higher than they had been in August 2003, yet 10-year bond yields were 0.3 percent lower and 30-year bond yields 0.5 percent lower. In the eurozone in July 2005, official short rates had been on hold at 2 percent for two years, but 10-year bond yields had fallen by 0.6 percent and 30-year yields by 1 percent.

There are several leading possible explanations. One is massive purchases of US government bonds by Asian central banks made necessary by their policy of intervention to prevent their currencies from rising against the dollar, which has created artificially strong demand for US bonds. This is potentially a powerful explanation not only because of the sheer size of Asian central bank funds, but also because such purchasers are not driven primarily by short-term profit maximization but rather by issues of security and economic policy. Hence they may be prepared to carry on buying such bonds long after they have ceased to be good value—which conventional analysis suggests they long since have.

Yet I am not altogether happy with this explanation. For a start, while bond buying by Asian central banks has been heavily concentrated on the

US market, the fall in bond yields has been a near-universal phenomenon. Admittedly, some of this could be explained by arbitrage between markets, but this explanation can be carried too far. Moreover, there have, after all, been plenty of bonds to buy as government deficits have been high in the US, the eurozone, and the UK.

In principle, the answer could be lax monetary policy, with money washing around the system as a result of the central banks' expansionary policies. Faced with excess liquidity, wealth holders have bid up the prices (i.e., bid down the yields) on the whole gamut of assets. This explanation has some force, not least because it would help to explain why all asset classes have been pretty strong—including equities. And money supply growth has been high in the UK and the eurozone, although notably not in the United States, where the conundrum is perhaps most puzzling.

Still, on its own, money supply growth is not an adequate explanation, because in normal conditions you might expect high rates of monetary expansion to arouse fears of inflation, with the result that, once you looked beyond very short-dated bonds, yields would be higher, reflecting the assumption of higher inflation and higher short-term interest rates in the future. But there is hardly any evidence of this effect in yield curves. Indeed, in mid-2005 in the UK, long bond yields were actually lower than 10-year yields. So if monetary expansion is the answer, it is an answer that leaves most of the question unaddressed—namely, why markets should have reacted so differently.

Perhaps the answer is that the markets believe that inflation is going to be very low and perhaps even that deflation will reappear. It would be right for markets to take this view of future price trends. Although the immediate deflationary danger appears to have passed, from current low rates of inflation, deflation is an ever-present danger. Nevertheless, although this is important in explaining the low level of nominal yields over the last decade, it is inadequate as an explanation of recent especially low bond yields, since a noteworthy feature is that *real* yields on inflation-linked bonds are extremely low everywhere. And it is low real yields that predominantly account for today's especially low nominal yields. These cannot be explained by the prospect of continued low inflation, or even the danger of deflation.

Too Much Saving

I think the essence of the answer is the forces making for deficient demand that I detailed above, which come down to a global tendency toward excess saving. A variant of this is the view that excess savings are located mainly in the western corporate sector. According to JP Morgan, in the last five years corporate savings have increased by $1,091 billion—and that is five times larger than the increase in emerging market savings.[14] The reason for such savings is not difficult to find. Indeed, it is intimately bound up with the central thrust of this book. It is a direct response to the equity bubble of the late 1990s. The bursting of that bubble has left many corporations with weakened balance sheets, which they are now trying to repair.

Nevertheless, there are some forms of the excess savings view that I do not accept, in any of its variants. We should put out of our mind the image of interest rates being beaten down by a continuing flood of savings. The Keynesian revolution of the 1930s taught us that bond yields are not determined by savings *flows* but rather by portfolio decisions about *stocks* of wealth. There may be large surpluses in the world—notably for Asian governments—but there are also some large deficits—notably in America—and surprise, surprise, in aggregate the two are exactly equal. Every shock, horror story about savings gluts could be matched with a similar story about shock, horror deficits.[15]

In order to explain what has happened to bond yields we have to look at the portfolio behavior of wealth holders: their views, hopes, and fears, and the constraints under which they operate. In that regard, there is one very obvious candidate explanation for low yields, namely the enforced preference for bonds by pension funds and insurance companies following the underfunding scares of the last few years. In essence, a large proportion of the investing community has now come to the conclusion that, in order to match its liabilities, it must hold a high proportion of its assets in bonds, more or less regardless of the rate of return.

This seems far more plausible as an explanation of low bond yields in the UK than in the US and scarcely any sort of explanation for low yields in the eurozone, where funded pension schemes, and hence the whole issue of underfunding, are very much the exception to the rule. But it is still too partial. For a start, it sits oddly with the fact that equities and most other assets have recently performed well. You would have expected a switch away from other assets and toward bonds to have produced weakness in these other assets.

The most powerful explanation for the "conundrum" is an amalgam of both the high savings and ample liquidity explanations, but with a difference. It is quite simply that the markets believe that because of the world's incipient shortage of aggregate demand, monetary authorities will be forced to keep real short-term interest rates very low for some time. The consequence of this belief is that the influence of low short rates spreads all the way down the yield curve. And the markets are right. The relevance of the high propensity to save is not that it leads to a flood of money on the markets seeking a profitable home, but rather that it depresses aggregate demand and that leads the policy authorities to set low short-term interest rates.

This interest rate explanation has several strengths. It explains why the move to low real yields has happened everywhere—because low real short rates will be with us everywhere. And it explains why all asset classes are pretty strong and why spreads between supposedly safe and risky assets have narrowed. This is the usual response when rates of return are low on conventional safe assets: a scramble for yield.

Equities and Pensions

You might think that the incipient economic weakness that underlies this view on interest rates should argue for a weak equity market. That is certainly a possible outcome, but it is not inevitable. After all, if the policy of ultra-low interest rates works perfectly then incipient economic weakness will not be realized. The danger will have been taken out in the form of ultra-low interest rates. Moreover, even if some of the incipient weakness were realized, so that profits performance were impaired, lower real interest rates and bond yields would temper the effects on equity prices.

Mind you, in this story there is still a very big risk for equities. The sharp plunge in bond yields has worsened the problems of pension fund deficits because future liabilities are discounted to the present at the long-term bond yield. And as pension deficits get larger, then so companies find themselves obliged to plug the gap with increased pension contributions, thereby weakening their profits—which, collectively, threatens to weaken the equity market, which threatens to increase pension fund deficits. And at some point this could prompt a panic out of equities and into bonds. In Chapter 2 I described this as a doomsday machine. Make no mistake, this machine is still in working order, and it continues to constitute a severe threat to the financial system.

And although the recovery of the equity markets in the two years after October 2003 helped dispel the worst fears about the pension system in the US and the UK, in some ways the underlying situation has continued to worsen. In the UK, by 2005, the number of workers without a pension (other than the inadequate state pension) had risen to 12.7 million.[16] Meanwhile, the combined deficits of local authority workers' pension funds stands at £30 billion ($45 billion).[17]

In the US, the Pension Benefit Guaranty Corporation has reported that on the basis of reports submitted for 2004, underfunding of defined benefit pension plans of US corporations has jumped 27 percent to $353.7 billion.[18]

A Change of Direction?

When will interest rates return to "normal"? The answer partly depends on what you think is normal. In the 1950s and 1960s, interest rates and bond yields were low across most of the world. The levels that ruled then are a much better benchmark for normality than the elevated levels of the 1970s and 1980s.

Even so, I do not believe that we will forever live in a world where real yields on inflation-protected bonds stand at not much more than 1 percent. When will the current ultra-low interest rate era end? Only when the private sector has recovered its confidence and balance sheet strength and Asia matures will monetary policy return to "normal." And the signs are that that is going to be some time yet. After all, as I argued above, the US equity bubble is not fully deflated and the deflation of the housing bubble has barely begun. And on a global scale, there are powerful reasons why demand is going to run below aggregate capacity in both the eurozone and in Asia.

But at some point in the future, the forces making for deficient aggregate demand will fade and the world will be able to grow rapidly. When this happens, real interest rates might then have to be abnormally *high*. But for now, that remains a distant prospect. The immediate task facing the policy makers is to ensure that huge global imbalances and the threat of protectionism do not plunge the world into another Great Depression.

Fending off Protectionism

So how can protectionist pressures be overcome? In Chapter 5 I discussed some of the arguments against globalization. They proved to be weak, but this is not enough to prevent the insidious spread of protectionist measures that could effectively kill off globalization. What makes protection so dangerous is that many of the arguments for it are so superficially attractive. Fending off the dangers and realizing the promise before us will require these arguments to be defeated and the various pressure groups that have coalesced behind them to be overcome.

This is more difficult than the economic textbooks make it seem. It requires political leadership of a high order. The benefits of economic specialization are all very well, but this is a difficult case to put to someone who is threatened with redundancy as a result of foreign competition. The threat is all too specific and immediate, whereas the potential benefits of trade are diffuse and difficult to grasp. Even when the benefits substantially outweigh the costs, as will be the case most of the time, this will not be obvious to most people. The typical worker or business person in the developed countries does not see the increase in markets but the competitive threat to their job or business from cheaper production in developing countries.

In many cases this is not surprising, because there may be little or no developing-country demand for the very things they are currently producing. How can car workers smile at the increased potential sale of medical equipment? How can the father who may be made unemployed by developing-country competition rejoice at the thought that his sons and daughters will eventually be employed producing the business services that a successful Chinese economy will demand from Europe and North America?

Moreover, there is a serious political problem in resisting pressure for protection because of the way the gains and losses are distributed. When the case is put for a particular industry to be protected against foreign competition, the potential gainers are plain to see. They are highly concentrated, know who they are, and are often highly organized. They are the workers employed in that domestic industry, its managers, suppliers, and shareholders.

The potential losers from protection are much more numerous, although as individuals they stand to lose relatively small amounts. Moreover, they may not recognize themselves as losers, and are rarely organized to resist the pressure for protection. They are the taxpayers who will foot the bill for the aid given to the protected industry, all those who are forced by protection to pay higher prices for inferior goods or services, and, most importantly, all those who are not able to benefit from the increased supply of other goods and services that would be made by all those workers, managers, suppliers, and equity capital if this industry were to be closed down and all those resources were to be deployed elsewhere.

Protection is particularly dangerous now because international trade apparently threatens millions of workers in the developed countries with low-cost competition, which they may well convince themselves (and others) is "unfair." Millions of manual workers have already been displaced and their position in the national labor markets weakened by foreign competition. As the developing countries become more sophisticated, the pressures extend well beyond manual workers into the heartlands of the middle classes. For people working remotely by computer, for instance, it may not matter a great deal for their employers whether they are based in Bangalore or Basel, but it will certainly affect the cost.

What makes the problem worse is that when workers in western societies with either no skills or skills honed to one particular industry are made redundant, or fail to find jobs in a traditional industry, it is often difficult for them to find other jobs. There really are some losers from international trade, and therefore some potential gainers from protection.

The Political Solution

It is up to all political leaders to promote the benefits of international trade and to resist the pressures from vested interests—not as an act of charity, but in their own countries' interests. This involves bringing home to people how much they benefit from trade.

However, this line of attack is not strong enough on its own to fend off protection. As part of the process politicians have to find ways of dealing with those people who lose from trade. There are four (noncompeting) ways for western countries to cope with this problem: generously compensate those adversely affected; encourage the reskilling and even re-education of people to improve their position in the labor market; free up domestic labor markets both to speed up the process of displacement and to ensure that displaced workers have the best chance of getting re-employed; and maintain buoyant demand conditions to maximize the chances of redundant workers finding new employment.

The third and fourth factors are the most important. The widespread consternation in old Europe at the power of globalization and the threat to jobs may seem irrational to an economist, but the fact is that within much of the EU if you lose your job it is not easy to get another. A 10 percent rate of unemployment is a very good reason to fear globalization. And the dangers of a slide into protectionism remain very serious. Europe has managed to limit the imports of Chinese textiles "by mutual agreement," but this does not disguise the fact that this is blatant protectionism. The annual growth of Chinese exports will be limited to between 8 and 12.5 percent, compared with increases of 500 percent in the previously restricted types in the first quarter of 2005.

It is no accident that within Europe, globalization in general and outsourcing in particular have aroused least opposition in the UK. That is because the UK's labor market works so well. After more than a decade of economic success and low unemployment, it is now widely believed that huge sectors of the economy can go into decline, accompanied by widespread job losses, and new opportunities can spring up, leaving the total number of unemployed the same or even lower.

Nevertheless, governments often find the approach of reducing the burdens on those who lose from trade less than seductive, particularly when it involves spending public money. It may be far more attractive simply to sort the problem out by imposing a tariff or quota and thereby letting "the foreigner" pay. It is easy to criticize the developing countries for such practices, which are very common there. These countries are cutting off their nose to spite their face. It happens because the interests of the government are not congruent with the interests of the country. And it is a mark of nondemocratic societies that when such a conflict of interests emerges, it is the interests of the government that prevail.

Yet this problem is hardly confined to the developing countries. The developed countries spend over $300 billion per annum on subsidies to their farmers, dwarfing the $50 billion they provide as development assistance to the developing countries. The protection of an ailing domestic industry was the approach taken in 2002 by the US, of all countries, in imposing tariffs of up to 30 percent on steel imports; tariffs that the WTO subsequently declared in violation of international trading rules. And in 2002 President Bush authorized $4 billion in subsidies to 25,000 American cotton farmers, which had the effect of lowering world cotton prices and thereby plunging West Africa's 11 million cotton-growing households into increased poverty.

Meanwhile, the EU operates an outrageously protectionist agricultural system that directly harms European consumers, taxpayers, and the peoples of many other countries, including poor farmers in Africa and aspirant EU members in eastern Europe. It spends $40 billion a year subsidizing the production and export of huge surpluses of cereals, sugar, and dairy products. Yet somehow this system staggers on without serious challenge.

There is hope for the future, nevertheless. As part of the Doha global trade round, the US proposed the complete abolition of all duties on industrial goods. This followed a similarly bold call by the US in July 2002 for a sharp cut in agricultural tariffs from a global average of 62 percent to 15 percent. The US also proposed substantial liberalization of trade in services. Naturally, these proposals met with the predictable response from industries within the US that would suffer, in particular the textile industry.

More worryingly, the US proposal on industrial goods initially met with a pretty negative response from the developing countries. Admittedly, under the proposal their rates of duty would fall much further because they start that much higher. However, the most important point is that yet again so many countries have failed to see that the abolition of tariffs is not some *quid pro quo* but rather something they should do in their own interests.

Most worrying of all, as I write in mid-2005, the fate of the Doha round of trade talks hangs in the balance.

Institutions and Ideology

Despite the alarming views of many people on the subject of international trade, the world's current ideological and institutional structure puts it in a strong position to resist the lure of protectionism. There were three main reasons why the globalized economic system, so brilliantly described by Keynes in the passage quoted at the beginning of Chapter 6, collapsed in the years between the wars. The first is economic instability, which was both cause and effect of the lurch toward protection. The second was straightforwardly ideological, the rise of antiliberal ideas: militarism, fascism, imperialism, nationalism, and communism. The third reason was rivalry between the Great Powers.

Today's position is radically different. As I have argued in this book, economic instability is still with us and it is vital that policy makers respond to the challenge of maintaining adequate aggregate demand. But our bulwarks against protectionism are much stronger. For a start, it is notable that the antiglobalizers are not linked to a clear ideology, nor are they rooted to a powerful social force such as the organized working class. Most of the antiglobalization protesters do not seek power and indeed reject organized politics. Moreover, no serious economists want to limit, still less reverse, economic integration. Accordingly, the intellectual climate remains favorable to continued liberal trade arrangements.

Meanwhile, the institutional structure of companies themselves makes them less susceptible to protectionist sentiment and pressures. It is striking that protectionist pressures tend to be strongest from nationally owned and operated industries such as steel and agriculture. The rise of the multinational company has greatly reduced the tendency, and the ability, of companies to identify with national interests. In fact, that is one of the antiglobalizers' own complaints. In addition, a web of international commitments and multilateral institutions makes it more difficult for protectionist interests to capture national legislatures. Lastly, all developed countries have abandoned the idea that wealth derives from acquiring or plundering territory.

So although in mid-2005 the protectionist threat is all too alive and well, there are good reasons to hope that it will be resisted.

Meeting the Challenge

For much of the time the capitalist system gets on pretty well without a major contribution from political leaders. However, there are occasions when they are thrust into a pivotal role. This is how it was in the 1930s. Despite the attempts of a generation of free-market economists to prove that the recovery from the Great Depression was due to the naturally recuperative powers of the US economy, it now seems pretty clear, as an older generation knew all along, that recovery came about as a result of aggregate demand stimulus. In Germany and the UK this was patently the case.

A heavy responsibility now rests on the shoulders of today's policy makers in both the developing and the developed world. Their position is rather like those men who, at Bretton Woods in 1944 and continuing after the war, fashioned the institutions that, after the ravages of the 1930s and the war years, gave the world 25 years of stability and rapidly increasing international trade and prosperity. They rose to the challenge of the time and gave the countries of the hallowed circle a generation of unparalleled prosperity.

In meeting their different challenges, today's leaders can achieve something greater, not only avoiding the catastrophe that could sink us into a new slump and achieving another golden age of rapid growth for the developed countries, but also facilitating the rapid advance of the rest of the world—thereby opening up the gateway to the economy of the future.

Index

About the Author

One of the City of London's best-known economists, Roger Bootle runs the consultancy, Capital Economics, which specializes in macroeconomics and the economics of the property market. He is also Economic Adviser to Deloitte, a Specialist Adviser to the House of Commons Treasury Committee, and a Visiting Professor at Manchester Business School. He was formerly Group Chief Economist of the HSBC Group and, before the change of government, he was a member of the former Chancellor's panel of Independent Economic Advisers, the so-called Wise Men.

Roger Bootle studied at Merton and Nuffield Colleges, Oxford and then became a Lecturer in Economics at St Anne's College, Oxford. Most of his subsequent career has been spent in the City of London.

He has written many articles and several books on monetary economics. *Money for Nothing* follows the success of *The Death of Inflation*, published in 1996, which became a bestseller and was subsequently translated into nine languages. Initially dismissed as extreme, *The Death of Inflation* is now widely recognized as prophetic. Roger is also joint author of the book *Theory of Money*, and author of *Index-Linked Gilts*.

A regular columnist on *The Sunday Telegraph*, Roger also appears frequently on television and radio.